THE LIFE AND WORKS OF ROBERT BAILLIE
(1602–1662)

St Andrews Studies in Scottish History

Previous volumes in the series are listed at the back of this book

THE LIFE AND WORKS OF ROBERT BAILLIE (1602–1662)

Politics, Religion and Record-Keeping in the British Civil Wars

Alexander D. Campbell

THE BOYDELL PRESS

First published 2017
The Boydell Press, Woodbridge

ISBN 978 1 78327 184 9

The Boydell Press is an imprint of Boydell & Brewer Ltd
PO Box 9, Woodbridge, Suffolk IP12 3DF, UK
and of Boydell & Brewer Inc.
668 Mount Hope Ave, Rochester, NY 14620–2731, USA
website: www.boydellandbrewer.com

A catalogue record for this book is available
from the British Library

The publisher has no responsibility for the continued existence or accuracy
of URLs for external or third-party internet websites referred to in this book,
and does not guarantee that any content on such websites is, or will remain,
accurate or appropriate.

This publication is printed on acid-free paper

Printed and bound in Great Britain by
TJ International Ltd, Padstow, Cornwall

Contents

Acknowledgements

A book is the product of many hours spent with one's own thoughts. But it is only through the beneficence of those around you that such a pursuit is made possible. This book, then, was made possible through many joyful years spent studying seventeenth-century Britain at two outstanding institutions: Queen's University and the University of Cambridge. My studies at the latter were generously supported by the Social Sciences and Humanities Council of Canada (SSHRC), the Lightfoot Trust, and the Archbishop Cranmer Trust and it was that funding which allowed for the initial research for this book to be conducted.

I first recollect being told about Baillie – and being urged to look at his archives – when I stumbled into the rooms of John Morrill, now emeritus doyen of early modern British and Irish history at Cambridge. When I returned to Baillie during the second year of my doctoral studies, I was still skeptical: should I write a biography? Thanks to the encouragement of my supervisor, Clare Jackson, I decided to dispense with my original plan and focus on Baillie. With countless supervisions and even more hours with mangled chapter drafts, Clare has seen this project through from start to finish. She pushed me relentlessly to improve my prose; question my evidence; and sharpen my conclusions. This book would not be half the finished product that it now is without her ceaseless encouragement and support throughout the last six years.

I was grateful to be awarded a two-year post-doctoral fellowship by SSHRC and to be given time to transform my doctoral research into a study worthy of a monograph. This award allowed me to return to my Canadian alma mater, Queen's University, and to reconnect with my old mentors. Jeff Collins acted as an excellent sounding board over more than one pint as we discussed ideas relating to Baillie, Thomas Hobbes, and early modern intellectual culture. The Institute for Advanced Studies in the Humanities at the University of Edinburgh coaxed me back across the Atlantic with the offer of an outstanding academic home in one of the world's most beautiful cities. It was in those months that I was able to put the finishing touches on the manuscript for this book. Having drawn extensively on archival resources, I am grateful for the assistance of the library staff in the Rare Books Room at Cambridge University Library, the National Library of Scotland, New College Library, and the Special Collections reading rooms at Edinburgh University Library and Glasgow University Library.

Finally, I simply could not have completed this book if I had been left to my own thoughts for the last six years. My friends and family in Cambridge and in Toronto have provided a constant source of distraction and relaxation, especially when the writing process got difficult. In particular, my fiancée, Jodie, has borne the brunt of my worries. She is my best friend and my closest ally and this book is as much a product of her sacrifices as it is a product of my two hands. If it were not for the kindness of my parents, Glenn and Kathy, and my sister, Emma, I would never have been able to embark on graduate studies in Cambridge and this project may never have begun. Nevertheless, what follows is the product of myself alone. All errors and omissions, though my colleagues may have tried to correct most of them, remain my own.

Abbreviations

Baill MS   Robert Baillie Papers, New College Library, Edinburgh.

Baillie, *Anabaptism*   Robert Baillie, *Anabaptism, the true fountaine of Independency, Brownisme, Antinomy, Familisme, and the most of the other errours, which for the time doe trouble the Church of England, unsealed. Also the questions of pædobaptisme and dipping handled from Scripture. In a second part of the Disswasive from the errors of the time* (London, 1647).

Baillie, *Antidote*   Robert Baillie, *A Scotch antidote against the English infection of Arminianism. Which little book may be (through Gods blessing) very useful to preserve those that are yet found in the faith, from the infection of Mr John Goodwin's great book* (London, 1652).

Baillie, *Appendix Practica*   Robert Baillie, *Appendix practica, ad Ioannis Buxtorsii epitomen grammaticæ hebrææ* ... (Edinburgh, 1653).

Baillie, *Catechesis Elenctica Errorum*   Robert Baillie, *Catechesis elenctica errorum qui hodie vexant Ecclesiam, ex nudis sacræ Scripturæ testimoniis, in brevibus ac claris quæstionibus ac responsionibus proposita. In gratiam studiosæ juventutis academiæ Glasguensis. Imprimatur, Edm. Calamy. Imprimatur, Edm. Calamy* (London, 1654).

Baillie, *Danger of Limited Episcopacie*   Robert Baillie, *The unlavvfulnesse and danger of limited episcopacie· VVhereunto is subioyned a short reply to the modest advertiser and calme examinator of that treatise. As also the question of episcopacie discussed from Scripture and fathers* (London, 1641).

Baillie, *Dissvasive*   Robert Baillie, *A dissvasive from the errours of the time: vvherein the tenets of the principall sects, especially of the Independents, are drawn together in one map, for the most part, in the words of their own authours, and their maine principles are examined by the touch-stone of the Holy Scriptures* (London, 1645).

Baillie, *Dissvvasive Vindicated*   Robert Baillie, *The Dissvvasive from the errors of the time, vindicated from the exceptions of Mr. Cotton and Mr. Tombes* (London, 1655).

Baillie, *Errours and Induration*   Robert Baillie, *Errours and induration, are the great sins and the great judgements of the time. Preached in a sermon before the Right Honourable House of Peers, in the Abbey-Church at Westminster, July 30. 1645. the day of the monethly fast: by Robert Baylie, minister at Glasgow* (London, 1645).

Baillie, *Historicall Vindication*   Robert Baillie, *An historicall vindication of the government of the Church of Scotland, from the manifold base calumnies which the most malignant of the prelats did invent of old, and now lately have been published with great industry in two pamphlets at London* … (London, 1646).

Baillie, *Ladensium*   Robert Baillie, *Ladensium autokatakrisis, the Canterburians self-conviction: or, an evident demonstration of the avowed Arminianisme, poperie, and tyrannie of that faction, by their owne confessions … Helped also in sundry materiall passages, wherein the author hath received better information* ([London], 1641).

Baillie, *Operis Historici et Chronologici*   Robert Baillie, *Operis Historici et Chronologici Libri Duo; In quibus Historia Sacra et Profana compendiose deducitur ex ipsis fontibus, a creatione Mundi ad Constantinum Magnum, et quaestiones ac dubia Chronologica, quae ex utroque Testamento moveri solent, breviter et perspicue explicantur et vindicantur* (Amsterdam, 1663).

Baillie, *Parallel*   Robert Baillie, *A parallel or briefe comparison of the liturgie with the masse-book, the breviarie, the ceremoniall, and other romish ritualls … By R.B.K. Seene and allowed* (London, 1641).

Baillie, *Review of Bramhall*   Robert Baillie, *A review of Doctor Bramble, late Bishop of Londenderry, his Faire warning against the Scotes disciplin. By R.B.G.* (Delft, 1649).

Baillie, *Satan the Leader in Chief*   Robert Baillie, *Satan the leader in chief to all who resist the reparation of Sion. As it was cleared in a sermon to the Honourable House of Commons at their late solemn fast, Febr. 28. 1643. By Robert Baylie, minister at Glasgow. Published by order of the House of Commons* (London, [1644]).

Coffey, *Samuel Rutherford*   John Coffey, *Politics, Religion and the British Revolutions: The Mind of Samuel Rutherford* (Cambridge, 1997).

EUL   Edinburgh University Library Special Collections, Edinburgh

FES   *Fasti Ecclesiae Scoticanae* (7 vols, Edinburgh, 1915–28).

GUL   Glasgow University Library Special Collections, Glasgow

LJB   Robert Baillie, *The Letters and Journals of Robert Baillie, A.M. Principal of the University of Glasgow. M.DC.XXXVII.–M.DC.LXII*, ed. David Laing (3 vols, Edinburgh, 1841–42).

NAS   National Archives of Scotland, Edinburgh

NCL   New College Library, Edinburgh

NLS   National Library of Scotland, Edinburgh

ODNB   *Oxford Dictionary of National Biography* (Oxford University Press, 2004, online edn).

Peterkin (ed.), *Records*   Alexander Peterkin (ed.), *Records of the Kirk of Scotland, Containing the Acts and Proceedings of the General Assemblies from the Year 1638 Downwards* (Edinburgh, 1843).

RSCHS   *Records of the Scottish Church History Society*

Scots Peerage   Sir James Balfour Paul (ed.), *The Scots Peerage: Founded on Wood's Edition of Sir Robert Douglas's Peerage of Scotland: Containing an*

Historical and Genealogical Account of the Nobility of that Kingdom (9 vols, Edinburgh, 1904–14).

SHR   *Scottish Historical Review*

Stevenson, *Revolution and Counter-Revolution*   David Stevenson, *Revolution and Counter-Revolution in Scotland, 1644–1651* (reprinted London, 2003).

Stevenson, *Scottish Revolution*   David Stevenson, *The Scottish Revolution, 1637–1644: The Triumph of the Covenanters* (reprinted London, 2003).

Conventions

Quotations preserve original spelling and syntax and any abbreviations have been expanded silently. The year is taken to begin on 1 January. All translations are my own, unless otherwise stated. All Scriptural citations are taken from the King James Version (KJV), unless otherwise stated.

Introduction

In 1661, Robert Baillie was languishing with an illness that would soon claim his life. Yet his troubles did not end with his health. Throughout his life, Baillie had witnessed riots, revolution and regicide, all whilst tactfully maintaining his standing as a minister in the Church of Scotland. He began his life as a loyal subject of James VI and I and he was to die in August 1662 as a loyal subject of Charles II. In the intervening years, however, Baillie had emerged as one of Scotland's most adept critics of Charles I's ecclesiastical policies and as a leading voice of the Covenanting regime. At the end of Baillie's tumultuous career, it was his life as Covenanter propagandist that came back to haunt him. Writing in September 1661 to John Maitland, earl of Lauderdale, at the royal court, Baillie was anxious to disclaim responsibility for the republication of an inflammatory pamphlet that he had written years earlier entitled *A Parallel or briefe comparison of the liturgie with the masse-book* (1641). In his *Parallel*, Baillie had cunningly argued that the essential facets of Roman Catholic worship were contained in the controversial Prayer Book that had been drafted by Archbishop William Laud of Canterbury and members of the Scottish episcopate, and which had provoked rioting on its introduction in July 1637. Hearing that 'these observations on the Scottish Service-book I writ twenty-four years ago' were now reprinted in London, Baillie beseeched Lauderdale that 'there is not a word of them reprinted but the title-page alone, by some cheating printer there, to make some old copies of the first and only impression sell'. Begging Lauderdale to 'clear my innocencie to his Majestie', Baillie explained that although he had 'written half-a-dozen little tractats against Books and Bishops, and near as many against Sectaries ... I would be loath now to reprint any of them'.[1]

Embarrassed by his former life as Covenanter propagandist, Baillie expressed a desire that his contributions to the ecclesiastical and political controversies of the 1640s and 1650s would be forgotten. Since Baillie wrote

---

[1] Robert Baillie to John Maitland, earl of Lauderdale, 9 September [1661], *LJB*, vol. III, pp. 478–9. Following the Restoration, the Scottish episcopate did not attempt to force ministers to use a set liturgical form, likely as a result of widespread opposition to an 'English-style' Prayer Book in the late 1630s. This may be considered a pyrrhic victory for the Covenanting revolution and one which has not been given sufficient attention in the historiography.

these words, historians have largely followed suit, overlooking Baillie's voluminous published and manuscript writings and his turbulent career. Apparent shifts in Baillie's allegiance at crucial junctures in 1638 and after 1660 have presented previous biographers with an apparent conundrum. How could an avid defender of episcopacy join the decidedly anti-episcopal Covenanters in 1638? How could this same individual seamlessly become the Covenanting regime's chief propagandist? And, then, twenty years later, how could he conform to the reintroduction of episcopacy whilst voicing no public protest? Answers to these and other questions pertinent to Baillie's life have either been ignored or dismissed altogether. Indeed, the only two modern biographical accounts of Baillie's life follow uncritically the conclusion of a hostile contemporary, who had argued that the tracts that Baillie had written for the Covenanters 'flowed rather from the instigation of other persons, than his own inclinations'.[2]

Such inconsistencies notwithstanding, Baillie remains a mainstay in the historiography of the period because of the lucid account of contemporary events that he preserved in his outgoing correspondence. Bequeathing to posterity a wealth of material illustrative of his times, David Laing's 1841–42 edition of the *Letters and Journals of Robert Baillie* has become a central source for historians studying 1640s and 1650s Britain. Indeed, the narrative threads of Baillie's letters have shaped historiography of the British Civil Wars for well over three centuries and they continue to this day to furnish one of the most accessible, contemporary accounts of those events. Thomas Carlyle complained of the 'breathless loquacity' of Baillie's epistolary style and the early twentieth-century Scottish Historiographer Royal, Peter Hume Brown, extolled Baillie's 'vividness and insight', comparing passages in his correspondence 'with anything in Clarendon'.[3] Baillie, the man, has largely been forgotten, whilst Baillie's words continue to be remembered for their brilliant portrayal of the British Civil Wars.

Yet Baillie was far more than a mere commentator on contemporary affairs and an avid collector of official documents. He was also an active participant in many of the debates over political and religious issues that he shrewdly recounted. No account of Baillie's *Letters*, then, is complete without prior acknowledgement of his role as pamphleteer in the religious debates of 1640s Britain. If his *Letters* show that he was concerned to document the conflicts from his own perspective, and his published works primarily showed

---

[2] Thomas Middleton, *An appendix to the history of the Church of Scotland* (London, 1677), p. 36. For the modern echoes of this partisan argument, see F.N. McCoy, *Robert Baillie and the Second Scots Reformation* (Berkeley, 1974), pp. 60, 218; David Stevenson, 'Baillie, Robert (1602–1662)', *ODNB* [accessed 26 March 2014]. Also see Stevenson, 'Mere Hasty Babblements? Mr Robert Baillie', in *King or Covenant? Voices from Civil War* (East Linton, 1996), pp. 17–39.

[3] Thomas Carlyle, 'Baillie the Covenanter', in *Critical and Miscellaneous Essays* (7 vols, London, 1839–69), vol. VI, pp. 206–37, at p. 213; Peter Hume Brown, *History of Scotland* (3 vols, Cambridge, 1905), vol. II, p. 452.

his acumen in engaging ideological opponents, his astonishing manuscript remains add numerous additional dimensions to this remarkable life. Baillie may have only spoken out once during his time attending debates at the Westminster Assembly, but this reticence stands in stark contrast to his confident deportment when negotiating on behalf of the Church of Scotland with the exiled monarch, Charles II, in 1649.[4] Much the same may be said about Baillie's surefootedness when engaging in protracted epistolary 'conferences' with recalcitrant parishioners or neighbouring ministers over points of theological orthodoxy. It was from his experience as a parish minister that Baillie honed the skills in disputation for which he became renowned and despised on both national and international stages. From his extensive notes and manuscript treatises on theological, philological and historical topics, Baillie emerges as a devoted university lecturer. He considered the printed material at his disposal insufficient for his teaching needs, so he composed from scratch his own works, specifically intended to be used as teaching aids during his career at Glasgow University. Three of these works appeared in print, and many more survive in manuscript. Beyond the lecture theatre, Baillie was also a dedicated preacher. There are only two extant volumes of Baillie's carefully handwritten sermon notes, yet these volumes dwarf in size all other surviving manuscript material, comprising at least half a million words in total. Coupled with the remarkable survival of documents for the period from 1637 to 1662 are a handful of sources providing evidence of Baillie's intellectual formation in the 1620s and his earliest lectures at Glasgow.

For the first time, this biography draws together discussion of Baillie's oft-cited *Letters and Journals* alongside analysis of his surviving corpus of manuscript and printed works. He emerges as a tortured and fretful figure, struggling to keep up with the shifting politics of his day. If an opportunity to challenge authority arose, Baillie first insisted on delaying any decision so that he could examine the scholarly volumes populating his personal library.[5] Time and again, he was hesitant to overcommit to any side of the conflicts tearing apart Scotland, England and Ireland, and throughout the latter half of his life he became obsessive about managing his legacy. More broadly, this book provides a new account of the Covenanting movement and Scotland's involvement in the Wars of the Three Kingdoms through the prism of Baillie's extraordinary archive. Baillie's surviving manuscript and printed works cast new light on the intellectual dynamics of the Covenanting movement in the 1640s and 1650s. The movement has long been characterized as ideologically homogeneous, but Baillie repeatedly voiced subtly dissonant

[4] Chad Van Dixhoorn, 'Introduction', in Van Dixhoorn (ed.), *The Minutes and Papers of the Westminster Assembly 1643–1652* (5 vols, Oxford, 2012), vol. I, p. 24.
[5] Through careful comparison of book lists in Baillie's manuscripts alongside catalogue entries in Glasgow University Special Collections, I have been able to identify, with confidence, approximately 500 titles that were once in Baillie's personal possession.

opinions about major issues regarding monarchical power, church government, liturgical reform and the Bible's authority. Despite outward shows of ideological unity, the Covenanters remained hopelessly divided amongst themselves and leading thinkers – Baillie included – held myriad opinions concerning the ecclesiastical and political reforms that ought to be exported into England. Through careful reassessment of the intellectual landscape of mid-seventeenth-century Scotland, then, this biography demonstrates, contrary to entrenched opinion, that pre-Enlightenment Scotland gave rise to a richly variegated, cosmopolitan and dynamic nation of thinkers.

A study of Baillie's political and religious writings opens a window onto an impressive array of intellectual trends prominent in the Scotland of his day. His writings show an assured command of source material, a calculating wit and a razor-sharp polemical edge. Hardly succumbing to the dictates of a hegemonic Calvinism, Baillie's theological interests interacted in creative and unexpected ways with other modes of thinking. Indeed, Baillie's orthodox theological beliefs drove him to search out novel – if ultimately misguided – solutions to apparently intractable questions regarding the antiquity and authority of Scripture. Finally, this book offers an opportunity for reflection on the creative processes of remembering and forgetting that informed early modern archival formation and early practices of life-writing. Considering that historians from the seventeenth century down to the present day have drawn on Baillie's *Letters and Journals* to furnish accounts of the Civil Wars, it is remarkable that no one has asked why Baillie went to such painstaking efforts to transcribe a selection of his outgoing correspondence in carefully organized volumes. Meticulous analysis of the compilation and transmission of Baillie's impressive manuscript remains provides a key to understanding the ways in which documentary survival shapes an individual's historical legacy. Despite Baillie's best efforts to manage his posthumous reputation, his memory remains contested and his life obscured to the present day.

I

What follows draws comprehensively on the collection of surviving documents both in print and in manuscript relating to Baillie's life. It is this paper legacy that comprises the building blocks of this biographical study. I will analyse the provenance and transmission of these documents later, but for now it is essential to familiarize readers with the contents and scope of Baillie's extant print and manuscript corpora. In one respect, this book provides a biographical and conceptual grounding for future readings of Baillie's *Letters and Journals*. It urges historians to take greater care when drawing on this and similar sources. After all, Baillie's correspondence survives because of decisions made by Baillie and his heirs to preserve and disseminate it. These acts, alone, are inscribed with numerous meanings essential to analysis of the content of the letters themselves. In another respect, though, this book sets aside Baillie's efforts to document and preserve evidence about the Civil Wars as only one of an array of intellectual concerns that he maintained throughout his life. Not every waking hour of Baillie's day was spent writing and transcribing his outgoing correspondence. In fact, as soon as the conflict in Scotland gathered pace, Baillie appears to have found himself preoccupied with his duties as a minister in Kilwinning, Ayrshire, and he deemed it necessary to enlist the help of amanuenses to transcribe his letters after he had drafted them.

Baillie may be remembered today for his biting comments about John Milton's views on divorce, or his glib assessment of the Solemn League and Covenant, but to contemporaries his renown stemmed, in the first place, from his published contributions to theological controversies.[6] In his own lifetime, Baillie authored fifteen published tracts through which he attracted both the praise and the criticism of leading churchmen and intellectuals of his day. Gisbertus Voetius acclaimed Baillie's 'keen judgment and indefatigable toil' as a Biblical scholar alongside Johannes Hornbeek's and Georg Horn's praise of 'the most renowned and revered D.D. Baillie'.[7] Baillie's *Ladensium Autokatakrisis* (1640) provided the most thorough critique of the Laudian episcopate, appearing in four editions and furnishing Continental theologians, such as Horn, with valuable evidence for their own treatises.[8] Writing in December 1640, Baillie remarked that his *Ladensium* offered 'sundrie countrie ministers ... much help' in framing a remonstrance against the English bishops.[9] An expanded version of Baillie's anti-Arminian speech at the Glasgow Assembly (1638), *An Antidote against Arminianisme*, was published in 1641 and 1652, the latter in response to John Goodwin's *Redemption redeemed* (1651). Baillie's *Parallel of the liturgie with the masse-book* (1641) provoked a response from the Restoration bishop of St David's, Laurence Womock.[10] Baillie's *Dissvasive from the Errours of the time* (1645) and *Anabaptism, the*

---

[6] For Baillie's attack on Milton's tract on divorce, see his *Dissuasive*, p. 116. For his oft-quoted appraisal of the Solemn League and Covenant, see Robert Baillie to William Spang, 26 July 1643, *LJB*, vol. II, p. 90.

[7] H.M.B. Reid, *The Divinity Professors in the University of Glasgow* (Glasgow, 1923), p. 97; Baillie, *Operis Historici et Chronologici*, n.p. ['Judicia Virorum Clarissimorum De Auctore et ejus Opere Historico-Chronologico'].

[8] It was printed in Amsterdam, 1640; Glasgow, 1640; London, 1641; and expanded with an appendix entitled 'Large supplement of the Canterburian self-conviction', and printed under the title, *The life of William now Arch-Bishop of Canterbury, examined* (London, 1643). I am grateful for discussions with Anthony Milton on this point. For Horn's use of Baillie, see Georgius Hornius, *De Statu Ecclesiae Britannicae hodierno, liber commentarius* (Danzig, 1647), 'Praefatio ad Lectorem'.

[9] Robert Baillie to the presbytery of Irvine, 12 December 1640, *LJB*, vol. I, p. 282. Baillie repeated to Spang in another letter that English opponents of Laud derived 'good help' from his *Ladensium* (*LJB*, vol. I, p. 286).

[10] Laurence Womock, *Beaten oyle for the lamps of the sanctuarie; or The great controversie concerning set prayers and our liturgie, examined in an epistle to a private friend: with an appendix that answers the paralell, and the most materiall objections of others against it* (London, 1641).

True Fountaine of Independency (1647) prompted rejoinders from the New England minister John Cotton and the Anabaptist John Tombes, to which Baillie responded in his *Dissvvasive from the Errors of the Time, Vindicated* (1655).[11] At the General Assembly's behest, Baillie composed *An Historicall Vindication of the Government of the Church of Scotland* (1646), refuting an earlier treatise by the former Scottish bishop John Maxwell.[12] During negotiations with Charles II in The Hague, Baillie responded to anti-presbyterian attacks from Bishop John Bramhall of Londonderry with *A Review of Doctor Bramble ... his Faire Warning* (1649), which, in turn, provoked responses from two prominent Restoration churchmen, Richard Watson and Robert Creighton.[13] During the Interregnum, Baillie published two pedagogical works on religious controversies and Hebrew: *Catechesis elentica errorum* (1654) and *Appendix practica, ad Ioannis Buxtorsii* (1654). Baillie's final, posthumous work, *Operis Historici et Chronologici* (1663) – a concise introduction to Biblical chronology – was printed three times in Amsterdam and Basel.[14] Recommended as an introduction to the complexities of Biblical chronology well into the eighteenth century, Baillie's *Operis* was studied by prominent figures such as Benjamin Wadsworth, President of Harvard University from 1725 to 1737, and John Adams, the second President of the United States.[15]

Baillie's published tracts provide another hitherto neglected layer to the story of his life, but it is only through the appreciation of his letters and pamphlets alongside his enormous archival remains that a clear picture may be seen. I make comprehensive use of Baillie's extant manuscripts, comprising over five hundred folio leaves and over three thousand quarto leaves. These manuscripts provide a broader chronological indication of the origins and

---

[11] John Cotton, *The way of Congregational churches cleared. In the former, from the historical aspersions of Mr. Robert Baylie, in his book, called a disswasive from the errors of the time* (London, 1648); John Tombes, *An addition to the Apology for the two treatises concerning infant-baptisme...In which the author is vindicated from 21 unjust criminations in the 92 page of the book of Mr. Robert Baillie, minister of Glasgow, intituled Anabaptisme* (London, 1652).

[12] See the letters Baillie sent to Alexander Henderson and David Calderwood, *LJB*, vol. II, pp. 372–4.

[13] See Richard Watson, *Akolouthos or A second faire warning to take heed of the Scotish discipline, in vindication of the first* (The Hague, 1651). The previous tract included a letter from Robert Creighton. This tract, along with those of Bramhall and Baillie, were reprinted together after the Restoration as *Three treatises concerning the Scotish discipline* (The Hague, 1661).

[14] Amsterdam, 1663; Amsterdam, 1668; Basel, 1669.

[15] For recommendations of *Operis Historici et Chronologici* as a good introduction to Biblical chronology, see Jacques Le Long, *Bibliotheca Sacra in Binos Syllabos Distincta* (Paris, 1723), p. 1053; Caspar Sagittarius, *Introdvctionis in Historia Ecclesiasticam Tomvs II* (Jena, 1720), p. 28; Johann Georg Walch, *Bibliotheca theologica selecta litterariis adnotationibvs instrvcta, tomvs tertivs* (Jena, 1762), p. 65. A copy of the Amsterdam 1668 edition in the Boston Public Library (Adams 22.2 Folio) is inscribed 'Benjamin Wadsworth His Book Anno Dominis 1687'. According to another ownership inscription, this copy was sold by Wadsworth to 'N. Williams' on 1 April 1695 before Adams probably purchased it at a later date.

genesis of many ideas which Baillie presented in published pamphlets or to which he briefly alluded in correspondence. They also help to cast Baillie in a variety of roles to which he devoted much of his time, but for which we have hitherto lacked sufficient documentation. Baillie's manuscripts are mainly preserved in New College Library, Edinburgh, where the collection comprises five shelfmarks: 'Baill MSS 1–5'.[16] 'Baill MS 2' and 'Baill MS 3' are early eighteenth-century transcriptions of Baillie's outgoing correspondence and they provide important evidence about the early uses and transmission of his manuscript correspondence, discussed in the final chapter. 'Baill MS 4' comprises three quarto volumes, containing the original transcriptions of Baillie's outgoing letters, interpolated with transcriptions of documents that Baillie sent to correspondents, some of which are not published in Laing's edition. Baillie annotated and corrected transcriptions throughout all three volumes of 'Baill MS 4', and his grandson, also Robert Baillie, used the blank pages left at the end of one volume to take notes on the contents of the correspondence. 'Baill MS 5' is a thick quarto volume containing over five hundred leaves of sermon notes in Baillie's hand. Sermons in this volume are dated between 1648 and 1651, spanning the period when the Covenanters' rule in Scotland crumbled and Oliver Cromwell seized control. Finally, 'Baill MS 1' is a single folio volume written entirely in a neat secretary hand. It was probably compiled late in Baillie's life because it contains items dated between 1627 and 1658 and includes corrections by Baillie. In chronological order, 'Baill MS 1' contains orations that Baillie gave at Glasgow University in 1627 and 1629; two 'conferences' on the lawfulness of kneeling to receive communion (c. 1634) and the Arminian tenet of the Saints' apostasy (1634–36); disputation theses on philosophical and theological subjects (undated); additional correspondence Baillie exchanged with his parishioners over patterns of worship (1643); surveys of controversies on presbyterian and congregational polities and Roman Catholic beliefs (1640s); and an unfinished treatise on the formal causes of justification (1658).

In addition to the New College manuscripts, another quarto volume of sermons, entirely in Baillie's hand, dating from 1637 to 1639, is in the National Library of Scotland.[17] Among David Laing's own manuscripts, preserved in Edinburgh University Library, there is an extant student notebook probably composed by Baillie in 1620 and a slim volume of notes taken by Baillie's son on sermons that he heard in Glasgow between 1650 and 1652, including many sermons preached by his father.[18] Finally, a quarto volume preserved in Glasgow University Library contains Latin tracts in various hands with

---

[16]   They are cited throughout this book as NCL, Baill MS 1–5. See the bibliography for a complete list of manuscripts that I have identified as belonging to, or having been produced by Baillie.

[17]   NLS, Adv.MS.20.6.4, Robert Baillie, Sermons, August 1637 to June 1639.

[18]   EUL, La.III.109, Robert Baillie, Student notebook, [c. 1620]; La.III.543, Robert Baillie [c. 1634–58], Sermon notes, c. 1650–c. 1652.

annotations and corrections by Baillie.[19] The majority of this volume comprises an early copy of Baillie's *Operis Historici et Chronologici*, including a preface that does not appear in subsequent printed editions. This volume also contains the only extant copy of a survey of controversies on episcopal church government, a tract that includes Baillie's most detailed statements concerning episcopacy.

II

Considering that critics of the Covenanters often attacked their unbending religious zeal, it is remarkable how little scholarly attention has been paid to the Church of Scotland after 1638.[20] Historiography of the English Civil Wars still engages with John Morrill's claim that they represented the last of the European Wars of Religion, but in Scottish historiography religion has been marginalized since David Stevenson's revisionist accounts of the field in the 1970s.[21] There has been no study of the Church of Scotland in the 1640s since Walter Makey's *The Church of the Covenant, 1637–1651* (1979), which presented the distinctively un-religious argument that rampant inflation encouraged the spread of revolutionary Calvinism amongst Scotland's ministry.[22] Laura Stewart's reappraisal of Covenanted Scotland presented political strife as the result of the negotiation of unequal and unstable power relations.[23] Her argument rests on the idea that the 'Covenanted state' was a 'confessional state', but her analysis does not attend to the complexities of religious belief and their impact on politics. Chris Langley, conversely, offers an initial foray into our understanding of the impact of civil war on parish kirks in Scotland.[24] These exceptions notwithstanding, religion still typically features as little more than a short-hand explanatory device or a catalyst for

[19] GUL, MS Gen 375.
[20] Not least in Charles I's unofficial rebuttal to the National Covenant, see Walter Balcanquhall, *A large declaration concerning the late tumults in Scotland, from their first originalls together with a particular deduction of the seditious practices of the prime leaders of the Covenanters* (London, 1639).
[21] John Morrill, 'The Religious Context of the English Civil War', *Transactions of the Royal Historical Society*, 5th Series, 34 (1984), pp. 155–78. For recent engagement with Morrill's claim, see Charles W.A. Prior and Glenn Burgess (eds), *England's Wars of Religion, Revisited* (Farnham, 2011). For Stevenson's revisions of the historiography of the Covenanting Revolution, see *Scottish Revolution; Revolution and Counter-Revolution; Alasdair MacColla and the Highland Problem in the Seventeenth Century* (Edinburgh, 1980); and *Scottish Covenanters and Irish Confederates: Scottish–Irish Relations in the Mid-Seventeenth Century* (Belfast, 1981).
[22] Walter Makey, *The Church of the Covenant, 1637–1651: Revolution and Social Change in Scotland* (Edinburgh, 1979).
[23] Laura A.M. Stewart, *Rethinking the Scottish Revolution: Covenanted Scotland, 1637–1651* (Oxford, 2016).
[24] Chris Langley, *Worship, Civil War and Community, 1638–1660* (London, 2015).

an ill-defined process of 'radicalization', obscuring the broader contours of religious debate that persisted during this period.

In this vein, historiographical interpretations of the post-Reformation Church of Scotland generally, and the Scottish Covenanters in particular, are still characterized by a narrative of internecine conflict between 'presbyterians' and 'episcopalians'. This stubborn historiographical trend may be traced back to the confessional accounts of the Reformation penned by David Calderwood and John Spottiswoode. It is remarkable, though, how little critical work has sought to revise the accounts presented in these works of partisan scholarship. Whilst studies have challenged these portrayals for the periods before 1638 and after 1660, analysis of the intervening years of Covenanting ascendancy remains unrevised.[25] The result is an obfuscating hermeneutic that fails to account for the nuances of printed and manuscript polemic and, more seriously, overlooks individual cases who do not easily conform to either category, as was the case with Robert Baillie.

Historiographical orthodoxy thus asserts that, in 1638, a large portion of Scottish adult males swore the National Covenant, pledging to defend the Church and its worship from 'antichristian' innovations, thereby succumbing to the influence of a small but powerful junto of 'radical' ministers, including Rutherford, Alexander Henderson and George Gillespie, and laity, such as Archibald Johnston of Wariston and Archibald Campbell, marquess of Argyll.[26] This powerful junto seized control of Scotland's civil and ecclesiastical institutions and, under the watchful eye of the zealous lawyer Wariston, rigorously policed Scottish beliefs, partly through close control of Scotland's printing presses.[27] Ideological fissures amongst the Kirk's ministry after 1638 tend to be explained as the result of latent 'episcopal' and 'Royalist' sympathies or exogenous factors, such as Oliver Cromwell's invasion of Scotland with a 'sectarian' army in 1651.[28] In reconstructing the formation

[25] For the earlier period, see Alan R. MacDonald, *The Jacobean Kirk, 1567–1625: Sovereignty, Polity and Liturgy* (Aldershot, 1998). For the later period, see W.R. Foster, *Bishop and Presbytery: The Church of Scotland, 1661–1688* (London, 1958). Also, see David George Mullan, 'Theology in the Church of Scotland, 1618–1640: A Calvinist Consensus?', *Sixteenth Century Journal*, 26 (1995), pp. 595–617.

[26] Stevenson catalogued extant signed copies of the National Covenant (1638) which suggested that the Covenanters enjoyed widespread support throughout Lowland Scotland. He published a similar survey of signed copies of the Solemn League and Covenant (1643). See David Stevenson, 'The National Covenant: A List of Known Copies', *RSCHS*, 23 (1988), pp. 255–99; Stevenson, 'The Solemn League and Covenant: A List of Signed Copies', *RSCHS*, 25 (1995), pp. 154–87.

[27] Kirsteen Mackenzie, 'A Glimpse Behind the Censor: Baillie and the Covenanting Printing Press', *Notes and Queries*, 60 (2013), pp. 42–3; David Stevenson, 'A Revolutionary Regime and the Press: The Scottish Covenanters and their Printers, 1638–51', *The Library*, 7 (1985), pp. 315–37.

[28] For this older view, see W.I. Hoy, 'The Entry of Sects into Scotland', in D. Shaw (ed.), *Reformation and Revolution: Essays Presented to the Very Rev. Hugh Watt* (Edinburgh, 1967), pp. 178–211; Gordon Donaldson, 'The Emergence of Schism in Seventeenth-Century Scotland', in Derek Baker (ed.), *Schism, Heresy and Religious Protest* (Cambridge,

of 'episcopal' and 'presbyterian' confessional cultures in late seventeenth-century Scotland, Alasdair Raffe has referred to the 'essential uniformity of mid seventeenth-century [Scottish] religious culture', while a prominent historian of the Jacobean and Caroline Church of Scotland has claimed that Scots who developed 'sophisticated thought[s]' about worship and theology before 1638 thereafter fell 'prey in such large proportion to [the] puerile nonsense' of a Roman Catholic 'conspiracy theory'.[29] By these accounts, a culture of fear successfully allowed radical presbyterian clerics and nobles to exploit widespread terror of Roman Catholic conspiracies in order to impose a homogeneous religious culture on Scotland.

Rather than asking why Baillie's ideas changed after a certain date, this biography asks how Baillie's religious and political ideas may have shaped, and were shaped by, the political changes of 1638 and 1660. Previous studies have cast 1638 and 1660 as watershed moments that, alongside the mass expulsion of episcopalian ministers in 1690 and the Disruption of 1843, rank as the most tumultuous periods in the Church of Scotland's history. It is precisely the chaos and apparent partisanship of this period that has contributed to its historiographical neglect. Any surviving works are considered as evidence of a radical form of presbyterianism, and are tacitly dismissed as conceptually uninteresting. This book, on the other hand, draws attention to the relative continuities in Baillie's thought across his career, according with recent historiography that has emphasized the consensual nature of Scottish religious culture before 1638 and after 1660.[30] By older accounts, the ministry and episcopate of the Jacobean and Caroline Kirk were united behind a 'Calvinist' theological consensus, and Reformed patterns of worship and discipline flourished because of the flexible and calculating implementation of reforms undertaken by local Kirk sessions.[31] After the re-establishment of episcopacy in 1661, moreover, at least two-thirds of ministers conformed because they were more committed to the maintenance of a Protestant national church than either a presbyterian or episcopal polity.[32] Scotland's

---

1972), pp. 277–94; Harry Escott, *A History of Scottish Congregationalism* (Glasgow, 1960).
[29] Alasdair Raffe, *The Culture of Controversy: Religious Arguments in Scotland, 1660–1714* (Woodbridge, 2012), p. 45; David George Mullan (ed.), *Religious Controversy in Scotland, 1625–1639* (Edinburgh, 1998), p. 13.
[30] With regards to the earlier period, a helpful discussion of the problems of these labels may be found in MacDonald, *The Jacobean Kirk*.
[31] On a 'Calvinist' consensus, see Mullan, 'A Calvinist Consensus?'; Mullan, 'Arminianism in the Lord's Assembly, Glasgow, 1638', *RSCHS*, 26 (1996), pp. 1–30; Mullan, 'Masked Popery and Pyrrhonian Uncertainty: The Early Scottish Covenanters on Arminianism', *Journal of Religious History*, 21 (1997), pp. 159–77. On worship and Protestant culture in the post-Reformation Kirk, see Margo Todd, *The Culture of Protestantism in Early Modern Scotland* (London, 2002), pp. 402–12.
[32] Robert Armstrong and Tadhg Ó hAnnracháin, 'Alternative Establishments? Insular Catholicism and Presbyterianism', in Armstrong and Ó hAnnracháin (eds), *Insular Christianity: Alternative Models of the Church in Britain and Ireland, c. 1570–c. 1700* (Manchester, 2013), pp. 1–27, at pp. 21–2. Also, see I.B. Cowan, 'The Covenanters: A

political elite were able to institute a predominantly Erastian episcopal settlement because of widespread anti-clericalism as well as the restored episcopate's failure to develop a convincing account of its *jure divino* status.[33] Likewise, many Scots who had hitherto shown presbyterian tendencies were reluctant to accord *any* ecclesiastical polity with *jure divino* status, thus further depleting the ranks of those Covenanters who refused to conform after 1662. Significantly, Scots were not required to adopt the Prayer Book, and the form of episcopacy that was re-established was not completely alien to Scots. At least seven out of fourteen members of the restored episcopate – including Archbishops Andrew Fairfoul of Glasgow and James Sharp of St Andrews – may be identified as 'Covenanters' before 1660.[34] Kirk sessions, presbyteries and synods continued to enforce discipline – albeit in a moderated form – alongside the restored episcopate.[35] In fact, this type of episcopal polity largely reflected that under which Baillie had grown up in the 1610s.

The transitions of ecclesiastical and political power that occurred in 1638 and 1660 appear even less momentous if we consider the fluidity of 'presbyterian' and 'episcopalian' identities evident in Baillie's writings. By one recent account, it has been suggested that it is more helpful to refer to 'presbyterian' tendencies, emphasizing that confessional identities were imperfectly formed.[36] Whilst this approach is useful, a further word of caution is required regarding the currency of confessional labels in religious historiography. In the pages that follow, I certainly make use of common labels, yet it is worth highlighting that many of the arguments I develop complicate traditionally held views about the intellectual preoccupations of a Scottish presbyterian during the Civil Wars. I would go so far as to argue that labelling individuals in religious historiography has injected a degree of confessional anachronism, transplanted, in a Scottish context, from the religious conflicts of nineteenth-century Scotland to the fertile soil of the seventeenth century.

Revision Article', *SHR*, 47 (1968), pp. 35–52, at p. 46; Raffe, *The Culture of Controversy*, pp. 33–4.

[33] Clare Jackson, *Restoration Scotland, 1660–1690: Royalist Politics, Religion and Ideas* (Woodbridge, 2003), ch. 5. In similar vein, David Mullan also suggested that the pre-Civil War episcopate had failed because of their 'want of an appreciable historic institutional dignity'. See David George Mullan, *Episcopacy in Scotland: The History of an Idea, 1560–1638* (Edinburgh, 1986), p. 196.

[34] Those that may be identified as Covenanters include Sharp (St Andrews), Fairfoul (Glasgow), George Haliburton (Dunkeld), James Hamilton (Galloway), John Paterson (Ross), Patrick Forbes (Caithness) and Robert Leighton (Dunblane). Those who may be definitively identified as opponents of the Covenanters include George Wishart (Edinburgh) and, the only survivor of the pre-1638 episcopate, Thomas Sydserf (Orkney). David Mitchel (Aberdeen), David Strachan (Brechin), David Fletcher (Argyll), Murdoch MacKenzie (Moray) and Robert Wallace (The Isles) do not have *ODNB* entries and other evidence of their pre-1660 allegiances is not readily available.

[35] W.R. Foster, *Bishop and Presbytery: The Church of Scotland, 1661–1688* (London, 1958).

[36] Armstrong and Ó hAnnracháin, 'Alternative Establishments?', p. 2.

Labels may often be used as convenient shorthand, but the interpretative baggage implied by their usage can potentially be misleading. If a minister like Baillie is described as a 'presbyterian' this often is taken to convey that Baillie held a predictable set of views on a range of issues. By such an account, we might expect Baillie to be a strict opponent of episcopacy, averse to kneeling to receive the communion elements, and a believer in a 'rigid' form of double predestination. The chapters that follow on Baillie's ecclesiology, liturgical writings and theology, respectively, all complicate these basic assumptions about what a 'presbyterian' might think about these topics.

In order to fashion a new and convincing account of Baillie's life and writings, then, this biography builds on a modest collection of studies that have uncovered points of ideological tension within the Covenanting movement. In an attempt to erase moments of embarrassing dispute amongst ministers obsessed with maintaining their 'godly' credentials, contemporaries and later historians have smoothed the edges of surviving source material and removed or destroyed evidence of disputes over key points of doctrine and policy. Baillie, more than perhaps any of his contemporaries, was careful to manage the documentary legacy that he left and our analysis here must attend to the reasons why some material may be preserved whilst other material – the existence of which may be inferred from other sources – was excluded or destroyed. Given the scarcity of Scottish primary material in contrast to the reams of material surviving for England at the same time, it is not unsurprising that relatively few historians have provided sustained accounts of intra-Covenanting disputes. Despite such evidentiary problems, studies have convincingly shown, for instance, that a group of so-called 'radical' ministers persisted with some degree of cohesion throughout the 1640s in their belief that the Glasgow Assembly of 1638 had not gone far enough in reforming worship in the Church.[37] A meticulous study of debates over ecclesiology at the Westminster Assembly has recently shown clear ideological differences amongst the Scottish delegates Baillie, Rutherford, Gillespie and Henderson when it came to finer issues regarding the power of particular congregations.[38] And the best study of religion in Interregnum Scotland convincingly argued that the cacophony of religious beliefs that followed Cromwell's invasion sprung from the influence of English ministers as well as from homegrown sources.[39]

Rather than asking why an apparently ideologically homogeneous culture of presbyterianism crumbled so quickly after the Restoration of Charles II, I contend here that it is more accurate to ask how the Covenanting regime

---

[37] David Stevenson, 'Conventicles and the Kirk, 1619–37: The Emergence of a Radical Party', *RSCHS*, 18 (1973), pp. 99–114; Stevenson, 'The Radical Party in the Kirk, 1637–45', *Journal of Ecclesiastical History*, 25 (1974), pp. 135–65.

[38] Hunter Powell, *The Crisis of British Protestantism: Church Power in the Puritan Revolution, 1638–44* (Manchester, 2015).

[39] R. Scott Spurlock, *Cromwell and Scotland: Conquest and Religion, 1650–1660* (Edinburgh, 2007).

maintained the appearance of a unified movement for as long as it did. Baillie's writings provide an ideal case study for exploding the historiographical tendency to cast Covenanting Scotland as torn between presbyterian and episcopal factions precisely because Baillie's intellectual commitments often blurred distinctions between these groups. Baillie's religious and political writings instead reflected the ambiguities of the Reformation settlement in Scotland. After 1560, the Church's polity remained in flux, its pattern of worship was cast in deliberately broad terms and its ministers' doctrinal beliefs remained subtly variegated. As a Reformed minister, Baillie aspired to maintain rigorous moral discipline in his parish, whilst leading worship according to God's Word.[40] Reformed ministers throughout Europe implemented these two broad ideals in a variety of manners, adapting them to local social, economic and political contexts.[41] Whilst Margo Todd and John Coffey have suggested that the post-Reformation Church of Scotland may be described as a 'Puritan church' – more fully reformed than the Church of England – it is more useful to think about the Scottish Church as a Reformed church.[42] First, this decision allows analysis of Baillie's ideas to transcend a simplistic binary opposition between 'presbyterian' and 'episcopalian' positions. In Scotland, ministers who evinced either presbyterian or episcopalian tendencies lacked detailed intellectual justifications for their respective platforms, in the way that Richard Hooker's *Laws of Ecclesiastical Polity* (1604) had provided for defenders of the episcopalian Church of England.[43] Baillie's writings about church polity, discussed below, reflected the more ambiguous settlement of the Church's polity at the Reformation. Secondly, this decision reorients analysis of Baillie's ideas to account for the influence of the rich variety of intellectual traditions of Reformed Europe, without precluding

---

[40] Philip Benedict, *Christ's Churches Purely Reformed: A Social History of Calvinism* (London, 2002), pp. 458–9.

[41] The precise ways in which this was affected throughout parish Kirks in Scotland is the subject of Todd's *The Culture of Protestantism*. Also, see, John McCallum, *Reforming the Scottish Parish: The Reformation in Fife, 1560–1640* (Farnham, 2010); Christopher R. Langley, 'Times of Trouble and Deliverance: Worship in the Kirk of Scotland, 1645–1658' (Ph.D. thesis, University of Aberdeen, 2012).

[42] Margo Todd, 'The Problem of Scotland's Puritans', in John Coffey and Paul Chang-Ha Lim (eds), *The Cambridge Companion to Puritanism* (Cambridge, 2008), pp. 174–88; John Coffey, 'The Problem of "Scottish Puritanism", 1590–1638', in Elizabethanne Boran and Crawford Gribben (eds), *Enforcing Reformation in Ireland and Scotland, 1550–1700* (Aldershot, 2006), pp. 66–90.

[43] *The First Book of Discipline* (1560) and *The Second Book of Discipline* (1578) offered little more than the bare outlines of church polity: a large reason why this issue became so hotly contested in the seventeenth century. The first detailed and persuasive account of the Kirk's presbyterian polity written by a Scot was either George Gillespie, *An assertion of the government of the Church of Scotland* (Edinburgh, 1641) or Samuel Rutherford, *A peaceable and temperate plea for Pauls presbyterie in Scotland* (London, 1642). On the emergence of presbyterian and episcopalian confessional identities, see Alasdair Raffe, 'Presbyterians and Episcopalians: The Formation of Confessional Cultures in Scotland, 1660–1715', *English Historical Review*, 125 (2010), pp. 570–98.

discussion of Baillie's contributions to English religious debates; indeed, the Church of England should be counted amongst Europe's Reformed churches.

This book resolves Baillie's thinking according to a broader set of themes that run through his extant writings, rather than analysing his writings through the prism of an idealized 'presbyterianism'. Approaching his writings, I ask what a work may tell us about Baillie's understanding of the problems of church government, for example, or his thinking on liturgical formulae. I explore the sources for his thinking on questions related to Reformed theology and show how his adoption of particular readings of texts may have strengthened his convictions. I also ask why Baillie chose to compose works in particular formats and what this might tell us about Baillie's diverse occupations as parish minister, polemic theologian, divinity professor and foreign diplomat. This enables a far more nuanced assessment of Baillie's writings than merely casting him against the backdrop of an ahistorical 'Scottish presbyterianism'. Although his writings may fall under a broad category, illustrative of presbyterian tendencies, Baillie's outlook here is developed from its disparate parts rather than by imposing a coherent vision from the outset.

III

More broadly, this biography casts serious doubt on interpretations of pre-Enlightenment Scotland as intellectually moribund. Its aims, though, are more constructive than they are destructive. Baillie's diverse and expansive corpus of surviving manuscript and published writings provide an ideal lens through which to re-evaluate the intellectual milieu of his day. Studies of the intellectual culture of post-Reformation Scotland have begun to transform engrained assumptions about the inherent narrow-mindedness of Scottish Calvinism. We have caught glimpses of the cosmopolitan outlook of early modern Scots, notably in John Coffey's biography of Baillie's contemporary, Samuel Rutherford.[44] Recent essays by Giovanni Gellera and Alasdair Raffe have uncovered and explained the early reception of Cartesian ideas in Scotland's universities.[45] This work continues to build on the foundations laid long ago by Christine Shepherd in her groundbreaking thesis on arts curricula and the adoption of 'New Scientific' thinking in seventeenth-century Scotland.[46] The book-gathering habits of polymaths, such as Sir John Scot of Scotstarvit, and the writings of theologians, such as Robert Leighton, have

---

[44] Coffey, *Samuel Rutherford*.
[45] Giovanni Gellera, 'The Philosophy of Robert Forbes: A Scottish Scholastic Response to Cartesianism', *Journal of Scottish Philosophy*, 11:2 (2013), pp. 191–211; Alasdair Raffe, 'Intellectual Change before the Enlightenment: Scotland, the Netherlands and the Reception of Cartesian Thought, 1650–1700', *SHR*, 94:1 (2015), pp. 24–47.
[46] Christine Mary Shepherd, 'Philosophy and Science in the Arts Curriculum of the Scottish Universities in the 17th Century' (Ph.D. thesis, University of Edinburgh, 1974).

provided glimpses of conceptual depth and variance hitherto neglected.[47] Indeed, rare-books librarians in Scotland's university libraries today are documenting, with remarkable care, ownership marks and marginalia that furnish details about provenance and reading habits unparalleled in an English context.[48] The humanist obsession with textual criticism and ancient languages influenced the writings of figures as ideologically diverse as George Buchanan and James VI and I.[49] Ramist logic held a short-lived and contentious influence over the reform of university curricula spearheaded by Andrew Melville, and carried out by teaching staff at institutions in Aberdeen, St Andrews, Edinburgh and Glasgow.[50] By the time that Charles II was restored to the throne in 1660 and Baillie was at the end of his life, Scotland was poised to enter a period of intellectual ferment. Newtonian physics took hold and was adopted more readily and quickly in Scotland than in England. Royalist ideas were formulated and given clearer historical roots than ever before, and presbyterian and episcopalian authors conceived of their rival ecclesiastical polities with greater clarity and exegetical precision than was ever necessary under the Covenanting regime of the 1640s.[51]

Despite such tantalizing glimpses, vestiges of an older interpretative paradigm still persist.[52] By this account, seventeenth-century Scotland was awash with an illiberal and hegemonic Calvinism that eschewed reason and scholarly rigour for the sake of blindly defending orthodoxy. Hugh Trevor-Roper thus eulogized Baillie as 'the confident grave-digger of Anglicanism ... the voluble, invaluable letter-writer, that incomparable Scotch dominie, so learned, so acute, so factual, so complacent, so unshakably omniscient, so infallibly wrong'.[53] Such dismissive accounts of seventeenth-century Scotland may be traced back to writers such as Samuel Johnson, who derided the effects that the 'waste of reformation' had exerted on Scottish culture, and Victorians such as Henry Buckle, who denounced the Church of Scotland's ministry for

---

[47] Crawford Gribben, 'Robert Leighton, Edinburgh Theology, and the Collapse of the Presbyterian Consensus', in Elizabethanne Boran and Crawford Gribben (eds), *Enforcing Reformation in Ireland and Scotland, 1550–1700* (Aldershot, 2006), pp. 159–83. An excellent outline of Scotstarvit's library may be found online at https://www.st-andrews.ac.uk/library/specialcollections/collections/rarebooks/named/scotcollection/

[48] See, for instance, the wonderful online material included in the digital catalogues for Glasgow University Library's Special Collections and the wealth of material included in the descriptions of book collections housed in St Andrews Library Special Collections.

[49] David Allan, *Virtue, Learning and the Scottish Enlightenment* (Edinburgh, 1993).

[50] Steven J. Reid, *Humanism and Calvinism: Andrew Melville and the Universities of Scotland, 1560–1625* (Farnham, 2011).

[51] Jackson, *Restoration Scotland*; Raffe, *The Culture of Controversy*.

[52] For another claim that this paradigm still holds sway, see Crawford Gribben, 'Introduction', in Gribben and David George Mullan (eds), *Literature and the Scottish Reformation* (Aldershot, 2009), pp. 1–20.

[53] Hugh Trevor-Roper, 'Scotland and the Puritan Revolution', in *Religion, the Reformation and Social Change* (London, 1967), pp. 392–444, at p. 401.

'prolong[ing] the reign of ignorance, and stop[ping] the march of society'.[54] In such accounts, Baillie is considered symptomatic of an 'intellectual fare … as uniform, as monotonous and as unpalatable as [Scots'] unvarying daily diet of salt-beef and oatmeal'.[55]

The assumption, *a priori*, is that Scots were so caught up with a particularly rigid brand of orthodox theology that all other intellectual concerns were set aside. Just as English Puritans in the 1650s cancelled Christmas and attempted to censure all other expressions of a loose, ungodly morality, Scottish presbyterians have long been characterized as utterly opposed to any forms of intellectual creativity. Reformed orthodoxy is typically considered inimical to intellectual innovation or change.[56] This is nowhere more evident than in the work of Jonathan Israel, who traced the genesis of modern conceptions of liberty, the state, individual rights, and secularism to the decidedly heterodox writings of Baruch Spinoza.[57] By this account, the willingness of Spinoza, Hobbes, Descartes and others to question the epistemological foundations of divine knowledge drove humanity to conceive of the world in terms divorced from 'superstitious' ways of thinking. If heterodox ideas drove intellectual change, or progress towards intellectual development, then it is assumed that orthodox theology led divines backwards to increasingly outdated systems of thought. It is hardly my contention here that Baillie should be considered an early figure of the Scottish Enlightenment. Rather, I am arguing that claims about the origins of this later intellectual culture have encouraged scholarly complacency towards the ideas and ways of thinking that held currency during Baillie's life.

To suggest that such characterizations are unfair, though, is not to go far enough in this critique. Such an understanding of Calvinist or Reformed theology persists even in studies by historical theologians more attuned to the complexities of theological debate. The Covenanters have featured regularly in accounts of the Reformed theological tradition in Scotland and more irregularly in discussions of Reformed theology broadly conceived.[58] For historical theologians working in a Reformed tradition, the documents written by the Westminster Assembly and the commentaries by Scottish and English participants comprise a body of evidence of a vibrant but cohesive and living

---

[54] Samuel Johnson and James Boswell, *A Journey to the Western Islands of Scotland and the Journal of a Tour to the Hebrides*, ed. Peter Levi (London, 1984), p. 48; Henry Thomas Buckle, *On Scotland and the Scotch Intellect*, ed. H.J. Hanham (Chicago, 1970), p. 12.

[55] Trevor-Roper, 'Scotland and the Puritan Revolution', p. 427.

[56] For a recent manifestation of this trend, see Sarah Mortimer and John Robertson (eds), *The Intellectual Consequences of Religious Heterodoxy, c. 1600–1750* (Leiden, 2012).

[57] Jonathan Israel, *Radical Enlightenment: Philosophy and the Making of Modernity, 1650–1750* (Oxford, 2001); Israel, *Enlightenment Contested: Philosophy, Modernity, and the Emancipation of Man 1670–1752* (Oxford, 2006); Israel, *Democratic Enlightenment: Philosophy, Revolution and Human Rights 1760–1790* (Oxford, 2011).

[58] Thomas F. Torrance, *Scottish Theology: From John Knox to John McLeod Campbell* (Edinburgh, 1996); M. Charles Bell, *Calvin and Scottish Theology: The Doctrine of Assurance* (Edinburgh, 1985).

theological tradition. There is a degree of intellectual variance *within* this tradition but, according to the foremost commentator, there are distinctive lines at which 'orthodoxy' becomes 'heterodoxy'.[59] These impenetrable boundaries of orthodoxy tend to transcend particular moments and create a sense that theologians in this tradition were always cognizant of their common, confessional identity. The Westminster Confession of Faith, for instance, is seen not as the outcome of complex and (embarrassingly) fractious debates in the 1640s but, rather, as a crucial document in the genesis of a Reformed tradition that stemmed from previous debates at Dort, and were only fully realized by Francis Turretin and Johann Heidegger who co-wrote the *Formula Consensus Helvetica* (1675). In these discussions, Covenanters typically play a less significant role perhaps because many of them failed to produce works of systematic theology akin to those of contemporaries in Geneva or Amsterdam. When the works of Rutherford, Gillespie and Baillie's colleague at Glasgow David Dickson are highlighted, they are typically discussed only insofar as they conform to, or depart from, the doctrines laid down by Knox, Calvin and the first generation of Reformers. Both intellectual historians and historical theologians have been far too susceptible to accepting at face value the Manichean rhetoric of Covenanting tracts that present the intellectual landscape of their day in black-and-white terms. Such rhetorical techniques deliberately brought areas of questionable ideological divergence into focus, in the process obscuring points of overlap that persisted.

Baillie's printed and manuscript output was informed by a simplistic rhetoric of 'orthodoxy versus heterodoxy', 'truth versus error' and 'good versus evil'. Yet these stark lines in the sand dissolve with the slightest breeze. Such rhetorical tactics, for Baillie, were essential to communicate to his readers in simple and accessible language the content of debates that had raged for centuries amongst incredibly learned theologians. This book adopts the perspective that currents of humanist, reformed-orthodox, empiricist and Ramist thinking persisted alongside, and in creative tension with, each other.[60] Rather than trying to chart Scotland's *progress* towards the early Enlightenment, this book throws into high relief the contours of Baillie's thought on myriad subjects. Historiography of the Covenanters' ideas is characterized by almost single-minded discussion of the genealogy and implications of the 'concept of the covenant'. As with discussions of Reformed theology, these treatments of Covenanting intellectual culture eschew distinctive individual contributions in favour of building a picture of intellectual trends that transcend historical time. Accounts of the social, legal and theological dimensions of covenanting

---

[59] For the classic formulation of what follows, see Richard A. Muller, 'Calvin and the "Calvinists": Assessing Continuities and Discontinuities between the Reformation and Orthodoxy', *Calvin Theological Journal*, 30 (1995), pp. 345–75, and 31 (1996), pp. 125–60.
[60] Thus, more in line with the work of scholars like Anthony Grafton. See his work on early modern intellectual culture, especially his essays in *Defenders of the Text: The Traditions of Scholarship in an Age of Science, 1450–1800* (Cambridge, Mass., 1991).

in early modern Scotland have endowed the National Covenant of 1638 and the Solemn League and Covenant of 1643 with nationalist significance; the latter agreement bound the Covenanters and English Parliamentarians in a pact of mutual defence to further religious reforms in Britain.[61] Whilst the National Covenant may not immediately appear to have been an expression of latent Scottish frustrations with a perceived demotion to provincial status after the regal union of 1603, Macinnes has claimed that the Solemn League and Covenant enshrined a plot to restructure the British state along 'confederal' lines, thus preserving a sovereign Scottish state.[62] Continued historiographical focus on the significance of the covenants with regard to the formation of the modern British state has distracted from 'the essential ideas behind, and implicit in, the covenants themselves'.[63]

To appreciate fully the intellectual diversity of Covenanting Scotland, it is not only essential to confront the ideas implicit in the covenants but, more importantly, it is also crucial to explore the ideas of their subscribers. For Baillie, the National Covenant and the Solemn League and Covenant represented potentially effective means to secure religious reforms in the Church of Scotland. Although his objectives for reform were shared by some Covenanters, they diverged from the aspirations of others. Indeed, some Scots who believed that the Church needed to be reformed nevertheless refused to subscribe the Covenants because they did not consider them to be the best means to this end.[64] Subscription of the Covenants did not entail wholesale adoption of a homogeneous 'Covenanting ideology'.[65] Whilst the ideas that

[61] Jenny Wormald, Lords and Men in Scotland: Bonds of Manrent, 1442–1603 (Edinburgh, 1985); S.A. Burrell, 'The Covenant Idea as a Revolutionary Symbol – Scotland 1596–1637', Church History, 27 (1956), pp. 338–50; Burrell, 'The Apocalyptic Vision of the Early Covenanters', Church History, 43 (1964), pp. 1–24; G.D. Henderson, 'The Idea of the Covenant in Scotland', in The Burning Bush (Edinburgh, 1957), pp. 61–74; J.B. Torrance, 'Covenant or Contract? A Study of the Theological Background of Worship in 17th Century Scotland', Scottish Journal of Theology, 23 (1970), pp. 51–76. For a discussion of covenanting from an English perspective, see Edward Vallance, Revolutionary England and the National Covenant: State Oaths, Protestantism, and the Political Nation, 1553–1682 (Woodbridge, 2005).
[62] Allan Macinnes, 'The "Scottish Moment," 1638–45', in J.S.A. Adamson (ed.), The English Civil War: Conflict and Contexts, 1640–49 (Basingstoke, 2009), pp. 125–52, at p. 138.
[63] E.J. Cowan, 'The Covenanting Tradition in Scottish History', in Edward J. Cowan and Richard J. Finlay (eds), Scottish History: The Power of the Past (Edinburgh, 2002), pp. 121–45, at p. 121. To some extent, Cowan does just that in his, 'The Making of the National Covenant', in John Morrill (ed.), The Scottish National Covenant in its British Context (Edinburgh, 1990), pp. 68–89. A doctoral thesis has also explored the origins of Covenanting thought, albeit it takes for its starting point the problematic assumption that post-Reformation Scots may be neatly divided into 'presbyterian' and 'episcopalian' factions. See Vaughan T. Wells, 'The Origins of Covenanting Thought and Resistance: c. 1580–1638' (Ph.D. thesis, University of Stirling, 1997).
[64] John Strang, Principal of Glasgow University, is one of the best examples of this ambiguous stance towards the Covenants.
[65] Allan Macinnes, 'Covenanting Ideology in Seventeenth-Century Scotland', in Jane

lay behind the National Covenant and the Solemn League and Covenant were certainly important, it is crucial to understand how Scots understood and incorporated 'covenanting' ideas into pre-existing intellectual frameworks. As Laura Stewart has recently argued, historiographical focus on the text of National Covenant has obfuscated 'subtle and ambiguous' responses which, in fact, sparked debates in Covenanting Scotland that exposed complex meanings of the relationships between Church and state, individual and community.[66]

IV

An intellectual biography is best suited to the task of illuminating how these complex relations were shaped and reshaped over the course of the conflicts in 1640s and 1650s Scotland. As a genre, it forces the author to focus on the life and opinions of one individual across time. It offers a window onto broader trends and currents at play in the intellectual, political and religious cultures of the day, whilst remaining grounded in the life and actions of a particular individual. A book-length biographical study is at least in part indebted to chance. The sources related to Baillie are particularly rich and cover most of his life, giving a unique glimpse at what it was like for one Scot to live through periods of conformity, rebellion and schism. It is not simply enough, however, to argue that Baillie *ought to* have a biography because a particularly large number of sources related to his life survive. As has been argued thus far, the sources relating to Baillie's life demonstrate that he held a remarkable awareness of the historical significance of the period in which he was living. The choice to write an intellectual biography, then, allows for the reconstruction of Baillie's milieu as well as offering historians the chance to reflect on early modern attitudes towards the preservation of a paper legacy.

Too often, as I have argued in this introduction, the history of seventeenth-century Scotland has been hastily dealt with in terms of a series of trends or chronologically expansive changes. Whether it was the eventual triumph of presbyterianism after 1690 or the rise of a particularly fertile form of secularism, these explanations deal in broad brushstrokes with a period of extraordinary diversity, but lamentably capricious documentary survival. In this regard, a shift to the study of 'biographical history' – as termed by one prominent practitioner – serves to undermine these narratives and

Ohlmeyer (ed.), *Political Thought in Seventeenth-Century Ireland* (Cambridge, 2000), pp. 191–220; Kirsteen M. MacKenzie, 'Presbyterian Church Government and the "Covenanted Interest" in the Three Kingdoms, 1649–1660' (Ph.D. thesis, University of Aberdeen, 2008).
[66] Laura A.M. Stewart, 'Authority, Agency and the Reception of the Scottish National Covenant of 1638', in Armstrong and Ó hAnnracháin (eds), *Insular Christianity*, pp. 88–106, at p. 102.

refocus attention on the individual life.[67] There is little understanding of what it was like for someone, like Baillie, to have been living, writing and engaged in academic inquiry in Scotland in this period. Outstanding work on kirk session and burgh records has gone some way towards uncovering the experience of attending worship in a church in the period following the Reformation of 1560.[68] My decision to focus on one thinker has allowed me to account for the ways in which individuals encountered and addressed myriad topics of study and how such endeavours intersected with their daily lives. Alternatively, I could have chosen to address a particular concept in common currency during the 1640s and 1650s amongst Scottish intellectuals and produced a conceptual history following in the method of Reinhart Koselleck's *Begriffsgeschichte* and exemplified in David Armitage's expansive *Civil War: A History in Ideas* (2016). Such an approach would still allow for thematic analysis that ranged across a broad period chronologically and included deep conceptual analysis. This would allow for discussions of the ways in which intellectual traditions of humanism, Ramism, empiricism and Reformed theology not only interacted, but were *used by a thinker* in their daily writings and scholarly pursuits. Yet such an approach would inevitably privilege the life of ideas as something separate from the mind of the individual. In this register, discussion easily becomes disjointed from the complexities of individual lives and, as a result, the account produced does not allow for contingencies of personal circumstance. Such an approach, to my mind, lends itself to a dehumanizing account of intellectual culture, divorcing it from the undeniably human acts of reading, writing, discussion and revision. A life is never straightforward and an attempt to impose retrospective coherence is bound to smooth rough-hewn edges and divert attention away from moments of tension and seemingly inconsistent decisions. Yet it is precisely such moments that may provide unexpected clarity or a new perspective on a well-trodden subject.

This book, therefore, situates Baillie's mind in its contemporary intellectual context.[69] My focus on Baillie allows not only for discussion of the ways in which ideas interacted in his mind, but for careful appreciation of the considerations that led Baillie to put pen to paper in the first place. Certainly there are discursive contexts that are cogent to analysis of Baillie's ideas – and these are addressed at length in what follows – yet there are also what might be termed 'vocational' or 'professional' contexts that were also hugely influential not just to the content of Baillie's writings but also to the forms

[67] Derek Beales, 'History and Biography: An Inaugural Lecture', in T.C.W. Blanning and David Cannadine (eds), *History and Biography: Essays in Honour of Derek Beales* (Cambridge, 2002), pp. 266–83.
[68] Todd, *The Culture of Protestantism*. Also, see Langley, *Worship, Civil War and Community*.
[69] In much the same way as intellectual history is typically written in the 'Cambridge School'. See Quentin Skinner, *Visions of Politics*, vol. 1: *Regarding Method* (Cambridge, 2002).

in which they survive. Baillie's writings are coloured by concerns and duties related to his employ as a minister, divinity professor and religious controversialist. Appreciation of the obligations of these roles fruitfully informs analysis of their intellectual content, whilst the texts themselves cast light on how Baillie undertook his duties on a daily basis. He wrote the things that he did, in the way that he did, because of a confluence of everyday practices that helped set the tone for his writings and that also provide the essential backdrop for understanding them.

This biography is, therefore, conceived as a starting point for future scholarship drawing on the sources related to Baillie's life. More boldly, it is intended as a key to understanding the complex ways in which a life, an archive and a biography are interrelated but not identical. As I argue in the final chapter, Baillie's surviving papers were preserved as the result of his self-conscious decision to document contemporary affairs, as well as the intentional decisions of generations of posthumous readers who combed through his works, transcribed working copies and ensured that the volumes made their way safely into the archives of the Church of Scotland. An intellectual biography is only possible because of the creation of this archive. Yet the archive itself was only created and preserved because of readers' interests in Baillie as witness of contemporary affairs. His 'letters and journals' may be more appropriately renamed 'historical collections' to demonstrate the significance of this claim. This biography asks a different set of questions of the surviving print and manuscript sources and it draws a narrative out of these documents that runs counter to the intentions of the very individual – Baillie – who first gathered these documents together.

There is also a problem of anachronism inherent in use of the term 'biography' when conceiving of the life of an individual from the early modern period.[70] This is starkly borne out if we consider briefly the assumed relationship between archival remains and an individual life that undergirds modern biography. Unlike modern biographers, Baillie and his contemporaries did not conceive of a life as something that gave rise to a discrete body of documents or papers.[71] Perhaps only with John Aubrey – working primarily after Baillie's death – do we begin to see the practice of life-writing becoming intertwined with efforts at simultaneously archiving an individual's life.[72] Writers now leave stashes of papers in their will to a designated custodian with express instructions on how to manage them and monitor access. American Presidents cap off their term in office with the foundation of a presidential library, expressly designed to house papers related to their

[70] For some reflection on these problems, see Adam Smyth, *Autobiography in Early Modern England* (Cambridge, 2010), pp. 1–14.
[71] For an expression of the currency of this assumption by a modern biographer, see Leon Edel, *Writing Lives: Principia Biographica* (London, 1984).
[72] John Aubrey, *Brief Lives with An Apparatus for the Lives of our English Mathematical Writers*, ed. Kate Bennett (2 vols, Oxford, 2015).

political career. Today, there is such a thing as the *personal* archive, or the *personal* library: repositories that exist expressly for the purpose of preserving evidence of an individual's life and their writings. In Baillie's case, however, his archive survives because he was interested in preserving material documenting the times in which he lived. It is only indirectly that these documents cast light on Baillie's life and thought and, even then, the information available is episodic, disparate and wanting in places.

This account of Baillie's life and writings began with my rediscovery of the surviving manuscript sources. I then moved outward from the sources, reconstructing the lineaments of Baillie's thought at particular moments and discussing his thinking in light of the relevant contexts. This, in fact, is where my choice to write a biography of Baillie has proved most useful. I have been able to dispense with labels whilst reading my sources so as to remain attuned to subtle dissonances, silences or other clues that might betray intellectual diversity. Rather than approaching the life of Robert Baillie as a coherent unit, I have returned to the archives in order to gather together all remaining evidence of his life. I have reassembled the extant papers to produce an account of Baillie's life and thought that allows for the fact that a human being often undergoes myriad changes of heart throughout their lifespan. Traditionally, biographers have likened a biography to a portrait. Yet such a metaphor creates the misleading impression that an individual's intellectual formation is static. Perhaps such a metaphor is suitable for a brief life or an entry in a biographical dictionary; however, a portrait, unlike that of Dorian Gray, does not alter as its subject ages. A life is comprised of countless instances of lived experience, spanning decades. It is a semi-permeable and translucent vessel, through which experiences and ideas are refracted, in which beliefs accrue and from which assumptions are discarded. During the decades of Baillie's life, it just so happened that the religious, political and social circumstances in which he lived underwent revolutionary change and he often played a role in how these events progressed.

This leads to a final consideration related to biography, memory and archives. Why are particular lives remembered whilst others are forgotten? And, for that matter, how is a life remembered? Baillie was not a unique thinker, nor was he one who was remembered long after his death for his published output. Baillie is remembered for his efforts in documenting events during his lifetime and this memory persists because he was particularly adept at preserving his personal papers. Yet it is not simply enough to say that, for the early modern period, lives that get remembered and written are those for which we are lucky enough to have access to sufficient source material. The mere survival of material does not make that material itself particularly illuminating or interesting. Set in a broader context of early modern history-writing and document collection, Baillie's efforts appear particularly remarkable, if not altogether novel. From relatively early on in the conflicts in Scotland over the Prayer Book of 1637, Baillie identified the time in which he lived as one of potentially dramatic upheavals. He persisted in documenting the progress of events because he must have trusted his instincts that future generations – not to mention contemporaries – would want to understand why Scots had reacted to their lawful monarch's actions in the ways that they did. In the progress of documenting his life and times, Baillie created an invaluable source for historians. Paradoxically, it was the character and content of this collection of impersonal letters and documents that simultaneously contributed to the creative processes of remembering and forgetting that have shaped Baillie's legacy ever since.

V

The following chapters present an account of Baillie's intellectual milieu with as much depth as the surviving documents permit. My analysis attends to nuances and omissions alongside the text itself, to arrive at a clearer understanding of the intellectual currents prevalent in Baillie's lifetime. In the process, Scotland emerges anew as a vibrant and bustling metropolis of cultural exchange and intellectual ferment situated on the periphery of an international 'Republic of Letters', and the Covenanters appear as a fractious group tenuously united in opposition to a series of common enemies.

Chapter 1 provides a chronological sketch of Baillie's life drawing on an array of archival and published sources to set the stage for the analysis that follows. In particular, this chapter addresses Baillie's intellectual formation through his formal education and it includes a discussion of the role that his correspondence played in his daily life. Chapter 2 illuminates the surviving evidence of his views concerning the limits and extent of monarchical power. In this vein, his ideas are distinguished from the tradition of 'monarchomach' authors, such as George Buchanan and the anonymous author of the *Vindiciae contra Tyrannos*, and his contemporary, Samuel Rutherford, and Baillie emerges as a proponent of a distinctive version of a form of monarchical loyalism prevalent amongst Covenanting elite. Chapter 3 situates Baillie's amorphous discussions of church government in the context of contemporary debates over the relative merits of presbyterian, congregational and episcopal forms. Whilst Baillie firmly dismissed any affinities that his ecclesiology held with congregational authors, he was far less hasty to dismiss some of the finer exegetical points prevalent amongst defenders of episcopacy. Chapter 4 traces the contours of Baillie's writings on theological controversies, showing the ways in which his opinions about what constituted 'orthodox' and 'heterodox' beliefs were malleable. For Baillie, 'Reformed orthodoxy' was not a clearly defined confessional position. More often, it was a stick with which he could beat opponents who, in his opinion, had failed to adhere strictly to a particularly severe set of standards.

Chapter 5 demonstrates Baillie's ambivalent views on liturgical reform. Baillie was a staunch supporter of kneeling to receive communion and, in fact, he defended a number of elements in worship deemed 'superstitious' by other Covenanting ministers. Nonetheless he emerged as *the* official critic of the Scottish Prayer Book of 1637. This chapter casts Covenanting opposition of the Prayer Book in a different light, and it reaffirms historiographical opinion that Charles I and Archbishop Laud were misguided in attempting such a brash reform of worship in Scotland. Chapter 6 situates Baillie's scholarly and homiletic approaches to the Bible alongside one another, highlighting the degree to which both exegetical methods were undergirded by a staunch defence of Scripture's self-sufficient authority. Although, in the pulpit, Baillie pruned his texts of content aimed at a more learned audience, his practice of opening up passages in a clear, accessible and relatable manner was closely informed by his scholarly understanding of the Bible. Finally, Chapter 7 returns to Baillie's archive and his manuscript 'letters and journals', exploring its collection and transmission. This biography concludes with a discussion of the impact that the creation of Baillie's archive has held over his legacy and, indeed, the influence that his own editorial decisions may have held over the ways in which he has been read and cited ever since.

Baillie was a remarkable individual, who lived in a period of unprecedented political and religious turmoil. His writings are unique amongst his compatriots and scholars must cast far and wide across different time periods and national contexts to find examples of individuals who engaged in similar practices of document collecting, editing and narration.[73] My aim in writing this biography is not to inflate Baillie's forgotten celebrity, nor to show that Baillie was a particularly novel thinker. Instead, I hope to inject the life and vigour back into an exceptionally diverse collection of writings that gave rise to them in the first place. Baillie's writings exhibit the drama of his day perhaps more than any other writer working in Scotland at the same moment. They go a long way towards reinvigorating study of a sorely neglected period in British historiography. And they raise questions that may move the study of this period beyond reductive dichotomies and unhelpful judgements. It certainly makes Baillie's own humility – frequently aired – appear in a far different light. Although he had 'publickly professed ... to be much fitter to be a scholler to others than a master to any', Baillie's writings demonstrate an extraordinary historical awareness of the significance of the period in which he lived.[74]

---

[73] For other similar examples, see James Amelang, *The Flight of Icarus: Artisan Autobiography in Early Modern Europe* (Stanford, 1998); Matthew Lundin, *Paper Memory: A Sixteenth-Century Townsman Writes his World* (London, 2012). Also pertinent will be Tom Hamilton's forthcoming work on Pierre de L'Estoile's accounts of the French Wars of Religion.

[74] Robert Baillie to John Young, [n.d.], *LJB*, vol. III, p. 261.

1

Biography and Intellectual Formation

I

Robert Baillie was born in 1602 in Glasgow. Much of what we know about Baillie's life is gleaned from the rich selection of extant documents that he produced himself; he was a meticulous chronicler of contemporary events. True to form, he recorded his precise time of birth on a blank leaf of a student notebook: Friday 30 April at 1:15 pm.[1] Later, Baillie explained that he had been born in the same street as the theologian John Cameron, who had been 'borne in our Salt-Mercat, a few doores from the place of my birth'.[2] The Saltmarket was a southern continuation of Glasgow's High Street, running from the Market Cross down to the River Clyde. At the turn of the seventeenth century, Glasgow's population was approximately 7,000 and the burgh was entering a period of sustained economic growth. Whilst eastern burghs such as Aberdeen and Edinburgh were better situated to exploit trade routes with Continental Europe, Glaswegian merchants developed the burgh as a hub of domestic trade and its craftsmen established profitable textile and metalwork industries.[3] In the 1650s, a captain in Cromwell's army, who had hitherto been critical of the Scottish towns he had visited, extolled the 'now famous and flourishing Glasgow', which he insisted should be considered the 'nonsuch of Scotland, where an English florist may pick up a posie'.[4]

Like most seventeenth-century ministers, Baillie's background was one of reasonably high social standing, only surpassed by leading merchants and landholders. In the nineteenth century, Laing incorrectly suggested that Baillie's

---

[1] EUL, La.III.109, Robert Baillie, Student notebook, [c. 1620], [fo. 110r]. The sentence reads: 'Robertus Baillize [sic] natio pridie Kal Mai hora sesquiquarta a meridie a 1602 die veneris'.

[2] Robert Baillie to William Douglas, 23 May 1660, *LJB*, vol. III, p. 402.

[3] Glasgow probably grew to about 12,000 people by 1640, making it similar in size to regional centres in England such as York, Norwich or Bristol: see R.A. Houston, *The Population History of Britain and Ireland, 1500–1750* (Cambridge, 1995), pp. 19–20. For Glasgow's economic prosperity, see T.M. Devine, 'Introduction: The Development of Glasgow to 1830: Medieval Burgh to Industrial City', in T.M. Devine and Gordon Jackson (eds), *Glasgow* (2 vols, Manchester, 1995), vol. I, pp. 6–10.

[4] Richard Franck, *Northern Memoirs, Calculated for the Meridian of Scotland: To which is added the contemplative and practical angle, writ in the year 1658* (Edinburgh, 1821), pp. 103, 107.

father was Thomas Baillie, a merchant and descendant of the Baillies of Lamington, a family of minor lairds.[5] According to Glasgow municipal records, published after Laing's account, Baillie's father was evidently James Baillie, a 'merchant, B[urgess] and G[uild] B[rethren]' of Glasgow, and his mother, Helen Gibson, was the daughter of Henry Gibson and Annabella Forsyth.[6] From surviving records it appears that Baillie had one sister, Christian, and no brothers. Nevertheless, we get a sense from Baillie's letters that he felt to be strongly linked to a wider, spiritual community of Scots. In many letters, Baillie addressed recipients as 'cousin' but this was not an expression of actual familial ties. More likely, it was intended as a term of affection, highlighting the close spiritual links that Baillie felt bound himself together with other godly individuals. Baillie frequently engaged in heated debate with 'cousins' such as John Creighton, the alleged Arminian, or John Rae, the zealous opponent of liturgical ceremonies, in attempts to convince them to revise misguided beliefs.[7] In such exchanges, Baillie insisted on theological precision and his proselytizing endeavours could, on occasion, provoke him to a frustrated outburst. In 1639, for example, writing to his brother-in-law, Henry Glen, Baillie doubted his effectiveness as a pastor, acknowledging that 'all that I am able to doe this twyse seven years, hes not moved yow, my onlie Brother, to amend bot one fault'.[8]

Baillie's own education in the principles of Reformed orthodoxy began at home and continued in Glasgow's grammar school, which he entered in November 1613, aged eleven. The school's demanding daily schedule and curriculum extended to instruction five days a week, beginning at 5 a.m. and finishing at 5 p.m., with students obliged to converse only in Latin during the school day.[9] Although not all students progressed to university, the school curriculum was largely intended to prepare students for rigorous Latin entrance examinations, and the academic staff at Glasgow University often interested themselves in curriculum standards. No documentation exists to confirm the particular course that Baillie followed, but in 1643 the university produced a revised curriculum for the school, provoked by an apparent decline in the quality of university applicants.[10] According to this revised curriculum,

[5]   Laing, 'Memoir', in *LJB*, Appendix, xxi–xxii.
[6]   James R. Anderson (ed.), *The Burgesses and Guild Brethren of Glasgow, 1573–1750* (Edinburgh, 1925), p. 81. For Helen Gibson's testament dated 18 April 1635, see *The Commissariot Record of Glasgow, Register of Testaments, 1547–1800* (Edinburgh, 1901), p. 189.
[7]   See NCL, Baill MS 1, Robert Baillie, 'A Conference by letters with a Canterburian minister anent the Arminian tenet of the Saints apostasie', pp. 1–135; ibid., Robert Baillie to John Rae, 14 June 1643, pp. 375–8.
[8]   Robert Baillie to Henry Glen, November 1639, *LJB*, vol. I, p. 229.
[9]   James Grant, *History of the Burgh and Parish Schools of Scotland* (2 vols, London and Glasgow, 1876), vol. I, pp. 162, 169, 161.
[10] Grant erroneously dated this curriculum to 1573 when the Privy Council had attempted to reform Scotland's burgh schools. For the Latin original, see Cosmo Innes (ed.), *Munimenta alme Universitatis glasguensis: Records of the University of Glasgow from its Foundation till 1727* (4 vols, Glasgow, 1854), vol. II, pp. 307–10.

Latin grammar and composition should be taught from texts by the Flemish humanist Johannes Despauterius, namely his *Grammaticae institutiones pars prima* (1512) and his *Syntaxis* (1509). Alongside grammatical and syntactical works, students were directed to read ancient and neoclassical authors such as Cicero, Terence, Ovid, Desiderius Erasmus and George Buchanan. Christian doctrine was also introduced via catechetical works such as Patrick Sharp's catechism, *Doctrinae Christianae brevis explicatio* (1599). Furthermore, Baillie would have attended school from 8 a.m. on Sundays for theological tuition before attending morning service, after which students discussed the sermon in Latin with their tutor before proceeding to the afternoon service.

Despite suggestions that the quality of education at Scotland's grammar schools declined after the Reformation, Baillie reflected positively on his experiences. Baillie subsequently acknowledged Robert Blair, a prominent nonconformist minister and one of Baillie's earliest known teachers, as having held significant influence over his early spiritual education.[11] Reflecting on 'those yeers of my childhood and youth', he later wrote to Blair that 'I were ungratefull if I should not acknowledge you after my Parents, the first and principall instrument' of his education.[12] In 1638, Baillie likewise wrote to his cousin in the Netherlands, William Spang, confirming that Blair had possessed the ability, 'greater than any man I know living, to insinuate the fear of God in the hearts of young schollars'.[13] Blair's own intellectual commitments and, by extension, his potential influence on Baillie are not easily categorized. If nothing else, Blair instilled in Baillie a strong belief in Scripture's self-sufficiency, which became an intellectual commitment evident throughout Baillie's published works. 'To be reading, meditating, and teaching philosophic notions', Blair wrote, 'distracted the mind more from divine contemplations.'[14] Refusing to conform to the Perth Articles in the 1620s, Blair was forced to resign his position at Glasgow University and to relocate to a parish charge in Bangor, County Down. Nevertheless, Blair proved a reluctant supporter of popular acts of presbyterian resistance to the Scottish Prayer Book in 1637. Throughout the 1640s and 1650s, Blair demonstrated little taste for playing a prominent role in public affairs. When the Church's ministry divided between Protestors and Resolutioners over criteria for admission into church services during the 1650s, Blair became more closely aligned with Baillie and the Resolutioner faction that sought to reincorporate erstwhile Royalists into the Church. Nevertheless, Blair remained alienated from the main body of Resolutioners because of his efforts to negotiate an end to the schism with the Protestors. Whilst Blair and Baillie held

---

[11] Thomas M'Crie (ed.), *The Life of Mr. Robert Blair, Minister of St Andrews* (Edinburgh, 1848), p. 9.

[12] Robert Baillie, 'For his Reverend and wel beloved Brother Master Robert Blaire, Minister of St. Andrewes', in *Historicall Vindication*, sig. A2r.

[13] Robert Baillie to William Spang, 'History of the General Assembly at Glasgow in 1638', *LJB*, vol. I, p. 174.

[14] M'Crie (ed.), *Life of Robert Blair*, p. 35.

distinct views on church government or particular liturgical issues, Blair's professed reluctance to engage in public controversies is also discernible in some of Baillie's later writings.

A characteristic aversion to public controversy may help to explain ambiguities in Baillie's intellectual development. Although he hailed from the west of Scotland – traditionally regarded as the main source of radicalism – like his mentor Blair, Baillie typically claimed to avoid unnecessary controversy. From one perspective, it might appear that Baillie always sought compromise and a suitable *via media* when engaging in debates. From another perspective, however, Baillie's reluctance to offend others might betray a deep-seated insecurity that he harboured throughout his life. Often quick to defend a position that garnered widespread support, Baillie was rarely one to strike out on his own and argue from a perspective considered unpopular. Throughout his career, Baillie's desire to maintain peaceful relations with neighbours led him to bide his time and remain noncommittal to various reforms until it appeared that opinions more generally had shifted in their favour. Unlike Blair, Baillie's initial forays into religious controversy indicated an instinctive insistence on the need to obey the authority of the Scottish episcopate. In 1610, James VI and I had restored the Scottish episcopate's powers of order and jurisdiction over the Presbyterian Church. Hence, Baillie was trained as a minister in an episcopal Church, under the metropolitan jurisdiction of John Spottiswood, subsequently best known for his apologetic account of episcopacy in the post-Reformation Church. Following his appointment to the archiepiscopal see of Glasgow in 1603, Spottiswood had played a central role in ecclesiastical and burgh politics. As archbishop of Glasgow, Spottiswood was also responsible for the appointment of burgesses and other office-holders, and since Baillie's father, James, was posthumously described in 1631 as a merchant and burgess of Glasgow, he may well have held his municipal office on Spottiswood's recommendation.[15] Connections between Baillie and Spottiswood were further confirmed when Baillie visited St Andrews in 1621, where he was evidently granted a private audience with Spottiswood.[16]

II

Baillie matriculated at Glasgow University in March 1617, and proceeded to receive, from his university education, a firm grounding in Aristotelian philosophy and the Bible. Characterization of the Scottish arts curriculum as 'surprisingly "secular"' cannot be sustained without qualification.[17] The arts degree was largely intended to train ministers for the Church. By the time

15 Anderson (ed.), *Burgesses and Guild Brethren*, p. 81
16 EUL, La.III.109, Baillie, Student notebook, p. 128.
17 Coffey, *Samuel Rutherford*, p. 63.

Baillie matriculated in 1617, logic, physics, metaphysics and ethics were all taught in a Reformed theological framework, with the intent of preparing students – should they choose – for postgraduate theological study.

In the early seventeenth century, there were universities in Glasgow, Aberdeen, St Andrews and Edinburgh. Scotland's universities retained distinctive characteristics that reflected the intellectual commitments of their academic staff, despite broad similarities in teaching systems and curricula.[18] Traditionally, one regent would take the same class through all four years of the arts course. Glasgow and Aberdeen introduced a 'professorial system' of teaching by the early seventeenth century, in which each regent specialized in one year of the curriculum, whereas St Andrews had reverted to the traditional 'regenting system' in the 1580s.[19] In the late sixteenth century, the theologian Andrew Melville introduced a humanist arts curriculum in Scotland that he personally implemented in Glasgow and St Andrews in the 1570s and 1580s, which later influenced curricula at Aberdeen and Edinburgh. According to this curriculum, first-year students studied Greek grammar and the rules of rhetoric; second-year students studied rhetoric and Aristotle's *Categories*; third-year students studied Aristotelian logic, ethics and politics; and fourth-year students studied physics, cosmography, history and basic Hebrew.[20] Although Melville had prescribed a uniform curriculum, variations emerged according to the intellectual predilections of regents at each university. In addition to emphasizing the need to study Aristotle in the original Greek, Melville had also sought to implement the use of textbooks by the French philosopher Petrus Ramus, noted for using logical principles as a tool to study other subjects. By the 1620s, however, evidently only regents at Edinburgh continued to teach Ramist texts.[21] In the first half of the seventeenth century, student notebooks continued to evidence a conservative focus on the study of Aristotle, whilst eschewing the study of Ramist manuals. Differences amongst regents emerged most noticeably in attitudes towards 'new' philosophies, such as René Descartes's metaphysics and Isaac Newton's physics; regents at Aberdeen integrated Cartesianism into graduation theses in the 1650s, whereas Glasgow's regents remained reluctant to teach Descartes's metaphysics well into the 1690s.[22]

---

[18] The best overview of the arts curricula in seventeenth-century Scottish universities is still Christine Shepherd's thesis. See Christine Mary Shepherd, 'Philosophy and Science in the Arts Curriculum of the Scottish Universities in the 17th Century' (Ph.D. thesis, University of Edinburgh, 1974).

[19] Ibid., pp. 18–23.

[20] For Glasgow's statutes instituting this curriculum reform, see Steven J. Reid, *Humanism and Calvinism: Andrew Melville and the Universities of Scotland, 1560–1625* (Farnham, 2011), pp. 79–81. For the text of the statutes, see 'Praelectionum et officii ratio a quatuor Professoribus Regentibus observanda', in Innes (ed.), *Munimenta glasguensis*, vol. II, pp. 45–6.

[21] Reid, *Humanism and Calvinism*, pp. 256, 265.

[22] Ibid., pp. 340, 319ff; Giovanni Gellera, 'The Philosophy of Robert Forbes: A Scottish Scholastic Response to Cartesianism', *Journal of Scottish Philosophy*, 11:2 (2013), pp. 191–211; Shepherd, 'Philosophy and Science', p. 318.

In 1617, Baillie entered Glasgow amidst rising tensions over James VI and I's proposed implementation of a set of liturgical reforms that came to be known as the 'Five Articles of Perth'. These articles introduced kneeling during communion, private baptism, private communion for the sick, confirmation by a bishop and the observance of Holy Days. Introduction of these articles in the Perth General Assembly of 1618 sparked widespread controversy over the king's powers in ecclesiastical matters and led to petitioning campaigns in Glasgow, Edinburgh and the Lowlands. As a student, Baillie was mentored by leading opponents of the Perth Articles, including Blair, David Dickson and Glasgow University's principal, Robert Boyd of Trochrig. In a prefatory letter to Boyd's posthumous *Epistolam Pauli Apostoli ad Ephesios* (1652), Baillie warmly recollected 'listening to the greatest part of this work … with so much delight, that the recollection of this former time still overwhelms my soul with great sweetness'.[23] For Baillie, Boyd and other teachers had shown outstanding care and attentiveness to their students' needs and, over thirty years later, he lavished praise on Boyd as a totem of Scottish erudition. In characteristically self-deprecating tones, Baillie concluded his panegyric to Boyd: 'Why not cut off the chattering magpie, so that the Nightingale may begin his final song?'[24]

These prominent opponents of the Perth Articles oversaw Baillie's study of Aristotelian philosophy. Whilst the humanist reforms that Melville had introduced to Glasgow in the 1580s still pertained when Baillie matriculated, significant curriculum changes had occurred. The university's statutes also provided only a bare framework for the arts degree, and regents could choose their own texts, with approval from the dean of the arts faculty.[25] There was 'limited' evidence that Melville's drive to teach Aristotle in its original Greek was successful, but the 'broader experimental spirit of Melville's curriculum', particularly his introduction of authors such as Ramus, had failed by the early 1610s.[26] Baillie's surviving student notebook largely supports a conservative, Neo-Aristotelian backlash against Ramus, but certain caveats are required. Baillie used this notebook during the fourth year of his degree (1620–21), based on the notebook's intermittent dates and content, which include excerpts from Porphyry and Johannes Sleidan's *Commentariorum de statu religionis et reipublicae Carlo V. Caesare libri XXVI* (1555).[27] The notebook is predominantly written in Latin, with diary entries and sermon notes in English.[28] The only Greek excerpts in Baillie's notebook appeared within

---

[23]   Robert Baillie, 'Ad Lectorem Epistola', in Robert Boyd, *Epistolam Pauli Apostoli ad Ephesios Praelectiones supra CC. Lectione varia, multifaria Eruditione, et Pietate singulare refertae* (London, 1652), n.p.
[24]   In the same letter, for instance, Baillie recollected Boyd's ability to quote the Greek Fathers 'perfectly from memory'.
[25]   Innes (ed.), *Munimenta glasguensis*, vol. II, p. 46.
[26]   Reid, *Humanism and Calvinism*, pp. 256, 265.
[27]   EUL, La.III.109, Baillie, Student notebook, pp. 111, 189.
[28]   For the sermons and diary entries see ibid., pp. 16–110, 126–36, 291–309.

passages copied from Latin treatises.[29] Notwithstanding, a set of disputation theses which Baillie later prepared for his own students in 1627 suggests that students were still expected to comprehend, and even to dispute, in Greek since all theses began with a quotation from Aristotle (or Porphyry) in the original Greek, followed by *consequentiae* in both Latin and Greek.[30] In line with a reaction against Ramist textbooks, Baillie studied rhetoric through the humanist Latin grammarian Julius Caesar Scaliger's *Poetics* (1561), rather than Talon's *Institutiones*.[31] Aristotle was also not the only ancient philosopher studied, as evidenced by brief notes on Platonic ideas, interspersed with commonplaces from Horace's Odes.[32] Interested in classical historical works, Baillie had evidently read Jean Bodin's *Methodus ad facilem historiarum cognitidem* (1572) in addition to Sleidan.[33] Nearly sixty pages of his student notebook are filled with notes on Roman emperors from Plutarch's *Lives* and about 120 pages are filled with notes on sermons to which Baillie had either listened or prepared himself.[34]

As a student, Baillie would have been introduced to subjects such as logic, ethics and metaphysics through the use of 'post-Ramist' compendia. These were probably used because they provided brief distillations of huge corpora of work that needed to be covered during the arts degree in comparatively short periods of study. For instance, Baillie took notes on Bartholomäus Keckermann's posthumous *Systema physicum* (1610) on the *praecognitae* of philosophy.[35] Read as one of sundry interpretations of Aristotle, such works were mainly admired for their formal qualities, particularly their brief and perspicuous organization.[36] Like Keckermann, Baillie drew on principles of Aristotelian logic as tools to inform the study and teaching of other disciplines such as theology and homiletics, as evidenced in passages from Keckermann dictated to Baillie by a regent. Under the heading *de subjecto et effecti* of philosophy, Baillie included notes on 'the study of theology' which was based on 'the accurate studying from the beginning of divine words in their original language'. Philosophy was 'the most useful and necessary [tool]' to raise and clearly explain difficult points of theology, whereby for the effective teaching of theology such questions could be laid out 'in their most

---

[29]   Ibid., pp. 1, 2, 5, 119.
[30]   NCL, Baill MS 1, Robert Baillie, 'Ex primariis Philosophiae partibus Thesium sylloge', pp. 10–22.
[31]   EUL, La.III.109, Baillie, Student notebook, pp. 211–47.
[32]   Ibid., pp. 7–14. Baillie also cited Plato in the *consequentiae* of some of his metaphysical theses, see NCL, Baill MS 1, Robert Baillie, 'Ex primariis Philosophiae partibus Thesium sylloge', pp. 11, 18.
[33]   EUL, La.III.109, Baillie, Student notebook, p. 247.
[34]   For Plutarch's *Lives*, see ibid., pp. 139–87. For the sermon notes, see ibid., pp. 16–110, 126–37.
[35]   See 'Quadam ex Keckermanni stystemate [sic] Physico excerpta et primum ex praecognitis Philosophicis', in EUL, La.III.109, Baillie, Student notebook, pp. 1–6.
[36]   Indeed Baillie refuted 'Keckermanni errores' alongside those of Zarabella and Julius Pacius in interpreting Aristotle, see NCL, Baill MS 1, 'De Mente Agente', pp. 6–7.

simple parts and pure or mixed propositions, whether in sacred scripture or in *systemate*'.[37]

Whereas Baillie completed the arts course at Glasgow University under the tutelage of leading opponents of James VI and I's liturgical innovations, prominent conformist ministers shaped his intellectual formation between 1621 and 1625. After the 1621 Parliament passed the Perth Articles into law, Boyd resigned his post as University Principal because, according to Baillie, 'he is resolvit not to obey'.[38] King James wished to reform Glasgow and St Andrews to be 'the principall fountayne of religion and good letters in Scotland', and thus appointed the theologian John Cameron to replace Boyd as Principal in 1621. Alongside Cameron, Baillie subsequently acknowledged the influence of William Struthers, minister of St Giles, Edinburgh. As Baillie later recounted, both Struthers and Cameron had encouraged him to 'some parts of conformity, which ... might have led me, as many my betters, to have run on in all the errours and defections of these bad times'.[39] Whilst Cameron did not arrive in Glasgow until 1622, and had abandoned his post by the following March, his short-lived tenure as Principal exposed Baillie first-hand to controversies over the royal supremacy and pan-European academic debates over Scriptural authority.[40] The nature of Baillie's encounter with Struthers is, however, more elusive. Baillie had probably heard Struthers preach as minister of the High Kirk in Glasgow between 1612 and 1614, but Baillie's above-quoted remark indicates that he may well have heard some of Struthers's sermons in Edinburgh in 1621 or 1622. As late as 1617, Struthers had opposed James's liturgical innovations, but by 1619, he had atoned for his initial opposition and started preaching sermons in Edinburgh urging conformity. Shortly thereafter, Baillie graduated MA from Glasgow University, and undertook a tour of Scotland during which he visited members of the Scottish episcopate, including John Spottiswood, archbishop of St Andrews and David Lindsay, bishop of Brechin, nonconformist ministers, such as William Scot of Cupar, whilst also hearing sermons in numerous parishes around Edinburgh and St Andrews.[41]

[37] EUL, La.III.109, Baillie, Student notebook, p. 5.
[38] Ibid., p. 69.
[39] 'Dedicatory epistle to Robert Blair', in Baillie, *Historicall Vindication*.
[40] For likely dating of Cameron's tenure from sometime in 1622 to March 1623, see Robert Wodrow, *Collections upon the Lives of the Reformers and Most Eminent Ministers of the Church of Scotland* (2 vols, Glasgow, 1834–45), vol. II, pt II, p. 161; John Cameron, *TA ΣΩΖΟΜΕΝΑ sive opera partim ab auctore ipso edita, partim post ejus obitum vulgata*, (Geneva, 1642), p. 446.
[41] For Baillie's description of these travels, see EUL, La.III.109, Baillie, Student notebook, pp. 127–8, 291–309.

III

Robert Baillie was admitted to the office of regent at his alma mater on 16 August 1625.[42] Having shown an inclination to defend royal religious policy, Baillie's role as regent enabled him to immerse himself in pedagogical duties and curriculum reform. As a regent on the arts course, Baillie may well have taught members of noble families who would later take a leading role in Covenanting opposition to Charles I; he also taught Archibald Johnston of Wariston, who was later responsible for drafting the National Covenant in 1638.[43] Baillie evidently championed implementation of more rigorous Hebrew language tuition, as explained in an oration delivered in 1629 that was entitled 'In praise of the Hebrew Tongue'. Believing that Hebrew needed to be taught from a young age, Baillie's suggested reforms would have extended further than Melville's earlier alterations to the arts curriculum. By contrast, Baillie regretted that the study of Hebrew was 'so restricted, as if [theology students] could easily cross this sea in a mere hull of a ship'.[44]

Baillie's diligence as regent later endeared him to several former students, especially Hugh, Lord Montgomery, eldest son of Alexander Montgomery, sixth earl of Eglinton.[45] Perhaps in repayment for his diligence as his son's tutor, Eglinton secured the vacant charge of Kilwinning, Ayrshire, for Baillie in 1631, much to his delight considering that since 1620 Baillie had yearned 'to die and liv in an landvart [i.e. landward or country] kirk that is offerit'.[46] Whether Baillie's ordination conformed either to 'presbyterian' or 'episcopal' practice, this moment did not significantly impact his later career trajectory as has previously been suggested.[47] Baillie's early misgivings about the Covenanting movement, discussed below, derived from various factors in his intellectual development and not simply from the style of his ordination. Notwithstanding, on 25 May 1631, Glasgow presbytery's minutes recorded Baillie's ordination, after a committee of parishioners from Kilwinning had appeared before the Glaswegian presbytery and Archbishop James Law on 20 April to consent to Baillie's admission to their church.[48] Evidently in the

[42] He did not, however, take his oath of office until September 1626, and his inaugural oration on the Aristotelian subject of the 'agent mind' is dated as having been presented in 1627. See Laing, 'Memoir', in *LJB*, Appendix, xxvi–xxvii; NCL, Baill MS 1, Robert Baillie, 'Oratio in Academiae Glasguensis comitiis habita a R.B. anno 1627 cum in Regentium numerum solemniter cooptaretur De mente agent', pp. 1–10.

[43] See Laing, 'Memoir', in *LJB*, Appendix, xxvii.

[44] NCL, Baill MS 1, Baillie, 'In Laudem Linguae Hebraeae', p. 24.

[45] Hugh matriculated at Glasgow on 29 February 1628 and, therefore, was taught by Baillie. See Innes (ed.), *Munimenta glasguensis*, vol. I, p. 80.

[46] EUL, La.III.109, Baillie, Student notebook, p. 293.

[47] For conflicting claims that Baillie received either episcopal or presbyterian orders, see Robert Aiken (ed.), *Letters and Journals written by the deceased Mr. Robert Baillie, Principal of the University of Glasgow* (2 vols, Edinburgh, 1775), vol. I, v; H.M.B. Reid, *The Divinity Professors in the University of Glasgow, 1640–1903* (Glasgow, 1923), p. 82.

[48] F.N. McCoy, *Robert Baillie and the Second Scots Reformation* (Berkeley, 1974), pp. 21–2.

early 1630s, the Scottish episcopate functioned in cooperation with local church courts in the ordination of ministers. Following his ordination, Baillie moved to the rural parish of Kilwinning, about thirty miles south-west of Glasgow. As Baillie later recalled, his Kilwinning congregation comprised 'a most loving and obedient people' whilst his patron, Eglinton, provided him and his young family with 'plentie of means, eight chalders of beer and meal … a good gleib [a portion of land assigned to a minister], a monie-dutie payed me for my manse'. In this rural idyll, Baillie had 'all my heart could wishe'.[49]

With his livelihood secured, Baillie married Lilias Fleming on 12 July 1632, with whom he evidently had eight children. Following Lilias's death in 1653, Baillie then married Helen Strang, with whom he had one child.[50] Baillie's youngest child, Margaret, who was born after 1656, became the mother of Clementine Walkinshaw, mistress of Prince Charles Edward Stuart ('Bonnie Prince Charlie'), and Margaret and her husband, John Walkinshaw of Barrowfield, later became the grandparents of the renowned eighteenth-century legal thinker Henry Home, Lord Kames.[51] For his part, however, Baillie rarely mentioned his wife or children in surviving correspondence. This apparent neglect is more likely indicative of the type of correspondence and documentation that Baillie selected for preservation. As we will see, Baillie transcribed a selection of outgoing correspondence that he hoped would comprise a historical record of the Church of Scotland under the Covenanters. Baillie's correspondence regarding personal and family matters simply did not factor into such a collection. With this qualification in mind, Baillie nonetheless displayed a startling nonchalance, as in the opening lines of a letter in 1634 to his cousin, John Creighton, indicating that he had received Creighton's previous letter 'in a sorrowfull time; some two hours efter the death of my onlie sone'. As Baillie continued, however, 'my greef was augmented when I read what you had sent': material defending Arminian theology.[52]

Baillie's subsequent notoriety stemmed from his adept handling of controversial religious disputes, but this was an undertaking that he had entered cautiously, if not reluctantly. Soon after marrying Lilias, her brother, Robert

---

[49] Robert Baillie to Henry Glen, November 1639, *LJB*, vol. I, p. 228.
[50] McCoy, *Robert Baillie*, pp. 24–5; *FES*, vol. VII, p. 395; Laing, 'Memoir', in *LJB*, Appendix, cxvi–cxxiii. McCoy erroneously only identifies five children and Laing failed to count Baillie's first son who died in 1634. Laing's family tree does an excellent job tracking some of Baillie's descendants to the nineteenth century. *FES*, vol. VII, p. 395.
[51] *FES*, vol. VII, p. 395. Also, see 'The Last Will and Testament of Mr. Robert Baillie August MDCLXII', in Laing, 'Appendix to the Memoir', *LJB*, lxxxvii–xc, cxvi–cxxiii; Hugh Douglas, 'Clementine Walkinshaw, styled countess of Albestroff (c. 1720–1802), mistress of Prince Charles Edward Stuart', in *ODNB* [accessed 1 February 2014]. I.S. Ross, *Lord Kames and the Scotland of his Day* (Oxford, 1972); Alastair J. Durie and Stuart Handley, 'Home, Henry, Lord Kames (1696–1782) judge and writer', *ODNB* [accessed 1 February 2014].
[52] NCL, Baill MS 1, 'A Conference by letters with a Canterburian minister anent the Arminian tenet of the Saints apostasie', p. 1.

Fleming, magistrate of Edinburgh, petitioned for Baillie's promotion to a more prominent charge in the Scottish capital, a charge that Baillie had no interest in pursuing. Stevenson has suggested that Baillie declined this proposed translation because 'at heart he was opposed to [Charles's religious policies]'.[53] Yet Stevenson's interpretation neglects the very real bonds that Baillie felt for his congregation. For his part, Baillie maintained that he was unwilling to desert his congregation for 'it were to break no[t] my heart alone, but manie hundreds that are glewed to myne'.[54] The underlying reason, however, seems to have been Baillie's discomfort with Edinburgh's religious climate. In June 1633, Charles's controversial coronation in Edinburgh, presided over by the Anglican bishop William Laud, had appeared alarmingly 'popish'. During the subsequent 'Coronation' Parliament of 1633, Charles had introduced legislation ratifying the Perth Articles of 1618 and had passed legislation reaffirming his royal prerogative and the monarch's right to determine ministerial dress, all the while carefully noting the names of those commissioners who opposed royal policy.

Developments in Charles's religious policy, together with tensions within the ministry over conformity, made Baillie resist moving to Edinburgh.[55] His own explanation candidly illustrated a latent sense of intellectual isolation by the 1630s. 'To avow and practise manie of the Englishe Ceremonies', wrote Baillie in private correspondence, and 'to count these schismatiques that holds it unlawfull to communicat with kneelers, yow know it to be verie hatefull doctrine to many; and yet this is my mind, and long soe has been'.[56] Although Baillie was inclined to defend ceremonial facets of worship, such as kneeling to receive communion, his aversion to Laud and the group of powerful prelates favoured by Charles I was clear. Intending to preach against 'all points of Arminianisme and Papistrie', Baillie responded to his brother-in-law, Fleming, explaining that he felt that this would be impossible in Edinburgh since the bishops could now 'put their brethren from their ministrie, yea cast them in the straitest prisones'. Why, Baillie concluded, 'should your love move yow to draw me under the first thunderbolt?'[57]

In Kilwinning, Baillie was evidently able to avoid provoking members of the Scottish episcopate and ruling class who appeared to support Laud's vision for further ecclesiastical reform in Scotland. Nevertheless, Baillie was still afforded plenty of opportunities to develop a reputation for himself as a religious controversialist. In two lengthy 'conferences by letters', written between 1634 and 1636, Baillie defended the royal supremacy and Reformed

---

[53]   David Stevenson, 'Robert Baillie', ODNB [accessed 1 February 2014].
[54]   Robert Baillie to Robert Fleming, December 1633, as quoted in Laing, 'Memoir', in LJB, Appendix, xxix.
[55]   For a discussion of these religious divisions, see David Stevenson, 'The Radical Party in the Kirk, 1637–45', Journal of Ecclesiastical History, 25 (1974), pp. 135–65.
[56]   Robert Baillie to Robert Fleming, December 1633, as quoted in Laing, 'Memoir', in LJB, Appendix, xxix.
[57]   Ibid., xxx.

orthodoxy.[58] In these two epistolary exchanges, with David Dickson and Creighton, respectively, Baillie defended kneeling to receive communion – one of the most controversial of the Perth Articles – and denounced the Arminian teaching that God's grace was resistible. Whilst these two manuscript treatises – the former comprising over three hundred folio pages and the latter, 130 folio pages – confirmed Baillie's skills at religious disputation, his aims in writing to Dickson, a close associate and lifelong friend, and Creighton, a family member, were to convince both men of the errors of their ways and to urge them towards repentance. Both of these 'conferences', in fact, appear to have been undertaken under the direction of Patrick Lindsay, archbishop of Glasgow, or at least with his knowledge that Baillie had engaged in such actions. Working in concert with one of the most prominent members of the Scottish episcopate, Baillie engaged in protracted disputes to try to police the bounds of conformity and orthodoxy as he conceived of them. In trying to corral these two individuals in a private forum, Baillie was attempting to maintain the appearance of a unified church capable of rebuffing the threat posed by Laud and the burgeoning 'Canterburian' faction.

IV

Baillie played a key role in identifying and charging Laud and his 'Canterburian' faction with corrupting the Scottish Church during the 1630s. In January 1636, a new book of Scottish canons was composed which bolstered royal authority over the Church and proscribed *ex tempore* prayer. On 20 December, the Privy Council passed legislation enjoining use of a Prayer Book in the Church of Scotland. A fortnight later, Baillie wrote to a colleague at Glasgow University, William Wilkie, describing this act as 'the matter of my greatest affliction'.[59] Thus started Baillie's richly descriptive outgoing correspondence, supplying a detailed narrative of contemporary events in mid-seventeenth-century Scotland, England and Ireland, until his death in 1662. The vast majority of Baillie's extant correspondence was addressed to his cousin, William Spang, minister of the Scottish Staple at Veere – a trade hub through which imports needed to pass before proceeding to other Dutch ports.[60] Before proceeding any further, it is crucial to address the scope and place of Baillie's surviving correspondence in our account of his intellectual development.

Although fragments and letters exist from an earlier date, Baillie's surviving

---

[58] NCL, Baill MS 1, Robert Baillie, 'A freindlie Conference betuixt tuo Ministers D. and B. anent the gesture of Communicants in the act of receiving the holie elements of the Lords Supper', pp. 158–210; NCL, Baill MS 1, Robert Baillie, 'A Conference by Letters with a Canterburian minister anent the Arminian tenet of the Saints apostasie', pp. 1–135.
[59] Robert Baillie to William Wilkie, Kilwinning, 2 January 1637, *LJB*, vol. I, p. 1.
[60] *FES*, vol. VII, pp. 547–8.

correspondence largely dates from 1 January 1637. Quantitatively, Baillie's preserved correspondence is large. By comparison with the correspondence of his contemporary Samuel Rutherford, Baillie's letters dwarf Rutherford's in terms of both the number of extant items and overall length.[61] David Laing's 1841–42 edition of the *Letters and Journals* contained 443 letters, providing a usable edition of all of Baillie's extant correspondence.[62] I have been unable to locate any additional letters of consequence.[63] The majority of Baillie's extant correspondence is composed of outgoing letters, a relative novelty for epistolary collections of early modern individuals, which usually include a majority of incoming letters. In some regards, then, the surviving collections are similar in character – though much smaller in size – to the letters books of the English diarist John Evelyn. Extant letters are addressed to eighty-two different recipients, albeit letters addressed '[f]or Scotland' or '[f]or Glasgow' suggest that some of these letters may have been circulated among groups of recipients.

Baillie's early intellectual formation, as has already been discussed, was influenced by trends in Continental intellectual culture, imported to Scotland through a flourishing book trade and promoted by leading figures such as Baillie's former mentor, Boyd, who had taught and studied at French Huguenot academies and Dutch universities. As Baillie matured, his letters highlight the extent to which his Continental European contacts proved critical to his intellectual development. Baillie's studies greatly benefited from long-standing Scoto-Dutch economic ties that had established large Scots communities in Veere, Middleburg and Amsterdam by the start of the seventeenth century.[64] Ships regularly made the short passage between the Netherlands and Leith, carrying letters and books. Although extant correspondence survives only between Baillie and five recipients in Continental Europe, nearly a quarter of all his extant letters were addressed to William Spang, Baillie's cousin and successively minister of Veere and Middleburg in the Netherlands.[65] Spang graduated MA from Glasgow University in 1625 and taught in Edinburgh before being appointed minister of the Scottish Church in the staple port of Veere in 1630.[66] Spang was probably responsible for introducing Baillie to two of the most renowned Reformed theologians

---

[61] Rutherford's correspondence is contained in just one volume, comprising 365 items. See *Letters of Samuel Rutherford*, ed. Andrew Bonar (Edinburgh and London, 1891).

[62] The only exception is a letter from Baillie to Wariston on church patronage and Wariston's response (see *LJB*, vol. I, pp. 237–41, vol. II, pp. 450–60). The originals, in Baillie's and Wariston's hands, are extant in EUL, La.I.298.

[63] There are two brief notes outlining Baillie's estate in NLS, MS.1036, fos 131r, 132r. I have not counted letters from the University of Glasgow's governing body signed by Baillie in the University of Glasgow archives.

[64] For a comparison of the religious dynamics of English and Scottish migrants in the Netherlands, see Keith L. Sprunger, *Dutch Puritanism: A History of English and Scottish Churches of the Netherlands in the Sixteenth and Seventeenth Centuries* (Leiden, 1982).

[65] By my count, there are eighty-five letters addressed to Spang.

[66] Ginny Gardner, 'Spang, William (1607–1664)', *ODNB* [accessed 11 August 2013].

of the mid-seventeenth century, Gisbertus Voetius, Theology Professor at Utrecht, and André Rivet, a French Huguenot minister and Theology Professor at Leiden with whom Baillie corresponded. Over the course of the British conflicts, Baillie also exchanged letters with a Scottish expatriate living in France and Switzerland, David Buchanan, who was best known as editor of the 1644 edition of John Knox's *History of the Reformation*, and Theodore Haak, the first German translator of John Milton's *Paradise Lost*. Based at Veere, a trade hub in the south-western Netherlands, Spang would have had ready access to the latest news and publications from both the Amsterdam book markets and further afield.[67]

Baillie wrote to his correspondents for a host of reasons associated with his personal intellectual formation and the dissemination of his own intellectual agenda. But interspersed amongst these letters are requests for books simply unavailable from Scottish presses. With the introduction of the Prayer Book looming, Baillie emerged as an adept religious controversialist. Yet the tracts that he wrote required the support of foreign printers and booksellers who, in turn, allowed him to develop his own ideas and continue to push Scottish literary culture in new and hitherto unexplored directions.[68] His surviving correspondence confirms a steady stream of book requests, reflecting a complex relationship between the importation of foreign books and its impact on Scotland's own literary culture. Domestic printing capacities continued to grow throughout the seventeenth century while authors, like Baillie, relied on foreign booksellers' wares, incorporating their content into works printed *both* at home and abroad. The increased output of Scottish presses during the 1640s reflected the political utility that leading Covenanters attached to the printed word. Although there was a pronounced peak in Scottish printing capacity under the Covenanters, such increases almost entirely comprised publication of official acts and proclamations. Scots, therefore, had to look abroad for a regular flow of more learned publications and Baillie's letters simply reflected long-standing practice.[69] In this way, Baillie's demands for foreign publications were directly linked to interests. In July 1638, for instance, Baillie was contemplating the civil magistrate's right to convene ecclesiastical assemblies and, beholden to foreign books for evidence, made a general request to Spang to 'direct me to all the wryters ye are able for my

---

[67] On the staple at Veere, see John Davidson and Alexander Gray, *The Scottish Staple at Veere: A Study in the Economic History of Scotland* (London, 1909).

[68] Themes of book and intellectual exchange between Scotland and Northern Europe are still shockingly understudied. For notable exceptions, see Esther Mijers, 'The Scottish–Dutch context to the Blaeu Atlas: An Overview', *Scottish Geographical Journal*, 121 (2005), pp. 311–20; John Cairns 'Alexander Cunningham, Book Dealer', *Journal of the Edinburgh Bibliographical Society*, 5 (2010), pp. 11–35.

[69] David Stevenson, 'A Revolutionary Regime and the Press: The Scottish Covenanters and their Printers, 1638–51', *The Library*, 7 (1985), pp. 315–37; Jonquil Bevan, 'Scotland', in John Barnard and D.F. McKenzie (eds), *Cambridge History of the Book in Britain* (6 vols, Cambridge, 1999–2012), vol. IV, pp. 687–700, at p. 697.

help of information'.[70] In May 1646, Baillie had a clearer idea of the authors needed to refute Erastian arguments articulated at the Westminster Assembly and asked Spang for works on ecclesiastical freedom by the Lutheran theologian Johann Rivius, the Dutch Reformed scholar Petrus Cabeljavius, and the Polish Reformed theologian Johannes Maccovius.[71] Pondering the complex subject of Biblical chronology, Baillie asked Spang to ask either Willem Apollonius or Alexander Morus for suggested readings, noting that Glasgow University's library already had 'Scaliger, Calvitius, [and] Lansbergius'.[72] Whilst it is difficult to judge how many of Baillie's requests were met, it would appear that Spang was relatively reliable. Baillie transcribed three letters from Spang in 1649, one of which included a list of ten books sent 'for the College' including Jan Huygen van Linschoten's *Navigatio ac itinerarivm in Orientalem* (1599) and Johannes Pontanus's *Rerum et urbis Amstelodamensium historia* (1611), 'both rare books, fit for Bibliotheks' and both still extant in Glasgow University's holdings.[73]

The degree to which Baillie was reliant on his correspondence with Spang and the Dutch book trade may be illustrated through the only protracted epistolary silence between Baillie and his cousin, during the First Anglo-Dutch War (1652–54), during which, according to extant correspondence, Baillie did not write to Spang for nearly three years. This resulted from a Dutch embargo on 'all commerce and corresponding out of these Provinces with England' and 'all places whatsoever that do resort under its power', including Scotland.[74] With conflict 'flameing betwixt the lands of our abode', Baillie explained that 'the passage being stopt, or difficult, and all corresponding betwixt any in these and thir parts being lyable to misconstruction, I choised rather to be silent than for that tyme to write'.[75] During this period, Baillie was still able to acquire scholarly works from London, but his first letter to Spang after the conclusion of hostilities clearly showed the extent to which he had become uninformed about Continental news and scholarly output.[76] 'What the world abroad is doeing we know noe more then the London Diurnall tells us,' Baillie complained. Was the theologian Claude Saumaise alive or dead? Was the Huguenot David Blondel alive or dead? And, most importantly, 'what new books are among yow?'[77]

[70] Robert Baillie to William Spang, 22 July [1638], *LJB*, vol. I, p. 93.
[71] Robert Baillie to William Spang, 15 May 1646, *LJB*, vol. II, p. 371.
[72] Robert Baillie to William Spang, 14 September 1649, *LJB*, vol. III, p. 101.
[73] William Spang to Robert Baillie, 7 March 1649, *LJB*, vol. III, pp. 70–1. For these copies, see GUL, Sp Coll B17-d.10 and Sp Coll Bl4-d.13.
[74] 'A Letter from Rotterdam, 15/25 December 1652', in S.R. Gardiner (ed.), *Letters and Papers Relating to the First Dutch War, 1652–1654* (6 vols, 1899–1930), vol. III, p. 170.
[75] Robert Baillie to William Spang, 19 July 1654, *LJB*, vol. III, p. 237.
[76] Baillie noted that he was able to obtain Gerardus Vossius's *Historicis Graecis* (1624) and *Historicis Latinis* (1627) from London. Robert Baillie to William Spang, 1 September 1656, *LJB*, vol. III, p. 256; Cairns 'Alexander Cunningham, Book Dealer'.
[77] Robert Baillie to William Spang, 19 July 1654,.

This silence casts the surrounding epistolary hubbub in perspective, high-lighting the impact that trade disruptions or other unforeseeable events could hold on these fragile lifelines of Scottish intellectual culture. Baillie was painfully aware of the fragility of early modern postal networks and these contingencies were often the cause for concern, as he expressed in his letters. Matters were made worse, since it appears that publications from London presses could be more readily available to Baillie via Dutch ports, than directly from London. As Baillie wrote to Spang in 1637, 'I have a mind to have some books from London if yow had any acquaintance there that would take paines to buy and send them to yow.'[78] Lacking an established infrastructure, the post in early modern Britain was notoriously unreliable, largely because the successful exchange of letters relied on finding messengers travelling to desired locations and locating recipients there. Baillie appears to have relied on various merchants and other individuals to carry his correspondence to Spang, but William and Thomas Cunningham (apparently unrelated) formed a vital and evidently reliable link. Whereas William was an official in the Customs House at Leith, Thomas was the Conservator of the Staple at Veere, and therefore the most senior figure in the Staple port's administration, having been appointed by the Scottish Estates to supervise trade.[79] Through their contacts in the busiest Dutch and Scottish ports, Spang and Baillie could sustain a protracted correspondence and exchange large amounts of books relatively easily. Despite the Cunninghams' assistance in their venture, Baillie's correspondence with Spang was still vulnerable to interception and miscarriage, especially during the Civil Wars. Baillie expressed anxieties that his correspondence may have been intercepted. Attendant anxieties sporadically manifested themselves in outbursts of frustration over Scotland's relative isolation, such as when Baillie sarcastically remarked to Spang that '[i]t is mervellous that in all our countrey we should have no word from over sea, more nor we were in America'.[80] On another occasion, Baillie's appre-hensions about the weakness of the post were more pronounced, because he was breaching protocol of the Westminster Assembly by disseminating news about the progress of its debates. In April 1644, Baillie believed that Spang's incoming letters had been intercepted, so Baillie 'wrote … under another name; but finding that all myne have come safe to your hand, I need not, I think, use any more that disguise'.[81]

---

[78] Robert Baillie to William Spang, 29 January 1637, *LJB*, vol. I, p. 10.
[79] For mentions of the Cunninghams, see *LJB*, vol. I, p. 62, vol. II, pp. 28, 163, vol. III, p. 71. Baillie also mentioned that letters were sent with a James Brown of Saltcots (vol. I, p. 69) and that he sent some books from London in 1646 with a 'Mr. Tirence' (vol. II, p. 364).
[80] Robert Baillie to William Spang, 29 January 1637, *LJB*, vol. I, p. 3.
[81] Robert Baillie to William Spang, 12 April 1644, *LJB*, vol. II, p. 163.

V

Baillie's remarkable command of an international network of correspondents, in no small measure supported his emergence as a critic of Archbishop Laud. Although Baillie subsequently became a leading propagandist for Covenanting opposition to Charles I, his initial response was uncertain. On the one hand, he vociferously opposed policies he regarded as manufactured by English bishops, including Laud and Bishop Richard Mountague of Norwich. Moreover, although his tracts supplying 'A Meditation upon the Canterburian faction' and 'A Meditation upon Antipuritanisme' were not published until 1641, Baillie indicated that they had been 'written, as now it stands, in the yeare 1633'.[82] On the other hand, however, Baillie remained a committed defender of royal ecclesiastical supremacy. Archbishop Patrick Lindsay of Glasgow therefore expected that Baillie would be willing to open the Synod of Glasgow that met in August 1637 with a sermon encouraging his audience 'to obey the Church Canons, and to practise the Service' – a request to which Baillie first responded with a 'flat refusall'.[83] Nevertheless Baillie prepared a sermon for this occasion, anticipating that his refusal would be denied, on the text 2 Timothy 4:2.[84] In this sermon, Baillie dwelt on a preacher's duty to 'be constant, to drau soules from sin both in season and out of season' – an equivocal message that could simultaneously be interpreted both as a call to conformity and as a veiled criticism of the Prayer Book. Yet Lindsay ultimately excused Baillie from preaching on this occasion, much to Baillie's 'great contentment ... for Mr. William Annan did preach that ch[apter] to his great danger'.[85]

Resentment of royal ecclesiastical policy exploded in the 'Prayer Book Riots' of July 1637. Although petitions were subsequently received from throughout Lowland Scotland, violent riots appear to have been limited to larger towns, such as Edinburgh and Glasgow. Such petitioning campaigns made it difficult for ministers, like Baillie, to profess obedience to Charles I without attracting fierce reprisals. Samuel Rutherford, for instance, had been banished to Aberdeen in 1636 for disputing with Bishop Thomas Sydserf of Galloway over the legality of liturgical ceremonies. During this period of domestic exile from 1636 to 1638, Rutherford's letters reveal plotting amongst an influential network of ministers and laity intent on undermining Caroline religious policy. By contrast, Baillie's letters from the same period reveal him experiencing a moral dilemma: 'the 35 yeir [of my life, i.e.

---

[82]   Robert Baillie, A Large Supplement of the Canterbvrian Self-conviction. Opening to the World, yet more of the wicked Mysteries of that Faction from their own Writs (London, 1641), p. 71.

[83]   Robert Baillie to William Spang, 4 October 1637, LJB, vol. I, p. 20.

[84]   As Baillie transcribed the text, 'I charge thee before God, to preach in season, and out of season' (LJB, vol. I, p. 20).

[85]   NLS, Adv.MS.20.6.4, Robert Baillie, Sermons 1637 to 1639, fos 45r, 50v.

1637] wes the worst that in this last age wes seen'.[86] Disaffected nobility and ministers, many of whom were part of Rutherford's nonconformist network, put 'poperie, idolatrie, superstition, in sundrie things which are innocent of these faults' and profess 'their mind to seperate'. Meanwhile, Scottish and English bishops 'add fewell to [their opponents'] flame' by introducing liturgical changes 'upon sole authoritie' and by enforcing conformity 'under the paines of depositione, excommunicatione and horning'.[87] Indeed, Baillie feared that widespread 'madness' might lead Scotland to ruin. Laud's interference in the Scottish Church's doctrine and liturgy had provoked such opposition that ministers and laity seemed intent on uprooting episcopacy, the Perth Articles and all other 'ungodly' innovations introduced since 1603. Although Baillie evidently feared that he 'may be killed, and my house burnt upon my head … my judgement cannot be altered by their motion'.[88]

As events gathered pace following the 1637 riots, Baillie was forced to decide whether or not to align himself with the opposition. By that autumn, critics of Charles's religious policies had organized themselves into a national governing body – 'the Tables' – and, the following February, Scots throughout the Lowlands swore the National Covenant.[89] A skilful piece of political propaganda, the Covenant invited Scots to pledge their abhorrence of 'the popish religion and tyranny' that threatened the 'subversion and ruin of the true reformed religion, and of our liberties laws and estates'. In effect, the Covenant renewed subscription of the 1581 'Negative Confession' by which Scots had forsworn adherence to Roman Catholicism. The suggestion that Baillie signed the Covenant to placate those in power neglects continuities in Baillie's thought.[90] The National Covenant was an ambiguously worded document which cast wide parameters so as to accommodate many divergent opinions. For his part, Baillie decided to subscribe on account of his underlying suspicions of the Romanizing English episcopate, as he explained in a letter to Alexander Cunningham, minister of Ettrick, in January 1638:

> For matters of ceremonies, I know no reason of changeing my minde; yea a late book, which others admire as a peece unanswerable, has made me more averse than I was from these mens doctrine and practises; *bot withall I am glad to joyne with them in opposing a common enemie.*[91]

---

[86] Robert Baillie to William Spang, 29 January 1637, *LJB*, vol. I, p. 5. For discussion of Rutherford's correspondence, see Coffey, *Samuel Rutherford*, pp. 45–8.
[87] Robert Baillie to William Spang, 29 January 1637, *LJB*, vol. I, p. 5.
[88] Robert Baillie to William Spang, 4 October 1637, *LJB*, vol. I, p. 24.
[89] Stevenson, *Scottish Revolution*, pp. 56–64.
[90] For this interpretation, see David Stevenson, 'Baillie, Robert (1602–1662)', *ODNB* [accessed 5 June 2013]; Stevenson, 'Mere Hasty Babblements? Mr Robert Baillie', in *King or Covenant?: Voices from Civil War* (East Linton, 1996), pp. 17–39, at pp. 37–8.
[91] Robert Baillie to Alexander Cunningham, 16 January 1638, *LJB*, vol. I, p. 28. Emphasis added. The 'book' to which Baillie referred was probably George Gillespie's *A Dispute against the English Popish Ceremonies* ([Leiden], 1637).

If the Covenanters' apparent ideological uniformity had been provoked by alterations to doctrine and worship, then Baillie argued that it was imperative that the Covenant could not offend the beliefs of any subscriber. Whilst a groundswell of opinion against the Prayer Book may have allowed disaffected nobility to seize control of Scotland's civil government late in 1637, Baillie's contribution to discussions surrounding the drafting of the Covenant in Edinburgh ensured that the movement remained unified. Surveying a draft of the text that had been prepared by Johnston of Wariston and the minister Alexander Henderson, Baillie insisted that the Covenant stipulated that 'Bishops and Ceremonies' were to be retained, not suspended *ex officio*, and particular passages were changed so that they *did not* 'import a Defence in armes against the King'. As Baillie admitted to Spang, he hoped that such alterations 'would content my scrupulous minde' and 'satisfie others who were of my judgement, whereof there was a great number'.[92]

This 'great number' of like-minded Scots, unwilling to countenance resistance and declare episcopacy 'unlawful', comprised a large portion of those members who attended the Glasgow General Assembly in December 1638.[93] Once again, however, Baillie appears to have been their lone spokesperson. Having convened the Glasgow Assembly in an attempt to placate Covenanting grievances, Charles soon lost control of its proceedings.[94] Spang subsequently reported that attendees at the Glasgow Assembly had been forced to carry arms due to reports of robbers and thieves on roads to Glasgow, confirming that broader social tensions remained high.[95] After attempting to manage the Assembly on Charles's behalf, the royal commissioner, James, marquess of Hamilton, withdrew in protest, but the ministers remained and repealed alterations in the Church's liturgy and polity, supported by the presence of Scotland's most powerful noble, Archibald Campbell, earl of Argyll.[96] The Assembly's legislation clarified what was deemed unacceptable in the Church, rather than determining how the Church's government and liturgy ought to be structured. Baillie was the only named individual to refuse to declare the Perth Articles and episcopacy 'removed and abjured', having declared them removed, but refusing to consider them 'abjured'. For Baillie, facets of discipline and worship could not be declared 'unlawful' simply because they had been deemed so by the Assembly.

Despite Baillie's voting record at the Glasgow Assembly, he reconciled himself with the Covenanting leadership and emerged as the movement's leading religious controversialist during the 1640s. Although Baillie's own

---

[92] Robert Baillie to William Spang, 27 February 1638, *LJB*, vol. I, pp. 52–3.

[93] Alexander D. Campbell, 'Episcopacy in the Mind of Robert Baillie, 1637–1662', *SHR* 93 (2014), pp. 29–55.

[94] The best narrative account of the Glasgow Assembly remains Stevenson, *Scottish Revolution*, ch. 3.

[95] [William Spang], *Rerum nuper in Regno Scotiae gestarum historia, seu verius commentarius* (Danzig, 1641), p. 81.

[96] For example, see *LJB*, vol. I, pp. 143–7.

views regarding liturgy and polity did not accord with those of all Covenanting ministers, he proved valuable to the Covenanting leadership because of his ability to denounce religious groups with whom the Covenanters disagreed ideologically. After the debacle of the Glasgow Assembly, Charles I confronted the Covenanters' affront to his sovereignty by launching two poorly planned 'Bishops' Wars' in 1639 and 1640 in an attempt to reassert royal authority. Although the need to finance his expeditionary forces required Charles to recall his English Parliament for the first time in eleven years, the English MPs refused to grant subsidies without airing grievances dating back over a decade. By his own account, the contents of Baillie's early pamphlets resonated equally with English and Scottish critics of Caroline religious policy. Prior to the Glasgow Assembly, Baillie had circulated two manuscript treatises criticizing the Scottish Prayer Book. As he explained in a letter to his close friend and Principal of Glasgow University, John Strang, these two treatises were intended to convince reluctant Scots (including Strang himself) that 'it is no lesse then popery in grosse which the Canterburian faction is now aiming at'.[97] One treatise was published in London in 1641 and reissued in 1661 as A Parallel of the Liturgy, with the Mass-Book.[98] Moreover, at the Assembly, Baillie and David Dickson had both been asked to 'make an oracon the next day to refute those Armynian points' maintained by an Edinburgh minister, David Mitchell, and a conformist divine from Aberdeen, Patrick Panter.[99] An expanded version of Baillie's speech was also later published in London, first in 1641, and later in 1652 with a preface identifying its target as the English puritan theologian John Goodwin, who, confusingly, held beliefs similar to those of the controversial Dutch theologian Jacobus Arminius.

Baillie also composed what was to become his most renowned work, Ladensium Autokatakrisis (1640, 1641 and 1643): a comprehensive invective against Laud and his closest English and Scottish intellectual sympathizers. In Ladensium, Baillie detailed the Laudians' manifest 'Arminianism', 'Popery' and 'tyranny' by supplying succinct summaries of their beliefs with extensive marginal citations from works by, inter alia, Laud, Andrewes, Bishop Francis White of Ely, Bishop Joseph Hall of Exeter and the royal chaplain, Peter Heylyn. In a letter to Archibald Johnston of Wariston in March 1640, Baillie indicated that Ladensium was intended to 'shew to the Churches abroad the true state of our controversies, and to waken up the spirits of our own countrymen ... [and] the rousing up of our slipprie neighbours of England'.[100] Owing to his adept denunciation of Laud and his sympathizers, Baillie attended treaty negotiations after the Second Bishops' War

---

97 Robert Baillie to John Strang, [after February 1638], LJB, vol. I, p. 69.
98 The other treatise, 'Some few Quaeries or doubts about the Scottish service booke', will be discussed in Chapter 7.
99 Peterkin (ed.), Records, p. 44.
100 Robert Baillie to Archibald Johnston of Wariston, 30 March 1640, LJB, vol. I, p. 242.

in Newcastle and London late in 1640, expressly 'for the convinceing of that praevalent faction'.[101]

In late 1640, London's booksellers heaved with protests against the political and religious dimensions of Charles I's personal rule. Baillie's indictments of Laud and, to a lesser extent, Thomas Wentworth, earl of Strafford, supplied fodder to Charles's disaffected subjects but, as legal and parliamentary proceedings began, Baillie's primary role became annalist rather than agitator. Whilst treaty negotiations continued between the Scots and Charles, Baillie attended the legal proceedings against that 'great *remora*', Strafford, and cries were also heard for impeachment of 'poor Canterburie … [the] pendicle at the Lieutenant's eare'.[102] Meanwhile Charles started to offer concessions to his opponents in a vain attempt to restore stability. To this end, Charles signed a warrant of attainder in May 1641 against his long-time confidant, Strafford, who was sentenced to death. As Baillie observed, 'the King is now verie sad and pensive … yet no man hes the least intention against him'.[103] Charles also assented to Scottish and English acts that preserved a clearer constitutional role for parliament. In the Scottish Parliament of 1640, the noble Covenanting leadership passed legislation that amounted to a 'constitutional revolution', guaranteeing that parliament would be called every three years and legally requiring the monarch to rule in conjunction with parliament.[104] As a condition of the Treaty of London (1641), the Covenanters required Charles personally to assent to the acts of the 1640 Parliament, thus approving both the Covenanters' civil and ecclesiastical reforms. Yet such concessions failed to stem the flood of unrest sweeping through Charles's kingdoms. Attending the Scottish Parliament of 1641 in person, Charles delivered news of an Irish Catholic uprising that became known as the 'Ulster Rebellion'. Attempting to regain control of his kingdoms, Charles tried to limit the powers of his English Parliament and, on 4 January 1642, entered the House of Commons and attempted to arrest five leading MPs including John Pym, John Hampden and Denzil Holles. This perceived abuse of royal privilege inflamed domestic opposition in England and on 22 August 1642, Charles raised his royal standard at Nottingham as civil war finally engulfed England, alongside Scotland and Ireland.

VI

Returning to Scotland from London in June 1641, Baillie discovered that the Covenanting movement was fracturing. '[A]ne verie evill spirit had

---

[101] Robert Baillie to Lilias Baillie, 5 November 1640, *LJB*, vol. I, p. 269.
[102] Robert Baillie to the Presbytery of Irvine, 15 March 1641, *LJB*, vol. I, p. 309.
[103] Robert Baillie to the Presbytery of Irvine, 7 May 1641, *LJB*, vol. I, p. 353.
[104] Stevenson, *Scottish Revolution*, ch. 7; Allan I. Macinnes, *Charles I and the Making of the Covenanting Movement, 1625–1641* (Edinburgh, 1991), ch. 8.

been stirring' rumours that leading Covenanter nobles Argyll and Rothes were guilty 'of highest treason', and, the previous summer, the marquis of Montrose and other nobles suspicious of Argyll's leadership had sworn the 'Cumbernauld Bond' to uphold the aims of the National Covenant and to resist 'the particular and indirect practising of a few'.[105] Within the Church, ministers remained divided over questions relating to the jurisdiction of presbyteries, synods and general assemblies over congregations. Since the General Assembly of 1640 had convened at Aberdeen, Baillie observed 'a continuall heart-burning' over the status of prayer meetings and other elements of worship which rendered church meetings 'scandalous debates'.[106] Baillie wished the Church to preserve an appearance of unanimity, but this proved elusive. At the opening of the General Assembly of 1641 in St Andrews, Andrew Ramsay preached a sermon 'as if our Kirk were presentlie burning with schisme' and, thereafter, Dickson urged all ministers who had previously conformed to Charles I's policies to repent and 'brought latelie our church to the brink of ruine'; a plea which 'did highlie offend very many', including Baillie himself.[107]

Amidst political crisis, Baillie was finally convinced to leave Kilwinning to accept a professorship of Divinity at Glasgow University in 1642. In this role, he assumed responsibility for teaching theology students religious controversies, Biblical chronology and 'Oriental' languages and he evidently welcomed the opportunity to develop and reform the university's theology and arts curricula. Soon after Baillie's appointment, however, members of the General Assembly decided that his talents were best deployed in the religious debates that had erupted in England. Covenanting leaders were becoming increasingly concerned about the Scottish Church's security following the collapse of church discipline in England, whilst English Parliamentarians suffered early military defeats at Roundway Down and Bristol during the summer of 1643. That August, four English commissioners arrived in Edinburgh to negotiate an alliance between the Scottish Covenanters and English Parliamentarians. These negotiations yielded a treaty known as the Solemn League and Covenant (1643) whereby the English and Scottish Parliaments pledged mutual defence, the preservation of the 'reformed religion' of the Scottish Church, and the 'reformation of religion' in England and Ireland 'according to the Word of god'.

The interests of the Solemn League and Covenant's signatories have attracted much historiographical debate. Whilst Stevenson has surmised that it represented Scottish 'imperial' ambitions to export presbyterianism abroad, Powell has suggested that Scots were willing to discuss the particular form a presbyterian polity might take, drawing attention to early attempts by Scottish commissioners at seeking rapprochement with English congregation-

---

[105] Robert Baillie to William Spang, 15 July 1641, *LJB*, vol. I, p. 356.
[106] Robert Baillie to William Spang, 20 August 1641, *LJB*, vol. I, pp. 358, 359.
[107] Ibid., pp. 359, 360.

alists.[108] Baillie may be selectively quoted to support claims that the Solemn League and Covenant represented Scottish 'imperial' interests, but such an interpretation overlooks his hopes for more general religious reform.[109] As Baillie observed from London in April 1644, 'the fruit of our victorie would be the advancement of religion, the joy of all the godlie, the settling of peace'.[110] Baillie had moved to the English capital soon after the Solemn League and Covenant had been agreed, as one of four ministerial commissioners representing the Scottish Church in the body convened to examine and reform the Church of England's liturgy, doctrine and discipline, subsequently known as the 'Westminster Assembly'.[111] While in London, Baillie hoped that the Scottish Church and its ministry could assist in reforming the English Church, but involvement did not necessarily entail the wholesale export of Scottish-style presbyterianism.

Baillie sat as a member of the Westminster Assembly from November 1643 until December 1646. Despite recording the debates over church government that dominated the Assembly's early years, he spoke publicly only once and then only to thank the Assembly's members for their hospitality on his departure in December 1646.[112] It appears that the reasons for Baillie's silence were twofold. First, Baillie was overwhelmed by the erudition of the other divines present. As he admitted to Spang, 'I professe my marvelling at the great learning, quickness, and eloquence, together with the great courtesie and discretion of speaking, of these men.'[113] Accordingly he deemed it better – and perhaps more conducive to the Assembly's efficiency – to let Gillespie, 'ane excellent youth', speak on the Scots' behalf.[114] Secondly, Baillie was frequently frustrated that the Assembly's 'longsomenesse is wofull', particularly since 'their Church and Kingdome lyes under a most lamentable anarchy and confusion. They see the hurt of their length, but cannot get it helped.'[115] Whilst ecclesiastical assemblies formed an essential part of the good government of the visible church, in Baillie's mind, they should primarily provide fora to produce swift and decisive resolutions of disputed matters.

Outside the Assembly's debates, Baillie encountered a disconcerting array of diverse religious beliefs and practices. Despite remaining silent in debates, Baillie actively supported presbyterian reforms in London and

---

[108] For a representative of the earlier view, see Stevenson, *Scottish Revolution*, p. 285. For the latter view, see Hunter Powell, 'The Dissenting Brethren and the Power of the Keys, 1640–1644' (Ph.D. Thesis, University of Cambridge, 2011), pp. 61–3.

[109] A good example that has been used to support such claims may be found in Robert Baillie to William Spang, 17 November 1643, *LJB*, vol. II, p. 103.

[110] Robert Baillie, 'Publick Letter', 2 April 1644, *LJB*, vol. II, p. 152.

[111] The best summary of the Westminster Assembly's work and aims may be found in Chad Van Dixhoorn, *The Minutes and Papers of the Westminster Assembly, 1643–1652* (5 vols, Oxford, 2012), vol. I.

[112] Ibid., vol. IV, pp. 378–81.

[113] Robert Baillie to William Spang, 7 December 1643, *LJB*, vol. II, p. 110.

[114] Robert Baillie, 'For Scotland', [late December 1643], *LJB*, vol. II, p. 117.

[115] Robert Baillie to William Spang, 7 December 1643, *LJB*, vol. II, p. 107.

staunchly opposed religious heterodoxy. He also cultivated extensive net-works of ministers, both in England and elsewhere, who primarily sought to promote a Presbyterian Church settlement.[116] For instance, Baillie was asked by Alexander Henderson to compose what became *An historicall vindi-cation of the government of the Church of Scotland* (1646) combatting aspersions cast on the Church of Scotland's 'tyrannical' discipline by the excommu-nicated bishop of Ross, John Maxwell.[117] Baillie's greatest concern, how-ever, was to denounce the deluge of heterodox religious beliefs that he and others encountered whilst in London. Another of Baillie's correspondents, the puritan minister of St Christopher-le-Stocks, London, James Cranford, preached a sermon that was later published, claiming that 'Amsterdam, Poland, Transilvania, places most infamous for heresies are now righteous, compared with England, London'.[118] Elsewhere Thomas Edwards, author of the prodigious heresiography *Gangraena* (1646), chided members of the English Parliament that, although 'Baal and his Priests' had been destroyed, 'with the Reformation have we not a Deformation, and worse things come in upon us then ever we had before?'[119] Echoing Edwards's sentiments, Baillie observed that in London 'every where the enemie is much stronger than was expected', and worryingly, 'schismes and heresies doe daily encrease in all the corners of the land'.[120]

Baillie dwelt specifically on the dangers of error, heresy and schism in two sermons that he preached, respectively, to the English Houses of Commons and Lords, as well as in a two-part heresiography entitled *A Dissuasive from the Errours of the Time* (1645 and 1646/47). In this context, Baillie's treatises were more concerned with denouncing enemies to reform rather than artic-ulating a separate ecclesiological vision. In the first part of his *Dissuasive*, published in November 1645, Baillie made a desperate attempt to alert oth-erwise godly ministers of the dangers of holding erroneous beliefs. In its pref-ace, he confessed an utter aversion to 'Polemick writings', before proceeding to plea for comprehension of ecclesiological differences with 'Independent' ministers, especially John Cotton, within a presbyterian polity. Baillie con-trasted this plea for comprehension of theological differences with Jeremiah Burroughs's *Irenicum* (1645) and petitions for toleration made by Roger Williams and John Goodwin.[121] A little over a year later, however, Baillie's

---

[116] Such efforts are explored further in Chapter 3.

[117] In Maxwell's *The burthen of Issachar: or, The tyrannical power and practices of the Presbyteriall-government in Scotland* (London, 1646).

[118] James Cranford, *Haereseo-machia: or, The mischiefe which heresies doe, and the means to prevent it* (London, 1646), p. 5.

[119] Thomas Edwards, *The first and second part of Gangraena* (London, 1646), 'Epistle Dedicatory to the Right Honourable the Lords and Commons Assembled in Parliament'.

[120] Robert Baillie to David Dickson, after 18 March [?] 1644, *LJB*, vol. II, p. 157; Robert Baillie to Robert Ramsay, 15 January 1646, *LJB*, vol. II, p. 336.

[121] Baillie, *Dissvasive*, 'For the Right Honourable the Earle of Lauderdaile, Lord Metellane', n.p.

tone had dramatically changed. Composing the second part of his *Dissuasive*, entitled *Anabaptism, the True Fountaine of Independency*, Baillie lamented that 'blasphemous heresies are now spread here more than ever in any part of the world; yet they are not only silent, bot are patrons and pleaders for libertie almost to them all'.[122] Whereas the first part of his *Dissuasive* represented a self-assured plea for congregational ministers to join with presbyterians in a unified English church, by the *Anabaptism*, Baillie had lost hope that presbyterian government could be satisfactorily established in England. 'Independent' and 'Erastian' factions in the House of Commons had conspired 'to be inclyned to have no shadow of a King; to have libertie for all religions; to have bot a lame Erastian Presbyterie; to be so injurious to us, as to chase us home with the Sword'.[123]

VII

With prospects of further reformation receding, Baillie returned to Edinburgh in January 1647. Despite opposition to presbyterian reforms articulated in the English Parliament, Baillie informed the Commission of the General Assembly – the interim governing body of the Church between General Assemblies – that the Church's commissioners had secured 'the four points of Uniformitie, which wes all our Church gave us in commission to agent [sic] in the Assemblie at Westminster'.[124] As Baillie indicated, the Westminster Assembly was about to produce a directory of worship, an outline of church government, a confession of faith, and a catechism. Following Charles I's surrender to the Scottish Army at Newark in May 1646, however, further religious legislation reached an impasse. Independent and presbyterian Parliamentarians, New Model Army members and presbyterian Scots all had competing interests in the ensuing peace negotiations as future forms of church government emerged as the most divisive issue, whilst Charles himself bided his time, hoping to muster a Royalist uprising. Briefly present at the Newcastle negotiations with Charles, Baillie reported to Spang that although 'the King took very weell with me', he had refrained from attempting to change Charles's opinion on church government, 'knowing his fixed resolutions'.[125]

Following months of fruitless negotiations, the Covenanters eventually relinquished control of Charles to English Parliamentary forces in January 1647 and returned home. The simultaneous rise of the New Model Army worried the Scots greatly, however, since it increased the likelihood that the king would conclude a treaty prejudicial to presbyterianism. Needing to

---

[122] Robert Baillie to David Dickson, 17 March 1646, *LJB*, vol. II, p. 361.
[123] Ibid., p. 362.
[124] Robert Baillie to William Spang, 26 January 1647, *LJB*, vol. III, p. 1.
[125] Robert Baillie to William Spang, 26 January 1647, *LJB*, vol. III, p. 4.

represent their interests in future negotiations, the Covenanters dispatched the earls of Lauderdale, Lanark and Loudoun to London. Observing the power shift towards the sectarian New Model Army, Baillie worried about the monarch's personal safety, confiding to Spang that 'these matters of England are so extremely desperate, that now twyse they have made me sick'.[126] Meanwhile, leading Covenanting nobles had begun to consider acceding to the king's demands and it had even been suggested that Charles should not be forced to subscribe the Covenants.[127] To this end, on 26 December 1647, Lauderdale, Lanark and Loudoun concluded a secret peace agreement with Charles, later known as the 'Engagement'. In exchange for Scottish military assistance, Charles agreed to implement a temporary ecclesiastical settlement in England, before convening an assembly of divines to determine a permanent settlement.[128] Whereas the majority of the Scottish Church's ministry and, importantly, Argyll denounced the 'Engagement' as a betrayal of the Solemn League and Covenant, Hamilton led a majority of nobles in support of the treaty.

For his part, Baillie initially welcomed the Engagement. Despite the New Model Army's rise in power, on hearing news of the Engagement in Edinburgh Baillie wrote to Spang, fearing that 'the pulpits sound loud against the dangers from Malignants [i.e. Royalists], but more softlie against Sectaries'.[129] In a manuscript spontaneously composed at the time and entitled 'My sudden thoughts ... of the motion of warre then in all mens mouthes', Baillie reasoned that a war against the 'sectarian' New Model Army was both expedient and necessary, as his fears of sectarianism's disruptive potential had doubtless become more acute whilst in London.[130] Baillie's inclination to support the Engagement may also have reflected his close relationship with Lauderdale.[131] It is unclear when the two men first met, but their correspondence confirmed a shared passion for scholarly pursuits and deep mutual respect. In 1643, Baillie had insisted that Lauderdale accompany the Scottish ministers delegated to the Westminster Assembly because 'it would be an injurie and disgrace to a youth, that brings, by his noble carriage, credit to our nation, and help to our cause'.[132] Meanwhile when imprisoned in the Tower of London in 1653, Lauderdale reflected on his friendship with Baillie, writing that he

---

[126] Robert Baillie to William Spang, 13 July 1647, *LJB*, vol. III, p. 9.

[127] Robert Baillie to William Spang, 1 September 1647, *LJB*, vol. III, p. 18.

[128] For the text of the Engagement, see S.R. Gardiner (ed.), *The Constitutional Documents of the Puritan Revolution, 1625–1660* (Oxford, 1906), pp. 347–53.

[129] Robert Baillie to William Spang, 27 March 1648, *LJB*, vol. III, p. 34.

[130] NCL, Baill MS 4/3, 'My sudden thoughts on saturday feb: 12 1648 of the motion of warre then in all mens mouthes', fos 9v–11v.

[131] Allan Macinnes has recently suggested that Baillie was Argyll's 'chief ministerial ally', yet such a claim cannot be sustained. See *The British Confederate: Archibald Campbell, Marquess of Argyll, c.1607–1661* (Edinburgh, 2011), pp. 17–18.

[132] Robert Baillie to Archibald Johnston of Wariston, 5 December 1643, *LJB*, vol. II, p. 107.

'could not but returne yow my acknowledgments for the continuation of your kindenes'.[133] At that time, Baillie's sporadic correspondence evidently provided the imprisoned earl with reassurance to 'obey [Baillie's] counsell' and endure persecution at Cromwell's hands. Seemingly content to await Baillie's letters patiently, Lauderdale confessed that he was 'not so easily subject to take the pett [to become impatient], especiallie at a friend of whose kindness I am so confident'.[134] In 1648, therefore, Lauderdale's involvement in negotiations over the Engagement may explain Baillie's initial optimism that its terms would be amenable to the interests of the Presbyterian Church.

Although Baillie's optimism was short-lived, he was reluctant to punish Engagers too severely. Following the defeat of Hamilton's pro-Engagement army by Cromwell in August 1648, a small but powerful junto seized power in Scotland. Described as the 'Radical Kirk Party' and led by Argyll, Wariston and Rutherford, it promptly punished ministers and laity alike for supporting the Engagement. In January 1649, the 'Act of Classes' then barred from public office any individual who had actively supported the Engagement, together with any ministers who refused to preach against it. In the months following the military defeat of the Engagement, the Kirk Party forced the Scottish Parliament to submit to the Church's limitations on civil office-holding, thereby establishing a theocratic regime that has subsequently been compared to revolutionary Iran.[135]

In January 1649, however, the Kirk Party's ascendency was abruptly halted with Charles's execution. 'One Act of our lamentable Tragedy being ended', Baillie grieved, 'we are entering again upon the scene.'[136] This violent act was widely deplored in Scotland and, on 5 February 1649, the Scottish Parliament declared Charles's eldest son, Charles II, king of 'Great Britain, France and Ireland'. Moreover, since this proclamation provoked further armed confrontation with Cromwell, the Covenanting regime became increasingly keen to gain support from the exiled Charles II. In March 1649, Baillie was chosen to go to The Hague to negotiate with Charles on the Church's behalf, being probably less likely to offend the exiled monarch than a more radical minister, such as Rutherford.[137] At The Hague, Baillie frantically tried to get leading divines, such as Gisbertus Voetius and André Rivet, and the Prince of Orange to supplicate on Scotland's behalf. Such efforts were in vain, however, because 'Old Royalist' members of Charles's exiled court, such as Edward Hyde, and members of the dispossessed episcopates, such as Bishop John Bramhall of Londonderry, had diluted sympathy towards the Scots, informing the new monarch of the Church's decisive opposition to Hamilton's Engagement. Bramhall, in particular, composed A faire warning, to take heed

---

133 The earl of Lauderdale to Robert Baillie, 17 December 1653, *LJB*, vol. III, p. 230.
134 The earl of Lauderdale to Robert Baillie, 14 March 1654, *LJB*, vol. III, p. 265.
135 Coffey, *Samuel Rutherford*, p. 53.
136 Robert Baillie to William Spang, 7 February 1649, *LJB*, vol. III, p. 66.
137 See Chapter 4.

of the Scotish discipline (1649), which portrayed the Church of Scotland as a tyrannical, anti-monarchical institution. Denouncing Bramhall's tract as 'a wicked pamphlet against our Church', Baillie sought to ameliorate perceptions of the Scottish Church abroad by publishing *A Review of Doctor Bramble … his Faire warning against the Scotes disciplin* in Delft a few weeks later.[138]

After negotiations with Charles II proved abortive, Baillie returned to Scotland convinced that the Kirk Party needed to mitigate proscriptions against past Royalists. Serving as a member of the Church's General Assembly in Edinburgh in 1649, Baillie witnessed further discussion about the deposition and forced transportation of ministers 'to the pitie and griefe of my heart'. For, as Baillie related to Spang, 'sundry of them I thought might have been, for more advantage every way, with a rebuke, keeped in their places; but there was few durst professe of much; and I, for my ingenuous freedom, lost much of my reputation, as one who was inclyning to malignancie'.[139] Trying to draw his colleagues away from the brink of schism, Baillie emerged as a defender of ministers such as William Colville, William Wilkie, Andrew Cant and his long-time friend John Strang, who had all been deposed from their charges for refusing to preach against the Engagement. Baillie was also attacked himself for denouncing the Act of Classes in Charles II's presence, although to have done otherwise would have been diplomatically unwise. Attacked as a 'malignant', Baillie recoiled: 'my unacquaintance with obloquie made my skin, at this first assay, more tender than needed'.[140] Such accusations continued during the Interregnum. In 1657, for example, the Glaswegian minister Patrick Colville reported that Wariston had told Cromwell that 'there was one of the Resolutioners [i.e. Baillie], who … stuck so close to these Resolutions' because he hoped to 'keep himself in a capacity to act for the King when opportunitie should offer'.[141]

To Baillie, however, it appeared that mistrust and suspicion were breeding schism within the Church because all 'chief men are whisperit to favour either sectaries or malignants'.[142] Despite his unease with the growing political rift, Baillie aligned himself with those ministers and laity who aimed at reconciliation and the preservation of a unified front against Cromwell's imminent invasion. Following Baillie's negotiations with Charles II in 1649, the Church and Committee of Estates sent another delegation to Breda in 1650, which secured an agreement with Charles to come to Scotland, although the ministry became deeply divided over the conditions that ought to be imposed. A majority of ministers including Baillie became known as the 'Resolutioners' and were prepared to grant clemency to former supporters of

---

[138] The earl of Cassilis, George Wynram, Robert Baillie and James Wood to the Commission of the General Assembly, 3 April 1649, *LJB*, vol. III, p. 87.
[139] Robert Baillie to William Spang, 14 September 1649, *LJB*, vol. III, pp. 91–2.
[140] Ibid., p. 92.
[141] Patrick Colville to Robert Baillie, 5 March 1657, *LJB*, vol. III, pp. 335–6.
[142] Robert Baillie to William Spang, 14 September 1649, *LJB*, vol. III, p. 93.

Hamilton's Engagement, allowing them to return to public or military offices if they repented. By contrast, a vocal minority, led by Wariston, Rutherford, James Guthrie and Patrick Gillespie and known as the 'Protestors', refused to allow such individuals to return to office. Cromwell's invasion of Scotland in 1650 exacerbated tensions amongst the ministry and, by the time of Charles II's eventual defeat at Worcester in September 1651, the Church of Scotland was deeply divided over the Protestors' refusal to accept legislation that removed the Act of Classes's rigid proscriptions, known as the 'Public Resolutions'. Furious, Baillie attacked the Protestor faction, vowing that 'the hands of lurking Joabs will in time be discovered'.[143]

The open accusations of malignancy that Baillie had faced in 1649 led him to eschew the bitter controversies that ensued. Shortly after Charles's return to Scotland, Robert Blair urged Baillie to steer clear of the Protestor–Resolutioner controversy: 'Get yow to your book and your work, and meddle not unhappilie to your prejudice.'[144] Accordingly, Baillie immersed himself in his university teaching in Glasgow during the 1650s, composing pedagogical treatises on Hebrew, religious controversies and Biblical chronology. All three, in Baillie's mind, represented an attempt to reform the curricula of Scotland's universities which lacked 'orthodox' introductions to important subjects. The first, *Catechesis Elentica Errorum* (1654), complemented the Westminster Confession of Faith by providing laity and ministers with proof texts against erroneous beliefs. In the same year, he published a study guide for students of Biblical Hebrew, entitled *Appendix practica ad Johannis Buxtorfii*. From 1650, Baillie also started compiling an introduction to the complex subject of Biblical chronology that was later posthumously published as *Operis Historici et Chronologici* (1663, 1668).[145] During this time, Baillie's wife and daughter were afflicted with 'a languishing disease'; his first wife, Lilias, died in 1653.[146] As Baillie explained to Spang in July 1654, his academic duties and his wife's protracted illness had diverted his attention away from writing treatises for publication, yet, with the publication of his first two Latin treatises, Baillie hoped that people might consider 'these testimonies of my faithfullness and diligence in my calling'.[147] At the same time, Baillie quietly contributed to debates with the Protestor faction, believing that his opinions were 'of that strain that might bring me to cumber [i.e. trouble]'.[148] In a long-delayed rejoinder to the congregationalist minister

---

[143]   Robert Baillie to David Dickson, 18 November 1650, *LJB*, vol. III, p. 109. Joab, the nephew of King David, conspired against the expectant monarch Solomon with David's eldest son, Adonijah. For this, David had him executed.

[144]   Robert Blair to Robert Baillie, 29 July 1650, *LJB*, vol. III, p. 105.

[145]   GUL, MS Gen 375, Robert Baillie, 'Opusculi historici et Chronologici', p. 23.

[146]   Robert Baillie to David Dickson, 28 April 1653, *LJB*, vol. III p. 219. Baillie mentions his wife's sickness again on pp. 222, 237.

[147]   Robert Baillie to William Spang, 19 July 1654, *LJB*, vol. III, p. 237. There are no extant letters from Baillie to Spang between 2 January 1651 and July 1654.

[148]   Robert Baillie to David Dickson, 21 May 1653, *LJB*, vol. III, p. 222.

John Cotton and the anabaptist John Tombes, Baillie explained that he had usually preferred to remain silent on account of his 'great aversenesse and constant disinclination from such publick appearances, and making of any noyse with my voice or pen'.[149]

Despite such protestations, Baillie was often confronted in Glasgow by one of the most controversial Protestor ministers, Patrick Gillespie. During the Protestor-Resolutioner controversy, Glasgow was the only burgh in Scotland in which a Protestor faction dominated ecclesiastical affairs. Whereas a faction of Protestors led by Guthrie, Rutherford and Wariston simply defended a more exclusive definition of who should comprise the visible church, Gillespie, John Carstairs and Francis Aird proved willing to work with Cromwell's government and defend congregational ministers.[150] In sermons preached in Glasgow in 1650 and 1651, Baillie denounced the dangers of ecclesiastical separation and monarchical loyalty, whilst simultaneously setting his son, Robert, to attend sermons throughout Glasgow's churches preached by Gillespie and his sympathizers, primarily in order to document their beliefs.[151] Having garrisoned in Glasgow for a few days in April 1651, Cromwell was offended by three sermons in which, as Baillie explained, each preacher 'gave a fair enough testimonie against the Sectaries'.[152] Whereas Baillie claimed to lack sufficient patience to discuss ecclesiastical matters with Cromwell, Gillespie and James Guthrie became 'the maine speakers', and Gillespie's willingness to debate evidently ingratiated him with Cromwell.[153] In February 1653, the English government appointed Gillespie Principal of Glasgow University and, the following year, Gillespie spearheaded negotiations with Cromwell over implementation of a system of 'triers and ejectors' used to manage ministerial appointments and suspensions in the Church outwith the authority of the Church's assemblies. As the diarist John Nicoll observed, in Glasgow 'matteris in Kirk Session were totalie gydit by [Gillespie], and none elected elders or deacons but by his approbation and accordance'.[154] For Baillie, Gillespie's cooperation with Cromwell denoted sympathy to congregational and separatist polities; as he lamented, Gillespie and 'our dissenting brethren' had thereby inflicted 'a wound almost incurable' on the Church.[155] This 'restless' man, Baillie wrote, had sacrificed his principles to garner English favour, thus seizing power in Glasgow and

---

[149] Baillie, *Dissvvasive Vindicated*, sig. Ar.
[150] Scott Spurlock, *Cromwell and Scotland: Conquest and Religion, 1650–1660* (Edinburgh, 2007), pp. 140–8.
[151] NCL, Baill MS 5, Robert Baillie, Sermons Jan. 1648 to Jun. 1652; EUL, La.III.543, Robert Baillie Junior, Sermon notes, [c. 1650–51].
[152] Robert Baillie to Robert Douglas, 22 April 1651, *LJB*, vol. III, p. 165.
[153] Ibid., p. 166; Robert Baillie to Andrew Kerr, 2 May 1651, *LJB*, vol. III, p. 168.
[154] John Nicoll, *A Diary of Public Transactions and Other Occurrences, Chiefly in Scotland, 1650–67*, ed. David Laing (Edinburgh, 1836), p. 205.
[155] 'Instructions for Mr. George Young, for Edinburgh', 8 April 1653, *LJB*, vol. III, p. 215.

disrupting the synod's processes with 'mere formalities of sederunts of meetings and niggie-naggies'.[156]

VIII

Following a decade of religious upheaval and continually haunted by fears of imminent imprisonment or worse, Baillie welcomed Charles II's restoration to the British thrones in 1660. Whilst Charles aimed to promote peace and stability in all his kingdoms, he proved more evasive regarding the nature of his desired church settlement in Scotland. In the negotiations that followed Charles's return to power, Baillie attempted to influence a presbyterian settlement in correspondence with other Resolutioner ministers, including Robert Douglas and James Sharp, and nobles such as the earls of Lauderdale, Glencairn and Middleton. Such debates, however, took place in London, so an aged Baillie only learned, through a trickle of correspondence, that a resurgent 'Canterburian faction' was attempting to restore 'Bishops and Books'.[157] Despite such recurrent fears, Baillie accepted Charles II's decision to appoint him as Principal of Glasgow University in January 1661.[158] Soon afterwards, however, on 6 September, Baillie's fears were confirmed when Charles issued a royal proclamation restoring episcopacy in Scotland. Baillie's quiescence over the restoration of episcopacy and his failure to resign as Principal have been taken to infer his tacit acceptance of the episcopal settlement. Baillie's correspondence, however, suggests a more complex picture.[159] As Robert Wodrow related, allegedly on the authority of Baillie's descendants, having received 'the offer of one of the new Bishopricks', Baillie may have 'declin'd it by reason ... of his dislike of the Episcopall Order', or because he did not wish to contradict previous statements, or because of 'the bad state of health that he was in'.[160] Nevertheless Baillie 'thanked God' he had 'peace of mind in his Low station of Principall'.[161] At the same time, rather than resigning his Principal's office or petitioning Charles directly, Baillie admonished Lauderdale and Glencairn for their failure to secure a presbyterian settlement. Whilst Baillie beseeched Glencairn to 'desert not our poor Church', he chided Lauderdale: 'fye on yow all who are about [Charles II]' failing to illustrate that episcopacy was unsuited to the Scottish Church.[162]

Such admonishments did not, however, extend beyond private

---

[156] Robert Baillie to David Dickson, 10 February 1653, *LJB*, vol. III, p. 208; Robert Baillie to James Wood, 14 February 1653, *LJB*, vol. III, p. 214.
[157] Robert Baillie to Lauderdale, 16 June 1660, *LJB*, vol. III, p. 406.
[158] Innes (ed.), *Munimenta glasguensis*, vol. IV, lxxxix–xc.
[159] Stevenson, 'Robert Baillie', *ODNB* [accessed 1 February 2014].
[160] NCL, Baill MS 3/1, [Robert Wodrow], 'Memoriall anent Principal Baillie', pp. 2–3.
[161] Ibid., p. 3.
[162] Robert Baillie to Glencairn, [n.d.], *LJB*, vol. III, pp. 475–6; Robert Baillie to Lauderdale, 9 September 1661, *LJB*, vol. III, pp. 476–8.

correspondence. Whilst Baillie feared the likely troubles arising from an episcopate restored outside the authority of presbyteries, he was unwilling at the end of his life to challenge Charles II's restored sovereignty. In a final biographical vignette, an ailing yet resolute Baillie described to his cousin, Spang, the opposition he had recently voiced to the newly consecrated arch-bishop of Glasgow, Andrew Fairfoul. Having met Fairfoul at the university, Baillie recounted that he 'excused my not useing of his styles, and professed my utter difference from his way; yet behoved to entreat his favour for our affaires of the Colledge'.[163] Another account of this meeting, supplied to the eighteenth-century presbyterian historian Robert Wodrow by Wodrow's father James, who had once been one of Baillie's students, stressed that Baillie 'accosted' Fairfoul, stating, 'Mr. Andrew, I will not call you my Lord. King Charles would have made me one of these lords; but I do not find in the New Testament that Christ has any lords in his house.'[164] A few months later, sometime after 18 August 1662, Baillie died in professed aversion to 'prelacy' but willing to submit to the new relationship between Church and state for the sake of stability.[165]

---

[163] Robert Baillie to William Spang, 12 May 1662, *LJB*, vol. III, p. 487.
[164] Robert Wodrow, *The History of the Sufferings of the Church of Scotland from the Restoration to the Revolution*, ed. Robert Burns (4 vols, Glasgow, 1830–35), vol. I, p. 288.
[165] For this likely date of death, see Baillie's final will and testament in Laing, 'Memoir', *LJB*, Appendix, lxxxvi.

2

Monarchical Power

Following the extensive reforms enacted at the 1638 Glasgow General Assembly in contravention of Charles I's command, war loomed between Scotland and England, but Robert Baillie hesitated to countenance armed resistance. Whilst Covenanters such as Samuel Rutherford voiced their support for war, Baillie was unsure whether Charles's alterations of the Scottish Church's doctrine and liturgy warranted such dramatic measures. After agonizing over the lawfulness of defensive arms, in February 1639 Baillie ultimately acquiesced, explaining to his cousin William Spang that he *did not* determine that resistance was lawful from reading '[David] Paraeus or Buchanan, or Junius Brutus, for their reasons and conclusions I yet scunner [i.e. shudder] at; bot mainly by Bilsone de Subjectione, where he defends the practise of all Europe ... who at diverse tymes, for sundry causes, hes opposed their princes'.[1] Baillie had become convinced of the lawfulness of defensive arms from reading *The True Difference betweene Christian Subjection and Unchristian rebellion* (1585) by the Elizabethan bishop Thomas Bilson, hardly an author commonly included in the canon of resistance theorists. On the one hand, Bilson had defended a robust conception of hereditary monarchy, arguing that religion could not justify rebellion. On the other hand, he asserted that subjects must resist a monarch when they cease to act in line with God's laws: Protestants may justly raise arms against their monarch if they reintroduced Roman Catholic beliefs into a national church.

Baillie's ideas concerning the foundation and limits of monarchical power distinguished him from his compatriot Rutherford, traditionally considered the main political theorist of the Covenanting movement. Baillie's political thought also challenges historiographical consensus that Covenanting political thought was predominantly influenced by late sixteenth-century 'monarchomach' authors such as George Buchanan, John Knox and 'Junius Brutus' – the anonymous author of *Vindiciae contra tyrannos* (1579).[2] Whilst

---

[1] Robert Baillie to William Spang, 12 February 1639, *LJB*, vol. I, p. 116. Robert Baillie's copy of *Vindiciae contra Tyrannos* (Amsterdam, 1610) is extant in the University of Glasgow Special Collections. See, GUL, Sp Coll Bi4-k.21.

[2] For example, see Stevenson, *Scottish Revolution*, pp. 133–4; I.M. Smart, 'The Political Ideas of the Scottish Covenanters, 1638–88', *Journal of the History of Political Thought*, 1 (1980), pp. 167–93; Allan Macinnes, *The British Revolution, 1629–1660* (Basingstoke, 2005), pp. 15–16, 114–16.

the influence of Buchanan's historical tract *Rerum Scoticarum Historia* (1582) remained pervasive on seventeenth-century Scottish intellectual culture, the influence of Buchanan's writings on resistance theory are more difficult to ascertain.[3] During the reigns of James VI and I and Charles I, writers consciously marginalized reliance on the radical resistance theories of the late sixteenth century in an attempt to defend their loyalty to the crown at a juncture when foreign Catholic threats loomed large.[4] Resistance to lawful authority in Britain became instinctively linked with subversive Jesuit practices, rather than with the religious liberation of the Scottish Reformation or the French Wars of Religion.[5] Indeed, contemporary critics of puritanism often seized on subtle resonances between puritan writings and 'monarchomach' texts to denounce the former as rebels.[6] The Scottish Royalist Sir James Turner, for instance, blamed the religious and political violence in Britain during the 1640s on the influence of Buchanan's *De Jure Regni apud Scotos* (1579).[7] Likewise, Peter Heylyn, the future biographer of William Laud, attacked the ideas of the puritan minister Henry Burton, on account of resemblances between Burton's arguments and those of Buchanan, 'Junius Brutus' and David Paraeus (a Palatinate divine who wrote a radical interpretation of the Biblical text Romans 13).[8]

Baillie's assertion quoted at the outset of this chapter, however, amounted to more than an act of rhetorical disassociation: it revealed a fundamental distinction between his political ideas and those of the Covenanting 'radical mainstream' exemplified by Rutherford's political treatise *Lex Rex* (1644). Historians who have argued that Buchanan, John Knox and the *Vindiciae contra tyrannos* exerted considerable influence on Covenanting resistance theory have largely focused on the thought of this small, radical group comprising, *inter alia*, Rutherford, Archibald Johnston of Wariston, George Gillespie and Archibald Campbell, marquess of Argyll. In the extreme, the ideas of this radical group have been taken as normative expressions of 'Covenanting thought' in the 1640s.[9] In Rutherford's case, his defence in *Lex*

[3]   John Coffey, 'George Buchanan and the Scottish Covenanters', in Caroline Erskine and Roger Mason (eds), *George Buchanan: Political Thought in Early Modern Britain and Europe* (Farnham, 2012), pp. 189–203.

[4]   Glenn Burgess, *Politics of the Ancient Constitution: An Introduction to English Political Thought, 1603–1642* (London, 1992); Burgess, *Absolute Monarchy and the Stuart Constitution* (London, 1996).

[5]   Glenn Burgess, 'Religious War and Constitutional Defence: Justifications of Resistance in English Puritan Thought, 1590–1643', in Robert von Friedeburg (ed.), *Widerstandsrecht in der frühen Neuzeit: Eträge und Perspektiven der Forschung im deutsch-britischen Vergleich* (Berlin, 2001), pp. 185–206, at pp. 189–90.

[6]   The term 'monarchomach' was coined by the Scot William Barclay as a hostile descriptor of French Huguenot resistance theorists.

[7]   Clare Jackson, 'Buchanan in Hell: Sir James Turner's Civil War Royalism', in Erskine and Mason (eds), *George Buchanan*, pp. 205–27, at pp. 205–6.

[8]   Peter Heylyn, *A Briefe and Moderate Answer*, in Joyce Lee Malcolm (ed.), *The Struggle for Sovereignty: Seventeenth-Century English Political Tracts* (Indianapolis, 1999), pp. 79–80.

[9]   Allan Macinnes, 'Covenanting Ideology in Seventeenth-Century Scotland', in Jane

Rex of Buchanan's historical narrative of the Scottish monarchy as elective was one factor that led his modern biographer to characterize him as a 'radical' thinker and an intellectual forbear of John Locke's populism.[10] Even if Buchanan's secular humanist sources of argumentation and his defence of tyrannicide in *De Jure Regni* proved uncomfortable for Biblically minded Covenanters like Rutherford, Buchanan remained 'a significant source for the Scottish Covenanters'.[11] Baillie would not have been comfortable with this conclusion considering, as this chapter shows, that Baillie's conception of the Scottish monarchy markedly diverged from Buchanan's assertion of its populist origins and limits.

This chapter represents the first exploration of a distinct, loyalist strain of Covenanting political ideas, of which Baillie is taken to be representative. Unlike Rutherford, Baillie never wrote a substantial political treatise, meaning that his political ideas must be reconstructed via works which discuss church polity in detail; specifically, *Ladensium Autokatakrisis* (1641), *An Historicall Vindication of the Government of the Church of Scotland* (1646) and *A Review of Doctor Bramble* (1649). Baillie's discussions of resistance, the nature of monarchy, and the relationship between the civil and ecclesiastical spheres were all closely linked with his aspirations for a British Presbyterian Church settlement. Throughout the 1640s, Baillie was worried that the eponymous Laudians were trying to secure an episcopal settlement, first, by regarding Charles I's powers as extra-legal, and second, once civil war had broken out, by promoting not only an episcopal settlement, but also by providing anti-presbyterian fodder to Erastians and Independents.[12] Presbyterianism's enemies therefore attacked the Scots for both their views on church polity and the impact that such a polity had on monarchical power. For Baillie, as for most Scots, presbytery and monarchy were mutually supporting institutions and, if both were established and governed according to the fundamental laws of the kingdom, they would not come into conflict.

Baillie changed his views regarding armed resistance, but he unfailingly advocated obedience to a monarch's lawful commands. Baillie's robust conception of the ancient Scottish monarchy derived from an account of its historical origins that provided legal limits on a monarch's lawful powers whilst, nevertheless, reaffirming the monarch's status as God's lieutenant on earth. Baillie's ideas thus emerge as remarkably Erastian in content. He preserved a distinctive separation of Church and state, characteristic of Scottish presbyterian writers at this point, but he also accorded a prominent role to the monarch and a state's civil jurisdiction as providing limits within which a church could act. After tracing Baillie's theoretical discussions of

Ohlmeyer (ed.), *Political Thought in Seventeenth-Century Ireland* (Cambridge, 2000), pp. 191–220. Also, see Smart, 'Political Ideas'.

10 Coffey, *Samuel Rutherford*, p. 181.
11 Coffey, 'George Buchanan and the Scottish Covenanters', p. 202.
12 Baillie, *Historicall Vindication*, pt II, p. 1.

monarchical power, it remains to be seen how these ideas may have impacted his allegiance when the unity of the Covenanting movement came under strain. Baillie's ideas are here characterized as a specifically Scottish brand of 'Presbyterian royalism' that combined religious zeal with a view of limited monarchy. Paradoxically, Baillie's pronounced monarchical loyalism and Erastianism more closely aligned him with nobles, such as Lauderdale, and clergy, such as James Sharp, who rose to prominence in Restoration Scotland as some of the most hardened persecutors of presbyterian nonconformity.

I

Baillie's writings demonstrate that discussions of obedience and resistance were not mutually exclusive.[13] The revolutionary writings on resistance theory produced by Buchanan and Knox did not create an insurmountable ideological divide between authoritarian monarchies and subjects agitating for greater freedom. Indeed, such currents of political thinking subsisted alongside, and in dialogue with, one another. For instance, puritans and conformist authors alike disputed definitions of a moderate *via media* of monarchical power in Elizabethan and early Stuart England. In a later context, Anglican churchmen writing before and after the Revolution of 1688 may have lacked a cohesive theory of revolution, yet it would be inaccurate to conclude that they were 'bereft of a considered case for resistance and that they must lamely acquiesce in despotism'.[14] This emphasis on shared conceptual similarities of conformists and puritans helps to explain why Baillie vacillated between passive obedience and active disobedience at the outset of the Covenanting Revolution in 1639, before reverting to a position of passive obedience at the Restoration in 1660. Puritans, bishops and laymen equally tried to reconcile frequently contradictory duties that Christians owed to God and their sovereign, in the process legitimizing resistance as the performance of a Christian duty.

Baillie's efforts to reconcile these conflicting duties may be seen in his earliest surviving letters, reporting on meetings of presbyterian ministers and laymen early in 1638 over the form and content of what came to be known as the National Covenant. Given Baillie's influence in these meetings, it appears appropriate to characterize the National Covenant as a restrained, conservative document.[15] I might go even further to describe it

---

[13]   In this vein, I follow the work of Glenn Burgess. See his 'Religious War and Constitutional Defence'; Burgess, *Absolute Monarchy*; Burgess, *Ancient Constitution*; Burgess, *British Political Thought, 1500–1660: The Politics of the Post-Reformation* (Basingstoke, 2009).
[14]   Ethan Shagan, *The Rule of Moderation: Violence, Religion and the Politics of Restraint in Early Modern England* (Cambridge, 2012). Mark Goldie, 'The Political Thought of the Anglican Revolution', in Robert Beddard (ed.), *The Revolutions of 1688* (Oxford, 1991), pp. 102–36.
[15]   As maintained, for instance, by I.B. Cowan, 'The Covenanters: A Revision Article', *SHR* 47 (1968), pp. 35–52 at pp. 38–9.

as deliberately ambiguous. As presbyterian nonconformists gathered support in Scotland against Laud's ecclesiastical reforms, the nascent Covenanting movement necessarily accommodated as broad a constituency as possible to command credibility and legitimacy. Such was Baillie's thinking when he later recalled the influence of the Scottish theologian John Cameron on his initial thoughts regarding the Covenant:

> Some other clauses also, whilk might have seemed to import a Defence in armes against the King, this I could not yield to in any imaginable case; for the grounds I had learned from Monsieur Cameron I had not yet leasure to try ... These were also changed; so that no word, I hope, remaines in this write, whilk, in any congruitie, can be drawne against the Prince.[16]

In formulating his response to the National Covenant, Baillie displayed a hallmark response that would characterize much of his career. Instead of jumping to a conclusion, or when faced with a particularly significant question over allegiance, Baillie professed in his correspondence the need to 'try the grounds' for a new position more thoroughly. When faced with a significant decision, he often retreated to his books to study the question and, it may be assumed, gauge popular responses, before committing himself to any one position. In the case of negotiations over the Covenant, Baillie added that a leading Scottish noble, John Campbell, earl of Loudoun, supported his amendments so as to 'satisfie others who were of my judgement, whereof there was a great number'.[17] After the regicide of Charles I in 1649, Baillie similarly defended the military and religious treaty concluded between the Scottish Covenanters and the English Parliament in 1643, known as the Solemn League and Covenant, as containing 'expresse Articles for the preservation of royalty in all its just rights in his Majestie and his posterity'.[18] Baillie evidently believed that the Scottish practice of covenanting in no way ran counter to the interests, position nor even the legal standing of the Stuart monarchy.

Baillie's concern that some Covenanters disregarded duties of obedience owed to Charles I for the sake of religious reform reflected his earlier inclination towards conformity, or at least towards passive obedience. Baillie considered the teachings of the theologian and fellow Glaswegian Cameron influential in tempering this stance, repeating his claim about the more conformist part of his political education in the dedicatory epistle to his *Historical Vindication* which explained that, during his undergraduate studies at the University of Glasgow, 'I came to be set at the feet of ... Mr. Cameron and Mr. Struthers, my very singular friends and excellent Divines ... [and] I was gained by them to some parts of conformity.'[19] Baillie was presumably referring to Cameron's brief, but tumultuous, tenure as the university's divinity

---

16 Robert Baillie to William Spang, 27 February [1638], *LJB*, vol. I, p. 53.
17 Ibid.
18 Baillie, *Review of Bramhall*, sig. a4r.
19 'Dedicatory Epistle to Robert Blair', in Baillie, *Historicall Vindication*.

professor. On 6 January 1623, Cameron had insisted that all members of the university take an oath of fidelity and supremacy and that daily prayers must include the names of the king and the royal family.[20] Meanwhile, the other individual to whom Baillie alluded, William Struthers, had taken similar steps to enforce the 1618 Articles of Perth whilst minister at Edinburgh. Struthers's *Looking Glasse for Princes and People* (1632) had been dedicated to Charles I, in celebration of the birth of his son, the future king Charles II, and had argued that monarchs remained subject only to God's judgement.

Baillie's inclinations towards obedience are best exemplified in sermons which he wrote between 1637 and 1639 and which are preserved in a manuscript volume in his own hand.[21] Ballie's sermons reflected a reluctance to countenance resistance, unlike the more inflammatory sermons of Rutherford preached at the English Houses of Parliament.[22] Alongside Baillie's willingness to support the implementation of ceremonial alterations, such as kneeling during communion, the tenor of Baillie's earliest surviving sermons lends qualified support to the suggestion that Laudian religious reforms of the 1630s may have enjoyed limited parochial support.[23] In Baillie's case, this appears to have been borne more out of habit than anything else. Having been educated first under Robert Boyd of Trochrig at Glasgow – before his deposition for opposition to James VI and I's liturgical reforms – Baillie had witnessed the disruptive effects of conscientious opposition to liturgical reforms. Baillie was prepared to accept that certain aspects of worship could be altered at will because, ultimately, Biblical precept did not provide a detailed outline of every last posture and phrase in divine worship. If such alterations enjoyed royal support, then the standard for resistance was set even higher. Without having proper time to study the Scottish Prayer Book, Baillie hedged his bets and we see him in 1637 and 1638 urging his parishioners to obedience.

In doing so, Baillie also downplayed his own personal suspicions about the Romanizing tendencies of Laudian churchmen responsible for drafting the Scottish Prayer Book. Parochial reactions to Laudian innovations were informed by more complex motivations than a simple decision to support their implementation or not. Soon after the Prayer Book's introduction in the summer of 1637, Baillie was still preaching sermons before his congregation in Kilwinning, Ayrshire, urging his parishioners to bide their time and to await guidance patiently.[24] In these sermons, Baillie emphasized the Christian duty

---

[20] On Cameron, see H.M.B. Reid, *The Divinity Principals in the University of Glasgow, 1545–1654* (Glasgow, 1917), ch. 5.

[21] The volume may be found in NLS, Adv.MS.20.6.4.

[22] For a discussion of Rutherford's sermons, see Coffey, *Samuel Rutherford*, pp. 142–5.

[23] Alexandra Walsham, 'The Parochial Roots of Laudianism Revisited: Catholics, Anti-Calvinists and "Parish Anglicans" in Early Stuart England', *Journal of Ecclesiastical History*, 49 (1998), pp. 620–51.

[24] Ibid., pp. 625, 646–7. This was due to the fact that Baillie had initially reserved judgement of the Prayer Book's contents until he was able to study a copy himself. See, for example, *LJB*, vol. I, p. 34.

of patience in the face of an ungodly sovereign, insisting that, in Apostolic times, some individuals had defended the Church with 'ther suord and they strek [their enemies] but this is a meins that Christ aproves no[t]'.[25] In October 1637, Baillie preached on the opening text of Romans chapter 13, emphasizing that God 'commands all saules to be subject to superiar pouer and never to resist them'. Christian subjects could either flee or forbear the commands of an unchristian magistrate but any form of resistance would cost Christian souls 'no lesse pric[e] than damnation'.[26] Christ should be taken as an exemplar in that he 'would not have any of his to oppose casar [and he] rebookit petir tell[ing] him he might perish with the hand, this is the faith and patienc of the Saintes to be establishit'.[27] Evils that befell the Church were signs of God's displeasure and parishioners should placate God through pious and disciplined worship. Despite Biblical examples of Christians resisting rulers, Baillie emphasized that prayer and supplication to God remained 'the churches weapons against Satan and the world, this procurs God to be on our syd and to defait our enemies'.[28] Although 'seditious rebellions ar verie naturall', Baillie insisted that 'they ar verie onChristian'. Neither David nor Christ encouraged their followers to oppose unlawful rulers with force. Since all Christian souls were subject to a superior power, Baillie continued (paraphrasing Romans 13), 'ther is no pouer but of God and the pouers that are be of God whosoever resisteth the pouer resisteth [God]'.[29]

Yet, as we know full well, Baillie did not stubbornly insist on the virtues of Christian patience for long. Baillie's instinctive belief that resisting a sovereign by arms was always unlawful was challenged by the circumstances that obtained in Scotland early in 1639. In particular, Baillie became convinced that defensive arms could be lawful after reading Bilson's *True Difference Betweene Christian Subjection and Unchristian rebellion*. Having distanced himself from monarchomach arguments, Baillie displayed a hallmark characteristic of what has been described as the fundamentally 'casuistical' nature of English puritan resistance theory.[30] Authors such as John Goodwin and William Prynne[31] sought clever, but hardly disingenuous, solutions to problems posed by the conflicting duties Britons owed to God and Charles I. Baillie attempted a reconciliation by explaining, in a letter to Spang in

---

[25] NLS, Adv.MS.20.6.4, Robert Baillie, Sermons August 1637–June 1639 (fo. 170r) fo. 19v. Not all sermons in this volume are dated; however, the order appears to be chronological. The last dated sermon was 29 April 1639 (fo. 162r). Foliation of this volume restarts after fo. 170r, all citations after this point begin with (fo. 170r) to indicate that the citation comes from the latter foliation.

[26] NLS, Adv.MS.20.6.4, Baillie, Sermons, fo. 63r.

[27] Ibid.

[28] Ibid., (fo. 170) fo. 19v.

[29] Ibid., (fo. 170) fo. 32r.

[30] Burgess, 'Religious War and Constitutional Defence'.

[31] See, for example, John Goodwin, *Anti-Cavalierisme, or, Truth pleading as well the necessity, as for the lawfulness of this present war* (London, 1642); William Prynne, *The Soveraigne Power of Parliaments and Kingdomes* (London, 1643).

February 1639, that the only way to save 'the King's authority among us ... [was to] hold off his armies by supplications, as hitherto we have done, or otherwayes also, in case of necessitie extreame and unavoidable'.[32] Describing what he regarded as the duty of 'Christian subjection', he insisted that in 'state-matters, we will meddle no further, then to pray for our dear father King Charles'.[33] Reflecting on the principle of absolute obedience defended by the group of Royalists known as the 'Aberdeen Doctors', Baillie concluded that such a stance was simply untenable and that subjects must always retain some recourse of action to resist unlawful commands. Baillie had been appalled to learn that the Aberdeen Doctors maintained that 'our whole estate, were they to be all killed in a day, or to be led to Turcisme [i.e. Turkism], to be spoiled of all liberty, goods, life, religion, all, yet they may make no kind of resistance'.[34] For Baillie, this conclusion was 'so horrible' and the reformers of Scottish and European churches were 'all to the contrare' that he insisted that there must be some cases in which armed resistance could be lawful.[35]

Without the least sense of the paradox in his position, Baillie argued that the best way to save the king's authority might be to resist his misguided attempts at ecclesiastical reform. Baillie's decision to distance his views on resistance from monarchomach authors also represented a critical statement on other Covenanting justifications of resistance. In the manuscript collection of Baillie's letters, immediately following Baillie's letter to Spang of February 1639 (quoted at the beginning of this chapter) is a copy of Alexander Henderson's 'Instructions for defensive arms', which circulated in manuscript among ministers indicating how they should justify impending war with Charles I to their congregations.[36] The placement of Henderson's 'Instructions' immediately after this letter, together with Baillie's evident preoccupation with questions over resistance, suggest that he may have been commenting directly on Henderson's tract. According to previous commentators on Henderson's tract, he had drawn on arguments 'previously put forward by Buchanan, Knox and other Calvinist writers': that is, precisely the same authors with whom Baillie disagreed.[37] There were, however, also

---

[32] Robert Baillie to William Spang, 12 February 1638, *LJB*, vol. I, p. 117.
[33] Ibid., p. 118.
[34] Baillie also cited the Aberdeen Doctors' *Duplyes* (who, in turn, may have been citing James VI's *Trew Law of Free Monarchies*) in the margins of his *Ladensium*, see p. 123 where they argued that 'The King is above the Law as both the author and giver of strength thereto.'
[35] Robert Baillie to William Spang, 12 February 1638, *LJB*, vol. I, p. 116.
[36] For the copy of this tract in Baillie's papers, see NCL, Baill MS 4/1, 'Hemmersons [sic] Instructions for defensive armes', fo. 131r. This treatise was published with the outbreak of the English Civil War as *Some Speciall Arguments which warranted the Scotch subjects lawfully to take up Armes in defence of their Religion and Liberty* (London and Amsterdam, 1642).
[37] John D. Ford, '*Lex, rex iusto posita*: Samuel Rutherford on the Origins of Government', in Roger Mason (ed.), *Scots and Britons, Scottish Political Thought and the Union of 1603* (Cambridge, 1994), pp. 262–90, at p. 264.

passages with which Baillie must have agreed; indeed Henderson concluded his 'Instructions' with a broad statement claiming that his position was supported by John Calvin and the 'most judicious lawyers and learned men, who have written *contra monarchimachos*'.[38] Presumably this caveat was, however, specifically included to placate more moderate Covenanters such as Baillie, and by enclosing this copy of Henderson's 'Instructions', Baillie was drawing his cousin's attention to specific passages with which he disagreed.

To illustrate which of Henderson's 'Instructions' distressed Baillie, we need to look at the expanded justification of defensive warfare contained in his *Ladensium Autokatakrisis* (1641), which included verbatim citations from the second edition of Bilson's *Christian Subjection*.[39] In the first place, Baillie differed from Henderson and other 'radical' Covenanters because of arguments that he *did not use*. These included arguments characterized as a 'private law' justification of resistance, namely ideas derived from the Roman civil law maxim *vim vi repellere licet* (it is lawful to repel force with force). Monarchomach authors used this claim to suggest that lesser magistrates may lawfully resist a monarch who broke the kingdom's laws. According to one historian, Knox and Buchanan and others exploited the individualistic 'and radically populist implications of the private-law argument' and extended this claim to justify private individuals resisting, and even killing, a sovereign.[40] In *Lex Rex*, for instance, Rutherford upheld the argument's 'radically populist implications', insisting that the power of life and death was not only given to kings and lesser magistrates, but also 'to a single private man in the just defence of his own life'.[41] Henderson likewise adopted this claim in his 'Instructions', stating that '[i]f a private man be found by the law of nature entitled to defend himself … against the prince or judge as a private man, invading him by violence … then, much more may the whole body defend themselves against all invasions whatsoever'.[42]

By citing Bilson, Baillie was drawing attention to passages in which the Elizabethan bishop had justified resistance as a collective action of the whole kingdom against one or two malevolent councillors, in defence of the laws of the realm. It is, therefore, unsurprising that there was no sense that a subject could lawfully *resist* a monarch in defence of the same monarch's authority since that authority was grounded on a specific set of fundamental laws. For

---

[38] Henderson, 'Instructions', in Stevenson, *History*, p. 359.

[39] See, Baillie, *Ladensium*, pp. 121–2. Given the pages Baillie cited (pp. 280, 94) he must have used the London edition of Bilson's treatise, published in 1586, one year after the first edition at Oxford. In this edition, the pagination resets at the beginning of each section and the citations are found in the third section. Baillie's first citation (*Ladensium*, p. 121) begins on p. 279 of Bilson's treatise.

[40] Quentin Skinner, *The Foundations of Modern Political Thought* (2 vols, Cambridge, 1978), vol. II, p. 210.

[41] Samuel Rutherford, *Lex, rex The law and the prince: a dispute for the just prerogative of king and people* (London, 1644), p. 49.

[42] Henderson, 'Instructions', in Stevenson, *History*, p. 359.

example, Baillie cited Bilson to the effect that 'not any private man may take the sword to redresse the Prince'.[43] In a sermon preached at some date in 1638, Baillie had argued that only Christian magistrates ought to defend true religion and 'no zeil sould mak privat men to ventur on publict reformation'.[44] In his *Ladensium*, he reiterated that resistance could only be initiated by the 'whole parliament': representatives of all subjects 'met together in Parliament' or 'their Commissioners in Parliament' – representative of the people's 'free consent' – to preserve England and Scotland's religion, laws and liberties by forcefully removing the influence of a few private men who were misleading Charles I.[45] Baillie rested his justification of resistance on a more conservative, 'constitutionalist' argument that focused on identifying the legal limits of sovereignty and the consequences if a magistrate exceeded those limits.[46] Moreover, this 'constitutionalist' justification of resistance usually distinguished between the person of a monarch and their monarchical office on the grounds that individuals who exceeded the limits of their office were only acting as private individuals. Hence, to counteract the distinctions drawn by Beza, Peter Martyr and Rutherford between the person and the office of monarchy, Baillie cited Bilson who claimed that, in discussing powers ordained by God, 'we do not meane the Princes private will against his lawes, but his precepts derived from his lawes, and agreeing with his lawes'.[47]

Given Baillie's insistence that only the whole representative body of the kingdom could raise arms in defence of Scotland's laws and religion, his sermons to his congregation in Kilwinning might be assumed to have focused on the duty of obedience since few, if any, of his parishioners would have been in the position to act as members of parliament. Notwithstanding, Baillie's charge was under the patronage of the Montgomery family, who held the earldom of Eglinton and were probably in regular attendance in Kilwinning. A copy survives, for example, of the baptismal sermon Baillie preached for Alexander Montgomery, who succeeded his father, Hugh, as earl of Eglinton in 1669, whilst Hugh's first wife had been buried at the parish church in the early 1630s.[48] Regarding Baillie's view of defensive arms, sermons in his notebook from 1637 to 1639 on the Book of Judges also contained clear justifications of resistance. Baillie's initial quiescence evolved into calculated hostility, as his perceptions of the Prayer Book changed, giving the impression that reception of Laudianism in the Scottish parish was fluid: from scep-

---

[43] Baillie, *Ladensium*, p. 121.
[44] NLS, Adv.MS.20.6.4, Baillie, Sermons, (fo. 170r) fo. 26r.
[45] Baillie, 'A Postscript for the personate Iesuite Lysimachus Nicanor', in *Ladensium*, pp. 10, 9; Baillie, *Ladensium*, p. 120.
[46] See, Skinner, *Foundations*, vol. II, p. 215.
[47] Baillie, *Ladensium*, p. 121.
[48] See NLS, Adv.MS.20.6.4, Baillie, Sermons, fos 82r–84r; Paul (ed.), *Scots Peerage*, vol. III, p. 451.

ticism to cautious opposition.[49] In his sermons, Baillie's exegesis of Romans 13 shifted to emphasize that St Paul's injunctions against resistance had meant that obedience to superior powers ordained by God only entailed obedience to commands in accordance with civil and divine laws. If God had commanded obedience to *all* commands of a superior magistrate, then that would yield the theologically unsound conclusion that God was the source of evil. Indeed, God displayed '[g]reat ongratitud [sic] when peic brings furth securitie and Sin'.[50] Baillie reminded his congregation that 'privat men mey no [resist] but a stat is not privat felouing ther laues … in our nation tirannie … was ever opposit'. Hence, Baillie recast the active opposition to unlawful commands as lawfully warranted, yet he still baulked at this conclusion and 'wish[ed] it mey never com to that[,] it is a grit plague but when war can no be divertit by no rasun the nixt is to mak for it diligently'.[51]

Like contemporary English puritans, Baillie redescribed resistance as 'defending' the laws, religion and liberties of the realm. His justification of resistance is thus more easily likened to arguments of Parliamentarians such as Philip Hunton, who minimized the significance of religion as a motivating factor in their war with Charles I.[52] Hunton, like Baillie, cited Bilson to the effect that from Romans 13 'nothing can be collected against any Resistance' for the passage referred to the exercise of lawful powers and the institution of lawful ordinances.[53] Glenn Burgess correctly argued that the Covenanters' propaganda 'more clearly and overtly' defended the Bishops' Wars as a war of religion than English tracts at the same time.[54] Nevertheless, in justification of the Bishops' Wars Baillie was at pains to stress that the Covenanters' 'defensive warfare' aimed to preserve the Church's liturgy, polity and doctrine because they were established by law. Refuting John Bramhall's suggestion that the Covenanters had raised arms 'meerly for Religion', Baillie later reminded the exiled bishop of Londonderry in 1649 that the National Covenant and Solemn League and Covenant had bound Scots in allegiance to the king's lawful commands.[55] According to Baillie, the Covenanters had defended Scotland against 'the violence also, which we see breathed out of the Bishops and their followers mouths'.[56] Baillie's three most political pamphlets – the *Ladensium*, *Vindication of the Government of the Church of Scotland* and his *Review of Bramble* – all blamed the subversive, self-interested and unlawful actions of the 'Canterburian faction' for trying to elevate royal

---

49 Cf. Walsham, 'Parochial Roots of Laudianism'.
50 NLS, Adv.MS.20.6.4, Baillie, Sermons, (fo. 170r) fo. 100v.
51 Ibid., (fo. 170r) fo. 105r.
52 See Glenn Burgess, 'England and Scotland', in Burgess, Howell A. Lloyd and Simon Hodson (eds), *European Political Thought 1450–1700: Religion, Law and Philosophy* (London, 2007), pp. 332–75, at p. 349.
53 Philip Hunton, *A vindication of the Treatise of monarchy* (London, 1644), p. 57.
54 Burgess, *British Political Thought*, p. 188.
55 Baillie, *Review of Bramhall*, pp. 88–9.
56 Robert Baillie to John Strang, n.d., *LJB*, vol. I, pp. 65–6.

power over law. Citing Bilson in his *Ladensium*, Baillie claimed that the 'people may plead their right against the Prince ... if a Prince should go about to subject his Kingdome to a forraine Realme, or change the forme of the Common-Wealth from Emperie [i.e. Empire] to tyranny'.[57] In a manuscript treatise containing maxims about the rights of magistrates (*de Majestatis jure*), written at some point in 1638, Baillie reiterated his belief that resistance was justified as a defence of a kingdom's constituent institutions, arguing that Christians 'ought not only to disobey but also to resist according to their strength [*pro viribus*]' when a 'contemptible magistrate or, if you prefer, a tyrant, destroys the church or state'.[58] By resisting such unlawful actions, true religion and pristine worship would be preserved intact and provided for in a timely fashion by the once tottering civil state.

In the vexed political climate of 1641, Charles's confused and panicked actions had provided Baillie with one of his strongest arguments in favour of the Covenanters' loyalty to the Stuart monarch. The Covenanters, Baillie reminded his readers, were simply engaged on the side of the English Parliament in defence of the religious reforms that Charles I had approved in the Scottish Parliament of 1641.[59] In effect, Charles's royal assent thereby absolved the Covenanters of any subsequent charge of treason, though supporters of the embattled Stuart monarch were not above suggesting that Charles had been forced to give his assent under duress. In his *Review of Bramble*, for example, Baillie argued that episcopacy and the Perth Articles were removed from the Church 'in no other than the ordinary and high path-way, whereby all burdensome Lawes and customes use to be removed'.[60] He thus resented the association that some Canterburian writers, such as Robert Creighton, the future bishop of Bath and Wells, drew between the Covenanters and the subversive intent of monarchomachs. Creighton wrote a preface to a reprint of *Akolouthos, or, A Second Faire Warning* (1651) by the royalist clergyman Richard Watson conceived as a reply to Baillie's *Review of Bramble*. In his prefatory letter, Creighton sarcastically apologized that Watson had been obliged to waste time in 'this business against Bailey', plunging himself into 'quagmires full of croaking Toads, and hissing Serpents, Covenants, Oaths, Perjuries, Assemblies, Reformations by blood, Knox and Buchanan, Consarcinations of trayterous plots'.[61] Elsewhere, when John Maxwell, the deposed bishop of Ross, alleged that the Covenanters approved of general assemblies holding the 'power to depose and kill Kings', Baillie responded that it was not 'just that John Knox['s] Assertions, long before

---

[57] Baillie, *Ladensium*, p. 121.
[58] NCL, Baill MS 4/1, 'Theses de Majestatis jure', fos 62v–64r, at fo. 63r.
[59] For example, see Baillie, *Review of Bramhall*, p. 84.
[60] Ibid.
[61] Robert Creighton, 'Dr. Creighton's Letter', in Richard Watson, *Akolouthos or A second faire warning to take heed of the Scotish discipline, in vindication of the first* (The Hague, 1651), sig. ¶4r.

any Assemblies were in Scotland, should be laid to their charge'.[62] Although Knox had contemplated killing the Catholic queen regent Mary Stewart, Baillie proceeded to justify the Scottish Reformation as taking place *with* Mary's consent. The Scots undertook 'no publike Reformation till first they had openly supplicated the Queen and gotten her allowance, and a promise of an Act of Parliament in the yeare 1558'.[63]

II

Baillie conceived of the Scottish (and English) monarchy as limited by funda-mental laws – essentially a sort of unwritten constitution – that preserved the lives, liberties and religion of each kingdom's subjects. Reference to Scotland's fundamental laws was common in both loyalist and radical Scottish political thought of the later medieval and early modern periods and there appeared to be no intrinsic opposition between ideas of *regnum* and *respublica*. If conflict arose, this was deemed to be the result of malpractice on either side.[64] The theme of misguided rule – characteristic of the writings of Baillie and many other critics of Caroline policies, both Scottish and English – allowed Baillie to focus on exposing the Romanizing efforts of Laud and other 'Canterburians', whilst simultaneously expressing unqualified loyalty to Scotland's ancient monarchy. Like most early modern Scots, Baillie believed that they were sub-jects of the most ancient and uninterrupted line of monarchs in the world. A national myth of origin, systematized by John of Fordun in the fourteenth century, claimed that the Scottish monarchy had been founded by Fergus MacFerquhard in 330 BCE, an alleged descendant of the eponymous Scota, daughter of an Egyptian pharaoh.[65] The means by which the Scottish mon-archy had been originally founded – whether by popular election or forcible conquest – held significant implications for early modern Scottish politi-cal ideas with a 'Buchananite' version of this foundation myth dominating mid-seventeenth-century political discourse.[66] Stemming from Buchanan's post-Reformation revival of the medieval chronicle tradition, this version argued that Scotland's monarchy had been originally elective and that, at certain historical junctures, the Scottish people had reasserted their right to choose who would occupy the throne and had even deposed particularly malignant monarchs without interrupting an unbroken monarchical lineage.

---

[62] Baillie, *Historicall Vindication*, Part I, p. 36.
[63] Ibid., Part I, p. 37.
[64] J.H. Burns, *The True Law of Kingship: Concepts of Monarchy in Early-Modern Scotland* (Oxford, 1996), pp. 286, 294.
[65] Many thanks to Roger Mason for clarification on this point about the mythical accounts of the Scottish monarchy's origins. See, also, Colin Kidd, *Subverting Scotland's Past: Scottish Whig Historians and the Creation of an Anglo-British Identity, 1689–c. 1830* (Cambridge, 1993), pp. 12–30.
[66] Ibid., p. xii.

Baillie did not explicitly dispute the originally elective nature of the Scottish monarchy, but he distanced himself from the more radical suggestion that the people thereby retained the right to depose a reigning monarch. Buchanan's *Historia* may have exerted a widespread influence over Covenanter political thought and acted as a primary source for Baillie on certain occasions, but his citations were noticeably selective.[67] '[S]ince the time our old ancestours did choose Fergus the first for their King', Baillie wrote, 'our subjection to the neerest Heire of that Race is now simply unchangeable' since the reign of Kenneth III (997–1005). Relatively easily, he reconciled this account of the Scottish monarchy's foundation with the notion of what he termed the 'divine institution of Kings'.[68] Baillie's adaptation of Buchanan's version of the monarchy's elective origins contrasted with the forcible conquest account that had been promoted, most notably, by James VI and I.[69] Likewise, Baillie contrasted his more qualified, elective account of the Scottish monarchy's origins with the account of John Corbet's *Ungirding of the Scottish armour* (1639) that claimed that the Scottish monarchy originated from conquest. He derided Corbet's insistence that 'Scotland is a subdued Nation, that Fergus our first King did conquer us by the sword, and establish an absolute Monarchie … giving to us what Lawes he thought meetest'.[70] Hence, any subject who denied obedience to the lawful commands of a superior was said to have sinned against God.[71]

Baillie's insistence on obedience to a monarch's *lawful* commands crucially distinguished him from those whom he claimed were arguing that obedience was owed to a king by virtue of 'royalitie alone'.[72] Accordingly, Baillie attacked Peter Heylyn for claiming that royal power was 'absolute and illimitate' and similarly reproved Maxwell for elevating royal authority above all law.[73] Whilst Maxwell had threatened to write an 'anatomie' of the British conflicts of the 1640s as a religious war, Baillie alleged that he had long been preoccupied with attaching 'the foure Limbes unto that Gorgons head of your Turkish Monarchy which some yeares agoe you set up at Oxford': referencing the parliament that Charles I had convened at Oxford in 1644.[74] Elsewhere, in his critique of Bramhall, Baillie argued that if Scottish liberties were made absolutely dependent on the king's will, civil

---

[67] This contrasts with Coffey's citation of Baillie's implicit usage of Buchanan in his 'Reply to Lysimachus Nicanor'. Coffey, 'George Buchanan and the Scottish Covenanters', p. 196.
[68] Baillie, *Ladensium*, pp. 127–8.
[69] Clare Jackson, *Restoration Scotland, 1660–1690: Royalist Politics, Religion and Ideas* (Woodbridge, 2003), p. 56.
[70] Baillie, *Ladensium*, pp. 127–8.
[71] Baillie, 'A Postscript for the personate Iesuite Lysimachus Nicanor', in *Ladensium*, p. 15.
[72] Ibid.
[73] Baillie, *Ladensium*, p. 123; Baillie, *Historicall Vindication*, pp. 3–7.
[74] Baillie, *Historicall Vindication*, p. 49.

society would revert to an anarchic state of nature. Popular liberties would only be secure so long as 'the sword and power remaines in their owne hand to preserve what they have obtained'.[75] Baillie's reading of royalist tracts was, however, not so selective as to overlook instances when Canterburians identified legal and institutional limits on monarchical power. After cataloguing all the Canterburians' 'tyrannical maxims', Baillie triumphantly concluded by exposing Laud's alleged hypocrisy, quoting a passage from the archbishop's *Conference with the Jesuit Fisher* (1639) wherein Laud had argued that 'the Statute Lawes which must bind all the Subjects, cannot be made but in, and by Parliament: the supreme Magistrate in the civill state, may not abrogate Lawes made in Parliament'.[76]

Baillie's sarcastic attack on Laud highlights the similarities between ostensibly antithetical early modern political theories of republicanism and monarchism when deployed against a looming Roman Catholic threat. Laud and Baillie were both terrified of the Jesuits' subversive tactics. Conflict arose when puritans and Canterburians began to characterize each other as 'Jesuitical' and debate inevitably polarized. After 1642, this helped to create a polemical atmosphere in England in which mere royal self-limitation in the coronation oath no longer provided sufficient grounds for preserving against misrule.[77] Baillie, by contrast, never went so far as to claim that the moral imperative for kings to rule according to law was no longer sufficient. Trust in a lawful monarch persisted for Baillie long after civil war had broken out in England. Ultimately, the English Parliament's revolutionary decision to try and execute the king resulted, in Baillie's mind, from the corrupting influence of Bramhall, Maxwell and their Canterburian colleagues, who had been 'cleare everters of the first foundations of trust betwixt Soveraignes and subjects'.[78] Baillie did not argue that the Canterburians, much less Charles I, had forced the Covenanters to seek a legal instrument with which to enforce the trust placed by subjects in their sovereign. After all, that was precisely the argument that, in putting Charles I on trial, the High Court of Justice had used to justify its existence.[79] Likewise, when Baillie addressed Charles II at The Hague on 27 March 1649, he notably failed to mention that the Scots would require Charles's subscription of the Solemn League and Covenant; rather, Baillie made a brief speech confirming a broad hope that Charles II would fulfil the duties or trusts of his office. Baillie hoped that Charles would

---

[75] Baillie, *Review of Bramhall*, pp. 18–19.
[76] Baillie, *Ladensium*, p. 128.
[77] See, for instance, Howard Nenner, 'Loyalty and the Law: The Meaning of Trust and the Right of Resistance in Seventeenth-Century England', *Journal of British Studies*, 48 (2009), pp. 859–70, at p. 860.
[78] Baillie, *Review of Bramhall*, p. 19.
[79] Howard Nenner, 'The Trial of Charles I and the Failed Search for a Bounded Monarchy', in Gordon J. Schochet (ed.), *Restoration, Ideology, and Revolution* (Washington, DC, 1990), pp. 1–21, at pp. 11–13. Also, see D. Alan Orr, *Treason and the State: Law, Politics, and Ideology in the English Civil War* (Cambridge, 2002), p. 176.

immediately fill 'the vacant Throne with your Majestie's most gracious and hopefull person', and confirmed that the Church's ministry was 'earnestly praying, that the light of the Lord's countenance may shyne so bright upon your Majestie's reign, that the very thick clouds of our present dangers and fears may flie away, and a new morning may spring up'.[80]

For Baillie, the legal limits of kingship derived from a covenant that was renewed by the monarch's coronation oath. Such a device was nothing more 'than nature requires of every society of men for their necessary preservation' and was based on the implicit trust Baillie vested in his monarch's word.[81] Although Baillie's *Ladensium*, in which some of the clearest statements of this trust occur, was printed before the outbreak of civil war in England – a key juncture for arguments about the need for an instrument of trust – Baillie republished the *Ladensium* in 1643 as *The life of William now Lord Arch-Bishop of Canterbury, examined* without undertaking any revisions, just as he had previously done between the work's first and second editions in 1640 and 1641. Specifically, Baillie objected to an argument found in the royalist defence of monarchical authority – John Weymss of Craigtoun's *Basileos hyperoche sive de regis primatu libellus* (1623) – from which Canterburian authors had subsequently concluded 'with applause' that 'all oathes and promises [the King] makes at his coronation are but of his meere free will and arbitrement, that by them all no true covenant or paction can bee inferred betwixt the King and his subjects'.[82]

Baillie's most convincing sources of authority on the legal limits of monarchy were parliamentary speeches delivered, and coronation oaths sworn, by James VI and I and Charles I. He used these documents to claim that the Covenanters opposed unlimited monarchy 'no more than our gracious Prince King Charles and his glorious Father King James'. Addressing the English Houses of Parliament in March 1610, for example, James VI and I had claimed that a 'Prince' would be a 'perjured Tyrant who would not gladly bound himselfe within the limits of his lawes' and that those who would 'assay by their flatteries to loose Princes from their pactions made with their people at their Coronation' should be considered 'vipers, pests and common enemies to princes and people'.[83] Elsewhere, Baillie cited a speech from Charles's third English Parliament in 1628, at which the 'Petition of Right' had been presented, to support the claim that most Christian princes,

---

[80] 'Mr. Robert Baillie's speech to King Charles the Second, March 27 1649: Spoken at The Hague in the King's Bed-Chamber, Tuesday, Three O'Clock in the afternoon', *LJB*, vol. III, pp. 84–5, at p. 85.

[81] Baillie, *Historicall Vindication*, p. 41.

[82] Baillie, *Ladensium*, p. 123. The citation from Weymss is found in *Basileos hyperoche* (Edinburgh, 1623), p. 18. The comment quoted is Baillie's interpolated between his marginal citations.

[83] Baillie, 'A Postscript for the personate Iesuite Lysimachus Nicanor', in *Ladensium*, p. 9. Baillie cited James's speech, printed in *The vvorkes of the most high and mightie prince, Iames by the grace of God King of Great Britaine, France and Ireland, defender of the faith, &c* (London, 1616), p. 531.

'and especially our gracious Soveraigne, are very well content to bee limited within the bounds of the lawes which themselves and their predecessors have setled in the Church and State of their dominions'; preservation of these laws was the royal prerogative's 'greatest glory'.[84] Baillie tactfully turned Charles's casuistry against the Stuart monarch a decade after the fact, pointing at such statements that – with hindsight – appeared disingenuous, insisting on their applicability. Hence, Baillie concluded in his *Historical Vindication* that 'all advised Princes abhorre' the suggestion that they are exempt from ecclesiastical discipline 'and confesse themselves to be subject to Ecclesiasticall Discipline … [for] Christianity is a body of Articles so straitly joyned that either all must be received or none'.[85]

In this context, Baillie preserved a quasi-Erastian role for the monarchy and parliament in passing legislation in favour of ecclesiastical acts. Acts of ecclesiastical assemblies had to stem from the authority of God's Word, but such acts were only given legal standing in a kingdom after ratification by king-in-parliament. For Baillie, Bramhall had therefore missed the mark in arguing that '[t]he [Scottish] Disciplinarians will sooner endure a Bishop or a Superintendent to govern them, than the Civil Magistrate'.[86] One modern commentator on the National Covenant claimed that 'in asserting the priority of divine authority [the Covenanters] were not so much subverting public authority as elevating the private authority of right-minded ministers'. '[M]oderate covenanters like Robert Baillie' found more comfort in the arguments of 'episcopalian adversaries who showed more willingness to preserve an area of indifference' in which subjects could fulfil the obligations of human law without having to ensure that it accorded 'in every detail' with divine law.[87] It appears that such an interpretation is correct to suggest that Baillie preserved a place for human laws outside the Church's aegis; indeed, Baillie adhered to this belief well after 1638 as evinced in his response to the pseudonymous Jesuit 'Lysimachus Nicanor', the royalist polemicist John Corbet. Whilst Corbet had argued that the Covenanters' 'doctrine of the Magistrate … is the head of Protestant Faith', Baillie retorted that this doctrine 'doth not concerne Religion at all'. According to Baillie, religion 'oblige[d] the conscience to give unto all Magistrats their due honour and obedience … the bounds and limits of that obedience … Religion medleth not with them till the civill lawes of States, and Empires have clearly defined them.'[88] Religious zeal was not subversive, but constitutive of the foundations of monarchy.

---

[84] Baillie, *Ladensium*, p. 120.
[85] Baillie, *Historicall Vindication*, p. 19.
[86] John Bramhall, *A fair warning to take heed of the Scottish discipline* ([Delft], 1649), p. 4.
[87] John Ford, 'The Lawful Bonds of Scottish Society: The Five Articles of Perth, the Negative Confession and the National Covenant', *Historical Journal*, 37 (1994), pp. 45–64, at pp. 62, 64.
[88] Baillie, 'A Postscript for the personate Iesuite Lysimachus Nicanor', in *Ladensium*, p. 6. Baillie repeated the assertion that ecclesiastical laws required 'civill sanction' in 1646. See Baillie, *Historicall Vindication*, p. 36.

Defending religion's role in encouraging honour and obedience to civil authorities, Baillie unsurprisingly accorded a prominent place to the royal supremacy in ecclesiastical affairs. In this context, Baillie's ideas challenge a common presumption that the Covenanters adhered to a strict separation of Church and state, which elevated the authority of the General Assembly *over* that of the monarchy. This 'Two Kingdoms' theory had been enshrined in *The Second Book of Discipline* (1578) and was based on the premise of Christ's sovereignty over the Church, which decreed civil magistrates' legitimate involvement in ecclesiastical affairs.[89] Although the theory has traditionally been ascribed to Andrew Melville, it is perhaps more accurate to acknowledge Melville as only one member – albeit a particularly vociferous one – of a minority of presbyterians in favour of removing monarchical power from the ecclesiastical sphere.[90]

Whilst the extent to which this 'Two Kingdoms' theory commanded widespread acceptance remains unclear, Baillie wholeheartedly supported *The Second Book of Discipline*, particularly those sections addressing the royal supremacy. Baillie did not, however, uphold this separation in order to restrict the scope of the monarch's powers, but rather on the grounds that the nature of such a separation proved that 'there is no better harmony in the world' than between a presbyterian polity and monarchy.[91] Rather than detailing his rationale, Baillie simply denied critics' claims that the seventh chapter of *The Second Book of Discipline* 'doe[s] trample on the Magistrats supremacy and Lawes'.[92] Instead, he upheld the Melvillian idea that 'the government of the Church and State are two really distinct policies, both ordained of God, which without his displeasure may not be confounded, nor ought to encroach one upon another'.[93] This was not, however, to grant ministers in a presbyterian polity any powers to rival those of their monarch; there was not any 'dominion, no Soverainity in Church officers, but a meer ministry under Christ'.[94] In fact, Baillie claimed – in remarkably Erastian vein – that, in Scotland, 'all the jurisdiction which the church there does enjoy, they have it with the consent of the Magistrat: all is ratified to them by such acts of Parliament as his Majestie doth not at all controvert'.[95] For Baillie, the injunction from Acts 5:29 to obey God, rather than man, did not imply that Christians ought to obey the ministry when the civil government acted contrary to God's Word.[96] In such situations, Christians ought rather to seek guidance from Scripture which, as seen, Baillie insisted should

---

[89] *The Second Book of Discipline*, ed. James Kirk (Edinburgh, 1980).
[90] Alan R. MacDonald, *The Jacobean Kirk, 1567–1625: Sovereignty, Polity and Liturgy* (Aldershot, 1998).
[91] Baillie, *Historicall Vindication*, p. 62.
[92] Baillie, *Review of Bramhall*, p. 17.
[93] Baillie, *Historicall Vindication*, p. 73.
[94] Baillie, *Review of Bramhall*, p. 56.
[95] Ibid., p. 21.
[96] Ibid., p. 56.

be interpreted as exhorting private individuals to passively obey ungodly magistrates.[97]

In addition to holding that presbytery and monarchy could exist harmoniously, Baillie suggested that a presbyterian polity strengthened the legal foundations of monarchy. In his *Historical Vindication*, Baillie claimed that the erroneous view that monarchy and presbytery were necessarily inimical to one another stemmed from the forgery promoted by the Jacobean archbishop of St Andrews Patrick Adamson, entitled *A declaration of the king's majesty's intention and meaning concerning the late acts of parliament* (1585).[98] The *Declaration* claimed to confirm James VI's approbation of acts of the 1584 Scottish Parliament at which Adamson had orchestrated the overthrow of presbyterian church government, but Baillie questioned the validity of Adamson's claim. Successive opponents of presbyterianism, including Archbishop Bancroft, and the allegedly Canterburian author of *Eikon Basilike* (1649), had subsequently seized on Adamson's fallacious claim to have written on James's behalf to condemn presbyterians as opposed to the royal supremacy, just as Corbet had purported to draft the fiercely anti-presbyterian *Large Declaration* (1639) on Charles I's behalf.[99] If the *Declaration* proved to be a forgery perpetrated by Adamson – one of the most notorious sixteenth-century opponents of Scottish presbyterians – then, in Baillie's mind, the historical basis of episcopal criticism of presbyterians crumbled.

In contrast to such allegedly slanderous accounts of presbyterian views, Baillie's conception of the royal supremacy was based on the writings of the moderate Elizabethan bishop Bilson, and the Irish bishop James Ussher, who had famously proposed a 'reduced episcopal' settlement during the 1640s and 1650s.[100] Both Bilson and Ussher championed a view of the royal supremacy that was more akin to Baillie's vision of distinctive, but equal, civil and ecclesiastical spheres operating harmoniously alongside each other. As has recently and persuasively been shown, the ambiguities of the Henrician establishment of the Church of England provided fertile territory for political debates throughout the seventeenth century, and Baillie's ideas likewise blurred the dividing-line between 'Presbyterian' and 'Erastian' conceptions of the royal supremacy.[101] For Baillie, it was significant that Bilson and Ussher, like the Covenanters, had refused to commit Maxwell's error in making 'the

---

[97] On the Geneva Bible annotations and their equivocal approbation and negation of lawful resistance, see Tom Furniss, 'Reading the Geneva Bible: Notes Toward an English Revolution?', *Prose Studies: History, Theory, Criticism*, 31 (2009), pp. 1–21.

[98] Baillie, *Historicall Vindication*, pt II, passim.

[99] Baillie, *Review of Bramhall*, sigs a2r–v.

[100] For Baillie's praise of Ussher, see 'A Large Supplement to the Canterburians Self-Conviction', p. 2. Also, see W.M. Abbott, 'James Ussher, Ussherian Episcopacy, 1640–1656 – the Primate and his "Reduction" Manuscript', *Albion*, 22 (1990), pp. 237–59, at p. 240.

[101] Jacqueline Rose, *Godly Kingship in Restoration England: The Politics of the Royal Supremacy, 1660–1688* (Cambridge, 2011), Introduction.

Magistrate the hand and fountaine of all Jurisdiction civill and Ecclesiastick'. Were such 'despotick' supremacy to be granted to king or parliament, it would 'shake the groundstones of all the Lawes of the Kingdome'.[102] By contrast, the Canterburians had gone much further than the 'moderate interpretations' of the royal supremacy posited by Bilson and Ussher.[103] As Baillie put it, Charles's 'Royall Supremacie we willingly yield to, so far as the fundamentall Laws of our Church and Kingdome extend it, yea, we make no question of it in that sense Bilson, and the old Bishops of England understood it'.[104]

Before exploring the scope of Baillie's version of the royal supremacy, it is worth considering Church–state relations from the General Assembly's perspective. Whilst opponents of presbyterianism claimed that, in such a polity, church assemblies dramatically limited the monarch's powers, they also argued that such assemblies limited a monarch's powers by encroaching on the civil sphere. According to Bramhall, it was the Covenanters' 'highest cheat … that Jesuiticall invention, (in ordine ad spiritualia,) they assume a power in worldly affairs indirectly, and in order to their advancement of the kingdom of Christ'.[105] Responding to Bramhall, Baillie argued that although the Covenanters claimed presbyterianism to be jure divino, this was no different from the episcopalian claim of a jure divino discipline and certainly did not cause presbyterians, ipso facto, to impinge unlawfully on the royal supremacy.[106] Recounting the historical relationship between the General Assembly and parliament in Scotland, Baillie argued that the 'forme of this proceeding established by the Parliament it selfe, does not import any subordination either of the lawes, or the Parliament to the Assembly'.[107] Despite the frustrating fortunes of presbyterian models in the post-Reformation Church of Scotland, there was clear and convincing evidence that a presbytery 'medles not to the prejudice of any civill Government which it finds established by Law'.[108] Accordingly, the problem was not that presbyterians claimed this jure divino status, but that Erastians and episcopalians claimed that church polity itself was adiaphorous:

> [N]o Presbiterian ever dreamed of any necessity, to change the government of the State, that it might be conforme to the Church; but many Episcopall and all Erastians doe hold the government of the Church to bee a matter of so indifferent arbitrary and changeable a nature, that it may well comply, and ought to be conformed to the model of every State wherein it requires to be entertained.[109]

---

[102] Baillie, Historicall Vindication, pt II, p. 15.
[103] Ibid., pt II, p. 14.
[104] Baillie, 'A Postscript for the personate Iesuite Lysimachus Nicanor', in Ladensium, p. 19.
[105] Bramhall, A fair warning, p. 19.
[106] Baillie, Review of Bramhall, pp. 48–55.
[107] Baillie, Historicall Vindication, p. 61.
[108] Ibid., p. 64.
[109] Ibid., p. 75.

Regarding the separate, but related, punitive measures of Church and parliament, Baillie contended that the General Assembly did not usurp civil powers, and no more 'power then what the Parliaments since the first Reformation have heartily allowed unto them'. When parliament chose to impose civil censure on a person found guilty by the General Assembly, its members applied a penalty which 'their wisedome findes meet to impose on a person who contemnes the Ordinances of God'.[110] The General Assembly never extended its authority 'to excommunicate, much lesse to dethrone any King'.[111] As Baillie pointed out, the king was required to be present – in person or by proxy through a royal commissioner – in all General Assemblies as a 'civil President'.[112]

Baillie did, however, deny the monarch a negative voice in his capacity as 'civil President', claiming that this opinion was shared by all presbyterians and Erastians. During peace negotiations in the 1640s between the Scots and Charles I, problems had arisen when Charles had refused to accept limits on his negative voice: a function that Baillie claimed had never been legally established in Scotland.[113] According to Baillie, all civil magistrates, especially the monarch, could act within ecclesiastical affairs insofar as such action accorded with God's Word. The monarch thus played a significant role in facilitating religious reform, which was so critical a role that Baillie conceded that 'we maintain no power of the Church to reforme and preserve Religion, but such as does well consist with that duty which God has laid upon the Magistrate, both for the reformation of Religion, and preservation of it when it is reformed'.[114] James VI and I was thus an exemplar, for Baillie, of how a Christian prince ought to act in support of ecclesiastical censures. James had not exercised ecclesiastical jurisdiction when he had punished men previously convicted for ecclesiastical crimes; rather he had only acted in his civil capacity, regulating the execution of discipline.[115] Following the destruction of royal power in England in 1649, Baillie indicated that 'there is no question for the convocating of ordinary assemblie, for extraordinary, no man in Scotland did ever controvert the Kings power to call them when and where he pleased'.[116] Appeals from the Church's ministry could not proceed directly from the General Assembly to the king, but 'in moderate Monarchies' it was normal practice to supplicate the king in court, whether in the General Assembly or parliament.[117]

---

110 Ibid., p. 33.
111 Ibid.
112 Ibid., p. 34.
113 Baillie, *Review of Bramhall*, p. 40.
114 Baillie, *Historicall Vindication*, pp. 75–6.
115 Ibid., pt II, p. 8.
116 Baillie, *Review of Bramhall*, p. 9.
117 Ibid., p. 23.

III

Now that I have established the conceptual outlines of Baillie's political thought and indicated some of the points at which he diverged from other Covenanters, it remains to be seen how Baillie's political ideas, particularly his emphasis on loyalty to the Stuart monarchs, influenced his allegiance at crucial junctures when strain was placed on the unity of the Covenanting movement. The printed output in Scotland from these years, or the subsequent historiography of the 'Scottish Revolution', suggests that the movement's political and religious leadership expressed the opinion of the vast majority of Scottish society. Certainly, the National Covenant was a remarkable document because of the extent of popular subscription.[118] Yet the Covenanters' unity was ultimately superficial, deriving from the existence of a common enemy in Laud and the need for popular action to combat his influence. Baillie himself appositely recognized the breadth of opinions encompassed within Covenanting ranks when he enumerated a number of royalist Scots, including the earls of Roxburghe, Traquair, Southesk and Lauderdale, who stood 'at the back of that long blasphemed Covenant' following Charles I's approval of the Covenanters' religious reforms in the 1641 Parliament.[119] More recently, Baillie has even been described as a 'conservative, the sentimental royalist', and a survey of some key moments in Baillie's Covenanting career supports a qualified version of this claim.[120] Accordingly, I stress here that Baillie's political ideas may be cast as a (slightly amended) Scottish equivalent of constitutional royalism or 'Presbyterian royalism'.[121] Rather than being characterized both by a commitment to the rule of law and by an absence of godly zeal, Baillie's version of royalist politics did not eclipse his attendant godly zeal for the sake of obedience to Scotland's fundamental laws; rather the former provided impetus to secure the latter.

Whilst the Covenanters evinced a latent loyalty to the Stuart monarchy throughout the 1640s and 1650s, at three crucial moments Baillie elevated attachment to his monarch over objectives of religious reform. In each instance, Baillie's fears regarding the increasing political power of 'sectarian' religious groups in both England and Scotland – radical Independents in the New Model Army, and the Scottish Protestors – prompted him to advocate measures to secure support from Charles I or Charles II. First, Baillie's Historical Vindication, which was specifically written to influence negotiations then underway between the Scots Army and Charles I at Newcastle in 1646, deemed it imperative for the Covenanters to reach a peace agreement with

---

[118] David Stevenson, 'The National Covenant: A List of Known Copies', RSCHS, 23 (1988), pp. 255–99.

[119] Baillie, 'A Postscript for the personate Iesuite Lysimachus Nicanor', in Ladensium, p. 8.

[120] F.N. McCoy, Robert Baillie and the Second Scots Reformation (Berkeley, 1974), p. 218.

[121] David Smith, Constitutional Royalism and the Search for Settlement, c. 1640–1649 (Cambridge, 1994).

Charles I, given the apparent rise in republican sentiment in the New Model Army, and growing opposition to the Covenanting Army in England. Baillie began writing the *Historical Vindication* at some point after 19 May 1646, which was the day on which the English House of Commons voted that the Scots Army was no longer required in England. On that day, Baillie wrote to the presbyterian historian David Calderwood requesting some historical documents which 'if you will be pleased to be againe at the paines to send … we shall readilie say something in answer to [Maxwell]'.[122] Baillie's tract was finished around 29 July, according to its dedication to Baillie's former tutor, Robert Blair. Moreover, in a letter Baillie wrote on 16 May 1646 to the Scottish minister conducting negotiations on the Church's behalf with Charles I, Alexander Henderson, he promised 'to send yow my thoughts, as yow desired, on King James's Declaration'; the substance of this was printed as the second part of his *Historical Vindication*.[123]

Baillie's correspondence during the summer of 1646 further reflects his increasing frustration at the unfavourable situation in which the Covenanters now found themselves. Charles had obstinately refused to grant the religious concessions demanded by the Covenanters because of the continued influence of 'Laudian' councillors at the royal court, but rumours of possible regicide and nascent republicanism left Baillie unwilling to surrender Charles to the New Model Army and abandon peace negotiations as a lost cause. Contrary to one recent historian who claimed that Baillie was Argyll's principal ally amongst the Church's ministry, Baillie's correspondence shows his increasingly close affinities with a group of moderate, even royalist, Covenanting nobles around the Newcastle negotiations.[124] 'Go matters as they will', Baillie dramatically lamented to Henderson, 'if men will not be saved, who can help it! And yet yow know that I was never among these who had greatest aversion from his person [i.e. Charles I], or least sympathie with his afflictions.'[125] If Charles would just 'doe his duty, in spight of all knaves, all would in a moment goe right, but if God have hardened him … this people will stryve to have him in their power, and make an example of him … every hour of his [i.e. Charles's] delay gives advantage to these men, who makes it their worke … to make him irreconcileable'.[126] With a tone of alarmism evident in his correspondence at this juncture, Baillie explained that if negotiations were delayed further some might take the opportunity to seize power and to ensure that 'we shall quickly establish ourselves in a republick, and forswear kings for ever'.[127]

An exchange of letters between Baillie and William Hamilton, earl of

---

122 Robert Baillie to William Spang, [June 1658], *LJB*, vol. II, pp. 373–4, quote at p. 374.
123 Robert Baillie to Alexander Henderson, 16 May 1646, *LJB*, vol. II, p. 371.
124 Allan Macinnes, *The British Confederate: Archibald Campbell, Marquess of Argyll, c.1607–1661* (Edinburgh, 2011), pp. 17–18.
125 Robert Baillie to Alexander Henderson, 19 May 1646, *LJB*, vol. II, p. 372.
126 Ibid., pp. 372–3.
127 Robert Baillie to Alexander Henderson, 18 July 1646, *LJB*, vol. II, pp. 381–2.

Lanark, in February 1646 further attests to Baillie's political alignments. Lanark's behaviour surrounding the Newcastle negotiations showed that he was intent on reconciling himself with the king's party and, then, playing a leading role in reconciling Charles to his Scottish subjects.[128] Responding to Lanark's concern that he was being slandered in both Scotland and England for his royalist leanings, Baillie reassured the young earl that compromise was essential. If the Scottish nobility could surmount their internal divisions, the survivors of these internecine struggles 'will gladly consent to that curse, which somewhere in the world is much desyred, and farr advanced, (though my heart did ever abhorre it,) that, when Kings and Princes are brought down, the power and following of the Nobles may be abolished'.[129] In a final attempt to sway Charles I's mind, Baillie engaged the help of William Murray, earl of Dysart and a former Gentleman of the Bedchamber, to remove all malignant influences from the royal court and the exiled court, specifically that of Thomas Hobbes, and to avoid inciting renewed conflict by raising Irish or French Catholic forces in his support. Justifying his blunt supplications, Baillie concluded that 'I have many good witnesses of my respects to monarchy, and to King Charles's persone, above many, if not all my fellows.'[130] In making his plea, Baillie was evidently acting without the knowledge of the radical Covenanting leaders Wariston and Argyll, writing to the former in October 1646 that, if Murray could 'draw from the King, at last, a satisfactorie answer, I wish my Lord Argyle and ye did come along with it'.[131]

Viewed from this perspective, Baillie sought to recover the failing image of the Scottish Church's presbyterian government as consistent with monarchy in the hope that he could sway moderate royalist and even – via Henderson – Charles I's own estimate of potential reconciliation with his Scottish subjects. After patiently enduring a dramatic reversal of previous religious reforms, God had finally accorded the Scots a chance, through the Solemn League and Covenant, to intervene in English affairs and thereby to secure godly reformation throughout Britain. As Baillie put it, in negotiating with Charles at Newcastle, all the Scots had sought was 're-establishing of the King in his throne the confirming of the Parliament, City, and Country in all their rights, the setling of Religion and peace according to the word of God, and the Lawes of the Land'. Despite these intentions, the Scots had been 'traduced and defamed by contumelious Libels in England, and that at London'.[132] Provoked by the apparent rise in republicanism, together with the exploitation of Maxwell's tract by 'opposites of Presbyteriall government', namely Independents and Erastians, who were denouncing the Covenanters'

---

[128] John Scally, 'William Hamilton, earl of Lanark', in ODNB [accessed 1 June 2012].
[129] Robert Baillie to William, earl of Lanark, [February 1646], LJB, vol. II, p. 355.
[130] Memorandum for William Murray, n.d., LJB, vol. II, p. 396.
[131] Robert Baillie to Archibald Johnston of Wariston, 27 October 1646, LJB, vol. II, p. 407.
[132] Baillie, Historicall Vindication, pp. 9–10.

objectives in London, Baillie thus set out to compose a tract – which became the *Historical Vindication* – reaffirming Scotland's commitment to presbytery and, most importantly, to limited monarchy.[133]

In similar vein, Baillie's initial support of the duke of Hamilton's royalist 'Engagement' in 1648, before his reluctant conformity to the Church's opposition, illustrates Baillie's willingness to accept significant religious concessions in order to preserve public order and prevent further sectarian violence. If Coffey is correct in claiming that Rutherford had written *Lex Rex* in 1644 to dissuade moderate Covenanters from compromising with Charles I, then the republication of Rutherford's tract in 1648, under the title *The Preeminence of the Election of Kings, or, A Plea for the Peoples Rights*, may be viewed as an attempt to sway opinion against Hamilton's royalist 'Engagement'.[134] The 'Engagement' treaty, which was secretly signed at Carisbrooke Castle on the Isle of Wight on 26 December 1647, pledged the Scots to invade England on Charles's behalf. In exchange, a group of prominent Covenanting nobles, namely Lanark, Loudoun and Lauderdale, sacrificed aspects of the Covenanters' religious demands for peace. Although the Solemn League and Covenant was to be approved by the English Parliament, neither Charles nor any unwilling Englishmen would be forced to swear it, and a presbyterian polity would be established in England for a trial period of three years after which an assembly of divines would meet to determine a permanent settlement.

Baillie's initial reaction to the Engagement is contained in a remarkable manuscript document entitled 'My sudden thoughts … of the motion of warre then in all mens mouthes'. Writing on the day that news of the Engagement arrived in Edinburgh, Baillie weighed the competing arguments for and against the treaty before resolving that 'my minde is inclined to conclude the lawfullnesse, expediency and necessity of a war with that evill partie [i.e. the New Model Army]'.[135] Baillie contended that 'this warre will reconceale all our divisions' and that, if any remained, who would 'preferr their owne interest' to those of their 'Religion, to their Countrey, to their King and his familie, I beleeve they would quickly become so contemptible creatures as no skill could enable them to remaine longer the head or considerable member of any party'.[136] If the Covenanters did not act, either the sectaries or English Royalists would triumph, before their attention turned towards Scotland. Baillie concluded with a pragmatic interpretation of Charles I's likely actions, evincing signs of a continued inclination to trust that Charles, once freed from 'Canterburian' influence, would act in line with the law:

---

[133]   Ibid., pt II, p. 1.
[134]   On the Engagement and the terms of the agreement as follows, see Stevenson, *Revolution and Counter-Revolution*, pp. 82–129.
[135]   NCL, Baill MS 4/3, 'My sudden thoughts on saturday feb: 12 1648 of the motion of warre then in all mens mouthes', fos 9v–11v, at fo. 10v.
[136]   Ibid., fos 10v–11r.

[A]s for the king, granting him not to be so farr changed as we wish, yet he is willing to doe what wee desire in suppressing sectaries and Papists, as for the prelaticall party wee trust the Presbiterian parliament, the City of London and wee joining togidder, will either persuad or make him giue to us in recompence of our Labours for him, that our gracious gift, his Bishops to be cast away, and they now being out, his negative voice could not bring them in.[137]

The Scots needed to act to 'vindicat our wrongs' and prevent the 'misseryes' that had followed after the Scots Army had surrendered custody of Charles to the Independent-dominated English Parliament in 1646.[138]

The decision to remove the Scottish Army from England early in 1647 proved to be a fatal miscalculation for the Covenanters as the power of the New Model Army increased, enabling it to purge the English Parliament of its presbyterian majority, erect the Court of High Justice and thereafter try and execute Charles I. Following Oliver Cromwell's military conquest of Scotland in 1651, the Covenanters decisively split between 'Protestors' and 'Resolutioners'. For his part, Baillie sided with the 'Resolutioners' who advocated reconciliation with repentant Royalists, whilst more radical Covenanters, such as Wariston, Rutherford and Baillie's arch-nemesis in Glasgow burgh politics, Patrick Gillespie, sided with the 'Protestors'. For Baillie, the decade of the 1650s was to become a period dominated by ecclesiastical strife primarily provoked by the sectarian Protestor faction. By the time of Charles II's Restoration in 1660, therefore, Baillie had become distraught by a preceding decade of turmoil and he was committed to supporting Charles II's restored rule throughout England, Scotland and Ireland.

Two salient characteristics of Baillie's letters at the Restoration are important in supplying an appropriate way to conclude this discussion of his political ideas. First, Baillie's political activities aligned him with Resolutioners who would subsequently rise to prominence in the Restoration Church or government. Between 1658 and his death in 1662, there are twenty-three extant letters from Baillie to James Sharp, future archbishop of St. Andrews, and to John Maitland, earl of Lauderdale and future Scottish secretary of state. Following the Restoration, Sharp became the focus of particularly bitter presbyterian ire on account of his suspected insincerity when deputed to negotiate on the Resolutioners' behalf in favour of a presbyterian settlement in London. Lauderdale, likewise, was an instinctive opportunist, who quickly distanced himself from presbyterian stalwarts in order to further his own political advancement.[139] More instructive, however, is the continuity

---

[137] Ibid., fos 11r–v.
[138] Ibid., fo. 11v.
[139] For a detailed, high-political narrative of the ecclesiastical settlement, see Godfrey Davies and Paul H. Hardacre, 'The Restoration of the Scottish Episcopacy, 1660–1661', The Journal of British Studies, 1 (1962), pp. 32–51. For the Resolutioner ministers' influence on negotiations over an ecclesiastical settlement in 1660, see Julia Buckroyd, 'The Resolutioners and the Scottish Nobility in the Early Months of 1660', Studies in Church History, 12 (1975), pp. 245–52.

between presbyterian Resolutioners and members of the restored political and ecclesiastical establishments in Scotland. Strikingly, on at least two occasions during the Interregnum, Baillie had asked the minister, James Wood, to forward his correspondence to their Resolutioner ally, Andrew Honyman, the Restoration bishop of Orkney and subsequent author of the *Survey of Naphalti* (1668), which was a damning critique of Rutherford's *Lex Rex*.[140] The intellectual lines along which the Resolutioners cohered thus encompassed thinkers such as Honyman who harboured outright hostility to radical Covenanting political thought, and it was these individuals, particularly Sharp and Lauderdale, in whom Baillie vested his hopes for securing a presbyterian settlement from Charles II. Following a year of uncertainty regarding the nature of the eventual religious settlement, Baillie's hopes for presbyterianism were dashed when Charles issued a royal proclamation re-establishing episcopacy on 6 September 1661.

Rather than stimulating popular support against this act, as the Covenanters had done in 1638, Baillie privileged his desire to maintain peace by supplicating the king through lawful channels, namely the Scottish nobility. Although Baillie's quiescence has hitherto been taken as evidence of his acceptance of episcopacy's re-establishment, his letters to Lauderdale and the earl of Glencairn, Lord Chancellor of Scotland, provide ample evidence of his aversion.[141] Baillie beseeched Glencairn, 'desert not our poor Church at this tyme … [p]ermitt not our gracious Soveraigne to be deceived'. If Glencairn did not act as a dutiful member of Scotland's nobility, representing the desires of the Church's ministry for a presbyterian settlement, Baillie presciently predicted that the restoration of episcopacy 'will cause a more generall grief and miscontent in Scotland, than any action of any of our Princes hes done' since the Reformation.[142] Baillie laid his aims bare in a particularly candid letter to Sharp. Albeit he 'behoved to dissuade [an episcopal settlement], which would but offend his Majesty' he was nonetheless 'loather in the least to offend [Charles II] than any mortall creature'.[143]

Baillie's privileging of public order over sectarian disruption, particularly regarding the re-establishment of episcopacy, led him to acquiesce, begrudgingly, to royal commands and thus to the settlement of the Restoration Church. In this sense, Baillie's reasoned silence and lawful supplication more closely aligned him with those writers who contributed to the Erastian climate of Restoration Scotland. Baillie's deference to civil authority as a key means to resolve religious strife was restated, for example, by a young royalist lawyer, and subsequent Lord Advocate, George Mackenzie, in his *Religio*

---

[140] *LJB*, vol. III, pp. 201, 212.
[141] Stevenson, 'Robert Baillie', *ODNB* [accessed 1 June 2012].
[142] Robert Baillie to William Cunningham, earl of Glencairn, [1661], *LJB*, vol. III, pp. 475–6. For Baillie's claims of the weight of opinion in favour of a Presbyterian settlement, see his letter to Lauderdale, ibid., p. 477.
[143] Robert Baillie to James Sharp, 29 August 1661, *LJB*, vol. III, p. 474.

Stoici (1663), which privileged public order and denounced religious persecution. In her recent reappraisal of Mackenzie's tract, Clare Jackson showed
that it presented a 'very public plea for peaceful religious practice' at a time
when widespread yearning for civil peace might induce a majority of Scots
to external conformity.[144] As Mackenzie argued, 'as every private Christian
should be tollerated by his fellow-subjects', worshipping God according to
his conscience, likewise Christians 'should conspire in that exteriour uniformity of worship, which the Laws of his Countrey injoins'.[145] In similar
vein, the former Resolutioner minister Honyman justified conformity to
the restored Scottish episcopate in his *Seasonable case of submission to the
church-government as now re-established by law* (1662). In his tract, Honyman
deployed arguments used by Resolutioners in the 1650s to persuade Protestors
to attend 'lawfully convened' synods in order to preserve a unified national
church. To avoid the 'exceeding great bitterness' that had torn Interregnum
Scotland apart, Honyman claimed that the restored episcopate should be
viewed simply as 'the Kings Majesties Commissioners in Causes ecclesiastical
for regulating the external order of the Church'. They were 'impowred [sic]
by the law of the land so to do' and it would, therefore, be 'hard to say, that
their power is not lawfull, and that obedience is not due to them'.[146] If such
obedience was not forthcoming, Honyman asked, would Scots acquiesce
in 'ecclesiastical Independency' or 'combine in clandestine Presbyteries'?
Ministers who entertained such opinions should consider how these actions
'shall be taken by the christian Magistrate, or how it shall relish of that spirit
of unity and love that should be amongst Christ's Ministers'.[147] Such considerations had certainly underpinned Baillie's decision to submit to Charles II's
restored Church and to accept prominent promotion as Principal of Glasgow
University in January 1661. Acquiescence to royal religious policy was essential in order to avoid plunging the British Isles back into sectarian warfare.

[144] Clare Jackson, 'Latitudinarianism, Secular Theology and Sir Thomas Browne's
Influence in George Mackenzie's *Religio Stoici* (1663)', *The Seventeenth Century*, 29 (2014),
pp. 73–94, at p. 74.
[145] George Mackenzie, *Religio Stoici* (Edinburgh, 1663), 'The Stoicks friendly addresse to
the Phanaticks of all Sects and Sorts', pp. 19–20.
[146] Andrew Honyman, *Seasonable case of submission to the church-government as now
reestablished by law* (Edinburgh, 1662), pp. 3, 16.
[147] Ibid., p. 13.

3

Presbyterian Church Government

The differences between episcopal, presbyterian and congregational polities were often porous and blurred. Even the polity of Robert Baillie's Scottish Church – hailed both at home and abroad as 'the best Reformed Kirk' – cannot easily be cast in a presbyterian mould without overlooking its similarities with episcopal and congregational polities. Yet seventeenth-century Scots and centuries of subsequent historiography may lead one to conclude that a clear divide emerged between proponents of episcopacy and presbyterianism at the Reformation Parliament of 1560. Such a dichotomous framework more accurately reflects, however, a characteristically sectarian historiography of Scottish Church parties from the early seventeenth century onwards. 'Presbyterian' tendencies emerged amongst a group of Scottish ministers following the Jacobean Union of the Crowns in 1603, reacting to royal absenteeism, fear of incorporating union with England, royal forbearance of Catholics and repeated prorogations of the General Assembly.[1] As it appeared that consensus over the Scottish Church's polity declined, contemporaries began to draft historical accounts that refashioned the post-Reformation Church as starkly divided between 'presbyterian' and 'episcopalian' factions. Composed during the reigns of James VI and I and his son, Charles I, David Calderwood's posthumously published *True History of the Church of Scotland* (1678) narrated the oppression endured and victories scored by presbyterian ministers against 'anti-Christian' bishops, whereas Archbishop John Spottiswoode of St Andrews provided an historical account of the lawfulness of episcopacy in his *History of the church and state of Scotland* that was completed before 1639, although not published until 1655.

The histories of Calderwood and Spottiswoode imposed retrospective coherence on the ecclesiological commitments of ministers within the post-Reformation Church, implying that such identities were becoming more clearly defined. Rhetorical coherence nevertheless continued to conceal conceptual ambiguities. Baillie's self-identification with a presbyterian polity, discussed in this chapter, remained largely a rhetorical construct deployed for polemical advantage in published pamphlets. Subtle resonances continued to subsist between proponents of presbyterian, episcopal

---

[1] Alan R. MacDonald, *The Jacobean Kirk, 1567–1625: Sovereignty, Polity and Liturgy* (Aldershot, 1998), pp. 179–80.

and congregational polities that were thereby overlooked. The porous divide between presbyterian and episcopal polities is traceable to the foundational documents of the Church of Scotland's polity, the First and Second Books of Discipline (1560 and 1578). The First Book of Discipline, for example, stipulated that the election of ministers 'appertaineth to the people, and to every severall Congregation', but if a particular congregation was 'negligent … the Church of the Superintendent with his councell, may present unto them a man whom they judge apt'.[2] Jurisdictional powers of both the whole congregation and the bishop (renamed a superintendent) were thereby retained. Curiously, powers of synods were not discussed at all, despite The First Book being unequivocally praised by subsequent generations of presbyterians.

Although The Second Book of Discipline was subsequently considered a high-water mark for presbyterianism in the post-Reformation Kirk, the Scottish episcopate remained unobjectionable to the majority of Scottish ministers. Often, however, it is the dissident ministers who have left more detailed records, thus skewing historiography to emphasize their complaints. Discontent emerged amongst presbyterian ministers at moments throughout the early seventeenth century when they felt that either king or bishops had encroached on their lawful powers. In 1606, a General Assembly was convened in Aberdeen without the king's authority, whilst James's subsequent policy of introducing greater 'congruity' between the established churches of England and Scotland provoked more widespread agitation.[3] In 1610, the General Assembly was prorogued indefinitely and two archiepiscopal courts of High Commission were established in St Andrews and Glasgow. Notwithstanding this increase in episcopal powers, presbyteries continued to function in concert with the presiding bishop, preserving a state of detente with opponents of the Jacobean Church. Although distinctive presbyterian tendencies may thus be detected, a 'presbyterian revolution' did not erupt for nearly another three decades. The lack of serious civil disturbances in Scotland before 1638 may be explained by several factors, not least a growth in the number of gathered churches or 'conventicles' that sought to preserve what their members considered to be a 'true' form of worship outside the parish church.[4] At the same time, the sustained civil peace throughout these decades also reflected the fact that a majority of the Church's ministry – who identified as 'presbyterians' or 'Covenanters' after 1638 – were evidently willing to live peacefully within an episcopal hierarchy. Most ministers were simply content to carry on their pastoral duties: neither too outspoken to

---

[2] The First Book of Discipline, 'The fourth head concerning Ministers, and their lawfull Election'.

[3] John Morrill, 'A British Patriarchy? Ecclesiastical Imperialism under the Early Stuarts', in Anthony Fletcher and Peter Roberts (eds). Religion, Culture and Society in Early Modern Britain: Essays in Honour of Patrick Collinson (Cambridge, 1994), pp. 209–37, at p. 214.

[4] The classic study of this tendency remains David Stevenson's 'Conventicles and the Kirk, 1619–37: The Emergence of a Radical Party', RSCHS,18 (1973), pp. 99–114.

defend the episcopal hierarchy nor too contrarian to oppose the bishops' powers publicly.[5]

Hazy definitions of the higher echelons of church government nevertheless were also quietly breeding controversy. In particular, the spread of allegedly 'heretical' or 'unscriptural' beliefs and liturgical practices became inextricably linked by Baillie (and other Covenanting reformers) with perceived deficiencies in the Church of Scotland's ecclesiastical polity. As Baillie argued in the opening of his survey of controversies about congregationalism, prevalent theological controversies called 'into question not only the government of the Churches, but also their constitution and standing'.[6] Baillie's ideas regarding church polity therefore emerged out of this ambiguous tradition of the Scottish Church's post-Reformation polity. Baillie's writings on church polity did not transcend this conceptually ambiguous heritage by justifying a 'perfected' form of presbyterianism. Rather, his support for a presbyterian polity accommodated aspects of episcopalism to an extent that has hitherto been underestimated, whilst firmly rejecting any facets of congregationalism.

Historians have only just started to focus on the exegetical similarities that godly Scots shared with congregational and separatist thinkers. An entrenched historiography, however, continues to cast episcopacy and presbytery across an insurmountable conceptual divide. This is a far cry from earlier historiographical debates on religious divisions of the English Civil Wars, which erected insurmountable divisions between 'Independents' and 'presbyterians'.[7] Nevertheless, such an entrenched hermeneutic continues to encourage overly cohesive descriptions of church polities that were in fact dynamic, malleable and susceptible to idiosyncratic definition. Having deemed the presbyterianism of the Scottish Covenanters 'self-consciously inflexible', David Mullan somewhat awkwardly asserted that, although presbyterians 'recoiled in horror from the congregational covenant', there existed an impulse in the 'direction of something like independency'.[8] Such seemingly contradictory expressions, though, may be more the result of a tendency

---

[5]   Thus, Margo Todd claimed that to the average Scot 'the Reformed religion's polity above the level of the session was very nearly irrelevant'. See Margo Todd, *The Culture of Protestantism in Early Modern Scotland* (London, 2002), p. 406.

[6]   NCL, Baill MS 1, Robert Baillie, 'Parageticorum Diatriba secunda de Congregationum Independentia', p. 431.

[7]   For some examples, see Tom Webster, *Godly Clergy in Early Stuart England: The Caroline Puritan Movement, c. 1620–1643* (Cambridge, 1997); Francis J. Bremer, *Congregational Communion: Clerical Friendship in the Anglo-American Puritan Community, 1610–1692* (Boston, 1994); J.R. de Witt, *Jus divinum: The Westminster Assembly and the Divine Right of Church Government* (Kampen, 1969); Lawrence Kaplan, *Politics and Religion during the English Revolution: The Scots and the Long Parliament 1643–1645* (New York, 1976).

[8]   David George Mullan, '"Uniformity in Religion": The Solemn League and Covenant (1643) and the Presbyterian Vision', in W. Graham (ed.), *Later Calvinism: International Perspectives* (Kirksville, 1994), pp. 249–66, at p. 260; Mullan, *Scottish Puritanism, 1590–1638* (Oxford, 2000), p. 131.

to isolate different ecclesiologies from one another. Instead, it is more help-ful to conceive of different polities on a spectrum. For instance, amongst Elizabethan and Jacobean presbyterians we may witness a 'diverse spectrum of English protestant thought' in which 'varying ecclesiological formulations emerged, changed and reconfigured'.[9] Hunter Powell's illuminating study of the ecclesiological debates of the Westminster Assembly showed that the Covenanters Samuel Rutherford and George Gillespie sought rapproche-ment with English congregationalist thinkers on fundamental points as late as 1644.[10] From this perspective, it was clearly possible for a persecuted, pres-byterian Scot during the Jacobean and Caroline reigns to adopt arguments for nonconformity shared by puritan brethren in England, Amsterdam and New England. Consequently, it is taken to be counter-intuitive to suggest that Covenanters who emerged out of this tradition of dissent might ever counte-nance, let alone defend, any form of episcopacy. The 'radical presbyterians' of the late sixteenth century, most notoriously Andrew Melville, opposed even a moderate form of 'reduced episcopacy' that coexisted with presbyter-ies in Scotland after 1581.[11] Following the writings of radical thinkers like Rutherford, whilst eschewing those of others like Baillie, it may be assumed that a homogeneous culture of *jure divino* presbyterianism existed amongst Scottish intellectuals prior to the restoration of episcopacy in the Church of Scotland in 1661.[12] As the leading historian of the post-Reformation Church of Scotland emphatically stated, '[t]o be a seventeenth-century Scottish pres-byterian entailed an uncompromising hostility to episcopacy'.[13]

The history of the post-Reformation Church's polity, as we have seen, was not so clear-cut and Baillie's writings reflected these ambiguities. Having identified himself as a presbyterian, he evinced restraint, and could even be moved to approbation, when discussing episcopacy. Presuppositions that a presbyterian writer must be completely averse to episcopacy are thus based on a narrow definition of what constituted 'episcopacy' and 'presbytery'.[14] Nevertheless, lines between the three categories of polity start to blur by con-sidering that authors defending each 'camp' drew on the same Biblical and Patristic sources. Differences between authors derived from shifting inter-

---

[9] Polly Ha, *English Presbyterianism, 1590–1640* (Stanford, 2011), p. 180.

[10] Hunter Powell, *The Crisis of British Protestantism: Church Power in the Puritan Revolution, 1638–1644* (Manchester, 2015).

[11] Margo Todd, 'The Problem of Scotland's Puritans', in John Coffey and Paul Chang-Ha Lim (eds), *The Cambridge Companion to Puritanism* (Cambridge, 2008), pp. 174–88, at p. 175.

[12] Alasdair Raffe, *The Culture of Controversy: Religious Arguments in Scotland, 1660–1714* (Woodbridge, 2012), p. 45.

[13] Mullan, *Scottish Puritanism*, p. 79.

[14] Another notable exception to this rule was Richard Baxter, whose post-Restoration ecclesiology sought a middle way that veered too far towards episcopacy for Baillie's liking. On Baxter's ecclesiology, see Paul Chang-Ha Lim, *In Pursuit of Purity, Unity and Liberty: Richard Baxter's Puritan Ecclesiology in its Seventeenth-Century Context* (Leiden, 2004).

pretative emphases, and ideological divisions proliferated.[15] Two of the most important Biblical passages concerning the powers of ecclesiastical juris-diction – or the 'power of the Keys' – were Matthew 16:19[16] and Matthew 18:17.[17] The 'power of the Keys' refers to the powers given to St Peter by Christ, in Matthew 16:19, when Christ said, 'I will give unto thee the Keys of the kingdom of heaven.' Both passages acted as proof-texts justifying acts of ecclesiastical censure, exhortation and excommunication by either church officers (a minister, a college of presbyters or a bishop) or the whole congrega-tion of a parish church. Individual interpretation of these passages depended on the signification of words such as 'I will give unto *thee*' or 'tell it unto *the church*'. Further controversy was fuelled by usage of both the terms *episcopus* and *presbyter* in Biblical passages discussing the practices of the Apostolic churches which included the Pauline letters to the Corinthians and the Acts of the Apostles. The most contested figures in the presbyterian–episcopal debate were those of Timothy and Titus, who could be interpreted as either bishops or presbyters, or a superintendent who retained facets of both. One means whereby the seemingly interchangeable use of these terms could be explained was to claim that a bishop was simply another term for a 'preaching pastor' tied to a particular church. The Patristic commentaries and epistles of Jerome, Chrysostom and Gregory of Nazianzus could lend support to such an interpretation of the episcopal office and this conception enjoyed widespread acceptance amongst the Jacobean episcopate of the English Church.[18] An author's self-fashioning as a polemical defender of episcopal, presbyterian or congregational platforms did not restrict their thoughts within neat catego-ries simply because of the latitude of exegetical licence that individuals were accorded in interpreting the same Scriptural proof-texts.

This chapter explores Baillie's conception of a presbyterian polity, con-firming that his version of presbyterianism showed marked affinities with episcopal polities, whilst diverging more drastically from congregationalism than some of his contemporaries. This is not to suggest that Baillie articulated a *unique* form of presbyterianism, and attention will be drawn to like-minded authors when appropriate. First, I discuss Baillie's stance towards episcopacy and illuminate several cases in which 'relics' of episcopacy were retained: instances in which Baillie deemed it necessary for temporary officers or qua-si-episcopal figures to exercise powers over church courts in a similar capacity to a diocesan bishop. Second, I discuss Baillie's critical stance towards congre-gational polities. Whilst Baillie's two Scottish colleagues at the Westminster

---

[15] For a concise summary of the relevant passages that follow, see Kenneth Fincham, *Prelate as Pastor: The Episcopate of James I* (Oxford, 1990), pp. 9–10.

[16] 'And I will give unto thee the Keys of the kingdom of heaven: and whatsoever thou shalt bind on earth shall be bound in heaven: and whatsoever thou shalt loose on earth shall be loosed in heaven'.

[17] 'And if he shall neglect to hear them, tell it unto the church: but if he neglect to hear the church, let him be unto thee as an heathen man and a publican'.

[18] Fincham, *Prelate as Pastor*, pp. 9–10.

Assembly – Rutherford and Gillespie – accorded a greater role to the parish congregation in acts of jurisdiction and order so as to reach an accommodation with a group of English congregationalists, Baillie rejected any concessions that undermined the absolute power of synods. I conclude here with a brief discussion of the Protestor/Resolutioner conflict that emerged within the Interregnum Scottish Church as a schism over definitions of the visible church. Baillie and the Resolutioners – representative of a majority of the Church's ministry in the 1650s – subscribed to an Augustinian definition of the visible church as *ecclesia mixta* of both elect and reprobate. On the other hand, Rutherford and Patrick Gillespie (brother of George) led the Protestor minority in justifying more rigorous standards for church membership that echoed English puritan insistence that the visible church should be comprised of 'visible saints'. Baillie's writings on church polity were primarily based on his desire to retain a unified, national church that could combat both antichristian tyranny and sectarian anarchy. Whilst Baillie gave expression to a distinctively 'presbyterian' tendency, it was only through the internecine ecclesiological conflicts of the 1650s that his opponents, the Protestors, arrived at a defence of a firmer, more inflexible conception of *jure divino* presbyterianism that would lead many into nonconformity after 1660. By contrast, Baillie's *modus operandi* helps to explain why erstwhile presbyterian Covenanters were prepared to conform to the re-established Scottish episcopate at the Restoration.

I

Baillie's attitude to episcopacy was more nuanced and less critical than has hitherto been assumed. Whilst an uncompromising hostility to episcopacy has been assumed to be a particular hallmark of *Scottish* presbyterians, it is not difficult to find instances when English presbyterians were clearly prepared to accept elements of an episcopal polity.[19] Although the polarization of Scottish polities may reflect the strongly confessional nature of post-Reformation historiography and the bifurcated character of episcopal and presbyterian perspectives, Baillie's actions at the Glasgow General Assembly of 1638 eschew such a framework. When the Assembly voted by a near-unanimous voice to 'abjure and remove' episcopacy from the Church of Scotland, Baillie was the only named dissenter, stating that he thought episcopacy should be 'removed' but that he could not declare the office 'abjured' according to the national church's laws and customs.[20] This curious dissenting opinion has

---

[19] Elliot Vernon, 'The Sion College Conclave and London Presbyterianism during the English Revolution' (Ph.D. Thesis, University of Cambridge, 1999), p. 8.
[20] 'An Account of the Proceedings of the General Assembly at Glasgow, in November 1638', June 1639, *LJB*, vol. I, pp. 157–8; Peterkin (ed.), *Records*, pp. 28–32; NLS, Wod. Fol.XXV, W. Wilkie to Walter Balcanqual, Glasgow, 26 December 1638, fo. 11r.

fuelled criticism of Baillie as one who primarily acted at 'the instigation of other persons'.[21] When Baillie finally joined the Covenanting ranks unequivocally, he had had to discard his 'episcopal' proclivities in favour of an undiluted form of presbyterianism. By contrast, Baillie's stance at the General Assembly represented a more fundamental ambiguity within Baillie's conception of church government than has hitherto been acknowledged.[22]

Baillie's dissent at Glasgow has led previous generations of historians to suggest that he was a proponent of a form of 'reduced' episcopacy until late 1638.[23] Despite noted shifts in emphasis after February 1639, Baillie's views on church polity remained consistent throughout his life, including a continued attachment to a form of episcopacy submitted to, and appointed by, presbyterian assemblies. Such an affinity could coexist with Baillie's aversion to proposals for 'reduced episcopacy' tabled in England in 1640 and 1641, although his relationship with at least one proponent of moderate episcopacy suggests ambivalence. Writing from London during negotiations for a treaty following the Second Bishops' War, Baillie recounted to his cousin that '[t]he Primate of Ireland [i.e. James Ussher], and a great faction with him, will be for a limited good and James Mitchell's calked [i.e. a rough copy of] Episcopacie'. Baillie did not, however, think that this faction could sway godly opinion because of their reluctance to speak out against 'any of the Canterburian abominations'.[24] Soon after the Covenanting revolution, the prominent Edinburgh minister James Mitchell had circulated proposals for a form of limited episcopacy – now lost – that Baillie considered an insufficient resolution to disputes of ecclesiastical polity. His position thus appears sympathetic with supporters of 'root and branch' reform of the English episcopate; an initiative spearheaded amongst London ministers and garnering signatures throughout England to petition demanding episcopacy's complete abolition. Nevertheless, mention of James Mitchell – one of the benefactors of a 1640 draft of Baillie's will and a frequent recipient of Baillie's letters written during the Westminster Assembly – indicated that he also associated with ministers supporting episcopal reform.[25] Such proposals, Baillie argued, would be insufficient considering the far-reaching abuses of episcopal government perpetrated by the Laudians. Archbishop William Laud of Canterbury and Bishops Matthew Wren of Ely, Richard Montagu of Norwich and Francis White also of Ely had defended the great extent to which episcopal powers could be carried and, for Baillie, such worrying precedents demanded more extensive reform.

[21] Thomas Middleton, *An appendix to the history of the Church of Scotland* (London, 1677), p. 23.

[22] For a fuller discussion of the consistency in Baillie's ecclesiology, see Alexander D. Campbell, 'Episcopacy in the Mind of Robert Baillie, 1637–1662', *SHR*, 93 (2014), pp. 29–55.

[23] Webster, *Godly Clergy*, p. 314.

[24] Robert Baillie to William Spang, London, 28 December 1640, *LJB*, vol. I, p. 287.

[25] See *LJB*, vol. I, pp. 13, 246, 268; vol. II, 219, 380, 392.

The Laudian episcopate's actions had left Baillie disenchanted with *almost* any form of episcopacy. Reacting to proposals for episcopal reform, published anonymously by the royal chaplain, George Morley, Baillie wrote that 'the verie name of a Bishop [should] not be retained', and repeatedly blamed the Laudian episcopate for the evils of schism, heresy and error that plagued the British churches of the 1640s and 1650s.[26] The Scriptural term *episcopus* had come to be invested with so many unscriptural connotations that Baillie derided any use in trying to retain it. Presbyterians, in general, had tended to argue that the terms *episcopus* and *presbyter* had been used interchangeably to refer to the same ecclesiastical office: an office that was invested by divine right with powers of order and jurisdiction. Debates with episcopalians arose over whether the proof-texts for these ecclesiastical powers referred to a single person or to a meeting of many officers variously called *episcopi* or *presbyteri*, or whether the terms, in fact, denoted two distinct orders of church officers. Further dispute arose over the precise nature of this form of 'primitive episcopacy'. Was the office primarily pastoral? Or, was a holder first meant to exercise powers of jurisdiction as a governor of the church? In discussing Baillie's views of episcopacy, it is therefore important to ask whether he was denouncing a particular type of episcopacy or episcopacy *tout court*.

Baillie's extensive anti-episcopal writings identified a particular type of 'English' or 'Laudian' bishop as unscriptural and inimical to godly church government. Baillie *never* denounced episcopacy in general, albeit the practical experience of living under the episcopate in 1630s Scotland tempted him to endorse such a proposition. By arguing that *episcopus* and *presbyter* referred to one and the same office, Baillie was obliged to insist that both terms were Scripturally warranted. To declare one unlawful would necessarily imply the other was likewise unlawful and thereby undermine any Scriptural basis of church officers. In January 1637, therefore, Baillie observed, 'Bishopes I love; but pride, greid, luxurie, oppression, immersion in saicular affaires, was the bane of the Romish Prelats, and can not have long good succes in the Reformit.'[27] For Baillie, the English term 'bishop' had come to denote much more than the office of a preaching pastor, through misguided interpretations of sources regarding the nature and character of the primitive episcopate.[28] More broadly, the pastoral role of an episcopate – described in Jerome's letter to 'Evagrius' or the fourth-century commentary on Paul ascribed to Ambrose – had often provoked clashes with duties stipulated by diocesan or national government amongst the Jacobean episcopate. Controversy over the interpretation of the offices of Timothy and Titus, for instance, had been ignited

[26] Baillie, *Danger of Limited Episcopacie*, p. 34. See, for example, Robert Baillie, 'A Postscript for the personate Iesuite Lysimachus Nicanor', in *Ladensium*, p. 29.
[27] Robert Baillie to William Wilkie, 2 January 1637, *LJB*, vol. I, p. 2.
[28] For Baillie's use of St Paul and Gregory of Nazianzus see, for example, Robert Baillie, *Prelacie is miserie: or, The suppressing of prelaticall government and establishing of provintiall, and nationall sinods, is a hopefull meanes to make a flourishing Church, and happie kingdome* ([London], 1641), p. 3.

in England with the publication of Adrianus Saravia's *De diuersis ministrorum Euangelii gradibus* (1590). Arguing for the divine origins of the superiority of bishops over presbyters, this tract had prompted publication of numerous *jure divino* justifications of episcopacy based on Scripture and Patristic sources.[29]

Justifications of the superiority of bishops led to claims that episcopacy was a mark of a 'true' church. This deeply worried Baillie, given his constant praise of non-episcopal Reformed churches abroad. A crucial shift in this debate occurred at Laud's instigation, both in his own Doctor of Divinity thesis which he defended in 1608 and in Joseph Hall's *Episcopacy by Divine Right Asserted* (1640), which Laud extensively edited. In his published and manuscript works, Baillie's criticisms mainly focused on Hall's tract, George Downame's *A defence of the sermon preached at the consecration of the bishop of Bath and Wells* (1613), Peter Heylyn's *Historie of Episcopacie* (1642) and also on the anti-*jure divino* arguments of Gersome Bucerus's *Dissertatio de gubernatione ecclesiae* (1618). For their part, Laud and other defenders of *jure divino* episcopacy were increasingly arguing that bishops were not only a distinct degree of presbyter, but also a distinct order. If episcopacy and its power of ordination did constitute a separate order, then ordination by presbyters 'could only happen outside the church's normal means of salvation'. In England, then, episcopacy slowly came to be regarded as occupying a 'central role in the constitution and nature of the church'.[30] Episcopacy was no longer simply part of a church's *melius esse*, but became part of its *esse*. If bishops were judged to be a distinct order by divine right, then the English Church's relationship with other Reformed presbyterian churches was threatened since it effectively accused such churches of heresy. Alarmed by this potential divergence from other Reformed churches, Baillie responded to the pseudonymous Jesuit Lysimachus Nicanor by emphasizing that the office of bishop 'is no way necessary in any Church, but removeable out of all'.[31] The 'manifold evils' of the English and Irish episcopates had demonstrated the 'needlesnesse' of the order.[32]

Not only did the Laudian bishops err in making a particular polity necessary but, Baillie argued, they were also abusing the powers of order and jurisdiction ascribed equally with presbyters to the Biblical office *jure divino*. The uniqueness of the post-Reformation polity of the Church of England should not be a cause for praise. '[W]hereever [sic], except in England', Baillie wrote, 'did any Protestant spoile all Pastors of all power, both of Ordination and Jurisdiction to put it in the hand of one Prelat.'[33] Baillie eagerly pointed out that the Laudian bishop of Ely, Francis White, had contradicted this tenet

---

[29] Jean-Louis Quantin, *The Church of England and Christian Antiquity: The Construction of a Confessional Identity in the 17th Century* (Oxford, 2010), pp. 95–8.
[30] Anthony Milton, *Catholic and Reformed: The Roman and Protestant Churches in English Protestant Thought, 1600–1640* (Cambridge, 1995), pp. 468–70.
[31] Baillie, 'Postscript', in *Ladensium*, p. 35.
[32] Ibid., p. 36.
[33] Baillie, *Historicall Vindication*, p. 79.

of his 'faction' by maintaining that a bishop could only alter ecclesiastical canons in convocation. In the margins of his *Ladensium*, Baillie cited this bishop's *Examination of a lawlesse pamphlet* (1637), in which White had argued that 'many learned persons are appointed to be assistants unto Bishops, and in our nationall synods in which al weightie matters concerning religion are determined, nothing is, or may be concluded, but by the common vote … of the convocation'.[34] In this context, the resonances with the limits of a Scottish superintendent's powers, as outlined in *The First Book of Discipline*, are striking.[35]

The recently deposed Scottish and English bishops had also erased any distinction between civil and ecclesiastical powers, vesting the same person with powers from both spheres. In attacking such powers, Baillie reflected a more widespread critique of the Scottish episcopate current during the 1630s. In Scotland, the Court of High Commission attracted most complaints about episcopal abuses whereby ecclesiastical office-holders were vested with authority to inflict corporal punishments against nonconformists. Originally erected in 1610 by royal letters patent and reconstituted twice by James VI and I in 1615 and by Charles I in 1634, the High Commission became the scourge of presbyterians.[36] Calderwood, for example, recorded fifty-six trials in his *History of the Kirk*, and Samuel Rutherford's trial and enforced exile to Aberdeen in 1636 at the hands of Bishop Thomas Sydserff of Galloway became an early rallying call for presbyterian opposition to Caroline religious policies.[37] Reflecting on such experiences, Baillie attacked the exiled Scottish bishop John Maxwell for being 'very impertinent' in alleging that presbyterian excommunication had been 'rash' and 'rigorous'. Rather, Baillie counselled Maxwell to remember how the Caroline bishops in Scotland had treated nonconformists, by 'imprisoning, banishing, Pilloring, stigmatizing the worthiest men for contradicting you in any one of your numerous ceremonies and traditions'.[38]

Whilst the Scottish bishops of the 1630s had appropriated superiority in executing ecclesiastical powers and added the potency of corporal punishment to charges of excommunication, they had also granted civil magistrates

---

[34] Baillie, *Ladensium*, p. 117. Citing Francis White, *An examination and confutation of a lawlesse pamphlet, intituled, A briefe answer to a late treatise of the Sabbath-day* (London, 1637), p. 22.

[35] The co-ordinate exercise of powers of ecclesiastical jurisdiction by superintendents and the ministry is especially evident in discussions of the limits on the powers of the superintendent. See, for example, *The First Book of Discipline*, 'The Fifth Head: Of Superintendents'.

[36] George I.R. McMahon, 'The Scottish Courts of High Commission, 1610–1638', *RSCHS* (1965), pp. 193–209.

[37] George I.R. McMahon, 'The Scottish Episcopate, 1600–1638', Ph.D. Thesis, University of Birmingham (1972), p. 143; NLS, Wod.Qu.LXXVI, 'The trew relatioun of my tryall before the High Commissioun', [ante 1617], no. 4; *Letters of Samuel Rutherford*, ed. Andrew Bonar (Edinburgh and London, 1894), pp. 135–6.

[38] Baillie, *Historicall Vindication*, p. 58.

'extraordinarie prerogatives … out of their [i.e. the bishops'] self-respect to their owne ambition and greed'.[39] Baillie directed his objection broadly against the 'flattery' that had subverted ecclesiastical laws and customs in both England and Scotland. Despite a marked tendency to portray presbyterianism as vital to a church's well-being, Baillie's defence of the ecclesiastical laws and constitutions of particular nations suggests that he retained a latent belief that ecclesiastical polity was essentially adiaphorous. Whilst Baillie defended the perspicuity of God's revealed Word in Scripture, there were certain points at which God's Word remained ambiguous, indicating that God had not outlined the specifics of an institution such as church government. In a manuscript survey of controversies over episcopacy that Baillie had prepared for his divinity students at Glasgow, he argued that God's counsel to the Church of Ephesus, revealed to Paul, was imperfect concerning matters of church polity.[40] Accordingly, Baillie did not attack English and Scottish episcopacy *per se*, but primarily the means by which it had been introduced and had also subsequently enlarged its powers. This 'wicked faction', Baillie wrote, accorded lawful sovereigns power 'to appoynt for the government of the Church in their dominions such Officers and Spirituall Courts, as they finde most meet, and agreeble to their temporall estates, to erect Bishops, and put downe presbyteries, to erect presbyteries, and put downe Bishops'.[41] Members of the Scottish episcopate had undermined human, ecclesiastical constitutions by submitting them to the will of individual bishops or the monarch. By contrast, Baillie did not make 'all the commandements of the Church to bee branches of the fifth command, and to bee obeyed as the precepts of God'.[42] Such canons, nevertheless, demanded observance by civil magistrates and could only be altered through lawful channels, being one of the foundations of a national church.

Ecclesiastical constitutions did not necessarily conform to God's will, but divine knowledge, as revealed in Scripture, provided a standard by which such laws could be judged. It was against such divine standards that Baillie judged English and Scottish episcopacy to be unlawful and requiring removal. Likewise, critics of the Laudian episcopate in England could allow 'for the possibility of primitive episcopacy without losing the powerful rhetoric of a call for abolition'. It is moot whether such calls for abolition tabled by the pseudonymous pamphleteer 'Smectymnuus' proposed the introduction of a form of 'presbyterian' polity or 'the most extreme form of primitive episcopacy'.[43] Straining the vocabulary available to discuss these polities obscures the similarities that existed between forms of 'episcopacy' and 'presbytery' even

---

[39] Baillie, *Ladensium*, p. 130.
[40] GUL, MS Gen 375, Robert Baillie, 'Parageticorum diatriba quarta de episcopatu', p. 125.
[41] Baillie, *Ladensium*, p. 125.
[42] Baillie, 'Postscript', in ibid., p. 27.
[43] Webster, *Godly Clergy*, p. 325.

as England was descending into civil war.[44] Distinctions between episcopacy and presbytery were not clear-cut. Indeed, the 'Smectymnian' pamphlets have been best characterized as reflecting a version of primitive episcopacy and Continental presbyterianism: a position 'more presbyterian' than Ussher's form of 'reduced episcopacy'.[45] Even after the short-lived triumph of the presbyterians at the Westminster Assembly, Baillie's writings on church polity continued to leave room for a version of primitive episcopacy, and whilst he would have abhorred the suggestion that his preferred polity was 'episcopal', he did not preclude inclusion of 'quasi-episcopal' officers.

Superintendents in the Dutch Reformed Church, for example, were so different from English bishops, Baillie wrote, 'as an Emperour in the dayes of Fabius Maximus, when the Senate ruled all, to an Emperour in the dayes of Tiberius or Nero, when an absolute Prince ... did governe all at his pleasure'. As Baillie concluded, '[t]he name is one, but the things are essentially different, and so farre distant as the East is from the West'.[46] Likewise, German churches that had retained superintendents should not be taken as evidence that Reformed churches retained bishops, writing that 'Superintendents are not Bishops' since all Lutherans abhorred concentration of the powers of jurisdiction and order in an individual officer.[47] A bishop was lawful only insofar as that individual exercised his powers by delegation from a presbytery. In this context, the primitive bishops of the early church had coexisted with a presbytery. These 'ancient bishops' were created by 'an humane Ecclesiastick constitution' that was not necessarily unlawful, but had also since fostered the spread of 'popery'.[48] In the primitive church, a bishop was chosen with the 'unanimous consent of the people' as a minister of a particular flock, with provincial and national synods overseeing lesser assemblies of believers. Such officers were 'no Lordly Bishops, save onely the Presbitors themselves, being all equall'.[49] Baillie echoed this sentiment in his *Catechesis elentica errorum* (1654) in which he argued that 'the office of bishop and presbyter is one and the same'.[50]

In his published pamphlets, Baillie's approbation of a primitive form of episcopacy was often markedly circumspect because he was engaging with proponents of a form of diocesan episcopacy.[51] Two manuscript

---

[44]   Polly Ha and Hunter Powell have, however, recently shown how presbyterianism could manifest itself in a variety of different ways. Ha, for instance, showed myriad ways in which Puritan ministers critiqued the English episcopate, see Ha, *English Presbyterianism*, pp. 52–5, 75–80.

[45]   Vernon, 'Sion College Conclave', pp. 60, 61.

[46]   Baillie, *Historicall Vindication*, p. 79.

[47]   GUL, MS Gen 375, Baillie, 'Parageticorum de episcopatu', p. 68.

[48]   Baillie, *Danger of Limited Episcopacie*, pp. 24, 25, 22. Also on *jus ecclesiasticum*, see GUL, MS Gen 375, Baillie, 'Parageticorum de episcopatu', p. 105.

[49]   Baillie, *Prelacie is miserie*, pp. 7, 8.

[50]   Baillie, *Catechesis Elenctica Errorum*, pp. 119–20.

[51]   In terms of entire pamphlets, Baillie directly engaged with the arguments of George Morley and John Maxwell. His works are nevertheless peppered throughout with refutations of arguments by a large group of 'Laudian' bishops.

works on episcopacy, however, reveal Baillie's position to have been more complex, whilst also providing examples of particular situations wherein Baillie was prepared to consider a form of episcopacy as lawful. The first treatise, entitled 'A discourse anent episcopacy', was written as an *ex post facto* defence of his stance at the Glasgow Assembly of 1638. At least two extant copies of this treatise survive and, from evidence in Baillie's letters and marginalia of the copy preserved among the Wodrow papers in the National Library of Scotland, this treatise evidently circulated to, and was read by, members of the Covenanting elite such as the marquess of Argyll, Archibald Johnston of Wariston and the earl of Loudoun.[52] The second treatise was entitled 'Parageticorum diatriba quarta de Episcopatu', and was written as part of a series of 'surveys' on ecclesiastical controversies that Baillie dictated to students at Glasgow University.[53] A likely date of composition for this latter treatise is more elusive. Whilst portions appear to have been written as early as 1643, internal evidence and Baillie's own preoccupations suggest that he substantially revised this tract following negotiations with Charles I on the Isle of Wight late in 1647.[54] Given Baillie's involvement in the heated political conflict that arose in Scotland following the so-called 'Engagement Controversy' of 1648, it is unlikely that Baillie had much time to draft the revised treatise until he had returned to his teaching duties in the early 1650s.[55] In any case, Baillie continued teaching on contemporary ecclesiastical controversies until his death in 1662, and the treatise's contents are probably representative of his lifelong views on the matter.

According to arguments in both manuscripts, either an episcopate could exist within a hierarchy of church courts subject to a prelate – as in the relationship between an English bishop, his court and episcopal commissioners – or, as Baillie preferred, bishops could be appointed on an *ad hoc* basis by presbyteries to fulfil particular acts of ecclesiastical jurisdiction, ordination or discipline.[56] The latter form of episcopacy was instituted only by ecclesiastical

---

[52] For the two copies, see NCL, Bail MS 4/2, Robert Baillie, 'A Discourse anent Episcopacie'; NLS, Wod.Qu.XXXI, Robert Baillie, 'A Discourse anent Episcopacie'. David Mullan published an edition of this tract based on the copy in the National Library of Scotland, in his *Religious Controversy in Scotland, 1625–1639* (Edinburgh, 1998). For potential readership, see Stevenson, *Scottish Revolution*, pp. 116–26.
[53] The only extant copy is found in GUL, MS Gen 375, pp. 57–171. This copy abruptly cuts off with a discussion of his adversaries' proofs from the epistles to Timothy and Titus on Baillie's third point: 'Tertium contra nos adversariorum telum hoc est ...'.
[54] See, for example, Robert Baillie to William Spang, 2 June 1643, *LJB*, vol. II, pp. 65, 72.
[55] The earlier manuscript edition of Baillie's *Operis historici et chronologici*, for instance, stated in the title that it was 'dictated to students of sacred theology at the University of Glasgow in the year 1650 and several [years] following'. This may be taken to suggest that Baillie had resumed composing pedagogical treatises sometime in 1650, including his 'Parageticorum diatriba de episcopatu'.
[56] NLS, Wod.Qu.XXXI, Robert Baillie, 'Discourse anent Episcopacie', fos 37r–v.

canon, implying that Scripture and Patristic sources did not explicitly condemn such a practice. For instance, justifying his dissent at Glasgow, Baillie
wrote that 'the constant moderators of dioceses of old, the superintendents of late were at most but of ecclesiastick appointment, brought in at
the Churches arbitriment and removeable when they are found inconven-
ient by that power of the church which first did erect them'.[57] The bishops
that had been deposed and excommunicated by the Glasgow Assembly did
not acknowledge such limits, but if the Church required 'ane new erection
of a lawfull episcopacie', such a new institution would differ 'from that we
have had'. Notwithstanding the legality of such a creation, and barring the
General Assembly's consent, Baillie seriously doubted that the Church of
Scotland would ever judge creation of such an office to be convenient.[58]

The exegetical basis of the powers of these temporary officers helped to
explain why episcopal critics could chide Scottish presbyterians for being
crypto-episcopalians. Alexander Henderson, perennial moderator of General
Assemblies from 1638 until his death in 1646, and the leading figure in
'British' religious negotiations, often bore the brunt of such attacks. John
Maxwell, for instance, called him 'the Scottish Pope', and Edward Hyde,
earl of Clarendon, referred to Henderson as 'their [i.e. the Scots'] metropolitan'.[59] Although my argument here endorses the validity of these polemical remarks, their potency also suggests why historians have hitherto been
reluctant to acknowledge latent debts to episcopal polities in Baillie's writings. Like Baillie, contemporaries remained acutely sensitive to this line of
criticism and thus tended to overcompensate with lengthy diatribes against
Caroline prelacy.

For Baillie, a temporary bishop was appointed either to prevent schism
from destroying a national church's unity or to preside over an ecclesiastical assembly as a moderator. Necessity determined these appointments
and it was left to a presbytery to decide when such extraordinary functions
should end. The appointment of such officers in the primitive church never
invested them *jure divino* with powers of order or jurisdiction that were not
also accorded to preaching presbyters. From Ephesians 4:11, Baillie outlined
the four Scriptural offices of the Church – Apostles, prophets, evangelists,
pastors or teachers – and concluded in Pauline fashion that 'episcopate and
presbytery are pastorate [*pastoratus*] and bishops and presbyters are pastors'.[60]
Ordination was given *jure divino* to the presbytery of Ephesus – not just the
meeting of presbyters but the 'office and grade of presbyter' as described by
Jerome and Calvin – which continued to exist even after the ordination of

[57] Ibid., fo. 37v.
[58] Ibid., fo. 38r et infra.
[59] John Maxwell, *The burthen of Issachar: or, The tyrannical power and practices of the
Presbyteriall-government in Scotland* (London, 1646); Clarendon, *History of the Rebellion*,
vol. I, p. 203.
[60] GUL, MS Gen 375, Baillie, 'Parageticorum de episcopatu', p. 117.

Timothy as a bishop: a delegation rather than relegation of powers of juris-diction.[61] Greek and Latin Fathers such as Cyprian, Tertullian, Irenaenus and Clement all maintained that the ordaining assemblies of Timothy and Titus were gatherings of presbyters.[62] Acts 20:17 and 28 both outlined the divine approbation of temporary, ambulatory pastors or bishops who were 'given by the Sacred Spirit the power of determining dogma, and expelling heretics from the church'. Yet Baillie was quick to affirm that the superior-ity maintained in these *loci* were during periods when the Church's polity was not firmly established.[63] Elsewhere, Baillie conceded that, in extraor-dinary circumstances, particular persons or pastors could ordain others, but such instances did not justify delegation of power but rather reflected the extraordinary exercise of powers that always resided with presbyteries.[64] Finally, Baillie cited the post-Apostolic practice of bishop-in-presbytery as justification of the Church of Scotland's practice of appointing a moderator. An ambiguous passage in Chrysostom's homilies did not prove the superiority of bishop over presbyter, but signified 'election to the office of president or moderator of the presbytery': an office not vested with specific powers outside the presbytery.[65] Baillie even showed a willingness to interpret the Seven Angels of Revelation 2 (representative of the seven churches of Asia) as a single moderator or bishop, although he argued that the use of the term *ecclesia* in this passage had been intended collectively, as representing the whole assembly of presbyters.[66] All conclusions of synods were such that have conjoined 'all determinations by divine inspiration and mandate with [those] of the presbyters who give their voice as if by pseudoepiscopate [*pseudoepis-copatus*], and all presbyters right of voting in synod overthrows the arrogance of private tyranny'.[67]

II

A sustained affinity between Baillie's writings on Presbyterian Church gov-ernment and episcopalian models becomes even clearer when exploring his critical appraisal of congregationalism. In this context, Baillie's position can be contrasted with the more congregationally inclined positions of Rutherford and Gillespie. Recent research has convincingly shown that, until mid-1644 (and arguably long thereafter), both Rutherford and Gillespie were 'more sympathetic' to the polity of the group of English congregationalist ministers

[61] Ibid., pp. 137, 128 [citing 1 Timothy 4:14 on the presbytery's imposition of hands in the ordination of Timothy].
[62] Ibid., pp. 137, 133ff.
[63] Ibid., pp. 127, 124.
[64] Baillie, *Dissvasive*, p. 200.
[65] Ibid., p. 154.
[66] Ibid., p. 163.
[67] Ibid., p. 161.

collectively known as the 'Dissenting Brethren'.[68] This sympathy was based not only on political pragmatism, but also on shared exegetical similarities. Hunter Powell's recent monograph has expanded on earlier observations to this end that have noted the propensity of 'radical' Covenanters – including Gillespie and Rutherford – to incline towards a polity that preserved the rights and power of a parish church's whole congregation, comprised of visible saints.[69] In these narratives, Baillie is often cast as a foil to the reconciliatory efforts of Gillespie and Rutherford, advocating a more clerical form of Presbyterian Church government which was similar to that of the English ministers Cornelius Burgess and Lazarus Seaman.[70] Given the previous focus on the writings of Rutherford and Gillespie, the particulars of Baillie's critique of congregationalism and its impact on his discussion of a presbyterian polity require further elucidation.

The main difference between the ecclesiologies of Rutherford and Gillespie on the one hand, and Baillie on the other, arose from divergent interpretations of the meaning of the 'church' in Matthew 18:17,[71] one of the most disputed proof-texts outlining powers of ecclesiastical censure and excommunication. In general, presbyterians interpreted the 'church' as the meeting of church officers (elders and pastors) in a presbytery, whilst congregationalists took the term to refer to a parish church's congregation. Resonance between Gillespie's and Rutherford's positions and those of English congregationalists appears in Gillespie's *Dispute against the English-popish ceremonies* (1637) and Rutherford's *Peaceable and temperate plea for Pauls Presbyterie in Scotland* (1642). Despite subtle differences, both Gillespie and Rutherford maintained that a particular church's congregation was the primary church which received the powers of jurisdiction *jure divino*. As Gillespie wrote, '[t]he power and authority of Binding and Loosing, Christ hath delivered to the whole church, that is, to every particular church, collectively taken'.[72] Whilst Rutherford reacted to Gillespie's strong congregational sympathies in his *Peaceable plea*, he also vested the power of the Keys in a particular congregation, but argued that the Keys conferred both 'authoritative' and 'popular' power. The power of the Keys that Christ gave to all believers was 'not formally a power of the keys, but a popular power about the Keys, whereby

---

[68] Hunter Powell, 'The Dissenting Brethren and the Power of the Keys, 1640–1644', Ph.D. thesis, University of Cambridge (2011), p. 111. This group included Thomas Goodwin, Jeremiah Burroughs, Philip Nye, Sidrach Simpson and William Bridge.

[69] Hunter Powell, *The Crisis of British Protestantism: Church Power in the Puritan Revolution, 1638–44* (Manchester, 2015). Mullan, *Scottish Puritanism*, p. 131; Coffey, *Samuel Rutherford*, p. 189; David Stevenson, 'The Radical Party in the Kirk, 1637–45', *Journal of Ecclesiastical History*, 25 (1974), pp. 135–65, at pp. 136–9.

[70] For instance, see Powell, 'Dissenting Brethren', p. 35.

[71] 'And if he shall neglect to hear them, tell it unto the church: but if he neglect to hear the church, let him be unto thee as an heathen man and a publican'.

[72] [George Gillespie], *A dispute against the English-popish ceremonies, obtruded upon the Church of Scotland* ([Leiden], 1637), pp. 181, 183.

popular consent may be given to key-bearers, for their election'.[73] Although the people retained certain powers of jurisdiction by divine fiat, execution of those powers was delegated – as much by divine warrant as by popular consent – to church officers.

Baillie's antipathy to the power of particular congregations can be dated to 1637, although his defence of a particular church's submission to a hierarchy of courts probably stemmed from his brief tutelage under John Cameron in the 1620s.[74] Whilst Baillie was also averse to the apparently arbitrary manner in which Charles I imposed the Scottish Prayer Book in 1637, as well as epis-copalian church government more generally at this time, his objections spe-cifically drew attention to how these 'innovations' might drive godly Scots to separatism. In this context, some groups of Scots designated as 'radicals' had shown support for private meetings, conventicles and tenets that could retrospectively be portrayed as 'Brownism' or separatism.[75] It was these pro-pensities amongst ministers such as Rutherford and Baillie's colleague at the University of Glasgow David Dickson, that Baillie regarded as a more imme-diate, internecine source of concern following announcement of the Prayer Book's pending imposition. 'I look for the most pitiful schism that ever [this] poor Kirk has felt,' Baillie lamented in January 1637, for 'poperie, idolatrie, superstition, in sundrie things which are innocent of these faults' provoked many ministers to a 'mind to seperate' on account of the present innovations. Writing to Spang in this way, Baillie also requested 'some good Treatises of Brounisme … for I feare to have too much use of such peeces'.[76] The bish-ops threatened the Scottish Church's cohesion by offering ministers such as Dickson and Rutherford an excuse to separate from its communion or, at the very least, to establish conventicles.

As opposition to the Laudian episcopate escalated with the imposition of the Prayer Book, therefore, Baillie appeared to be scrambling to maintain a unified, national front in opposition. He was primarily concerned here with maintaining unity amongst Scots rather than allowing individual congrega-tions to go their own way, led towards separatism by individual ministerial personalities. Baillie elaborated his critique of congregational polity most fully in the tenth chapter of his *Dissuasive*, entitled 'Independency is con-trary to the Word of God', which he translated verbatim in his Latin trea-tise, 'Parateguorum Diatriba secunda de Congregationum Independentia'.[77] It was startling, Baillie argued, that groups of ministers refused to conform to the practice of the established church and, *in extremis*, separated from

---

[73] Samuel Rutherford, *A peaceable and temperate plea for Pauls Presbyterie in Scotland* (London, 1642), p. 3.
[74] See Dedicatory epistle to Robert Blair in Baillie, *Historicall Vindication*.
[75] Stevenson, 'Radical Party'; Stevenson, 'Conventicles and the Kirk'.
[76] Robert Baillie to William Spang, 29 January 1637, *LJB*, vol. I, pp. 5, 12.
[77] The treatise can be found in NCL, Baill MS 1, Robert Baillie, 'Parageticorum Diatriba secunda de Congregationum Independentia', pp. 431–44. The introductory sections of both this and the published version are unique.

its communion and moved to either the Netherlands or America. Whilst less radical groups had not separated from communion with the Church of England, they had nevertheless established autonomous, parochial bodies exercising powers of order (ordination of church officers) and jurisdiction (censure, exhortation and excommunication) outside the national church's aegis. Exacerbating the alleged anarchy of congregational beliefs, Baillie was clearly frustrated that proponents of 'Independency' had avoided standardizing their platform of church government.[78] This situation changed, however, with the publication of John Cotton's influential *Keys of the Kingdom of Heaven* (1644). Having carefully avoided attacking presbyterians directly, Cotton demonstrated that he was 'reaching out to the Scots' to achieve a compromise on church polity. Cotton's tract also appeared at a time when Baillie was unsuccessfully trying to obtain critiques of Independent ecclesiology from Continental divines.[79] Baillie's frustration with Cotton's tract peaked when he heard that the Dutch divine Gisbertus Voetius was prepared to approve the *Keys* as consonant with Dutch polity.[80] Baillie deemed this unacceptable as Cotton's tract showed that 'Independents' were those who defended the 'full liberty of such a Church [i.e. a parish church] to discharge all the parts of Religion, Doctrine, Sacraments, Discipline, and all within it selfe without all dependence, all subordination to any other on earth ... so that the smallest Congregation ... may not be controlled by any Orthodoxe Synode'.[81]

The problems posed by Cotton's *Keys* help to explain the rhetoric of Baillie's *Dissuasive* and *Anabaptism, the true fountain of Independency* (1647), both of which were, paradoxically, published when presbyterian fortunes in England and Scotland were at their apogee. In both works, Baillie drew together various tenets of congregationalist, Brownist and anabaptist ecclesiologies in order to tar all with one broad brushstroke. The threat posed by the sort of presbyterian–Independent allegiance sought by Cotton in the *Keys* compelled Baillie to place congregationalism at the head of a slippery slope towards anarchy. Whereas Independents might be said to have 'misplaced' the power of the Keys, anabaptists and their 'offspring', the Brownists or Separatists, destroyed 'the Keys of heaven' altogether, by overturning all forms of church government.[82] At the root of the problem, Independents held that all power is 'in the Congregation, without any subjection to any other Superiour'.[83] For Baillie, this tenet of non-subjection appeared to be either 'the root or the fruit, either the mother or the daughter of all the rest of their errors' and eliminated any effectual means to remedy heresy, error

---

[78]   Baillie, *Dissvasive*, p. 101.
[79]   Ibid., pp. 158, 161.
[80]   Robert Baillie to William Spang, 1 November 1644, *LJB*, vol. II, p. 240.
[81]   Baillie, *Dissvasive*, p. 198. Cf. NCL, Baill MS 1, Baillie, 'Parageticorum de Congregationum Independentia', p. 432.
[82]   NCL, Baill MS 1, Baillie, 'Parageticorum de Congregationum Independentia', p. 431.
[83]   Baillie, *Dissvasive*, p. 111.

and schism.[84] The Independents 'borrowed in full' the 'Brownist' polity, further corrupting it by allowing all 'non-fundamental' errors to flourish where Brownists simply would have continued to separate.[85]

In this way, Independency, paradoxically, became a preservative of heresy. Yet it also appeared to mark the return of far more radical beliefs concerning the nature of church government. For Baillie, anabaptists represented the extreme manifestation of this opposition to a cohesive, national church government, and to confirm the threat, Baillie cited the English anabaptist John Tombes's 'Exercitation', a Latin treatise against infant baptism that was presented to the Westminster Assembly in January 1644, and Tombes's *Apology or Plea for the Two Treatises* (1646), which defended his earlier tract.[86] Not only would anabaptists establish 'an intolerant and unfettered tyranny' in church government, but they would also dissolve all standing and binding ecclesiastical government (*Ecclesiarum statum et compagem dissolvant*) and deny that Scripture had established any 'formal essentials'. In effect, anabaptists and Brownists argued that all established ecclesiastical constitutions were illegitimate and could not bind individual Christians to any form of obedience.[87] As anabaptists entirely disregarded all notions of obedience to higher authorities or institutions lawfully established, Baillie bewailed 'this new glorious light of the Kinghood (as they call it) of every individuall of the people'.[88] Anabaptists even cited the example of the Church of Corinth in Acts to prove that women, pastors and men *equally* executed powers of ordination and jurisdiction.[89] For Baillie, a balance needed to be achieved between a bishop's overextended powers over a church of believers – the subjection of many private consciences to the will of one – and subjection of acts of order and jurisdiction to the determination of a congregation's unanimous majority – the subjection of acts of ecclesiastical power to the private consciences of many. Baillie, however, insisted that the latter option fostered anarchy and rendered powers of jurisdiction impotent.[90]

Taking a familiar presbyterian line of criticism against congregational polities, Baillie argued that a devolution of powers of order and jurisdiction to particular congregations ran contrary to the practice of the 'best' Reformed churches. Before the 1640s, puritans had permitted a degree of latitude on

---

[84] Ibid., p. 112.
[85] Ibid., pp. 105–6.
[86] Baillie, *Anabaptism*, sig. b4r. Tombes's 'Exercitation' was published as *Two Treatises* (London, 1645) and immediately gave rise to numerous responses including one by Stephen Marshall, whose sermon on baptism provided Tombes with original impetus to write his tract. Although Baillie possibly had just read and responded to the printed version of this tract, it is more likely that he would have read the manuscript version previously submitted to the Westminster Assembly.
[87] NCL, Baill MS 1, Baillie, 'Parageticorum de Congregationum Independentia', p. 431.
[88] Baillie, *Anabaptism*, sig. a3r.
[89] Baillie, *Dissvasive*, p. [229]. Cf. NCL, Baill MS 1, Baillie, 'Parageticorum de Congregationum Independentia', p. 442
[90] Baillie, *Dissvasive*, p. 122.

points of polity by focusing on the importance of justification through the preached word. Their only overarching ecclesiological goal was to maintain unity in a national church.[91] *In extremis*, church polity could be placed within the economy of grace and salvation permitting more radical puritans to argue that *nulla salus extra ecclesiam* ('there is no salvation outside an established church').[92] Whilst Baillie unfailingly stressed the importance of maintaining a unified national church – that is, distinct national churches in England and Scotland – he resolutely insisted that Independency was not conducive to such an end. The government of the Scottish Church, Baillie railed, as well as 'the same discipline of the Churches of France, Holland, Switz, Geneva, as also the Politie of the High Dutch and English, and all the rest who are called Reformed, is turned upside downe by Independency'. For Baillie, congregational principles destabilized any form of authority except that of 'their divine and beloved Independency'.[93] Congregationalism was the means by which true Christianity would become endlessly fractured.

Unity could only be maintained if particular congregations submitted to provincial and national synods, as Baillie found reaffirmed by the practice of the Apostolic Churches. 1 Timothy 4:14 – describing the ordination of Timothy – and Acts 2:44 – 'And all that believed were together' – suggested to Baillie that a presbytery did not exist within one congregation, but exercised powers over many. Allusion to the unity of the 'Church' in these cases was taken to indicate a unity of souls 'distributively' across many locations because there were simply too many members of the churches to congregate in a single place.[94] The necessity of maintaining unity amongst many congregations, subjected to a hierarchy of courts, was supported not only by the practice of the Synod of Jerusalem 'but [also] of the holy Ghost'.[95] Additionally, the principle of nature, or *juris naturalis*, that the lesser ought to be subject to the greater, reinforced Baillie's justification by necessity and divine fiat.[96] Yet Baillie was careful to outline that divine warrant of a hierarchy of synods did not entail that decrees of superior assemblies bound the lesser with the force of divine right. Whereas the Scriptural writings of the Apostles reflected God's immediate Word, the Apostles' actions and decisions in the Church remained those of fallible men. For example, the Synod of Jerusalem, which in Acts 15 sent commands to the Churches of Antioch, Syria and Cilicia, did not prove that a synod held a power to command

---

[91] Peter Lake, *Moderate Puritans and the Elizabethan Church* (paperback edn, Cambridge, 2004), pp. 3, 16–17, 21.

[92] See, for example, Conrad Russell, 'Arguments for Religious Unity in England, 1530–1650', *Journal of Ecclesiastical History*, 18 (1967), pp. 201–26.

[93] Baillie, *Dissvasive*, p. 215.

[94] Ibid., pp. 199–201, 202–5. Cf. NCL, Baill MS 1, Baillie, 'Parageticorum de Congregationum Independentia', pp. 433, 434.

[95] Baillie, *Dissvasive*, p. 207.

[96] Ibid., pp. 211–12. Cf. NCL, Baill MS 1, Baillie, 'Parageticorum de Congregationum Independentia', p. 439.

lesser gatherings with divine authority. '[M]eerely Divine, and more than Ecclesiastick Authority of these Decrees in their first Formation, is not made good from this.' As Baillie continued, all acts which are now 'registred [sic] in Scripture' were 'meerely indifferent'.[97] The various churches were 'legally subject to the Decrees of that Synod' because they had delegated commissioners to act on their parishioners' behalf.[98]

The legal 'consociation' of particular congregations into presbyteries and synods also needed to be maintained in order to prevent schism and to curb the spread of heresy effectively. Rather than granting Christians greater liberty, Baillie argued that congregational churches paradoxically tyrannized over individual conscience through unduly harsh and frequent processes of excommunication. Since 'the church' in Matthew 18:17 referred to a supervisory body of presbyters, two or three 'witnesses' in a congregation alone could not decide an individual's spiritual fate. If delegation of decision-making to a superior assembly did not occur, then Baillie believed that 'Christs order is not kept, and the Church gets wrong'.[99] If one followed congregationalist readings of Matthew 18, and limited progression from the lesser to the greater to a particular church, 'the Lords medicine were not meete to cure very many ordinary and daily scandals'. This might occur, for example, if a neighbouring church offended a parishioner; if the 'Church offending' was both judge and defendant; or, if a parishioner was 'scandalized' by his own church or a majority of that church. In congregational polities, a parishioner's only bulwark against heresy was their pastor's orthodoxy. Should a pastor transgress, there would be no remedy: 'Independency bindes the hands of presbyteries and Synods. Pastors of neighboring Congregations, have no power to binde, or expell that ravenous wolfe: in the destroyed flock there is no Pastor, but the wolfe himselfe.'[100]

By contrast, Baillie defined the discipline of a presbyterian church in remarkably lenient terms. Proceeding in a 'spiritual Method evidently fitted for the gaining of hearts', the Church of Scotland and other Reformed churches rid themselves of heretical teachings.[101] This was only possible if 'subordination established by Christ be extended, not onely without the bounds of one Parish, but as farre and wide as the utmost limits of the Church universall'.[102] The extent to which this hierarchy could extend suggested the rationale of Christ's command: an admonition from two, three or a greater

---

[97] Baillie, *Dissvasive*, pp. 207, 208. Cf. NCL, Baill MS 1, Baillie, 'Parageticorum de Congregationum Independentia', p. 437.
[98] Baillie, *Dissvasive*, p. 207. Cf. NCL, Baill MS 1, Baillie, 'Parageticorum de Congregationum Independentia', p. 437.
[99] Baillie, *Dissvasive*, p. 191.
[100] Ibid., p. 212. Cf. NCL, Baill MS 1, Baillie, 'Parageticorum de Congregationum Independentia', p. 439.
[101] Baillie, *Dissvasive*, p. 7.
[102] Ibid., p. 211. Cf. NCL, Baill MS 1, Baillie, 'Parageticorum de Congregationum Independentia', p. 439.

authority had more 'gravity and wisedome' than that 'of one alone' and a delinquent party was supposed to be struck with more 'feare, shame, and reverence'.[103] Such subordination in no ways left 'the Session of a Parish prejudged'. Rather, this form of presbyterian government ensured that a congregation's session had 'warrant to take the cognition of things common to it selfe with the Neighbouring Congregations'.[104]

Significantly, Baillie defended the autonomy of a parish church's session, rather than the autonomy of the whole congregation. A crucial point of debate during the Westminster Assembly arose over definition of the *ecclesia prima*, since that was the body invested with powers of order and jurisdiction *jure divino*.[105] This was also the point at which Rutherford and Gillespie sought rapprochement with the 'Dissenting Brethren', by preserving a greater role for the people in executing the powers of the Keys at the lowest level of a presbyterian system. For Baillie, all power of jurisdiction and ordination was granted by divine warrant to presbyters (or 'preaching elders'), eliding any role in church government for private members of a congregation. This placement of ecclesiastical power in the presbytery was much more widely accepted by puritan ministers and became one of the foundations of the 'presbyterian' majority at the Westminster Assembly.[106] Refuting the arguments of episcopalian authors, Baillie wrote that in Matthew 18:17, 'Christ committed the cognition of all ecclesiastical causes from the first admonitions to the final exposition, not to one bishop but to many presbyters.'[107] Such presbyters congregated together in a presbytery, which lay between a congregational session and provincial synod in a hierarchy, and the presbytery was made 'the first and ordinary subject of Ordination, and of sundry acts of Jurisdiction'.[108]

Whilst Baillie excluded private persons from any role in selecting ministers and other church officers, he did not completely deny lay power in the church. During debates at the Glasgow Assembly in November 1638 over the legality of lay elders electing commissioners to the Assembly, Baillie emerged as an ardent defender of a role for the laity.[109] By contrast, in the Restoration Church of England, a church typically associated with strong

---

[103] Baillie, *Dissvasive*, p. 210. Cf. NCL, Baill MS 1, Baillie, 'Parageticorum de Congregationum Independentia', p. 438.

[104] Baillie, *Dissvasive*, p. 227. Cf. NCL, Baill MS 1, Baillie, 'Parageticorum de Congregationum Independentia', p. 441.

[105] See Session 84, 30 October 1643, in Chad Van Dixhoorn (ed.), *The Minutes and Papers of the Westminster Assembly, 1643–1652* (5 vols, Oxford, 2012), vol. II, p. 233.

[106] Vernon, 'The Sion College Conclave', p. 107. Carol G. Schneider, 'Roots and Branches: From Principled Nonconformity to the Emergence of Religious Parties', in Francis J. Bremer (ed.), *Puritanism: Transatlantic Perspectives on a Seventeenth-Century Anglo-American Faith* (Boston, 1993), pp. 167–200.

[107] GUL, MS Gen 375, Baillie, 'Parageticorum de episcopatu', p. 156.

[108] Baillie, *Dissvasive*, p. 113.

[109] Stevenson, *Scottish Revolution*, pp. 105–8. For Baillie's description of his defence of the electoral powers of lay elders, see *LJB*, vol. I, pp. 98–9.

lay involvement, lay officers at best held an office responsible for the over-sight, rather than the exercise, of ecclesiastical jurisdiction.[110] This distinc-tion not only held true for Baillie, but it also sheds greater light on latent complexities in the Melvillian 'Two Kingdoms' theory. In one vein, Baillie's writings may be said to support the suggestion that Scottish 'clericalist' pres-byterians evoked a 'moderate version of Andrew Melville's theory of Christ's two kingdoms'.[111] Returning to Bucerus's *Dissertatio de gubernatione eccle-siae*, Baillie defended the parity of a pastor, bishop and preaching elder in Scripture, albeit this order was 'superior to a ruling Elder, or presbyter'.[112] In this context, Baillie's clericalist version of presbyterianism may be jux-taposed alongside that of Lazarus Seaman, Thomas Gataker and Cornelius Burgess, whose preferred polities in the 1640s 'reflected residual traces of their episcopalian tradition'.[113] In a tract prepared at the Glasgow Assembly, Baillie expanded on the relationship between lay elders and presbyters, sum-marizing historical precedents in favour of lay elders. Citing *The First Book of Discipline*, he argued that if a minister 'be worthie of admonition, they that be the elders, must admonish him, for correction they must arrest him, and iff he be worthie of deposition, he with consent of the kirk and Superintendent may depose him'.[114] Such checks existed because otherwise 'one minister may governe lyke a pope his patronage without elders'.[115] By granting the church's officers-in-presbytery the power of the Keys alone, some force needed to be in place to ensure that groups of heretical ministers could not corrupt a national church. This lay power, which he argued was Scripturally based and approved by the practice of the post-Reformation Church, was the primary means by which Baillie mitigated the power of a church's ministry.

III

In practice, the Church of Scotland was not immune from internecine dispute and alleged ministerial and lay corruption. From as early as 1647, fault-lines within its ministry started to appear over the question of whether or not the Covenanters should make further concessions regarding ecclesi-astical polity to Charles I so as to secure a treaty and thereby outmanoeu-vre the English Independent party in peace negotiations. Such fault-lines

---

[110] Jacqueline Rose, *Godly Kingship in Restoration England: The Politics of the Royal Supremacy, 1660–1688* (Cambridge, 2011), p. 77.
[111] Vernon, 'The Sion College Conclave', p. 111.
[112] Baillie, *Danger of Limited Episcopacie*, p. 17. This highlights another of the issues with the Scriptural term *presbyter*, namely that it could be taken to refer variously to a preach-ing elder, lay or ruling elder, bishop, minister or pastor.
[113] Powell, 'Dissenting Brethren', p. 86.
[114] NCL, Baill MS 4/1, 'The pouer of elders provit from the constitutions of our church', fo. 127v.
[115] Ibid., fo. 128v.

ultimately erupted in the so-called 'Protestor/Resolutioner' schism of the 1650s, described in the previous chapter.[116] On one side, the 'Protestors' – most prominently Rutherford, Patrick Gillespie and Johnston of Wariston – maintained that church membership (and, by extension, eligibility to hold office) should be limited to godly 'true' believers. The evils that had befallen the Scottish Church since the short-lived triumph of presbyterianism in the mid-1640s were all taken to be signs of God's displeasure. On the other, 'Resolutioners' garnered the opinion of a majority (upwards of 750 of 900 parishes) of the Church's ministry – including Baillie, Robert Douglas and James Sharp – who argued that the visible church was an *ecclesia mixta* comprised of both the saved and the reprobate.[117] Accordingly, royalist sympathizers who had publicly repented should be permitted to rejoin the Church and hold public office, to help prevent the spread of sectarianism and heresy and rebuff Cromwell's invasion force that threatened Scotland from July 1650. Arguments to exclude 'malignant' Royalists were unjustified and a means by which a narrow faction had begun to undermine a unified national polity. As Baillie wrote of the Protestors, 'they will exclude such multitudes for one cause or another that the end will be the setting up of a new refined congregation of their own adherents'. From an English perspective, Richard Baxter explained the Protestors' position less polemically: persecution had driven some Scottish presbyterians to sectarianism 'so that their Congregations were, through necessity, just of Independent and Separating Shape, and outward Practice, though not upon the same Principles'.[118] Protestor thought has previously been explored, but the ideas of their Resolutioner rivals have not received similar attention. This chapter thus concludes with a discussion of Baillie's reaction to the Protestor/Resolutioner controversy, paying particular attention to contested ecclesiological points.

Baillie attacked the Protestors' views on ecclesiastical polity in a note drafted for Robert Douglas detailing his criticisms of the preface to Rutherford's *Survey of the Survey of that Summe of Church-Discipline Penned by Mr. Thomas Hooker* (1658).[119] Aside from this short manuscript, Baillie's letters provide the only other evidence of his criticisms of the Protestors. In his *Survey*, Rutherford had criticized the congregational ecclesiology advo-

---

[116]   The best study of this factional conflict is Kyle David Holfelder, 'Factionalism in the Kirk during the Cromwellian Invasion and Occupation of Scotland, 1650 to 1660: The Protester–Resolutioner Controversy' (Ph.D. Thesis, University of Edinburgh, 1998).

[117]   See, for instance, Stevenson, 'Radical Party', p. 165. Here Baillie is quoted as describing the Visible Church as a 'mixed multitude': a major point of contention with the Protestors. On the relative size of Protestor and Resolutioner factions, see Holfelder, 'Factionalism in the Kirk', pp. 296–7.

[118]   Both as quoted in Stevenson, 'Radical Party', p. 164.

[119]   The recipient of this critique is provided by a marginal note in an early eighteenth-century transcription of the 'Letters and Journals'. See NCL, Baill MS 2/4, 'R. B's animadversions on Mr Rutherford's preface to his survey of Mr Hookers survey. To Mr Douglas', p. 553.

cated by the puritan minister from Hartford (Connecticut) Thomas Hooker, but Rutherford's critical stance was not supported by Baillie, despite ostensibly offering a 'presbyterian' critique of congregationalism. Whilst definition of the visible church could distinguish presbyterian and congregational thinkers, divisions of opinion on this point also distinguished differences amongst thinkers with presbyterian tendencies.[120] Baillie was more critical of Rutherford's strain of presbyterianism on account of its affinities to an ecclesiology based on a church of visible saints. Indeed, Rutherford was correct in detecting considerable discrepancies between the theory and practice of presbyterian government. If such a divide could be bridged, he wrote, 'the question of the constitution of visible Churches should be a huge deal narrower'.[121] Bridging this divide was, however, simply impossible in Scotland during the 1650s. For his part, Baillie could not contain his 'greef and scandale' at the ideas articulated in Rutherford's tract, lamenting that his compatriot appeared willing 'to spit in the face of our mother church'.[122]

Notwithstanding, Baillie's attack on Rutherford's preface was tempered by his earlier readings of Brownist, Independent and anabaptist treatises. Baillie's ecclesiology was undergirded by an Augustinian notion of the universal visible church as *ecclesia mixta* – comprised of both reprobate and elect – and by a strong sense of the necessity of maintaining a unified national church.[123] Although Stevenson has contended that 'Independent or sectarian ideas' did not influence Protestor writings on church polity – rather ascribing this divide to the influence of 'English puritan ideas', a tradition of Conventicles and recent developments in federal theology – Baillie's conception of the visible church was articulated in dialogue with such thinkers.[124] Engaging with Cotton and others in his *Dissuasive*, for example, Baillie described the 'nature of a visible Church' as 'such a body whose members are never all gracious … [i]t is not like the Church invisible, the Church of the Elect. It is an heterogeneous body, the parts of it are very dissimilar, some chaffe, some corne, some wheat, some tares.' Elsewhere, moreover, Baillie held that 'every member of a visible Church is not in truth and sincerity a Believer and Saint'.[125]

By contrast, the Protestors apparently sought to set a requirement of visible regeneration for admission to communion. A requirement of 'godliness' was not, however, necessarily what animated Rutherford's stance, since he

---

[120] Ha, *English Presbyterianism*, pp. 66–7. Also on this point, see Powell, 'Dissenting Brethren', p. 83.
[121] Samuel Rutherford, *A Survey of the Survey of that Summe of Church-Discipline Penned by Mr. Thomas Hooker* (London, 1658), sig. a4v.
[122] NCL, Baill MS 4/3, Robert Baillie, [Review of Samuel Rutherford's Preface to the *Survey of the Survey*], fo. 247r.
[123] Vernon, 'The Sion College Conclave', pp. 93–4.
[124] Ibid., pp. 163–4. On the impact of federal theology, see J.B. Torrance, 'Covenant or Contract? A Study of the Theological Background of Worship in 17th Century Scotland', *Scottish Journal of Theology*, 23 (1970), pp. 51–76.
[125] Baillie, *Dissvasive*, pp. 159, 165.

may equally have been motivated by political concerns. As Rutherford wrote, 'the admitting of many known unsufficient, and unqualified, and scandalous Ministers and Elders to office in the house of God ... is to us no part of this Government [of the Church]'. The Protestors did not claim to be the 'godly in Scotland', nor did they 'ever say [they were] the onely, or all the godly in Scotland; but sure we was [sic] either looked on as of the same way'.[126] Baillie seized on this circumlocution and condemned Rutherford for effectively maintaining that the visible church should comprise only the elect. The Resolutioners were not simply 'receiving to the Covenant and church fellowship men who againe and againe had broken there ingadgment'. Rather, they had required public repentance of 'malignants' before readmission and even when such men proved 'they ar hypocrits, so long as there hypocrisie does not appear [it] will not be counted a fault except by Novatians and Donatists'.[127] Invoking the name of the third-century antipope Novatus, and the fourth- and fifth-century heretics Donatists, Baillie drew attention to the severity of the Protestors' ecclesiology. Novatus had refused to allow lapsed Christians back into communion with the Catholic Church after penance (claiming that only God could do this), whilst Protestors maintained that the visible church could be comprised only of visible saints. For Baillie, restitution of repentant sinners to the universal visible church was not an act reserved for God's will alone, but was an act of ecclesiastical jurisdiction.[128] To suggest otherwise would be to justify separatism. In the face of persecution, the stipulation that a church could only comprise those who had given proof of their regeneration was simply a means to strengthen 'the armie of the calumniating Sectaries' by proving the necessity of separation.[129]

For Baillie, the Resolutioners' stance on presbyterian government was not 'popish', 'prelatical' or 'tyrannous'.[130] By contrast, Rutherford had struck a contentious chord when he alleged that Resolutioners made obedience to 'Prelaticall acts' of synods necessary. The hierarchy of courts and unwavering obedience of the lesser to the greater all resembled the type of subjection required in an episcopal polity. Rather than answering this charge directly, Baillie appealed to acts of the General Assembly and the practice of presbyterians 'beyond sea'. The Resolutioners maintained no other form of subordination than that 'which since our late reformation from 1638 to 1648 was in ordinarie practice among ws w[ithou]t all question'.[131] Drawing a line at the acts of the General Assembly of 1648 was therefore significant. In the following year, the 'Radical Party' had taken a much more severe line against those prepared to repent for their involvement in Hamilton's

---

[126] Rutherford, A Survey of the Survey, sigs a4r, a4v.
[127] NCL, Baill MS 4/3, Baillie [Review of Rutherford], fo. 249r.
[128] NCL, Baill MS 1, Baillie, 'Parageticorum de Congregationum Independentia', p. 437.
[129] NCL, Baill MS 4/3, Baillie [Review of Rutherford], fo. 249r.
[130] For instances of this criticism, see Rutherford, A Survey of the Survey, To the Christian Reader.
[131] NCL, Baill MS 4/3, Baillie [Review of Rutherford], fo. 247v.

'Engagement', whilst Baillie had maintained that nobles, such as the earls of Loudoun and Lauderdale, should be readmitted to public office. Even assemblies that demanded obedience to acts that appeared to run contrary to God's law should be obeyed because such synodic acts were made according to law, Scripture, reason and 'all churches of all nations both friends and adversars'. Ecclesiastical polity, thus, remained in some regards for Baillie a thing that was indifferent or unclearly delineated in divine law. Every particular of ecclesiastical jurisdiction could not possibly have been outlined in Scripture and, therefore, Baillie's critique of the Protestors' polity revealed a growing division over whether presbyterianism was *jure divino*. By contrast, the Protestors refused to be 'obedient to the ordinarie judicatories of the Kirk', because they were 'made up of persons so faultie as no subjection was due to them'.[132] Some element of faith in the composition of church courts was required because the alternative – 'that everie particular person may and must follow the judgment of his owne braine' – was a recipe for anarchy.[133] For the Protestors of the Interregnum, much like the nonconforming presbyterian authors of the decades following the Restoration, God had given clear and immutable expression to a perfect form of presbyterian church government. In conflicts over the relationship between ecclesiastical jurisdiction and God's will during Interregnum Scotland, therefore, we may also see the seeds of more boisterous claims of *jure divino* presbyterianism made after 1660.

IV

Baillie's writings on church polity defy straightforward categorization. Whilst he identified himself as a 'presbyterian' and vigorously defended efforts towards introducing presbyterianism in England, the exegetical particulars of his position showed similarities with an episcopal polity whilst firmly eschewing any form of congregationalism. This is not to suggest that presbyterianism was simply a hybrid or *via media* between a 'top-down' model of ecclesiastical power and a 'bottom-up' model. Rather, there were significant differences amongst ministers who self-identified as presbyterians. Baillie's conception of presbyterian church government evinced similarities with divines such as 'Smectymnuus', who advanced proposals for reduced episcopacy early in the 1640s, whilst sharply diverging from the type of presbyterianism advocated by Rutherford and Gillespie. Within the constellation of ideas considered as 'presbyterian', Baillie's views retained a place for a temporary or extraordinary bishop, whilst completely eliminating any possibility for parish congregations to exercise powers of ecclesiastical jurisdiction.

These exegetical similarities with proponents of episcopacy suggest that Baillie's primary concern was to combat the threat posed by sectarianism

[132] Ibid., fo. 248r.
[133] Ibid.

111

to the unity of a national church. It was never a simple question of iden-tifying bishops as 'popish and Antichristian' and simply doing away with the institution altogether.[134] Above all, Baillie sought to preserve a unified national church that comprehended all Scots within its communion. For this reason, as seen in this and the previous chapter, Baillie started to sym-pathize with Royalists from 1647 onwards, showing a willingness to reach agreement with either Charles I or Charles II, even if this entailed sacrificing the Covenanters' ultimate aim of securing presbyterian reforms throughout Britain. Faced by the threat of an influx of sectaries via Cromwell's invasion force, Baillie and his fellow Resolutioners increasingly came to believe that the only hope for a satisfactory ecclesiastical settlement rested in Charles II's restoration. After years of fighting and inconclusive debates among English divines over alternatives to diocesan episcopacy, Baillie turned to the Stuart monarchs to restore peace and stability.

Political considerations as well as a growing conceptual divide, therefore, both played a role in the bifurcation of presbyterian tendencies and the rise of a more comprehensive formulation of *jure divino* presbyterianism in the Restoration. If the overriding priority for Baillie's conception of church polity was to maintain a unified national church comprised of all Christians, then his submission to a restored episcopate in 1661 may be cast in a dif-ferent light. After a decade of clear schism within the Church of Scotland, an episcopate may well have appeared the most effective means to secure peace. Although episcopacy was not Baillie's polity of choice, he accepted its reintroduction without public protest. By accepting the office of Principal of Glasgow University in 1661, Baillie effectively signalled his willingness to accept whatever form of church polity Charles II and his Scottish Council thought fit to implement. This act of public acquiescence notwithstanding, in private letters to Sharp and Lauderdale Baillie expressed grave concerns over the apparent decision 'to bring back upon us the Canterburian tymes'. Should Lauderdale have been involved in promoting the 'introduction of Bishops and Books … I thinke yow a prime transgressor, and lyable among the first to answer to God for that great sin'.[135] Similarly, Baillie confessed to Sharp in 1661 that 'the ma[t]ter of our changes [in church government] lye near my heart', fearing that bishops 'will hasten my death; yet I make no noyse about them'.[136] Accordingly, Baillie's protests were restricted to private

---

[134] David George Mullan, *Episcopacy in Scotland: The History of an Idea, 1560–1638* (Edinburgh, 1986), p. 1.

[135] Robert Baillie to John Maitland, earl of Lauderdale, 18 April 1661, LJB, vol. III, p. 459.

[136] Ibid., p. 458. This occurred after Sharp had written to Lauderdale expressing his outrage at the Protestor faction and arguing that Lauderdale ought to show his full sup-port for episcopacy, lest more Englishmen think he was sympathetic to presbyterianism. See 'Fragment of a Letter from James Sharp to the Earl of Lauderdale', [end of 1660] in Osmund Airy (ed.), *The Lauderdale Papers, 1639–1667* (3 vols, London, 1884–85), vol. I, pp. 56–60.

correspondence with Sharp and Lauderdale and a meeting with the newly consecrated archbishop of Glasgow, Andrew Fairfoul. On meeting Fairfoul in 1662, Baillie was convivial and only expressed his dissent in a calculated manner. Receiving the archbishop, along with a number of nobles, including Glencairn and Middleton, with 'seck and ale the best of the towne', Baillie related to Spang how he had 'excused [his] not useing of [the archbishop's] styles, and professed my utter difference from his way; yet behoved to entreat his favour for our affaires of the Colledge; wherein he promised liberallie'.[137]

For Baillie, reconciliation, rather than revenge, was required. Whilst Baillie's final utterances evinced a strong aversion to episcopacy, his acceptance of a prominent university position and his willingness to work with the new archbishop of Glasgow confirm the premium he was willing to place on peace and stability. Baillie died in August 1662 long before nonconformist presbyterians suffered persecution in the period later known as the 'Killing Times' during the late 1670s and early 1680s. It is tempting to speculate that Baillie's stance during the Restoration would have followed a similar reconciliatory line to that of his Resolutioner colleagues. By the mid-1660s, most Resolutioner ministers evidently agreed that a moderate form of episcopacy – that of 'constant moderators' – was consonant with the Covenants.[138] Baillie's writings on church polity indicate that he would likewise have been able to justify such a claim. A minister's presbyterianism did not necessarily entail complete aversion to episcopal church government.

---

[137] Robert Baillie to William Spang, 12 May 1662, *LJB*, vol. III, p. 487.
[138] Holfelder, 'Factionalism in the Kirk', p. 300.

4

Reformed Theology

In typically spirited fashion, Hugh Trevor-Roper characterized seventeenth-century Scottish religion as 'dictatorial, priestly, theocratic', and perhaps best styled 'intolerant'.[1] In a more recent appraisal of Robert Baillie's theological writings, the authors described them as a 'fierce, intemperate defence of Calvinist orthodoxy'.[2] In similar vein, historical theologians have criticized Baillie, Samuel Rutherford and James Durham for diverging from Calvinist theology in their introduction of a strict framework of federal theology. Whilst acknowledging that Calvinism was 'not monolithic', such studies have highlighted differences across historical periods between, for instance, John Knox's theology and that of Rutherford, or between federal theologians of the mid-seventeenth century, such as David Dickson and Durham, and those of the eighteenth century's 'Marrow' controversy, such as Thomas Boston.[3] Elsewhere, the Covenanters' theology has been described as 'the faith of the Gospel on fire'. By supporting other Reformed confessions alongside their own, Protestant Scots 'had one Rule of Faith and they had one and the same attitude towards it'.[4] By such historiographical accounts, seventeenth-century Scots had a clear and uncontested vision of what constituted theological 'orthodoxy' and were unwilling to accept any deviations from this norm.

By contrast, this chapter suggests that Baillie's conception of orthodox theology was more malleable and contextually determined than such historiography suggests. His writings on theological controversies may appear, *prima facie*, to present an inflexible vision of Reformed orthodoxy, but such a conclusion neglects subtleties of his theology. Characterization of Baillie as an obstinate and intolerant theologian partly reflects the Manichean rhetoric

[1] Hugh Trevor-Roper, 'Scotland and the Puritan Revolution', in *Religion, the Reformation, and Social Change* (London 1967), pp. 392–444, at pp. 397, 417.
[2] David Loewenstein and John Marshall, 'Introduction', in Loewenstein and Marshall (eds), *Heresy, Literature and Politics in Early Modern English Culture* (Cambridge, 2006), pp. 1–10, at p. 3.
[3] M. Charles Bell, *Calvin and Scottish Theology: The Doctrine of Assurance* (Edinburgh, 1985), pp. 10–11. On the Marrow controversy, see D.C. Lachman, *The Marrow Controversy, 1718–1723: An Historical and Theological Analysis* (Edinburgh, 1988).
[4] James Macleod, *Scottish Theology: In Relation to Church History since the Reformation* (Edinburgh, 1974), pp. 99, 101.

of the theological disputations in which he participated. Baillie's published and manuscript theological writings were exclusively framed as refutations of 'heterodox' or 'erroneous' beliefs and such polemical works were 'central to [presbyterian] campaigns' for ecclesiastical reform in 1640s Britain.[5] For most early modern theologians, disputes over matters of faith were conducted in a scholastic style, whereby disputants refashioned their positions as fundamentally opposed to that of opponents. Accounts of debates may imply that disputants were separated by insurmountable divides, but such divisions were not deeply wrought. English puritans could disagree among themselves over the extent of God's grace, for example, but they would nevertheless have been willing to coexist in communion with each other. It was significantly more serious to separate from communion with other Christians than to disagree over abstract theological points. This chapter highlights points of ambiguity, nuance and leniency demonstrated by Baillie in debates. He was realistic about the practicalities of contemporary theological debates: they had progressed to a point where it was relatively easy for two like-minded theologians to develop contrasting views over any number of exegetical minutiae. To curb tireless academic debate from spilling over into the parish and to preserve a unified national church, Baillie recognized that it was necessary to accept conceptual disagreement. This chapter thus helps to explain why Baillie, the author of some of the most acerbic critiques of theological error in the 1640s, may also legitimately be deemed 'the tolerant Robert Baillie'.[6]

This chapter situates analysis of Baillie's theological writings within the context of seventeenth-century Reformed orthodoxy. Historiography on this subject has undergone extensive revision, the outlines of which are important to recount in some detail. Richard Muller's magisterial revisionism has questioned older interpretative paradigms and exerts a dominant influence on most studies.[7] Most significantly, Muller challenged the so-called 'Calvin against the "Calvinists"' model that had argued that later Reformed theologians sharply diverged from Calvin's ideas. Scottish historical theologians writing in this vein had argued that Robert Rollock's introduction of an organizing framework of federal or covenantal theology in the late sixteenth century, drawing on the writings of Heinrich Bullinger and Zacharias Ursinus, blunted Calvin's emphasis on God's absolute sovereignty by highlighting a series of mutually binding agreements between God and humankind. Muller, by contrast, conceived of Reformed orthodoxy as a continuous tradition, emerging from the writings of all non-Lutheran Reformers, and

---

[5] Ann Hughes, *Gangraena and the Struggle for the English Revolution* (Oxford, 2006), p. 22.
[6] G.D. Henderson, *Religious Life in Seventeenth-Century Scotland* (Cambridge, 1937; reprinted 2011), p. 44.
[7] Richard A. Muller, *The Unaccommodated Calvin: Studies in the Formation of a Theological Tradition* (Oxford, 2000); Muller, *After Calvin: Studies in the Development of a Theological Tradition* (Oxford, 2003).

encompassing considerable 'variety and breadth'.[8] He emphasized the movement's general continuity by devising a rough periodization of Reformed
theology – 'early orthodoxy', 'high orthodoxy' and 'late orthodoxy' – wherein
changes were marked by generational shifts rather than by intellectual divergence.[9] Within this framework, Baillie's writings bridged the periods of early
orthodoxy (1618–40) and high orthodoxy (c. 1640–85). More broadly, the
former period was marked by the publication of significant documents such
as the Irish Articles (1615) and the Canons of Dort (1619) that lay the confessional groundwork for the 'Second Reformation', whilst the latter period
witnessed increasing theological and confessional precision as 'new and
highly defined internal conflicts' emerged within the movement.[10] At the
same time, 'high orthodoxy' was also a period when Cartesian rationalism
and Socinianism challenged the validity of divine knowledge revealed in
Scripture.

This chapter takes Muller's revisions as a starting point, but challenges
the broad coherence that he accorded to a tradition of Reformed orthodoxy.
Muller is, himself, a Reformed theologian who approaches historical contributions to these debates as living texts that comprise the historical identity
of his own faith. The conception of a Reformed orthodox *tradition*, therefore,
predisposes historians to expect authors writing in that tradition to react in
a particular way to a view about, *inter alia*, salvation, grace or free will. If said
author responded in a way that diverged from expectations, such dissonances
might be explained away or ignored altogether to smooth the edges of the
historical theological tradition being described. In Baillie's case, an expecta-
tion that he would disapprove of Arminian soteriology, for example, might
be accurate, but Baillie's diverse and unfixed attitudes towards theologians of
different beliefs challenges such expectations. Whilst nascent confessional
identities may often have led authors to defend their own beliefs vigorously,
theologians of divergent beliefs nevertheless extensively interacted and
defended one another precisely because confessional identities remained so
fluid and unstable in the 1640s and 1650s. Consequently, Muller's revisionism created certain blind spots that disregarded points of cross-fertilization
between an amorphous Reformed orthodoxy and a diversity of visions of toleration or ecumenism. A rhetoric of Christian or Protestant reunion also
offered an effective tool to be refashioned by authors across a spectrum of
theological beliefs.[11] Baillie's objective of doctrinal purity did not sacrifice,
but was rather undergirded by, aspirations of ecclesiastical unity. In the early

---

[8] Richard A. Muller, 'Approaches to Post-Reformation Protestantism: Reframing the
Historiographical Question', in *After Calvin*, pp. 3–21, at pp. 15–16.
[9] Ibid., pp. 4–7.
[10] Ibid., p. 6.
[11] Anthony Milton, '"The Unchanged Peacemaker"? John Dury and the Politics of
Irenicism in England, 1628–1643', in Mark Greengrass, Michael Leslie and Timothy
Raylor (eds), *Samuel Hartlib and Universal Reformation: Studies in Intellectual Communication*
(Cambridge, 1994), pp. 95–117, at pp. 95–8.

modern period, expressions or acts of 'tolerance' did not necessarily entail positive acknowledgement of religious diversity, but could rather be a calculated action to avoid some greater evil.[12] Whilst the ideal of toleration certainly provoked outcry from Baillie in print, his experience as a parish minister and member of various ecclesiastical institutions brought him into contact with the realities of everyday coexistence. In practice, toleration was rarely based on the assumption of an individual's right to religious freedom, but was frequently pursued as a pragmatic means of promoting social harmony.

This chapter, therefore, argues that despite Baillie's apparently rigid definition of Reformed orthodoxy, his thinking could accommodate elements of theological diversity in order to maintain peace and unity. It is divided into four sections, the first of which examines how Baillie defined 'heresy' and 'error', before briefly discussing the authorities on which his theological arguments were based. Since Baillie rarely gave positive expression to his theological commitments, they must necessarily be reconstructed from his criticisms of prevalent theological errors. As the first section argues, Baillie often blurred categories of 'fundamental' and 'non-fundamental' errors to further a specific polemical argument. The following two sections discuss how Baillie critiqued prevalent theological errors by first examining his criticisms of Arminian theology which appeared to privilege human free will over God's absolute sovereignty, then by exploring how Baillie's stance towards proponents of a hypothetical-universal conception of God's grace and Socinian critiques of the triune Godhead. Whereas Baillie showed a willingness to laud, and even to support, the publications of proponents of the former position, he – along with most other Reformed theologians – denounced as heretical the Socinian challenge to Christ's divinity. The final section establishes the limits of Baillie's conception of orthodox theology, and specifically examines the latitude Baillie was prepared to concede to theologians of divergent beliefs. Although resolutely opposed to freedom of conscience or reconciliation with the Roman Catholic Church, he can be shown to have countenanced the possibility of a loosely defined confessional reunion amongst Reformed Protestants. Whilst Baillie's rigid defence of orthodoxy set him in opposition to other irenic contemporaries, the bitter legacy of sectarian violence left him adamant that theological dispute could not be permitted to undercut the foundations of Church and state.

I

Baillie's discussions concerning the nature of heresy and error help to establish why he believed that members of the visible church should not hold

---

[12] Alexandra Walsham, *Charitable Hatred: Tolerance and Intolerance in England, 1500–1700* (Manchester, 2006), Introduction.

particular beliefs. Although Baillie first arrived at his definitions of 'error' and 'heresy' during debates over Arminian theology in the 1630s, such definitions were also applied to the 'heresiographies' that he wrote during the 1640s enumerating the religious errors he witnessed in civil war London. A heretical belief, in general, was regarded as one that contradicted a 'fundamental' tenet of Christian faith, whereas a theological 'error' contravened a secondary or non-fundamental matter of faith. Problems arose, however, on account of disagreements amongst Reformed theologians over what constituted a fundamental and non-fundamental tenet of faith. Whilst anti-Trinitarian beliefs could easily be cast beyond the acceptable pale of orthodoxy, the Arminian doctrine of free will was arguably not 'heretical' but instead a very serious error. Members of the Westminster Assembly were acutely aware of the nuanced differences that existed over what constituted 'fundamental' articles of faith and were accordingly reluctant to produce a definitive statement defining heresy.[13]

To presbyterians like Baillie, the apparent deluge of heretical teachings in the 1640s rendered it imperative that attempts be made to denounce all allegedly novel theologies. As the erstwhile authority of the established Church of England lapsed during the 1640s, London in particular witnessed a rapid proliferation of Separatist and Independent congregations that challenged the authority of London presbyterian ministers whilst promoting a diversity of idiosyncratic theological beliefs. Together with English heresiographers such as Thomas Edwards, Ephraim Pagitt and Thomas Cranford, Baillie responded by engaging in an unapologetic smear campaign producing works that have been described as 'pretty haphazard' in method and lacking theological precision.[14] In particular, the rigour that was absent from Baillie's categorization of diverse theologies meant that it was not underpinned by a consistent definition of what constituted fundamental and non-fundamental tenets of faith. This may partly also be explained by the fact that the Scots had made no official attempts to define heresy during the 1640s and 1650s. For their part, most Covenanters preferred a black-and-white characterization of orthodoxy and heterodoxy, as enshrined in the National Covenant (1638) and Solemn League and Covenant (1643), which bound Scots to uphold 'true religion'. Such an approach was very similar to that of the London presbyterians who conflated heretical beliefs with erroneous beliefs to sharpen the polemical edge of their tracts. For Baillie, the rhetorical benefit of this imprecision was that it enabled him to adopt a more rigid stance on defining 'orthodoxy' when appropriate, whilst also permitting more lenient opinions to be aired at other junctures.

Baillie first formulated his definition of heresy in 1634 in an exchange

---

[13]   John Coffey, 'A Ticklish Business: Defining Heresy and Orthodoxy in the Puritan Revolution', in David Loewenstein and John Marshall (eds), *Heresy, Literature and Politics in Early Modern English Culture* (Cambridge, 2006), pp. 108–36, at pp. 114–15.
[14]   Ibid., pp. 110–11.

with the Paisley minister John Crichton. Baillie believed that Crichton had claimed that a heretical opinion was not a valid ground on which to excommunicate an individual or to separate from a more widely corrupted Church. For Baillie, a heretic was 'a person who obstinatlie mantaines an error against a principall and fundamentall part of Religion'.[15] Elsewhere, in a set of theses on the origin of sectarian errors, Baillie expanded this definition, explaining that heresy was a species of religious error, more generally defined as 'deviation from truth revealed in Sacred Scripture ... with the appearance of truth'.[16] This position, however, included a crucial distinction by which Baillie distanced himself from those he identified as Laudians, on one side, and proponents of freedom of conscience on the other: his principle of self-condemnation which, as seen below, accorded a particular place of authority for Scripture and confessions of faith. Clarifying this point, Baillie insisted to Crichton that '[a] man that is an haeretick sinneth being condemned of himself αὐτοκατάκριτος' (Titus 3:10).[17] Subsequently, Baillie revised his exchanges with Crichton on this subject for his inaugural lecture as divinity professor in 1642 which was entitled 'On the Self-Condemnation of Heretics'.[18] The principle of self-condemnation also informed the structure of Baillie's polemical pamphlets. This conceit to let his enemies' erroneous ways speak for themselves was common among polemicists in the 1640s. Despite the appearance of extensive verbatim quotations with citations it is still crucial to understand that such evidence was gathered to further a particular, partisan case. After all, Baillie rarely accorded his interlocutors the chance to prove their innocence through citation of their own words. His *Ladensium, Dissuasive* and *Anabaptism* all included extensive quotations from authors under attack in order to illustrate particular points on which Baillie argued that his opponents had erred.

Self-condemnation needed to be judged by an external rule, for otherwise a man could not be deemed self-condemned if he believed what he taught was true.[19] There were only two 'judgment seats of haeresie considerable to ws', namely, that of God (as revealed in Scripture) and that of the Church. The third possibility of conscience was not distinguishable from God since a well-informed conscience was ordered 'according to Gods judgment declared

---

[15] NCL, Baill MS 1, Robert Baillie, 'A Conference by Letters with a Canterburian minister anent the Arminian tenet of the Saints apostasie', [1634–36] pp. 57–8.
[16] NCL, Baill MS 1, Robert Baillie, 'Theses a sacra Theologiae studiosis diebus lunae hora locoque solitis discutiendae De primariis Sectariorum erroribus', p. 445.
[17] NCL, Baill MS 1, Baillie, 'Conference by Letters', p. 59.
[18] Robert Baillie, 'Diatriba Prooemialis, in publicis Academiae comitiis recitata, cum Theologicas Praelectiones auspicarer de haereticorum Autocatacrisi, anno 1642 Jul. 6.', in *Operis Historici et Chronologici*, II, pp. 99–106. Also see the MS copy, corrected in Baillie's hand, NCL, Baill MS 1, Robert Baillie, 'Diatriba Prooemialis', pp. 68–76.
[19] NCL, Baill MS 1, Baillie, 'Conference by Letters', p. 59; cf. Baillie, 'Diatriba Prooemialis', in *Operis Historici et Chronologici*, II, p. 100.

in his word'.[20] Setting up conscience as a separate judicature in cases of theological error, Baillie continued, would mean that, in cases of heresy, there would be two possible sources of 'truth' against which to judge the offence: conscience and Scripture.[21] In typically brisk style, Baillie dismissed the possibility of any variance in Scripture's meaning and, simultaneously, established himself (and other ministers) as a viable interpreter of Scripture's *right meaning*. He would never have claimed privileged access to knowledge about God's divine will, but in his written polemic Baillie often backed himself into a corner making any other understanding of his position impossible.

There was little consistency with which Baillie applied the term 'heresy' to a particular belief and, in fact, he appeared reluctant to make too liberal use of the term. Baillie explicitly referred to blasphemous ideas about the Godhead as 'heretical' and included the ancient heresies of Arius and Nestorius, and contemporary ones articulated by Faustus Socinus and Conrad Vorstius. Echoing equally reluctant efforts in England to define 'heretical' beliefs, Baillie denied deeming Arminians to be heretics on the grounds that he did not know anyone who 'does pronounce the doctrine of of [sic] conditionall praedestination an haeresie'.[22] Elsewhere, Baillie admitted that Luther's doctrine of the 'local presence' of Christ in the Eucharist and the Arminian doctrine of reprobation were 'not to be fundamentall'.[23] Writing during the 1630s, Baillie maintained some distinction between fundamental and non-fundamental errors and their relative significance. The difference between contradiction of a fundamental and non-fundamental tenet of faith was that the former was 'so cleare, so immediat, so materiall, that the errour about it is damnable haeresie' whereas the latter was 'so obscurlie deducit, that the errour in it stands weel with grace and salvation'.[24] Yet he was also able to elide this distinction simply by emphasizing the seriousness of any error. For instance, Baillie required his divinity students to debate the proposition that even 'trifling errors' (*leviusculi errores*) which did not undermine fundamentals of faith, nor delayed charitable works, might still endanger an individual's salvation.[25] Both heresy and error could be held to challenge divine truth with false doctrines.[26]

Baillie, Richard Vines, Thomas Edwards and other presbyterian heresiographers writing during the Civil Wars in England were, in effect, trying to reassert the traditional positions of Reformed orthodox belief. In Baillie's case, the traditional position, or, more precisely, methodological principle, of

---

[20] NCL, Baill MS 1, Baillie, 'Conference by Letters', p. 63.
[21] Ibid., p. 64.
[22] Ibid., p. 58; Coffey, 'Ticklish Business' pp. 108–36.
[23] NCL, Baill MS 1, Robert Baillie, 'A freindlie Conference betuixt tuo Ministers D and B. anent the gesture of Communicants in the act of receiving the holie elements of the Lords supper', p. 348.
[24] Ibid., p. 347.
[25] NCL, Baill MS 1, Baillie, 'Theses a sacra Theologiae', p. 445.
[26] Ibid., p. 447.

Reformed orthodoxy was *sola scriptura*.[27] It was not so important for Baillie to define fundamentals as to justify the nature of the authority from which arguments for theological truths were derived. His search for divine knowledge, or 'truth', began and ended with Scripture, albeit also according a particularly important role to the authority of religious confessions. It was the papacy's most wicked deception, Baillie argued, to affirm 'the Word of God to be blocked by a Chimera and indeed darkness'.[28] Accordingly, although all Christians could interpret Scripture, Baillie criticized imperfect editions. A perfect Latin or vernacular edition of Scripture could only be compiled by careful consultation of Greek and Hebrew texts to correct numerous errors accrued over centuries.[29] In this context, Baillie's concern with Biblical philology reflected the increased specificity introduced into Reformed theological systems in the seventeenth century as new techniques in textual analysis of Scripture opened new avenues of theological criticism and argumentation.[30] Philology and Biblical hermeneutics became a means by which theological systems might be both supported and attacked and, in the midst of this shifting scholarly terrain, Baillie scrambled to maintain a clear delineation of orthodox belief.

Baillie's philological methods sought to justify the perspicuity and self-sufficiency of divine knowledge as revealed in the Hebrew texts of the Old Testament. Since all matters affecting a Christian's path to salvation could be clearly and completely discerned from careful Biblical study, Baillie often attacked opponents for being 'skeptical' of the clarity of God's Word in Scripture. This aversion to scepticism was a common trope in Scottish anti-Arminian writings and the centrality of this criticism cannot be underestimated.[31] The claim that an author was a 'skeptic' reflected Baillie's entrenched view that Scripture provided comprehensive and perfect knowledge about the natural world and God's divine will. Moreover, Baillie's use of the charge 'skeptic' indicated that the designated offender had touched a raw nerve. Unwilling to accept that Biblical authority might be insufficient to describe certain points of obtuse theology, Baillie could hurl this label to discredit a writer thoroughly in his readers' eyes. When Baillie prepared a small Latin compendium of the most common theological errors, along with brief Scriptural refutations, the first chapter, 'Contra Scepticos', castigated all who diminished the gravity of errors.[32] Baillie wrote this précis, the *Catechis*

---

[27] This is addressed at greater length in Chapter 6.
[28] NCL, Baill MS 1, Robert Baillie, 'Commentariolus de praecipuis Pontificiorum erroribus', p. 427.
[29] Ibid., pp. 423–4.
[30] Richard Muller, 'Ad fontes argumentorum: The Sources of Reformed Theology in the Seventeenth Century', in *After Calvin*, pp. 47–62.
[31] Coffey, *Samuel Rutherford*, p. 120; David George Mullan, 'Masked Popery and Pyrrhonian Uncertainty: The Early Scottish Covenanters on Arminianism', *Journal of Religious History*, 21 (1997), pp. 159–77.
[32] Baillie, *Catechesis Elenctica Errorum*, pp. 1–4.

elentica errorum, not only as a handbook for his university students, but also to serve as a supplement to the Westminster Confession of Faith (1646) and the Larger and Shorter Catechisms (1647/48).[33] Whenever men began to dispute about 'truth', therein 'the Paganisme of the old Scepticks is lyke to be renewed'. 'Atheists' such as Thomas Hobbes had formulated their episte-mologies under the assumption that divine knowledge was completely inaccessible.[34] Like the Dutch theologian Gisbertus Voetius, Baillie abhorred the anti-Aristotelian conclusions of the new Cartesian science as well as René Descartes's attack on Reformed theology. Voetius's defence of his character-istically succinct exposition of Reformed doctrine in a debate with Descartes emphasized the instrumental role of human reason in formulating the 'con-tents of faith', rather than its normative role.[35] Such arguments resonated with Baillie who often praised and sought support from Voetius in his letters.

II

Baillie believed that Arminian theologians questioned the perspicuity of God's revealed Word in order to mitigate disagreements between Reformed theologians and Rome. Studies of Jacobean and Caroline religious ideas in Scotland have followed the concerns articulated by historians of early modern England in primarily focusing on questions about the political and theolog-ical significance of the impact of Laudianism.[36] The 'Calvinist consensus' in the Jacobean Church of England – whereby most theologians upheld a sote-riology of absolute double predestination – was disrupted by the innovatory catalyst of Arminianism, converting puritanism into a dissident movement and igniting conflict in the 1640s.[37] Whilst this thesis became central to revisionist accounts of the causes of the English Civil Wars, it remained dis-tinguished from the work of other revisionist accounts by placing a coherent ideology of Arminianism at the core of the account, characterized as a peculiar

---

[33] Ibid., sigs A2r–A8v.
[34] For Baillie's discussion of Hobbes as an atheist, see Robert Baillie to William Spang, 11 November 1658, *LJB*, vol. III, p. 388.
[35] Aza Goudriaan, *Reformed Orthodoxy and Philosophy, 1625–1750: Gisbertus Voetius, Petrus van Mastricht, and Anthonius Driessen* (Leiden, 2006), pp. 11, 37. For the dispute between Voetius and Descartes, see René Descartes, *Epistola Renati Des-Cartes ad celeber-rimum virum D. Gisbertum Voetium* (Amsterdam, 1643).
[36] In Scotland, see David George Mullan, *Scottish Puritanism, 1590–1638* (Oxford, 2000); Mullan, 'Masked Popery'; Mullan, 'Arminianism in the Lord's Assembly, Glasgow 1638', *RSCHS*, 26 (1996), pp. 1–30; Mullan, 'Theology in the Church of Scotland 1618–1640: A Calvinist onsensus?', *Sixteenth Century Journal*, 26 (1995), pp. 595–617.
[37] Nicholas Tyacke, 'Puritanism, Arminianism and Counter-Revolution', in Conrad Russell (ed.), *The Origins of the English Civil War* (London, 1973), pp. 119–43. Tyacke has tempered his thesis in 'The Puritan Paradigm of English Politics, 1558–1642', *Historical Journal*, 53 (2010), pp. 527–50. For opposition to Tyacke, see Peter White, 'The Rise of Arminianism Reconsidered', *Past and Present*, 101 (1983), pp. 34–54.

theology of grace, a pronounced anti-Calvinism and a novel vision of the visible church. Following these arguments, more recent work on the established Church in Scotland has similarly identified a broad 'Calvinist' consensus on the theology of grace. In Scotland, it was the introduction of liturgical innovations and the propensity of episcopal writers to cite extensively from the Church Fathers that unnerved those of a more puritan disposition. Whilst such accounts of the Scottish Church have rightly accepted that a spectrum of opinion can be accommodated under the heading of 'orthodoxy' before becoming undiluted Arminianism, searching for theological evidence of a Calvinist/Arminian dichotomy may also obscure more nuanced positions. More recent contributions, notably from Anthony Milton, have not explicitly challenged the rise of Arminianism thesis, but have instead drawn attention to the theological diversity found within the early seventeenth-century Church of England.[38]

Whilst it is correct, as one prominent commentator has done, to describe Baillie's theology as 'infralapsarian and limited atonement Calvinism', it is precipitous to characterize it as 'unexceptional'.[39] In brief, Baillie held that God made an absolute decree from eternity designating a particular group of fallen humans for salvation and condemning the rest to reprobation. Christ's mediating sacrifice atoned only for sins of the elect, whilst all humanity enjoyed the benefits of the Covenant of Grace freeing them from the need to fulfil the strictures of the Covenant of Works. Although Baillie's soteriology denied any role for man's free will in affecting salvation, he maintained that an absolute decree of predestination did not predetermine all human action.

The theology of the Dutch theologian Jacob Arminius and his followers, known as Arminians or 'Remonstrants', presented an affront to Baillie's theology by curbing God's absolute sovereignty in order to preserve man's free will.[40] Arminius posited that God's grace was universal and men were free to choose whether or not to accept it. Not only did men have to choose to accept God's grace, but they also had to persevere in living a righteous life in order to attain salvation. In Muller's opinion, however, Arminius's ideas represented a sharp deviation from Reformed orthodoxy in insisting that 'the divine rule of the created order is limited and that this limitation provides the only conceivable ground of human freedom'.[41] Such a conclusion, however, is based on the benefit of hindsight. At the time, Arminius and successive leaders of the movement, Jan Uytenbogaert and Simon Episcopius, attracted

---

[38] Anthony Milton, *Catholic and Reformed: The Roman and Protestant Churches in English Protestant Thought, 1600–1640* (Cambridge, 1994).

[39] Mullan, 'A Calvinist Consensus?', p. 595.

[40] The 'Remonstrants' derived from their Remonstrance of 1610 which challenged the soteriology of John Calvin, Theodore Beza and the Belgic Confession (1566). On Arminius, see Richard A. Muller, *God, Creation, and Providence in the Thought of Jacob Arminius* (Grand Rapids, 1991).

[41] Ibid., p. 281.

extensive support and ignited debate in the Dutch Reformed Churches with Franciscus Gomarus and the Contra-Remonstrants. Theological dispute turned into political intrigue, however, as the Remonstrants were quickly accused of conspiring with Spanish occupiers of the Southern Netherlands, and Prince Maurice of Nassau became involved on the Contra-Remonstrants' side. With Maurice's backing, the Synod of Dordrecht was called in 1618 – with delegates from the Reformed German principalities, the Low Countries and Britain – which condemned the Remonstrants' teachings in the Canons of Dort (1619).[42] It was only through the dictates outlined in the Canons of Dort that Arminius's theology was placed beyond the pale of orthodox belief. In no small part were these decisions motivated by political considerations. It was no wonder, then, that those theologians who might be considered as 'Reformed orthodox' could still attract criticism for expressing views that resembled those of Arminius and the Remonstrants.

From Baillie's earliest surviving manuscript treatise, a 'conference' with his cousin Crichton on the Arminian tenet of the Saints' apostasy, compiled from letters written between 1634 and 1637, to his final tract 'De formali causa justificationis', begun in 1658, Arminius's theology remained continually in Baillie's sights.[43] Whilst his *Ladensium* unsurprisingly contained extensive illustrations of how the 'Canterburian faction's' Arminian errors inclined them towards reconciliation with Rome, the continued prominence of concerns over Arminian errors in Baillie's *Dissuasive* and *Anabaptism* is more remarkable, given the expansion in theological diversity that had emerged in England during the 1640s. In his *Dissuasive*, for example, Baillie alleged that the theology of the congregational minister John Cotton verged on Pelagianism, being the notion that salvation could freely be chosen or rejected by men because their will was untainted by original sin.[44] In this way, Baillie's theological critiques of such works might appear as little more than variations on an anti-Arminian theme, which was pursued throughout his life. At the Restoration, Baillie's *Parallel* was republished, once again drawing readers' attention to his central claim that the Laudians affirmed 'all the Articles of Arminius'.[45] Baillie had not authorized republication and, in fact, he was quite embarrassed by his tract's reappearance. Nevertheless, as

---

[42] Although the delegation was referred to as 'British' the only Scot present was Walter Balcanquahall, but he held no official commission from the Scottish Church. For a discussion of the composition of the 'British' delegation, see Anthony Milton (ed.), *The British Delegation and the Synod of Dort (1618–1619)* (Woodbridge, 2005), p. xxvii.

[43] Baillie's posthumous publication, *Operis Historici et Chronologici*, was completed before he began drafting this tract, see Robert Baillie to William Spang, [June, 1658], *LJB*, vol. III, p. 369. Baillie's *Operis Historici et Chronologici* contained a dissertation in the second part entitled 'Amica per epistolas de Praedestinatione Collatio cum Theologo Ladensi', which was a translation of a portion of Baillie's correspondence with Crichton.

[44] Baillie, *Dissvasive*, p. 57.

[45] Baillie, *Parallel*, pp. 94, 95.

he explained in a letter to Lauderdale, 'I remaine fully in the mind I wes then in.'[46]

In an English context, a distinction has been drawn between the divergent backgrounds of Dutch and English Arminians, showing that the former often lived outside the Dutch Reformed Church whilst the latter occupied influential positions within the Church of England.[47] For Baillie, however, such divergent manifestations of Arminianism were, in his words, 'two long black ugly hornes' of the same theological errors.[48] It did not matter whether they existed within or outside an established Church. For Baillie, both expressions of this theology were equally dangerous. Whereas the Dutch Arminians inclined towards the anti-Trinitarian teachings of Conradus Vorstius and Faustus Socinus, the 'British Arminian with the Ancients will abhor the Extravagancies of Vorstius and Socinus, yet their heart is hot and inflamed after the abominations of Rome'.[49] In England, the Romanizing writings of Richard Montagu had particularly aroused Baillie's fears that the British Churches were set to return under papal aegis. Yet Baillie blurred this distinction for polemical effect, attacking Montagu for his 'Vorstian impiety' in making God subject to man's contingent will.[50]

To substantiate the 'Canterburians Self-Conviction', in 1639 Baillie notably sent the Scottish minister Alexander Cunningham to Cambridge, Oxford and London to collect a range of printed and manuscript works in order to establish first-hand the theological affinities of Samuel Ward, William Beale and John Cosin. From Cunningham, Baillie probably acquired a manuscript treatise written by Montagu and circulating in England, which he used in his manuscript entitled 'Some few Quaeries or doubts about the Scottish service booke'.[51] According to Baillie, Montagu maintained the Remonstrants' tenets of election, redemption, grace, free will and perseverance contrary to the Lambeth Articles (1595) and the Canons of Dort (1619). Even more unsettling, however, was the fact that despite Archbishop Laud's clear acknowledgement of these errors in the English Church, Laud still refused to censure erroneous individuals and stamp out their teachings.[52]

Baillie's most extensive discussion of Arminian errors is found in his

---

[46] Robert Baillie to Lauderdale, 18 April 1661, *LJB*, vol. III, p. 460.
[47] See Nicholas Tyacke, *Anti-Calvinists: The Rise of English Arminianism, 1590–1640* (Oxford, 1987), pp. 87–105.
[48] Baillie, *Antidote*, p. 20.
[49] Ibid., pp. 18–20.
[50] Baillie, *Ladensium*, pp. 16–18.
[51] 'My instructions to Mr. Alexander Cunighame [sic]', n.d. *LJB*, vol. I, pp. 225–8. For an edition of this tract, see Anthony Milton and Alexandra Walsham (eds), 'Richard Montagu: "Concerning Recusancie of Communion with the Church of England"', in Stephen Taylor (ed.), *From Cranmer to Davidson: A Church of England Miscellany* (Church of England Record Society, 7) (Woodbridge, 1999), pp. 69–101. For Baillie's citation of this tract, see NCL, Baill MS 4/2, Robert Baillie, 'Some few Quaeries or doubts about the Scottish service booke', fo. 66v.
[52] Baillie, *Ladensium*, pp. 16–18.

correspondence with Crichton. The fact that Baillie initiated this correspondence at the urging of Archbishop Patrick Lindsay of Glasgow supports claims that the Church of Scotland was united behind a 'Calvinist consensus' on the point of grace during the 1630s.[53] Yet it was Crichton's anomalous beliefs that Baillie interrogated for the next three years, thereby producing the most detailed articulation of a standard set of anti-Arminian arguments to which Baillie returned throughout his life. Following accusations of Arminian sympathies, Baillie opened the correspondence to discern the truth and, if need be, to convince Crichton that his ideas were heterodox.[54] Analysis of this exchange not only confirms Baillie's detailed knowledge of Arminian writings and proofs, but also reveals the primary intent of Baillie's anti-Arminian writings as being to convince holders of such tenets of their manifest errors and to persuade them to return to orthodoxy. In this context, his *Antidote* was intended to provide the wider public with a distilled version of the chief points of the Arminian controversy and thereby to swell the ranks of the godly to attack the 'main fortresses of Antichrist': theological errors.[55] Baillie's first assault was on Crichton's belief that the elect could fall totally and finally away from God's grace. According to Baillie, the tenet of the Saints' apostasy 'hath most shew of reason' but was, nevertheless, 'against the truth of God'.[56]

Baillie's engagement with Arminian theology forced him to reconcile his conception of God's absolute sovereignty with human free will. In his discussions with Crichton, Baillie introduced a common set of distinctions to explain Scriptural passages from which Arminians argued that the elect could resist God's grace. Luke 8:13, for example, stated that 'Manie beleeve with joy for a while; when tentation maks fall away'.[57] In this case, a distinction between temporary and true faith needed to be drawn: the former could be present in both the elect and the reprobate, whilst the latter was only present in the elect and could not be lost.[58] In drawing this distinction, Baillie acknowledged a debt to his former tutor, Cameron, who had also proved a major influence on Moses Amyraut's theology, discussed below. Just as different types of faith could be discerned, Baillie also argued that it was necessary to differentiate between a fall of degrees and a 'totall fall'. If a church fell, as in the Biblical case of Ephesus, a fall by degrees did not indicate that the

---

[53] Mullan, 'A Calvinist Consensus?'
[54] Citations are drawn from the copy, in the hand of an amanuensis, but corrected throughout by Baillie, in NCL, Baill MS 1, Baillie, 'Conference by Letters', pp. 1–135. There is also a partial copy (excluding the Latin dissertations on heresy and predestination, included in *Operis Historici et Chronologici*) in the hand of another copyist and extensively corrected by Baillie, apparently in preparation for publication, in NCL, Baill MS 4/2, fos 2r–42v.
[55] Baillie, *Antidote*, To the Reader.
[56] NCL, Baill MS 1, Baillie, 'Conference by Letters', p. 2.
[57] Ibid.
[58] Ibid., pp. 2, 17, 18, 35–6.

church had no 'true grace'.[59] True believers – those who had received God's grace through election – could not sin to death. The certainty of perseverance among those God had elected to salvation was thus central to Baillie's soteriology; indeed it was the 'chiefe ground of all the comfort that the soule of man hath in this miserable pilgrimage'.[60]

The certainty of perseverance also underpinned Baillie's belief in an absolute decree of predestination. If God's decree was ultimately unknowable, however, the question remained as to how Christians ought to find assurance that they were one of the elect. Elsewhere, the Covenant of Grace has been acknowledged as the mainstay of English puritan assurance. Whilst this reciprocal agreement between humankind and God, secured in Christ's sacrifice, could offer a basis for assurance in dialogue with Antinomian theologians, Baillie's debate with Crichton claimed that assurance was also firmly based on God's absolute decree. Leading a pious and righteous life and upholding the agreement of the Covenant of Grace played an important role in both Arminian and Reformed theologies. Whilst good works could be a sign of election for Baillie, assurance was only reliable if election was based on God's absolute decree and not on man's contingent will.[61] In the case of election, Arminians argued that election was based on foreseen merits, faith and perseverance, partly drawing on Luis de Molina's concept of *scientia media*, or middle knowledge. By this view, God not only had knowledge of his own nature and freedom to decree a certain state of affairs, but also knowledge of the contingent future. Whilst Arminians derived their argument for election based on foreknowledge from this notion, Molina had originally used it to defend an absolute divine decree.[62] In common with contemporary Augustinian theologians, Baillie offered proofs from Scripture, Church Fathers (mainly Augustine and Prosper) and syllogistic reasoning to refute this argument, claiming that such 'gifts' were signs, rather than causes, of election. 'Praedestination to grace,' Baillie stated, 'hath no faith nor perseverance, nor anie other grace praevious to it.' The pious action of purging of sins, as detailed in 2 Timothy 2:20–1, was thus an effect of God's prior election.[63]

In his correspondence with Crichton, Baillie recognized that most of his cousin's arguments and proofs were derived from Gerardus Vossius's *Historia Pelagiana* (1618), a tract that the Dutch humanist had written in an attempt to reconcile Arminians with the mainstream of Reformed orthodoxy. Vossius's *Historia* provoked a subtle, but unquestionably anti-Arminian, response from the Irish antiquarian James Ussher in his *Gotteschalci et Praedestinationae*

---

[59] Ibid., pp. 35–6, 4, 22.
[60] Baillie, *Antidote*, p. 104.
[61] NCL, Baill MS 1, Baillie, 'Conference by Letters', pp. 3, 15, 33, 50, 122.
[62] W.L. Craig, *The Problem of Divine Foreknowledge and Future Contingents from Aristotle to Suarez* (Leiden, 1988), chs 7 and 8.
[63] NCL, Baill MS 1, Baillie, 'Conference by Letters', pp. 101, 102.

Controversiae (1631). In this context, analysis of Baillie's reactions both to Ussher's tract and to Crichton's use of Vossius sheds light on the rigidity of Baillie's anti-Arminian discourse. The Vossius–Ussher dispute concerned the orthodoxy of Augustine's later anti-Pelagian writings on predestination and perseverance and was deliberately couched in historical terms to avoid explicitly taking sides with either the Remonstrants or Contra-Remonstrants. The Remonstrant Petrus Bertius, amongst others, had argued that Augustine's later writings represented a radical departure from both his earlier works and the earlier Greek and Latin Fathers on the efficacy of God's grace. Vossius largely concurred in this reading of Augustine, albeit his judgement, as expressed in a letter to Laud in 1632, was that it was equally incorrect to lend too much credence to the importance of free will in the pre-Augustinian Fathers as it was to argue that the Fathers had all maintained the irresistibility of grace.[64]

By contrast, Ussher defended Augustine's orthodox views of grace and predestination that precluded any role for free will, in what has been described as a 'typically oblique' history of the ninth-century German theologian Gottschalk of Orbais.[65] Baillie likewise believed that Ussher should have more explicitly denounced Vossius. Gottschalk was an obscure German monk who had provoked the ire of Archbishop Hincmar of Rheims for teaching a doctrine of double predestination and limited atonement. Although Gottschalk had been imprisoned and tortured, the Council of Valence (855) had reversed Hincmar's decision and, in Ussher's words, supported 'the orthodox opinion on predestination of Gottschalk and, equally, Augustine'.[66] Whilst Ussher dedicated his rejoinder to Vossius partly as a show of respect, the dedication was also used as a subtle means of drawing Vossius's attention to Ussher's amended reading of Augustine. Moreover, Baillie also believed that Ussher's work committed 'the errour of Vossius in his manifold calumnies of that poor man [i.e. Gottschalk] and all the race of the imaginarie predestinarians'. Despite highlighting Vossius's errors, Baillie deemed Ussher's work akin to giving someone 'ane intoxicat cup with great comendatione of the win[e]', whilst pointing 'at a stern or tuo of the black venome' therein. To Baillie's mind, Ussher should have written a more forceful refutation of Vossius, devoid of scholarly pleasantries. If the testimony of antiquity was, in fact, as complex as Ussher's and Vossius's histories showed, 'it were good to knou it certainly', so that, concerning tenets of the regeneration of baptized infants and the perseverance of the elect, 'we might … leave antiquitie in a Catholick corruption, and stand by sole scripture our best ground'.[67]

---

[64] Jean-Louis Quantin, *The Church of England and Christian Antiquity: The Construction of a Confessional Identity in the 17th Century* (Oxford, 2011), pp. 173–83. Also, see Petrus Bertius, *Hymenaeus desertor. Siue de sanctorum apostasia problemata duo* (Frankfurt, 1612).
[65] Alan Ford, *James Ussher: Theology, History, and Politics in Early-Modern Ireland and England* (Oxford, 2007), p. 155.
[66] Ussher, *Gotteschalci*, as quoted in ibid., p. 156.
[67] NCL, Baill MS 4/1, Robert Baillie to [Sir James Fullerton?], Kilwinning, 29 August 1636, fo. 7r.

Baillie's reaction to Ussher's calculating treatment of Vossius confirmed that he was concerned not only about Arminian ideas, but also particularly about attempts by divines to reconcile Arminian theology with Reformed orthodoxy. This did not mean that Baillie was wholly insensitive to nuances in the Ussher–Vossius dispute; he recognized that Vossius was amongst a group 'who are not plaine syders with the Arminians' and that Vossius was an 'Arminian in sundrie things not in all'.[68] Nevertheless, Baillie believed that Vossius's reading of the Fathers was fundamentally flawed, and in formulating his attack, Baillie resolved not to concede any ground over the disputes that had arisen concerning Arminius's theology, echoing the equally hardline statement of Reformed orthodoxy found in the *Synopsis purioris theologiae disputationibus* (1625), written by Antonio Walaeus, André Rivet and Johannes Polyander.[69] Baillie frequently attacked Vossius's judgement in questioning the authenticity of citations from Greek and Latin Church Fathers as, for example, when Vossius had questioned whether Athanasius had actually written a treatise arguing that God's decree caused good works.[70] Defending himself against Baillie's criticism, Crichton vainly tried to claim, from Vossius, that both the semi-Pelagian (based on foreseen faith) and Augustinian decrees of election were absolute. Yet Vossius's reconciliatory efforts, according to Baillie, had led him to overlook that if the decree was considered 'in order administered or executed, preconceived within the divine intellect' a decree based on foreseen faith must be conditional.[71] Nevertheless, Baillie's refusal to countenance Vossius's reconciliatory arguments led him into circular argumentation confirming his complete refusal to yield ground on the definition of God's decree required to secure human freedom.

III

Whilst Baillie's maintenance of an absolute decree of predestination could be held to have entirely eliminated free will, Antinomians, Amyraldians and Hypothetical Universalists, and Socinians conversely challenged the moral implications that Baillie drew from his soteriology. First, Antinomians embraced an absolute decree which they suggested freed humanity from any moral responsibility. If God had preordained everyone from eternity either to paradise or damnation, then there was little point in strictly adhering to moral laws whilst living. Of course, those preordained to be saved would *naturally* be inclined to uphold these standards and they would, of course, appear to do so with little trouble. But, in any case, no human action determined how you could fare in the afterlife. To combat such troublesome opinions,

---

[68] NCL, Baill MS 1, Baillie, 'Conference by Letters', pp. 24, 52
[69] Ibid., p. 56.
[70] Ibid., p. 125.
[71] Ibid., p. 127: 'in ordine dispositumis aut executionis in mente divina praeconceptae'.

some Covenanters might imply that they 'bore responsibility for their own eternal destines', signifying that 'Calvinism' was ultimately an 'unstable doctrine'.[72] Identifying sources of instability or 'tensions' in Reformed theology, however, inevitably detracts from the apparent coherence with which early modern theologians tended to view their own doctrines.[73] For his part, Baillie evidently saw no inconsistency in the relationship between good works and God's absolute decree when he argued that Augustine understood 'not any decree to the end of glorie so absolute as does exclude the midses [i.e. mediation] of grace'.[74] Modern attempts to identify apparent inconsistencies are nevertheless approaching Calvinist theology in a similar manner to that of some seventeenth-century critics such as the Antinomian William Dell and the New England divine Anne Hutchinson.

In his *Short Story of the rise ... of the Antinomians* (1644), the colonial governor John Winthrop provided Baillie with extensive ammunition to attack Antinomians. Writing as a hostile observer of the 'free grace controversy' during the 1630s in Massachusetts, Winthrop recounted the teachings of a group of theologians who argued that God had given men grace freely and that they were not bound to adhere to the moral strictures of the Mosaic Law.[75] These Antinomians attacked the mutuality of the Covenant of Grace, the second Covenant in a schema of federal theology outlined by Robert Rollock in the late sixteenth century and, later, more fully developed by Rutherford and Gillispie.[76] In contrast to the emphasis placed by Baillie on God's absolute decree in his dialogues with Arminian critics, in attacking Antinomians he underscored the importance of religious duties stipulated in the Covenant of Grace as a source of assurance.[77] A shift in emphasis is also evident when comparing Baillie's theological treatises and his sermons. God's decision to give Christ as an atoning sacrifice, freeing humanity from the strictures and punishment of fulfilling the Covenant of Works, was predicated on the condition that humanity continued to live in accordance with the Moral Law. The Covenant of Grace that came in the person of Christ 'is Gods band he set doun clairly by Christ and the apostle to give us lyf an salvation who will tak it with faith and be thankful'.[78] Although God's grace was free, evidence of such grace did not free Christians from living a pious life. To this charge, the Antinomian response was that all 'conscience of sin' demonstrated that an individual was actually reprobate, and *not* elect. Christians determined to be part of the elect through their profession of the

---

[72] Mullan, 'Masked Popery', p. 175.
[73] Muller, 'Approaches', pp. 11–13, 21.
[74] NCL, Baill MS 1, Baillie, 'Conference by Letters', p. 110.
[75] For the Antinomian controversy, see Michael P. Winship, *Making Heretics: Militant Protestantism and Free Grace in Massachusetts, 1636–1641* (Princeton, 2002).
[76] J.B. Torrance, 'The Covenant Concept in Scottish Theology and Politics and its Legacy', *Scottish Journal of Theology*, 34 (1981), pp. 225–43.
[77] Winship, *Making Heretics*, pp. 12–25.
[78] NLS, Adv.MS.20.6.4, Robert Baillie, Sermons August 1637–June 1639, fo. 92r.

Holy Spirit dwelling within them were not bound to any duty of holiness.[79] This belief in the perfection of the saints was scrutinized by Baillie in his *Dissvvasive Vindicated* (1655), through engagement with the writings of John Cotton and Hutchinson. Whilst Baillie believed it was important to recognize saints' failings in order to encourage godly behaviour, Cotton was cast as a Montanist. Baillie was, however, inconsistent in articulating his criticism, having previously accused Cotton of Pelagianism or, in other words, the belief that all humankind was unaffected by Original Sin and were free to act righteously. In the *Dissvvasive Vindicated*, Baillie suggested that only those saints with the spirit of God personally living in them could enact 'spirituall' or good works.[80] Accordingly, Baillie had found it more effective during the 1640s to depict both Cotton and the Canterburian faction with a broad, Pelagian brush-stroke; during the Interregnum, he was more concerned to associate Cotton's congregational ecclesiology with the advance of prophetic or 'enthusiastick' preachers into the once-unified Church of Scotland. According to Baillie, Cotton overemphasized the nature of free grace by arguing that 'the union of Christ with the soul is compleat before and without all acts of faith'.[81]

Whilst Antinomians challenged Baillie's insistence on the necessity of leading a devout and pious life, Baillie's belief in a particularist theology of grace also placed him in opposition to the ideas espoused by the French theologian Moses Amyraut. Proponents of an absolute decree of double predestination, such as Baillie, were frequently attacked by Arminians and Antinomians for making God the author of sin. Baillie's engagement with Amyraut on this point distinguished him not only from Amyraldianism and its closely related theology of hypothetical universalism, but also from otherwise 'orthodox' proponents of a supralapsarian soteriology. For his part, Amyraut defended the view that God gave all humans *sufficient* grace through Christ's atoning sacrifice, but only gave grace *efficient* for salvation to the elect. Amyraut made God's will – as opposed to God's decree – conditional, arguing that all men should be saved, but that the reprobate man 'was not interested'.[82] In this schema, since the power of God's will was rendered dependent on man's acceptance of its actions, sin could be explained as instances when man chose to ignore or defy God's will. Since the Canons of Dort, widely taken by Reformed divines as a standard of orthodoxy, did not define clearly the extent of God's grace, Amyraut's position sparked protracted debates within French, Dutch and Swiss churches and prompted renowned divines such as André Rivet, Willem Apollonius and

---

[79] Baillie, *Dissvasive*, p. 61.
[80] Baillie, *Dissvvasive Vindicated*, pp. 20–2. For his previous denunciation of Cotton as Pelagian, see Baillie, *Dissvasive*, pp. 165–7.
[81] Baillie, *Dissvvasive Vindicated*, pp. 26–7.
[82] F.P. van Stam, *The Controversy over the Theology of Saumur, 1635–1650* (Amsterdam, 1988), pp. 167–74.

Pierre du Moulin to defend a particularist theology of grace. Amyraut's ideas likewise divided the Westminster Assembly, as Baillie observed to his cousin Spang in October 1645 that 'Unhappilie Amiraut's Questions are brought in on our Assemblie. Many more loves these fancies here than I did expect.'[83]

Baillie's identification of English proponents of Amyraldianism neverthe-less requires qualification. Proponents of 'Amyraldianism' and 'hypothetical universalism' are often conflated erroneously. Whereas British proponents of hypothetical universalism, such as Preston, Ussher and John Davenant, did not oppose the Reformed *ordo decretorum*, the order of God's eternal decrees of election and redemption, Amyraut represented a 'far more radical' depar-ture from Reformed orthodoxy by placing the decree of election *after* the decree to give Christ. In doing so, 'the object of predestination becomes, in effect, redeemed mankind' rather than just fallen or unfallen mankind, and Baillie seems to have acknowledged this distinction.[84] In his *Ladensium*, Baillie compared Amyraut's theology to 'some small twigs of one article of Arminius' and, in January 1646, castigated the French divine's 'vanitie and pride' for causing divisions within the Huguenot Churches.[85] Conversely, in his previously quoted letter of 1636 discussing another proponent of hypo-thetical universalism, Ussher, Baillie cast Ussher as 'that most eminent and great man' – as a leading defender of Reformed orthodoxy who would 'tend to the glory of God, [and] to the good of his Church'.[86] Sometimes, the dis-tinction between Amyraut and hypothetical universalists can be identified in Baillie's misleading characterization of a theologian's pedigree. The English divine Richard Baxter, for example, was criticized by Baillie for evincing affinities with Amyraut, although in a recent study of Baxter's theology his beliefs have been characterized as being closer to the 'moderate Calvinism' of Ussher, Davenant and Joseph Hall.[87] Whilst Baillie argued that Baxter's *Aphorismes of Justification* (1649), much like Amyraut's writings, was 'stuffed with grosse Arminianism', Baillie was nevertheless despondent, for he 'love[d] and highly esteeme[d] [Baxter], for much good I find in his writs' and his 'manifest piety'.[88]

Baillie's anxieties about Baxter's views, together with his admiration for Ussher, suggests that he remained ambivalent towards hypothetical univer-salists, whilst defending a resolute hostility to Amyraut's theology, although

[83] Robert Baillie to William Spang, 1 September 1656, *LJB*, vol. III, p. 324.
[84] Jonathan Moore, *English Hypothetical Universalism: John Preston and the Softening of Reformed Theology* (Grand Rapids, 2007), pp. 217–20.
[85] Baillie, *Ladensium*, p. 8; Robert Baillie to William Spang, [1646], *LJB*, vol. II, p. 342.
[86] NCL, Baill MS 4/1, fo. 7r.
[87] Paul Chang-Ha Lim, *In Pursuit of Purity, Unity and Liberty: Richard Baxter's Puritan Ecclesiology in its Seventeenth-Century Context* (Leiden, 2004), pp. 156–89.
[88] Robert Baillie to Simeon Ashe, 31 December 1655, *LJB*, vol. III, p. 304. For Baillie's perception of the links between Amyraut and Baxter, also see p. 324; NCL, Baill MS 1, Robert Baillie, 'Tractatus de formali caussa Justificationis seu potius de justitia Christi imputata et hominis inhaerente', p. 475.

he was probably most alarmed by Amyraut's potential to foster schism amongst French Protestants. Baillie's willingness to forbear, and even publicly to defend, proponents of hypothetical universalism emerges clearly in consideration of his relationship with his friend and predecessor as Principal of Glasgow University, John Strang. Furthermore, Baillie's intermediate stance between a rigid particularist theology of grace and a more universal conception, as found in Strang's works, suggests that hypothetical universalism was not required to defend a particularist reading of Christ's sacrifice against 'anti-Calvinists'.[89] In 1646, Strang's alleged affinities with Amyraut's teachings on the authorship of sin led the General Assembly to examine his doctrines and, the following year, forced Strang to subscribe a statement confirming that he assented to the Synod of Dort's articles.[90] In his sworn statement, Strang accorded a more significant soteriological role to man's free will, arguing that God decreed the election and reprobation of man from eternity, 'foirseeing that [man] would abuse his freewill and so fall'.[91] Strang prefaced the document submitted to the General Assembly in 1647 with a refutation of those who held doctrines of sin that 'aggrie not w[ith] the counsell of Dort'.[92] From the 'Life' of Strang which Baillie wrote in June 1658 and subsequently prefixed to Strang's posthumous *De interpretatione et perfectione scripturae* (1663), it appears that Strang disagreed with the particularly strong role accorded to God's sovereignty by Rutherford and the English theologian William Twisse.[93] Strang was unconvinced by their solution to the problem of necessitarianism, which sought to 'make a distinction betwixt the cause of sinne and the author of sinne, quilk indeed I vnderstand not'.[94] For his part, Rutherford later quoted Strang's description of this type of reasoning as 'dark and not intelligible'.[95]

For Baillie, Strang's doctrine of sin did not represent sufficient reason for the General Assembly's censure. Indeed in his biographical account of Strang, Baillie carefully defended Strang's orthodoxy in an account that made little effort to hide his sympathetic view of his deceased mentor and friend's orthodox credentials. Commenting on the proceedings against Strang in 1647 in a letter to Spang, Baillie explained that Strang 'handles these Questions in such a way that I doe pryze the man's ingyne and learning ... and thinks him now among the best schollars of the Reformed Church'.[96] Nevertheless Baillie still had reservations about the dispute between Strang and Rutherford and Twisse: 'I do not like [Strang's] withdrawing from the Divine decree the act

---

[89] Moore, *Preston*, pp. 212–13.
[90] See Peterkin (ed.), *Records*, pp. 454, 482.
[91] NCL, Baill MS 4/2, 'Dr. Strangs stateing his owne quaestion, 1647', fo. 274r.
[92] Ibid., fo. 273v.
[93] Robert Baillie, 'Vita Autoris ad Lectorem, Glasgua V. Cal. Junii, 1658' [n.p.], in John Strang, *De interpretatione et perfectione scripturae* (Rotterdam, 1663).
[94] NCL, Baill MS 4/2, 'Dr. Straings quaestion', fo. 273v.
[95] Samuel Rutherford, *Influences of the Life of Grace* (London, 1659), sig. a2r.
[96] Robert Baillie to William Spang, 2 June 1647, *LJB*, vol. III, pp. 5–6.

and entitie of *any* sinne … [b]ut I fear those he refutes shall be found in alse dangerous errors.' Insisting that ecclesiastical assemblies should 'medle not with such subtile questions', Baillie recommended that they should rather be reserved for dispute in 'the schools'.[97]

In addition to his willingness to forbear subtle doctrinal differences with the hypothetical universalist Strang, Baillie's letter to Spang also suggests that his doctrine of sin was distinct from that of Rutherford and Twisse. Baillie accorded a more prominent role to free will by holding an infral-apsarian view of God's decree of election and reprobation, as opposed to Rutherford and Twisse's supralapsarianism. Since the Dort articles had been deliberately framed in order to accommodate both infra- and supralapsarian-ism, scholars have largely dismissed the significance of differences between Reformed theologians on this point. Baillie's most explicit statement of his doctrine of sin is found in a sermon to the English House of Lords which he preached in July 1645. Whilst Baillie's presentation of a doctrine of sin in this format is instructive, sermon literature was nevertheless a less rigorous medium for expressing theological propositions than formal treatises. Whilst acknowledging that the doctrine of sin was 'exceeding dark' – an implicit nod towards Strang's opinion – Baillie distinguished between the 'matter and form' of sin, before illustrating three acts of God's 'actuall providence about the matter and form of sin' in terms of God's 'concourse', 'efficacious permis-sion' and 'judiciall tradition'.[98] In the first two cases, Baillie evidently agreed with Rutherford. God's concurring influence over the events of the world as the 'first and universall' cause did not make him the cause of sin's effects, 'for effects are denominate from the second and particular causes'. As divine *concursus* did not cause particular sins, God's withdrawing his influence like-wise did not cause sin. Sins only followed from such permissive acts 'not as effects, onely as consequents'.[99] Strang likewise argued that 'God hes willed and decreed the permission of sinne, but it cannot be properlie or rightlie' said that 'God euer decreed sinne'.[100] Whilst Baillie distinguished himself from Strang by insisting that God's 'judiciall' infliction of sin was a means of punishing humankind, he differed from Rutherford and Twisse by maintain-ing that 'all sinfull actions be immediately the works of the sinner alone … [they] flow from the reprobate mindes and vile affections of the sinners'.[101]

If Baillie was to maintain a more prominent place for free will as the main cause of sin, he had to account for contingent human actions within his con-ception of the decree of reprobation. Both Strang and Baillie maintained a standard exposition of infralapsarian predestination from eternity, based on

---

[97] Ibid., pp. 5, 6.
[98] Baillie, *Errours and Induration*, pp. 9, 7–8.
[99] Ibid., p. 9; cf. Coffey's discussion of Rutherford on this point, *Samuel Rutherford*, pp. 125–7.
[100] NCL, Baill MS 4/2, 'Dr. Straings quaestion, 1647', fo. 274r.
[101] Baillie, *Errors and Induration*, pp. 10–11.

God 'foirseeing that [man] would abuse his freewill and so fall b[y] transgression of Gods love from his integritie'.[102] Hence, for Baillie, God's decree of reprobation was *not* based on foreseen sin, as David Mullan has erroneously suggested.[103] Baillie explicitly refuted this suggestion, along with the claim that election was based on foreseen faith and perseverance, for such an argument meant that actual sin would 'fall out with as great certaintie as is to be found in the infallible praescience of the omniscient God'.[104] God's decree of reprobation from eternity was separated from the operations of God's ordinary providence. Drawing on Aristotle, Baillie argued against Bellarmine and Arminius that *necessarium* and *voluntarium* may coexist within the same person.[105] Whilst God left the reprobate to act without the assistance of grace, 'the want of grace or God for not giving of grace to reprobats is no wayes the cause neither of ther sins heere nor of there torments hence'.[106] This cause was firmly ascribed to man's will, albeit within a world inextricable from divine *concursus*.

Whilst Baillie's engagement with Strang's complex beliefs primarily addressed theological minutiae, dividing the ranks of notable Reformed theologians into ever-smaller groups, Socinians, by contrast, challenged the core of Reformed theological beliefs by questioning the ubiquity and divine nature of the triune Christian Godhead. Thus far, the complexities of Baillie's relationship with Arminianism, Antinomianism, Amyraldianism and hypothetical universalism have been examined to show how Baillie's systematic criticisms placed him vis-à-vis other Reformed theologians. His refutation of the so-called 'Socino-Remonstrant' Conradus Vorstius's heterodox conception of the Godhead in his *Tractatus theologicus de Deo sive de natura et attributis Dei* (1610) illustrated the limits to Baillie's orthodoxy in ways that resonated with most other Reformed theologians. Whilst the denunciation of Socinianism as heretical was common to Reformed theologians, Baillie attacked Vorstius in much the same way as he attacked irenic theologians, such as Baxter, Ussher, Hugo Grotius and John Dury, namely, for undermining the authority of divine knowledge as revealed in Scripture.[107] Discussion of Baillie's 'Diatriba de Dei simplicitate' thus provides an appropriate segue into the final section of this chapter.[108] Whereas Reformed theologians such as Ussher and Baxter exhibited restraint in their discussions of Arminian

---

[102] NCL, Baill MS 4/2, 'Dr. Straings quaestion', fos 273v–274r. For another statement of Baillie's infralapsarianism, see *Operis Historici et Chronologici*, I, p. 3.
[103] Mullan, 'A Calvinist Consensus?', p. 606 where he cited NCL, Baill MS 1, Baillie, 'Conference by Letters', p. 114.
[104] NCL, Baill MS 1, Baillie, 'Conference by Letters', p. 110.
[105] Ibid., p. 114.
[106] Ibid., p. 111.
[107] Sarah Mortimer, *Reason and Religion in the English Revolution: The Challenge of Socinianism* (Cambridge, 2010), pp. 55–62.
[108] Baillie, 'Diatriba de Dei simplicitate, num quicquid in Deo est, Deus sit?', in *Operis Historici et Chronologici*, II, pp. 106–21.

theology, the ideas of Faustus Socinus, on which Vorstius drew, were universally denounced as heretical. Socinus had argued that religion must be freely chosen by humanity, who received divine knowledge through application of 'human ideas' to Biblical interpretation.[109] As the orthodox concept of the Trinity, three persons in one substance, or *homoousios*, determined by the Council of Nicaea (325), was not based expressly on Scripture, Socinians challenged both the Divinity of Christ and the conception of a triune Godhead. The principle of *sola scriptura* was not the harbinger of peace, but rather brought 'a sword of such sharpness as to pierce to the dividing asunder of the joints and marrow of Protestantism'. Hence debates between antitrinitarians and trinitarians in early modern England focused on definitions of the 'right' interpretation of Scripture.[110]

Drawing on Socinian authors, Vorstius challenged the Trinitarian, infinite and omnipotent nature of the Godhead, and his *De Deo* was notorious throughout Reformed Christendom. In 1612, James VI and I had issued a declaration protesting against Vorstius's appointment as professor at Leiden and, during the Synod of Dort, members of the British Delegation repeated James's request that *De Deo* be burned.[111] For his part, Baillie was prompted to produce a refutation of Vorstius's arguments following remarks by Crichton on the divine attributes which obliged Baillie to ask if Crichton believed Vorstius was a heretic. Baillie's attack focused on the uncertainty with which Vorstius discussed the divine attributes. Echoing attacks made on Vorstius by the Palatinate divine David Paraeus, Baillie objected to Vorstius's language, using *videtur* – 'it seems that' – to start propositions and, like Socinus, applying languages of philosophy and jurisprudence to Scripture.[112] In this context, such an historical approach to Scripture – as taught by Socinus – exposed rampant inconsistencies in the metaphysical formulation of the Godhead. 'The question about divine simplicity', Baillie argued, 'is of greatest moment amongst all theologians, Papists as well as Protestants.'[113] The dispute was not simply one of transcendental speculation. In arguing, for example, that God's decrees were not of God's essence but accidents, Vorstius had restricted God's absolute sovereignty far more radically than Arminius. For Baillie, such a claim appeared to promote Arminian arguments

---

[109] Mortimer, *Reason and Religion*, p. 2.

[110] Norman Sykes, 'The Religion of Protestants', in S.L. Greenslade (ed.), *The Cambridge History of the Bible: The West from the Reformation to the Present Day* (Cambridge, 1963), vol. III, p. 178 as quoted in Paul C.H. Lim, *Mystery Unveiled: The Crisis of the Trinity in Early Modern England* (Oxford, 2012), p. 13.

[111] *His Maiesties declaration concerning his proceedings with the States generall of the Vnited Prouinces of the Low Countreys, in the cause of D. Conradus Vorstius* (London, 1612); W.B. Patterson, *King James VI and I and the Reunion of Christendom* (Cambridge, 1997), pp. 262–3.

[112] Baillie, 'Diatriba de Dei simplicitate', in *Operis Historici et Chronologici*, II, p. 109; David Paraeus to Conrad Vorstius in Matthew Slade, *Cum Conrado Vorstio ... De blasphemiis, haeresibus et Atheismus* (Amsterdam, 1612), p. 62.

[113] NCL, Baill MS 1, Baillie, 'Conference by Letters', p. 110.

for the autonomy of free will. As God could only be known through his active providence on earth, and if such providential actions were merely accidental qualities of the Godhead, Baillie feared that Vorstius risked undermining the authority of divine knowledge derived from Scripture by separating God's actions from his being.

IV

This final section discusses the limits of Baillie's conception of 'orthodoxy' as illustrated through his involvement in debates over Christian reunion and toleration. As seen above, the increased popularity of Arminian, Socinian, Amyraldian and Antinomian theology drove Baillie and like-minded theologians throughout Britain and Continental Europe to enforce their definitions of 'orthodoxy' by emphasizing the severity of *any* theological error. For his part, Baillie avoided discussions regarding what should be deemed heretical, or opposed to a fundamental article of Christianity, leading him to adopt a more rigid view of orthodoxy than many of his contemporaries. Underlying this rigid stance towards theological pluralism was his firm insistence that divine 'truth' could be clearly discerned in Scripture, which even led him to denounce the reconciliatory efforts of his former mentor, Robert Blair, during the Protestor/Resolutioner conflict of the 1650s. Nonetheless, Baillie's beliefs did not lead him to advocate the endless proliferation of new churches in order to purify the visible church of corruptions. Accordingly, this chapter concludes by showing how Baillie reconciled his strong belief in the unity of the visible church with his rigid exposition of 'true' Christian doctrine.

Despite notable revisions of the history of toleration in early modern Europe, primarily written by social and cultural historians attuned to the complex and interrelated ways in which these concepts were implemented, intellectual historians have tended to continue searching for the roots of qualities resembling modern, positive concepts of 'toleration' as acceptance of religious diversity.[114] In such narratives, the Covenanters, and specifically Baillie, are perennially cast as *bêtes noires*, especially in histories encompassing traditions of rational religion. In the nineteenth century, Henry Buckle famously asked how the Scots could have 'long been liberal in politics, and illiberal in religion'.[115] Meanwhile in the 1960s, Trevor-Roper argued that 'Arminianism or Socinianism, not Calvinism, was the religion of the pre-Enlightenment. Calvinism, that fierce and narrow re-creation of medieval scholasticism, was

---

[114] See Walsham, *Charitable Hatred*; Benjamin Kaplan, *Divided by Faith: Religious Conflict and the Practice of Toleration in Early Modern Europe* (Cambridge, Mass., 2007). For an overview of the current research, see Jeffrey R. Collins, 'Redeeming the Enlightenment: New Histories of Religious Toleration', *The Journal of Modern History*, 81 (2009), pp. 607–36.
[115] H.T. Buckle, *On Scotland and the Scotch Intellect*, ed. H.J. Hanham (Chicago, 1970), p. 161.

137

its enemy.'[116] More recent accounts of Socinian rational religion and unique thinkers, such as John Goodwin, have concluded with careful suggestions as to how their subjects may have exerted some influence over John Locke's thoughts on toleration, a perspective also explored in reverse, through analysis of 'Socinian' tendencies in Locke's thought.[117] Such studies, however, focus on exceptional divergences in early modern intellectual culture, rather than providing a more contextually grounded understanding of the practical demands exerted on that intellectual culture itself. Thinkers from the so-called Great Tew Circle might stand out as trailblazers in a dark, illiberal past, but it is crucial not to overlook the particular demands that that past society exerted over a writer's beliefs. Dismissing 'Calvinist' theologians like Baillie as obstinately opposed to programmes for toleration or ecumenism obscures the practical considerations that influenced a theologian's decision to accept a narrow degree of theological pluralism.

Baillie's emphasis on the perspicuity of Scripture aligned him with contemporary groups who, for various reasons, emphasized Scripture's ambiguities. Baillie would, for example, have agreed with Richard Vines who preached to the English House of Commons in 1646, insisting that 'to make conscience the final judge of actions, is to wipe out the hand-writing of the Word of God'.[118] For Baillie, Vines was one of the 'ablest' presbyterian ministers in England and one of his 'late dear friends'.[119] But proponents of freedom of conscience, such as John Milton, attacked Baillie, Vines and other presbyterians as priestly suppressors of individual conscience. Milton's sonnet 'On the New Forcers of Conscience' also contained a veiled attack on Baillie who, along with Thomas Edwards, had criticized Milton's views on divorce:

> Men, whose life, learning, faith, and pure intent
> Would have been held in high esteem with Paul,
> Must now be named and printed heretics
> By shallow Edwards and *Scotch What a'ye call*.[120]

Whilst Milton's denunciation of 'Scotch What a'ye call' correctly attacked Baillie for casting a wide net when condemning 'erroneous' theologians, he disregarded Baillie's desire to achieve a unified, inclusive ecclesiastical

---

[116] Hugh Trevor-Roper, 'The Religious Origins of the Enlightenment', in *The Crisis of the Seventeenth Century: Religion, the Reformation and Social Change* (Indianapolis, 1967), pp. 179–218, at p. 199.

[117] Mortimer, *Radical Religion*, pp. 233–41; John Coffey, *John Goodwin and the Puritan Revolution: Religion and Intellectual Change in 17th-Century England* (Woodbridge, 2006), pp. 291–7; John Marshall, *John Locke: Resistance, Religion and Responsibility* (Cambridge, 1994).

[118] Richard Vines, *The Authour, Nature, and Danger of Heresie* (London, 1662), p. 45.

[119] Robert Baillie to John Campbell, earl of Loudoun, 25 December 1646, *LJB*, vol. II, p. 414; Robert Baillie to Francis Rous, 6 September 1656, vol. III, p. 326.

[120] *Milton's Sonnets with Introduction, Notes, Glossary and Indexes*, ed. A.W. Verity (Cambridge, 1916), p. 27. Emphasis added. For Baillie's attacks on Milton, see *Dissvasive*, p. 76.

settlement, which was a goal shared with other presbyterian heresiographers, such as Edwards.[121] Baillie also praised Jeremiah Burroughes's *Irenicum* (1645), which supported a form of limited toleration whilst 'exploding' the 'abomination' of liberty of conscience and specifically that which had been advocated by the English puritan John Goodwin and the founder of the Providence Plantation in New England Roger Williams.[122] Establishing conscience as the sole judge of error led 'Brownists', Baillie argued, to advocate endless separation from those who manifested the least corruption of sin.[123] Enthusiasts championed an individualistic and experiential theology based on the reception of saving knowledge directly from God without the mediation of Christ or Scripture.[124] Such a 'liberty to beleeve' undermined the 'principall Articles of Christian Religion' and raised the authority of 'things of the mind and matters of opinion'.[125] Whereas this might lead to a more persecutory and exclusive image of the visible church than Baillie was willing to accept, liberty of conscience also led the Independents to refuse to exclude anyone from communion unless they had committed a 'fundamental error'.[126] Accordingly, Baillie blurred the distinction between 'fundamental error' and 'heresy' to condemn the 'grosse' errors of Arminians who the Independents evidently would not exclude from communion. If this was the case, and 'if Arminian, Socinian, Anabaptistick, Antinomian ... errours be declared not fundamentall, what shall we say of ... most of the Popish Tenets that are no wayes so grosse?'[127]

Baillie likewise attacked Laudians and Arminians for denying that the Church of Rome was heretical, declaring it a 'true church' and taking steps towards reconciliation.[128] In minimizing the heresies of Rome, Baillie complained that the Laudians 'so subtilized' the nature of heresy 'that so farre as in them lies it is now quite evanished in the aire, and no more heresies are to be found on the earth'.[129] Baillie also criticized irenic authors such as George Cassander, Archbishop Marco Antonio De Dominis of Spalato and Hugo Grotius because they diminished the significance of theological error and heresy. In Scotland, the 'Cassandrians' William Forbes and James Wedderburn – whose manuscripts were discovered in Aberdeen by the Covenanters and published in Baillie's 'Large Supplement' to his *Ladensium* – had argued that there was no heresy and idolatry in Rome, only 'abuse and

---

121 Hughes, *Gangraena*, pp. 18–22.
122 Baillie, *Dissvasive*, 'Epistle Dedicatory', sig. *2r.
123 Ibid., p. 23.
124 Ibid., pp. 79–82.
125 Baillie, *Anabaptism*, sig. 4r–v.
126 Baillie, *Dissvasive*, p. 130.
127 Ibid.
128 Milton, *Catholic and Reformed*, pp. 128–72.
129 Baillie, *Ladensium*, p. 63. Also see Baillie's chapter, 'Num Ecclesia Romana sit Ecclesia vera?', in NCL, Baill MS 1, Baillie, 'Commentariolus', pp. 428–30.

scandal'.[130] In this context, it was the Romanizing writings of Forbes and Wedderburn, rather than their alleged Arminianism, that informed Baillie's critique, supporting Mullan's willingness to challenge the extent to which Arminian ideas had spread throughout Scotland. Baillie even suspected that Laud's interest in the efforts of the Scottish ecumenist Dury to promote reunion with the Lutheran churches was merely a ploy to bring the British churches back under papal authority.[131]

Baillie staunchly challenged theologians who appeared to be advocating reunion with Rome because he considered the Roman Church to be heretical and the pope the Antichrist. Such was the basis of Baillie's criticism of Robert Shelford's controversial *Five Pious and Learned Discourses* (1635). The final section of Shelford's work, 'A treatise shewing the Antichrist not to be yet come', rejected identification of the pope with the Antichrist and called for reconciliation. Despite ceremonial differences amongst 'Papists, Protestants, [and] Lutherans ... yet still our head Christ by Baptisme standeth upon our bodie, and the substance of the Gospel is entire and whole amongst us'.[132] In Baillie's words, Shelford 'comes home to [the Jesuit scholar, Robert] Bellarmine', identifying the Antichrist with an individual, namely, 'a Jew preaching formall blasphemies against Christs natures and person thre yeeres and an halfe'.[133] Baillie even cited evidence that Laud was actively seeking to diminish the ceremonial distinctions between the Church of Scotland and Rome. In the new Scottish Prayer Book of 1637 – discussed more fully in the next chapter – Baillie observed how the Scottish bishops had termed adoration of the bread 'the Popish adoration', but Laud 'on the margine with his owne hand directeth to scrape out the word Popish'.[134] In such ways, Laud and his followers had removed 'the mayne impediment[s]' dividing Protestants from the Roman Church. Namely, Laud sought to undermine the pan-Protestant decision to make 'the Popes Antichristianisme, their chiefe bulwarke to keepe all their people from looking backe towards that Babylonish Whore'.[135]

By removing these rhetorical preservatives against Roman heresy, the Laudians were able to claim, much to Baillie's chagrin, that the Roman and British churches were of the 'same religion'. Baillie further levelled these criticisms against Montagu's Romanizing tendencies in his *Antidiatribae ad priorem pautem diatribarum J. Caesaris Bulenger* (1625) and in Montagu's manuscript tract on Roman Catholic recusancy in England.[136] In the latter tract, Montagu

---

130 Baillie, 'Large Supplement', in *Ladensium*, p. 20.
131 Baillie, *Ladensium*, pp. 31–4.
132 Robert Shelford, 'A treatise shewing the Antichrist not to be yet come', in *Five pious and learned discourses* (London 1635), p. 235. For Baillie's citation of this passage in his discussion of the Laudians' position towards Roman Catholics, see Baill MS 4/2, 'Some few Quaeries or doubts about the Scottish service booke', fo. 59r.
133 Baillie, *Ladensium*, pp. 36–7.
134 Ibid., p. 55.
135 Ibid., p. 35.
136 Ibid., p. 38; Milton and Walsham (eds), 'Concerning Recusancie', pp. 69–101

argued for the shared Christianity of the Roman and English churches, whilst defending the latter's autonomy by drawing on Gallican criticisms of papal temporal authority. In Baillie's *Ladensium*, John Pocklington and Laud – or *Cassandrianis Britannicis* – were likewise accused of claiming that the Church of England and Rome were of the 'same religion'. For Pocklington, despite some differences, there was 'no schisme betwixt Papists and Protestants' and Protestants remained in 'union and communion with the Church of Rome in all things ... necessary for salvation'.[137] Baillie also accused Christopher Potter, dean of Worcester, of claiming that the Church of England and Rome did not differ in 'fundamentals', but rather that 'the truths that the Papists doe maintaine, are of force to hinder all the evill that can come from their errours'.[138] Baillie's fears were rekindled at the Restoration, when he complained to Sharp about the influence of a 'neo-Laudian' party at Charles II's court – including Peter Heylyn, Matthew Wren and John Bramhall – who were 'most expresse and bitter for all Arminianisme, for the farre most of Poperie, as much as Grotius maintains'.[139]

Baillie's attacks on the Laudian Church's stance towards Rome were largely based on the authority granted to tradition over Scripture. In the Jacobean and Caroline Kirk, emphasis on Patristic authorities became a crucially divisive factor between presbyterian Scots and their conformist opponents. For Baillie, the Canterburians appeared to adopt Bellarmine's Jesuitical emphasis on 'Scriptures imperfection, and doctrinall traditions'.[140] In his 'Commentariolus' on the errors of the Roman Church, Baillie similarly attacked the claim that many doctrines necessary for salvation could not be found in Scripture.[141] In an incomplete tract composed around 1658, 'On the Formal Causes of Justification', Baillie attacked William Forbes's *Considerationes modestae et pacificae* – his 'wicked dictates', as Baillie observed to Lauderdale – for drawing on extra-Scriptural authority.[142] Together with Forbes, Baillie excoriated De Dominis and Grotius for neglecting the significance of post-Reformation controversies over justification. Diminishing theological controversies by all possible prudence (*cordato*) and with a good conscience (*cum bona conscientia*) led those seeking Christian concord to weaken in their defence of truth. In seeking reconciliation among Protestants, Scripture's necessary truths (*necessariae veritates*) could not be set aside.[143]

A lax attitude towards the controversy over justification did not only correlate to an author's emphasis on Patristic authority. Baillie was also concerned that Baxter's *Aphorismes of Justification* (1649) strayed from orthodoxy, on

---

137 Baillie, *Ladensium*, p. 43.
138 Ibid., pp. 43–4.
139 Robert Baillie to James Sharp, 16 April 1660, *LJB*, vol. III, p. 400.
140 Baillie, *Ladensium*, p. 64.
141 NCL, Baill MS 1, Baillie, 'Commentariolus', pp. 426–7.
142 Robert Baillie to John Maitland, earl of Lauderdale, 16 June 1660, *LJB*, vol. III, p. 406.
143 NCL, Baill MS 1, Baillie, 'Tractatus de formali caussa Justificationis', p. 462.

account of Baxter's reluctance to defend Scriptural truths.[144] In a prefatory epistle to his *Aphorismes*, Baxter had attacked divines who became 'Creed makers themselves' and obscured Scriptural texts. Despite remaining unsure on many points of justification from his own reading of Scripture, Baxter nonetheless believed that there was 'a strong probability of what I have written therein'.[145] Such an assertion illustrates Baxter's rigorist approach to the principle of *sola scriptura*, which led him to denounce any confessional document that did not retain Biblical language. By contrast, Baillie believed that Scripture should be probed to uncover its inherently truthful meaning, and this conviction distinguished Baillie from Baxter and like-minded divines, such as Davenant, Hall and Ussher, who sought reconciliation by accepting Scriptural ambiguity on finer doctrinal points. It was also common for Baillie and other presbyterian divines to be attacked for being too rigorous in defending truth. In 1641, Dury wrote to Baillie, following the first edition of Baillie's *Ladensium*, in which Baillie had condemned Dury's ecumenical programme on account of Dury's brief association with Laud. Dury reminded Baillie that 'it is a dangerous matter to take upon us to iudge and condemne others'; it was easier to be too charitable than too rigid in censure.[146]

Whereas Baxter emphasized Scripture's sole authority, albeit as an often obscure and ambiguous body of knowledge, Baillie argued that Scripture's meaning was clear and that Reformed confessions of faith contained reliable accounts of Scripturally based doctrine. A concordance of these Reformed confessions, a 'harmonie of Confessions', was, to Baillie, a means by which to judge orthodox opinion on doctrinal points.[147] Elizabethan and Jacobean divines had commonly stressed the harmony of Reformed confessions to refute Roman Catholic accusations that Protestant Christendom was hopelessly splintered.[148] The high esteem in which Baillie held confessional and catechetical documents was evident when he attacked Brownists who denounced any need for such authorities in their separatist churches, and Arminians, who allegedly complained that 'none of the churches confessions made for our tenet'.[149] In his treatise on justification, Baillie approved the proceedings of the Contra-Remonstrants at Dort who had denounced the Remonstrants' articles by Scriptural proofs, the Confessions and Catechisms of Belgium and the Palatinate, and the decrees of national synods that accorded with the Belgic Confession.[150] Baillie's strict adherence to the decisions of church councils – whether national, or the ancient ecumenical councils – helped elucidate the authoritative relationship he viewed between

[144] Ibid., p. 475.
[145] Richard Baxter, *Aphorismes of Justification* (London, 1649) sigs a2v, a7r.
[146] Sheffield University Library, Hartlib Papers 2/3/3a–4b, John Dury to Robert Baillie, The Hague, 27 January 1641.
[147] NCL, Baill MS 1, Baillie, 'Conference by Letters', p. 61.
[148] Milton, *Catholic and Reformed*, p. 377.
[149] Baillie, *Dissvasive*, p. 30; NCL, Baill MS 1, Baillie, 'Conference by Letters', p. 28.
[150] NCL, Baill MS 1, Baillie, 'Tractatus de formali caussa Justificationis', p. 467.

Scripture and confessional documents. In synods, questions of doctrine and heresy were answered by 'making deductions from the grounds of scripture towards the questions in hand'.[151] Scripture was not obscured, but rather clarified by decisions of church councils.

In Scotland, the authority Baillie accorded to church councils was strenuously tested by the Protestor/Resolutioner conflict during the 1650s and even led him to oppose reconciliatory efforts made by his former tutor, Robert Blair. Whilst the Resolutioners managed to secure majorities in the General Assembly and Committee of Estates, the Protestors convened separate synods and denounced all acts passed by the General Assembly of 1651. Recognizing that the schism was largely based on these acts' legality, Blair proposed to Baillie in March 1652 that 'not only debates about former resolutions, but determinations, acts, censures, all be quite laid' aside. Although both sides in this conflict had erred, Blair 'would preferr one act of oblivion' to secure peace.[152] In response, Baillie showed just how far he was willing to stand on the authority of 'lawful' assemblies. '[F]or the quite laying aside all the acts of the last Assemblie [of 1651]', Baillie wrote, 'and that men censured shall not make so much as the least acknowledgement for all their ... very evill Remonstrance ... I doubt it acceptable to God'.[153] In a letter written to his fellow Resolutioner James Wood, Baillie confessed that he would rather be excluded from ecclesiastical office than accept repeal of the General Assembly's acts.[154]

V

Despite Baillie's opposition to efforts for Christian reconciliation or toleration, his unwavering pursuit of Scriptural 'truths' did not lead him to advocate endless division to purify the visible church. Instead, a desire for peace and unity animated most of Baillie's writings. In responding to Blair, for example, Baillie prefaced his criticism by reminding his former tutor 'how gladlie I would be at union in any tollerable termes'.[155] In 1637, three years before Baillie denounced Dury's ecumenical programme in his *Ladensium*, Baillie had written to Spang, '[c]oncerning Duraeis business, when ever I hear of the advancement of it, I am refreshed; yow neid put no questione on our side, for we did ever earnestlie sute it'.[156] Baillie rarely envisaged sacrificing the authority of Scriptural 'truth', and the dictates of Reformed confessions of faith and church councils for the sake of ecclesiastical reconciliation.

---

[151] Baillie, *Dissvvasive Vindicated*, p. 48.
[152] Robert Blair to Robert Baillie, 23 March 1652, LJB, vol. III, p. 175.
[153] Robert Baillie to Robert Blair, 1 April 1652, LJB, vol. III, p. 176.
[154] Robert Baillie to James Wood, 1 April 1652, LJB, vol. III, p. 177.
[155] Robert Baillie to Robert Blair, 1 April 1652, LJB, vol. III, p. 176.
[156] Robert Baillie to William Spang, 29 January 1637, LJB, vol. I, p. 9.

Baillie's defence of Strang's orthodoxy, however, suggests that he accepted that Scripture could sometimes be less clear on finer theological points that should not be allowed to disrupt national churches. This implicit acknowledgement of Scripture's ambiguity on theological minutiae highlights a tension in Baillie's writings between his acerbic denunciations of error and his desire to avoid religious strife. In the preface of his belated rejoinder to Cotton and Tombes in 1655, Baillie confessed his 'great aversenesse and constant disinclination from such publick appearances, and making of any noyse with my voice or pen, in this exceeding clamorous and tumultuous generation'.[157] This passage was, in one sense, a common plea made by an author at the start of a particularly critical tract. It was seen as unchristian to denounce co-religionists so roundly, so some such feeble gesture needed to be made towards the personal torment that had preceded publication.

In another sense, though, this disclaimer serves as a useful clue as to why so many of Baillie's theological works remained in manuscript during his lifetime, whilst also highlighting the factors that weighed on Baillie's decisions to publish. It appears that Baillie took into consideration what profit might come from furthering, in such a public and accessible form, a debate between otherwise 'godly' individuals. In the Church of Scotland, ministers often discussed the controversies of the day both in presbytery and in session – apart from their parishioners – but also in their sermons, at the front of their congregation. It was no secret to church-going Scots that Reformed Christendom was under strain through damaging internecine conflicts. Nevertheless, Baillie carefully weighed up his options and shrewdly understood the benefits as well as the harm that could follow print publication. This viewpoint, moreover, reinforces earlier arguments concerning Baillie's writings on church polity. In formulating his presbyterian vision, Baillie emphasized the importance of incorporating as many subjects in a kingdom into a unified national church as possible. The visible church was to be a peacefully unified conglomerate of elect and reprobate, instructing Christian souls in the particulars of God's 'true' and clearly revealed will. Whilst Baillie was often amongst the most zealous advocates of further theological reformation, he nevertheless recognized that such a pursuit must be controlled to prevent endless conflict and schism.

[157] Baillie, *Dissvvasive Vindicated*, sig. Ar.

5

The Five Articles of Perth, the Scottish Prayer Book and Church Discipline

The Five Articles of Perth (1618) and the Scottish Prayer Book (1637) loom large in the history of the Church of Scotland as two miscalculated, liturgical 'innovations' that galvanized presbyterian opposition to the Scottish episcopate. Historiography tends to draw a clear connection between these two sets of controversial reforms, arguing that opposition to the former presaged opposition to the latter. Following the Union of the Crowns, it is commonly argued, James VI and I and, later, his son, Charles I, were intent on reforming worship in the Scottish Church to ensure it more closely resembled that of the Church of England. In 1618, a General Assembly at Perth enacted the so-called 'Five Articles of Perth', enjoining private baptism, private communion for the infirm, episcopal confirmation of youth, observance of Holy Days and kneeling to receive communion. Whereas these reforms were enacted through a General Assembly and parliament, Charles I introduced the Prayer Book by his prerogative alone, issuing a proclamation through the Scottish Privy Council commanding its usage in December 1636. In 1637, after consultation with members of the Scottish episcopate, a version of the Anglican Book of Common Prayer was introduced for use in Scottish services.[1]

Historiographical orthodoxy purports that the introduction of these reforms exacerbated latent tensions concerning the Church's polity, thereby undermining the efficacy of its episcopate.[2] Divergent reactions to the Perth Articles and the Prayer Book have, similarly, been explained in terms of changes in Scottish politics. Opposition to the former set of reforms lacked any significant political backing, thus denuding protests of disruptive power. Combined with the reluctance of the Scottish Privy Council and other local authorities to enforce conformity to the Perth Articles, peaceful relations

---

[1] Gordon Donaldson, *The Making of the Scottish Prayer Book of 1637* (Edinburgh, 1954), pp. 41–59; Joong-Lak Kim, 'The Scottish-English-Romish Book: The Character of the Scottish Prayer Book of 1637', in Michael J. Braddick and David L. Smith (eds), *The Experience of Revolution in Stuart Britain and Ireland: Essays for John Morrill* (Cambridge, 2011), pp. 14–32.
[2] Alan R. MacDonald, *The Jacobean Kirk, 1567–1625: Sovereignty, Polity and Liturgy* (Aldershot, 1998), pp. 179–80, 186–7; David George Mullan, *Scottish Puritanism, 1590–1638* (Oxford, 2000), pp. 318–21; Laura A.M. Stewart, *Urban Politics and the British Civil Wars: Edinburgh, 1617–1653* (Leiden, 2006), pp. 176, 182.

were maintained in Scotland.[3] By contrast, in 1637, the politically weak 'Anti-Articles' movement was reinforced as a result of unconstitutional encroachments on traditional landholding and judicial rights.[4] The 1636 Book of Canons, moreover, strengthened royal and episcopal control over the Kirk, essentially obliging civil authorities to enforce conformity.[5] The Canons controversially included no mention of the Church's presbyterian courts and made it an offence punished by excommunication to deny that the monarch was the head of the Church. Accordingly, if ministers such as Robert Baillie, Andrew Ramsay or William Colville had hesitated to condemn kneeling at communion in the 1630s, by 1638, a coterie of 'radical' presbyterians were able to exploit fears of the 'idolatrous' Perth Articles to convince moderates of the need to eradicate episcopacy.[6] In other words, radicals such as Samuel Rutherford and George Gillespie seized control of the Scottish Church in 1638 and forced moderate ministers such as Baillie to abandon their more nuanced beliefs over divine worship.[7]

The differences between these two reforms are thrown into high relief if we look at Baillie's contrasting reactions to them. Whereas Baillie presented an exhaustive defence of kneeling at communion, he unequivocally denounced the Prayer Book as 'popish' and 'idolatrous'. As he explained in a letter of January 1638 to a minister in Glasgow, John Maxwell, whilst the king and his bishops 'troubled us bot with ceremonies, the world knowes we went on with them ... bot while they will have us, against standing Lawes, to devoire Arminianisme and Popery ... shall we not bear them witnes of their oppression though we should die for it, and preach the truth of God'.[8] His writings disrupt a straightforward narrative of presbyterian dissent gathering force from the late 1610s to the late 1630s. His divergent opinions of these liturgical changes were undergirded by beliefs about the theological implications of the reforms themselves. He clearly distinguished between mere 'ceremonies' and 'Arminianisme and Popery'. Moreover, as will be seen at the end of this chapter, Baillie's engagement with the intellectual cases for and against liturgical change may be detected in the ways in which he carried out his duties as a parish minister. It is not to be claimed that Baillie's practice as a minister impacted his intellectual programme, or vice versa. Rather, this

---

[3] Laura A.M. Stewart, 'The Political Repercussions of the Five Articles of Perth: A Reassessment of James VI and I's Religious Policies in Scotland', *The Sixteenth Century Journal*, 38 (2007), pp. 1013–36, at p. 1036.

[4] Stevenson, *Scottish Revolution*, pp. 42–55; Allan I. Macinnes, *Charles I and the Making of the Covenanting Movement, 1625–1641* (Edinburgh, 1991), ch. 6.

[5] Joong-Lak Kim, 'Firing in Unison? The Scottish Canons of 1636 and the English Canons of 1640', *RSCHS*, 28 (1998), pp. 55–77.

[6] Laura Stewart, '"Brothers in Treuth": Propaganda, Public Opinion and the Perth Articles Debate in Scotland', in Ralph Houlbrooke (ed.), *James VI and I: Ideas, Authority, and Government* (Aldershot, 2006), pp. 151–68, at p. 162.

[7] Mullan, *Scottish Puritanism*, pp. 62–6, 228.

[8] Robert Baillie to John Maxwell, 16 January 1638, *LJB*, vol. I, p. 30.

chapter highlights striking points of similarity that suggest theory and practice were closely linked together in his mind.

Whilst the legal and political mechanisms of their introduction were open to similar criticisms, the tendency to lump together opposition to these liturgical reforms has obscured the significance of the Perth Articles and the Prayer Book in their own right, in the context of worship in the post-Reformation Church of Scotland. Such an approach has also downplayed the novelty of the Prayer Book itself. Since 1560, worship in the Church had been loosely defined as consisting of the preached word and administration of the sacraments.[9] *The First Book of Discipline* (1560) had provided a skeletal outline whereby administration of the sacraments was to be conducted according to the 'Order of Geneva', the liturgy used by John Knox in Geneva and introduced into Scotland in 1564 – and communicants were to sit to receive the communion elements since this was the 'most convenient' posture.[10] *The Second Book of Discipline* (1578) primarily delineated the relationship between civil and ecclesiastical jurisdictions, only including a general stipulation that ministers should teach the Word of God and administer the sacraments 'as God's word prescribes to him'.[11] Protestantism was thus introduced much more peacefully and thoroughly in Scotland than in England because little further attempt was made to define an exact pattern of worship. The localized nature of ecclesiastical discipline in parish church sessions enabled a 'measured, flexible and comprehensive' implementation of reforms that adapted pre-existing practices to a Reformed pattern of worship in ways that did not offend parishioners' mores.[12] In the average parish kirk, most parishioners might only have encountered the controversial injunction to kneel on a biannual basis, but the reforms introduced by the Prayer Book would have been immediately evident in weekly services.[13]

This chapter, therefore, evaluates Baillie's contrasting reactions to the Perth Articles and the Prayer Book in light of current discussions about popular religious experience in early modern Scotland. Baillie's reactions to these changes to worship add a new layer to understandings of the origins and progress of opposition to such ecclesiastical policies in Scotland. In turn, Baillie's nuanced and calculating reactions cast prevailing assumptions about

---

[9]   The best discussion of worship in the Kirk is found in Margo Todd, *The Culture of Protestantism in Early Modern Scotland* (London, 2002), chs 1 and 2. Also see Donaldson, *Scottish Prayer Book*, pp. 3–40; William D. Maxwell, *A History of Worship in the Church of Scotland* (Oxford, 1955), pp. 43–77.

[10]   *The First Book of Discipline* (1560), Heads 1 and 2. *The Liturgy of John Knox: Received by the Church of Scotland in 1564* (Glasgow, 1889).

[11]   *The Second Book of Discipline* (1578), ch. 4 'Of the Office-Bearers in Particular, and First of the Pastors or Ministers'.

[12]   Todd, *The Culture of Protestantism*, p. 403.

[13]   Stewart, *Urban Politics*, p. 178; I.B. Cowan, 'The Five Articles of Perth', in Duncan Shaw (ed.), *Reformation and Revolution: Essays Presented to Hugh Watt* (Edinburgh, 1967), pp. 160–75; Todd, *The Culture of Protestantism*, p. 89.

worship in Covenanted Scotland in new light. The first section lays out Baillie's defence of kneeling to receive the communion elements, showing that it was consonant with both his liturgical theology and his understanding of the civil magistrate's right to determine areas of Scriptural indifference. This section shifts attention away from the well-trodden terrain of arguments against the Perth Articles put forward by critics such as David Calderwood, instead focusing on a lengthy manuscript treatise, hitherto unstudied, in which Baillie tried in vain to convince his colleague David Dickson to encourage parishioners to kneel at communion. The second section revisits Baillie's criticisms of the Prayer Book, showing that his arguments derived from careful study of its contents, read alongside the writings of its creators. Baillie's opinion of the Perth Articles in no way predisposed him to take a particular view of the Prayer Book. Indeed, nuanced views regarding worship continued to hold currency throughout Scotland well after the first subscriptions of the National Covenant in 1638. This chapter, therefore, concludes with discussion of some of the fragmentary evidence illustrative of Baillie's liturgical views during the 1640s, showing how these views impacted on his interactions with parishioners. Whilst Covenanting propaganda necessarily sought to promote an image of Scots united in their defence of 'true worship', the reality of Baillie's dealings with parishioners in Glasgow suggests a very different picture. Baillie struggled to maintain unity within his congregation that comprehended all eligible communicants. To this end, he engaged in 'conferences' or other efforts to negotiate the readmission of parishioners into communion with the Kirk. Tensions amongst the Church's ministry and its parishioners over right worship continued to fester and such latent tensions suggest that the Covenanters' anti-Laudian rhetoric was perhaps more nuanced and calculating than hitherto acknowledged.

I

Introduction of kneeling as one of the Perth Articles in 1618 encountered widespread disapproval.[14] Observance was to be enforced by individual ministers and members of the episcopate, and non-observing ministers could face punishments, such as warding, after a trial by the episcopal Court of High Commission. In effect, however, the Perth Articles were a 'public relations disaster' for James VI and I. Even his Scottish bishops were reluctant to enforce conformity to the Articles, and kneeling became such a conten-

---

[14] There have been a number of studies of the debates that followed the introduction of the Perth Articles. See John D. Ford, 'The Lawful Bonds of Scottish Society: The Five Articles of Perth, the Negative Confession and the National Covenant', *Historical Journal*, 37 (1994), pp. 45–64; Ford, 'Conformity in Conscience: The Structure of the Perth Articles Debate in Scotland, 1618–38', *Journal of Ecclesiastical History*, 46 (1995), pp. 256–77; Stewart, 'The Political Repercussions'.

tious subject in Scotland – as opposed to England – that godly Scots would have had trouble accepting, for instance, claims by the English puritan Stephen Denison that kneeling was a 'thing indifferent'.[15] Amid widespread anti-Catholic anxieties, Scottish critics believed that kneeling at the communion table implied either that the elements contained the real presence of Christ's body and blood or that communicants were worshipping the elements in an act of idolatry. Partly as a result of this heightened sensitivity to 'Romanizing' elements of worship among Scots, historians have hitherto focused on opposition to the Perth Articles, discussing defences of them only insofar as their arguments related to those of opponents such as William Scot and Calderwood.[16] Moreover, discussion of arguments *in favour* of the Perth Articles has been confined to discussion of printed texts deploying scholastic legal vocabulary in debates, ignoring altogether the sacramental significance of a parishioner's posture at the communion table discussed at length in a rich and understudied manuscript literature.

Whereas opponents of kneeling such as Calderwood and Rutherford attached sacramental and theological significance to posture at the communion table, Baillie denounced such inferences as inflammatory. In 1636, for instance, Rutherford had insisted that kneeling was tantamount to 'idolatry' in exchanges with Bishop Thomas Sydserff of Galloway, copies of which circulated in manuscript.[17] As Rutherford had argued, 'I think I see idolatrie in kneiling, which is sufficient to scare me from it.'[18] Baillie disagreed and, writing to William Spang in June 1637, commented that 'I like not weill … [Rutherford's] conclusions and reasonings in a pamphlet of his, goeing athort our people … wherein he will have our kneilling black idolatrie.' The problem, Baillie continued, was that Rutherford had claimed that Sydserff interpreted the article in question as enjoining 'reverence, to the mysterious elements' which was a position that Baillie denied even 'Papists' would defend.[19] Baillie's unwillingness to regard kneeling as idolatrous was reflected in his refusal to vote the Perth Articles 'abjured' at the General Assembly held in Glasgow in 1638. As he explained at this Assembly, abjuration of the Perth Articles would have encouraged schism within the Church because 'all shall be abjured who practised them'.[20]

---

[15]   MacDonald, *The Jacobean Kirk*, pp. 158, 170; John Coffey, 'The Problem of "Scottish Puritanism", 1590–1638', in Elizabethanne Boran and Crawford Gribben (eds), *Enforcing Reformation in Ireland and Scotland, 1550–1700* (Aldershot, 2006), pp. 66–90, at p. 87.
[16]   Such is the case in Stewart, '"Brothers in Treuth"'; Stewart, 'The Political Repercussions'.
[17]   For an extant manuscript of this document, see NLS, MS 15948, pp. 322–44. This manuscript has been published in David George Mullan (ed.), *Religious Controversy in Scotland, 1625–1639* (Edinburgh, 1998), pp. 82–99.
[18]   Samuel Rutherford and Thomas Sydserff, 'Ane discussing of some arguments against cannons and ceremonies in God's worshipe', [1636], in Mullan (ed.), *Religious Controversy*, p. 91.
[19]   Robert Baillie to William Spang, 29 June 1637, *LJB*, vol. I, p. 9.
[20]   Peterkin (ed.), *Records*, p. 170.

This stance reflected Baillie's belief that the posture taken by parishioners at communion was indifferent (*adiaphora*) in Scripture. At the time that he was writing, a handful of vocal colleagues in the Scottish pulpit had begun to argue that such facets of worship could not possibly have been left undefined and, thus in the light of divine law, a thing indifferent. If particular elements of worship were indifferent in light of the precepts laid down in God's Word, then it was potentially divisive to maintain that one posture at communion was 'necessary', whilst another was 'idolatrous'. Theological hair-splitting, Baillie believed, was unduly restrictive of contingencies arising from accepted practices and local variances across a national church. Baillie developed his thoughts on kneeling in a collection of manuscript tracts written between 1634 and 1636, aimed at convincing David Dickson, minister of the nearby parish of Irvine, that it was potentially divisive to formulate too strict a pattern of 'true' worship. This section analyses the arguments that Baillie articulated in these manuscript works, since they represent his most sustained engagement with the controversial subject of kneeling. Moreover, an exclusive focus on these manuscripts is necessary partly because of their sheer size: the largest, entitled 'A freindlie Conference betuixt tuo Ministers D. and B. anent the gesture of Communicants', extends to more than two hundred folio pages.[21] Moreover, this focus is justified because Dickson was a leading opponent of the Perth Articles and close associate of other opponents of kneeling such as Calderwood and Rutherford.[22]

For Baillie, adoration of the elements was idolatrous, but the simple act of kneeling was not. As he explained in his manuscript 'conference' with Dickson, to claim that kneeling was inherently idolatrous was a 'spurre' to ecclesiastical schism and based on 'misapplied citations of popish writers' which subsequently misled 'ignorant people' to believe that 'all kneelers doe of necessitie committ that same idolatrie which Papists doe in the adoration of their images upon apparentlie false grounds'.[23] In this sense, Baillie showed a concern with determining the legal and moral status of *adiaphora*, a central feature of the Perth Articles debates. Baillie's efforts to define the

---

[21]   See NCL, Baill MS 1, Robert Baillie, 'A peacable consideration of a paper against Kneeling', pp. 152–8; NCL, Baill MS 1, Baillie, 'A freindlie Conference betuixt tuo Ministers D and B.', pp. 158–373. A Latin translation of a portion of the latter tract is also extant in this volume, see NCL, Baill MS 1, Baillie, 'Duorum studiosorum de genuculatione; quam vocant per literas Collatio', pp. 137–52.

[22]   On Dickson's associations with the so-called 'Radical Party', see David Stevenson, 'Conventicles and the Kirk, 1619–37: The Emergence of a Radical Party', *RSCHS*, 18 (1973), pp. 99–114; Stevenson, 'The Radical Party in the Kirk, 1637–45', *Journal of Ecclesiastical History*, 25 (1974), pp. 135–65.

[23]   NCL, Baill MS 1, Robert Baillie, 'A freindlie Conference betuixt tuo Ministers D and B. anent the gesture of Communicants in the act of receiving the holie elements of the Lords supper', p. 331. Elsewhere, Baillie cited Calvin's *Institutes* book 4, chapter 17, sections 35 and 36 and the Council of Nice as denouncing 'adoration of the Sacrament and prostration befor the bread to adore Christ within it', but not specifically against kneeling (p. 175).

status of *adiaphora* reflected his anxiety that 'radical' ministers held such strict beliefs about 'true' worship that they would separate from communion with the Kirk in order to avoid involvement in services that did not conform to their models. In his correspondence with Baillie, Dickson argued that every particular element of divine worship was clearly set out in Scripture. In 1619, the dissemination of beliefs, such as Dickson's, may have encouraged hundreds of Edinburgh parishioners to attend communion services outside the town's limits, where observance was not enforced by parish ministers, or to worship privately in conventicles.[24] Alarmed by such responses, Baillie accorded considerable latitude to the lawful officers of a national church to define particulars of divine worship that he held to have been left indifferent or ambiguous in Scripture.[25]

Whilst it was not unprecedented for parish ministers to defend the act of kneeling, or simply to allow parishioners to continue to receive the communion elements by kneeling at the table, it is notable that Baillie had defended its lawfulness before becoming a Covenanter. After the Perth Assembly, some ministers ignored the prescribed changes in posture at communion, whereas others, many of whom would later become Covenanters, adopted the new posture in worship.[26] For Baillie, acts passed by the lawful institutions of a national church should be obeyed insofar as they related to points of Scriptural indifference. Although it was not unjust for a General Assembly to change a canon – even those in long and uncontested use – it was potentially divisive 'to abjure it as contrare to some article of the Confession of Faith'.[27] Before the General Assembly held in 1639, Baillie also sought Dickson's support for two proposed acts that would have removed potential opprobrium attached to more 'conservative' Covenanters, like himself, for maintaining that the Perth Articles were 'not to be unlawfull, not to be against God's word, or abjured by our church, or any church'.[28] To declare an article, such as kneeling, 'abjured' implied that the General Assembly had reason to regard such an act as contrary to Scripture. By contrast, for Baillie, since Scripture remained ambiguous, it was much more effective to declare the Articles 'inexpedient'.

Potentially more serious difficulties arose when legislative bodies attempted to make canons necessary to salvation. Following the threefold discussion of Christian liberty found in Calvin's *Institutes*, Baillie explained that 'we are obliged to obedience in the particular enacted, but our conscience is absolutelie free: our practise is free lykwayes *extra rationem contemptus et scandali*,

---

[24] Stewart, 'The Political Repercussions', pp. 1024–5.
[25] On *adiaphora* as a defining feature of the split between moderate and radical puritans in England, see Peter Lake, *Moderate Puritans and the Elizabethan Church* (paperback edn, Cambridge, 2004), pp. 242–68.
[26] Mullan, *Scottish Puritanism*, p. 76.
[27] NCL, Baill MS 1, Baillie, 'A peacable consideration', p. 155; Robert Baillie to Archibald Johnston of Wariston, [20 December 1638] *LJB*, vol. I, p. 178.
[28] Robert Baillie to David Dickson, 21 July 1639, *LJB*, vol. I, p. 180.

as Calvine teaches'.[29] Although room remained to draw more subversive conclusions from Calvin's tenets of Christian liberty, they also could be drawn on to encourage deference to established powers. Calvin's emphasis on obedience was made clear when Baillie defended the paradoxical state-ment that an unlawful change in worship could be both lawfully followed and unlawfully opposed, since the method by which a canon was introduced did not change the legality of the decree itself. Baillie thus begged Dickson to remember that, at Perth,

> the changer is our Prince, his laufull commands God commands to obey, shall those become unlaufull commands to ws befor the object be proven unlauful? As for intentions, charitie, that is to say Christianitie obleises [obliges] ws ever to think weil wher we have tolerable arguments, and that to this hour we have more nor [i.e. than] probabilities for the kings good intention in his changes, I know nought to the contrare, nether in the Praelats except suspicion whilk I hope to be false.[30]

If the Church, with Charles I's consent, were to declare kneeling removed and sitting to be a 'rite institute' then Baillie insisted he would be obliged to keep his personal views regarding Scriptural indifference on this point 'in prisoun and never to vent it for any mans hand'.[31]

If Baillie's opinions about kneeling did not hinge on whether or not its prescription was lawful, then he must have been satisfied that kneel-ing accorded with Scriptural precept. Accordingly, Baillie's correspond-ence with Dickson primarily addressed the question of which aspects of the Words of Institution – those Scriptural passages describing the Last Supper – were essential or integral to the correct practice of communion.[32] Defenders of conformity to the Perth Articles, like Baillie, were trying to negate the symbolic meanings of ceremonial gestures in the hopes of preserving local variance of liturgical practice and, by extension, a unified national church. For his part, Dickson insisted that sitting was, in fact, necessary and the only instituted 'table gesture' suitable to receive the communion elements. By contrast, Baillie held that sitting is 'not necessar, not institute, not unchangable' and that 'kneeling in the sacrament is Laufull'.[33] To claim that sitting – or kneeling, for that matter – was the posture instituted by Christ in Scripture 'layes on the conscience a burden where Christ hath made free' and also made the author of such a suggestion 'superstitious' by

[29] NCL, Baill MS 1, Baillie, 'A freindlie Conference betuixt tuo Ministers D and B.', p. 220. For Calvin's account of Christian liberty, see John Calvin, *Institutes of the Christian Religion*, trans. F.L. Battles (Atlanta, 1975), vol. VI, pp. 1–56.

[30] NCL, Baill MS 1, Baillie, 'A freindlie Conference betuixt tuo Ministers D and B.', p. 183.

[31] Ibid., p. 185.

[32] These include the accounts in the Gospels of Matthew, Mark and Luke, as well as Paul's account to the Corinthians, 1 Corinthians 11:24–5.

[33] NCL, Baill MS 1, Baillie, 'A freindlie Conference betuixt tuo Ministers D and B.', p. 158.

putting 'himself in Christs roome to mak significant rites and to joyne them as necessar parts to the holie sacrament'.[34]

Although this dispute revolved around differences of opinion regarding correct interpretations of Scripture, modern commentators have hitherto disregarded this aspect of the Perth Articles debate. To support the claim that sitting or a specific 'table gesture' was instituted by Christ at the Last Supper, Dickson and Baillie both agreed that Christians should follow Christ's example, but differed over the extent of imitation. Baillie criticized Dickson for making his rule to be whether something was 'fit' for imitation or not since to do so would be 'to joine with Scripture the light of reason, as a necessar fellow to mak up a perfite directer in the worship of God'. As Baillie pointed out, this was the same tenet that a previous generation of readers had challenged in Richard Hooker's *Laws of Ecclesiastical Polity* (1593) as 'somewhat worse then the Popish joining of tradition and scripture', which Baillie believed 'did open a large doore for humane inventions'.[35] Such reasoning would open a door to human innovation, by allowing interpreters to claim that those features deemed accidental to the circumstances surrounding the Last Supper were in fact essential, despite being inferred only from schematic portrayals of the event in Scripture.

In contrast to Dickson's definition of the Words of Institution, which he had extended to encompass the most minor elements of the sacrament's administration, Baillie adhered to a narrower definition of Christ's Institution, reflecting means adopted by some ministers to encourage discontented worshippers to return to their parish churches, rather than worshipping under nonconformist ministers or at conventicle. At Easter services in 1620, for example, Thomas Sydserf, then minister of Edinburgh, offered members of his kirk session the option of receiving the sacrament either standing, sitting or kneeling.[36] According to William Scot, a prominent opponent of kneeling, many parishioners who had hitherto left Edinburgh's churches returned once they received assurance that their ministers would not strictly insist on kneeling.[37] Whilst critics of kneeling insisted that this practice merely introduced confusion into the sacrament's administration, this shrewd compromise appears to have gained currency and may have undergirded quiescence in Scotland during the initial years of the Laudian episcopate. In May 1636, for instance, the archbishop of Glasgow enquired whether Glasgow's ministers obeyed the Book of Canons (1636), specifically 'anent geniculation'. Glasgow's presbytery records include responses from

---

[34] Ibid., p. 175.
[35] NCL, Baill MS 1, Baillie, 'A freindlie Conference betuixt tuo Ministers D and B.', pp. 162, 302.
[36] David Calderwood, *The History of the Kirk of Scotland*, ed. T. Thomson and D. Laing (8 vols, Edinburgh, 1842–49), vol. VII, p. 436.
[37] Stewart, 'The Political Repercussions', p. 1025; William Scot, *An Apologetical Narration of the State and Government of the Kirk of Scotland since the Reformation*, ed. David Laing (Edinburgh, 1846), p. 268.

thirteen ministers. James Scharpe 'answered he gave nor the communion kneeling, nor gave it out of his owne hand', whereas another, John Strang, answered that he 'keepit good order', and yet another explained that he 'gave not communion out of [his] owne hand', nor did he preach 'vpon good fryday'.[38]

Writing in 1634, familiar with local variance as it obtained throughout Glasgow's parish kirks, Baillie's defence of kneeling suggested that he may have enforced table gesture at communion in a similar way. This remains unclear since the kirk session records for Kilwinning are not extant for the period of Baillie's ministry. In his debate with Dickson, however, Baillie insisted that all facets of divine worship not explicitly mentioned in Scripture remained *adiaphora* that could, and did, vary according to time and place. The Institution simply comprised 'the words of the institution' and nothing else: 'all rites significant are expresslie mentionit within the termes of the institution'.[39] Christ's precept of imitation – 'do this in rememberance of Me' (Luke 22:19) – 'does stick onlie on the substantiall part not on the changable circumstances of those actions' and only applied to those elements of the Last Supper's account that furthered 'his purpose and were agreeable to the nature of the Sacraments'.[40] It was perfectly legitimate to deduce from the express words that communicants should receive the elements with 'humilitie, modestie, sobrietie', but deciding whether a specific 'table gesture' was included in Christ's institution necessitated discussion 'of the institution in a farre stricter sense'.[41] Baillie argued that the significant elements of worship were those that could be 'deduced by such a cleare and immediat consequence from Scripture' that all 'orthodoxe Divines' have hitherto accepted such claims.[42] Communicants were bound to *idem specie* 'or to that which doth carie both the nature and name with the rite used by Christ'; for instance, 'we have libertie to use whit, red, old, new wyne, Spanish, French but it must be wine'.[43] Christians were bound to the same kind of practice in essence, but not to accidental qualities such as the same number, time, place or posture. Such decisions had also been left to Christ's free choice in Scripture; as Baillie observed, 'Paul [also] gives warrand to change [what] is no institute'.[44] To support this claim, Baillie also cited Calvin, Beza and Robert Rollock's *In*

---

[38] Mitchell Library, Glasgow, CH2/171/3/1, Glasgow Presbytery Records, 1628–40, fo. 60r.

[39] NCL, Baill MS 1, Baillie, 'A freindlie Conference betuixt tuo Ministers D and B.', p. 163.

[40] Ibid., pp. 245, 189. On the imitation of Christ, see Giles Constable, 'The Imitation of the Divinity of Christ', in *Three Studies in Medieval Religious and Social Thought* (Cambridge, 1995), pp. 145–68.

[41] NCL, Baill MS 1, Baillie, 'A freindlie Conference betuixt tuo Ministers D and B.', p. 214.

[42] Ibid., p. 255.

[43] Ibid., p. 169. Also discussed again at p. 313.

[44] Ibid., pp. 194, 213.

Evangelium sanctum Johannem commentarius (1600), insisting that they had all likewise denied that there was any proscribed 'table gesture' in Christ's institution.[45]

Attempts to provide more extensive definitions of the Institution's terms only emerged in seventeenth-century Scottish debates after the introduction of the Perth Articles. In England, conformist divines such as Bishop Lancelot Andrewes of Winchester and Bishop John Buckeridge of Rochester 're-sacralized the act of kneeling' by arguing that it was necessary to show reverence to the elements; in Scotland, Baillie accused nonconformist divines, such as Calderwood, of overemphasizing the sacramental significance of table gestures.[46] Reviewing his position that 'table gesture' was not intended to be a rite instituted, Baillie claimed that 'all writers befor M. Catherwood [i.e. David Calderwood] are against the institution of sitting'. As Baillie saw it, Calderwood's *Perth Assembly* (1619) or, as Baillie called it, 'his Perth nullities', was the first printed work to make the claim that a particular posture at communion was Scripturally instituted.[47] On several points, Baillie cited David Lindsay's *True narration of all the passages of the proceedings in the generall assembly of the Church of Scotland* (1621 and 1625), a critical appraisal of Calderwood's *Perth Assembly*, as a valid defence of the Perth Articles that had yet to be successfully refuted.[48] Elsewhere, Baillie looked to precedents in the post-Reformation Church of Scotland to support the claim that gesture at communion was indifferent. For the most part, 'Christian writers' described the practice of standing from Pasch to Whitsunday at prayer and communion, whilst also maintaining that such a posture was 'changable in the sacrament'. Likewise, *The First Book of Discipline* was regarded as ambiguous, having simultaneously approved the practice of Geneva (standing) and stipulating that communicants should sit, evidently reflecting what Baillie took to be Knox's belief that both sitting and standing were legitimate postures. Elsewhere, Baillie claimed that the Leiden theology professors Johannes Polyander, André Rivet, Antonius Walaeus and Antoine Thysius had determined in their jointly authored 'summe of pure Divinite', the *Synopsis purioris theologiae* (1625), that all gestures at communion were 'indifferent' and, even in an English context, Baillie cited Thomas Cartwright as having

---

[45] Ibid., p. 329.
[46] Lori Anne Ferrell, 'Kneeling and the Body Politic', in Donna B. Hamilton and Richard Strier (eds), *Religion, Literature, and Politics in Post-Reformation England, 1540–1688* (Cambridge, 1996), pp. 70–92, at p. 82.
[47] NCL, Baill MS 1, Baillie, 'A freindlie Conference betuixt tuo Ministers D and B.', p. 174. Baillie took this name from the extended title of Calderwood's work, *Perth assembly. Containing 1. The proceedings thereof. 2 The proofe of the nullitie thereof. 3 Reasons presented thereto against the receiving the fiue new articles imposed. 4 The oppositenesse of it to the proceedings and oath of the whole state of the land. An. 1581 5 Proofes of the unlawfulnesse of the said fiue articles, viz. 1. Kneeling in the act of receiving the Lords Supper. 2. Holy daies. 3. Bishopping. 4. Private baptisme. 5. Private communion.* ([Leiden], 1619).
[48] NCL, Baill MS 1, Baillie, 'A freindlie Conference betuixt tuo Ministers D and B.', pp. 218, 235, 267.

'abhorred geniculation' but willing to accept sitting and standing as 'things indifferent'.[49]

Whilst Baillie certainly feared threats to the Church's unity, his tracts defending kneeling also highlighted his concerns that opponents were introducing novel interpretations of what constituted true worship in order to contest royal policies. Accordingly, Baillie charged Dickson with having 'made table gesture truelie a sacramentall seale not onlie signifieing to ws our heavenlie honour, but also … our adoption, justification, freindship with God'.[50] The problem with such a claim was that it maintained a 'needles symbolizing with Papists' over the particulars of sacramental worship.[51] By adding sacramental seals to the proceedings of communion, Dickson was committing the same error for which Protestant Reformers had criticized the papacy: adding novelties to worship. It was the duty of reformers to 'cut off corrupt parts of worship but addit none of new'.[52] Whilst Baillie hoped that subscription of the National Covenant would serve to excise 'Laudian' corruptions in the Church of Scotland's worship, he remained anxious that some members of its ministry were insisting on too strict a conception of what such worship ought to comprise.

II

Baillie's critiques of the Scottish Prayer Book of 1637 were the product of extensive research and careful reflection rather than an extension of opposition to the Perth Articles. Tendencies to assume that a minister's opposition to one liturgical 'innovation' invariably entailed opposition to all liturgical 'innovations' neglect the fact that individuals like Baillie did not view all alterations to church worship in the same way. Ultimately, most ministers were probably willing to admit some degree of change in worship that they would have deemed acceptable and, therefore, not an 'innovation' per se. This approach has also concealed the jarring novelty of the Prayer Book in the context of worship in the post-Reformation Church of Scotland. Critiques of the Prayer Book have been crudely discussed as little more than inflammatory polemic. Gordon Donaldson, for instance, dismissed Baillie's Ladensium and Parallel of the Liturgy with the Mass-Book as 'mere hysterical rants, as often as not concerned not with what was in the book but with what was not in it'.[53] David Mullan echoed such remarks, doubting the veracity of Baillie's insistence that Laud, John Cosin and other English anti-Calvinists were intent

---

[49] NCL, Baill MS 1, Baillie, 'A freindlie Conference betuixt tuo Ministers D and B.', p. 174. Also see p. 351 where Baillie cites Knox's practice in Geneva, George Wishart in Wittenberg, and Cartwright who 'was indifferent for standing or sitting'.
[50] Ibid., p. 328.
[51] Ibid., p. 329.
[52] Ibid., p. 349.
[53] Donaldson, Scottish Prayer Book, p. 71.

on returning Britain to the See of Rome's aegis, by judging such claims to be 'patently false'. As Mullan put it, otherwise 'intelligent' men such as Baillie 'set aside their critical faculties in the heightened passions of the 1630s' and simply joined the chorus of 'frequently mindless diatribes and rants'.[54] More balanced appraisal of the Prayer Book's reception has concluded that critics of Laud's policies confused his sacramentalism with Roman Catholicism.[55] Whilst it was clearly misguided to allege a genuine inclination amongst members of the English episcopate to return their Church to Rome, many puritan authors nevertheless considered anything but outright condemnation of the Roman Catholic Church as tantamount to positive acceptance of Rome's authority in the late 1630s. In this context, Baillie highlighted alarming tendencies he detected amongst members of the English and Scottish episcopate that, if taken to their logical conclusion, might seem to threaten just such an apostasy.

Baillie's correspondence indicates that he only arrived at a negative reception of the Prayer Book after extensive reflection on its text in contrast to more vehement critics, such as Rutherford, who rallied opposition before the Prayer Book had even been printed.[56] In a letter written on 27 February 1638, the day before the first subscription of the National Covenant, Baillie recollected that his first inclination had been to submit to the Prayer Book's dictates and 'construct all that cause from authoritie' – much as he had done in his defence of kneeling.[57] On the one hand, the Church of Scotland's canons and officers ought to be obeyed, but on the other, the Prayer Book had been introduced outside the lawful channels of ecclesiastical legislation (that is, a General Assembly) by a proclamation of the Privy Council. In 1638, George Gillespie had similarly argued that if a Prayer Book was to be introduced, 'then it ought to come in by a lawfull manner: by a general assemblie'.[58] As rumours emerged concerning the Prayer Book's allegedly 'Popish' content early in 1637 – including, Baillie mused, 'a very ambiguous prayer … looking much to Transubstantiation' – he resolved to 'suspend my judgement till I see the Booke'.[59] Baillie's previous record of conformity evidently led Archbishop Patrick Lindsay of Glasgow to request that he preach a sermon that would 'incite [his] hearers to the obedience and practice of the Canons of our Church and Service-Book' on 25 August.[60] The archbishop's request, however, was met with reluctance and a series of feeble excuses by which Baillie tried to avoid this obligation. Baillie pleaded that he could not

[54] Mullan (ed.), *Religious Controversy*, p. 10.
[55] Kim, 'The Scottish-English-Romish Book', p. 31.
[56] Stevenson, *Scottish Revolution*, p. 47.
[57] Robert Baillie to William Spang, 27 February [1638], *LJB*, vol. I, p. 34.
[58] [George Gillespie], *Reasons for Which the Service Booke, Urged upon Scotland Ought to Bee Refused* (Edinburgh, 1638), sig. Cr.
[59] Robert Baillie to William Spang, 29 January 1637, *LJB*, vol. I, p. 4.
[60] Robert Baillie to Patrick Lindsay, archbishop of Glasgow, 14 August 1637, *LJB*, vol. I, p. 12.

undertake such a task because he had 'not studied the matters contained in the bookes' and the little he had read had left him 'no wayes satisfied'. This was further compounded by 'the great displeasure [he] found the most part, both of pastours and people wherever I come, to have conceaved against [the Prayer Book]'.[61] Baillie was unsure of how events in Scotland would develop and, at this early juncture, he was not willing to take a public stand either for or against the recently published Prayer Book. Notwithstanding his reluctance to preach on this occasion, Baillie prepared a sermon in case his request to excuse himself was disregarded, and the text survives in manuscript.[62]

Baillie's language in his draft sermon was noticeably guarded and can be read as a subtle criticism of set forms of worship. Since 1560, the Scottish Church had never followed a liturgy akin to the English *Book of Common Prayer*. Outlines for worship found in the *First* and *Second Book of Discipline* allowed for considerable variety in divine worship throughout Scotland.[63] Accordingly, most ministers and parishioners were likely to oppose any attempt to institute set forms of worship, especially when evidently composed by leaders of a foreign episcopate. To understand Baillie's evasive language in this draft sermon, it is crucial to distinguish between his reluctance to declare both episcopacy and the Perth Articles 'abjured' at the Glasgow Assembly and his unambiguous opposition to the Prayer Book (along with the Books of Canons and Ordination and the Court of High Commission). In the cases of episcopacy and the Perth Articles, as has been shown, Baillie acknowledged that both contentious elements related to things indifferent. By contrast, the vote concerning the Prayer Book at the Glasgow Assembly had asked if its members believed the liturgy should be 'rejected and condemned' and *not* 'abjured and removed'.[64] Speaking in the Glasgow General Assembly shortly after Baillie had read an abridged version of his 'Quaeries' manuscript, Alexander Somerville, minister of Stronsay, echoed Baillie's differentiated stance on the Prayer Book and the Perth Articles. 'For as long as there was nothing concludit but the Five Articles, many were deceeved with their indifferencie; but now their courses [i.e. the bishops'] are discovered, and it is weill knowne now they are leading us toward Rome.'[65] As the moderator of the Glasgow Assembly Alexander Henderson objected, the Prayer Book had 'bein brought into the Kirk without warrant' but it also contained elements (that is, popish elements) 'abjured in our National Confessione of Faith we have latelie subscryved'.[66] Indeed, before the Glasgow Assembly convened, Charles I

---

[61] Ibid.
[62] See NLS, Adv.MS.20.6.4, Robert Baillie, Sermons, August 1637 to June 1639, fos 45r–50v.
[63] Todd, *The Culture of Protestantism*, pp. 1–23, 402–12.
[64] See Peterkin (ed.), *Records*, pp. 163–4. Cf. *Acts of the General Assembly of the Kirk of Scotland*, pp. 9–10.
[65] Peterkin (ed.), *Records*, p. 164.
[66] Ibid.

had already relented and not enforced use of the Prayer Book on account of the violent opposition its introduction had aroused.

When he had been asked to preach in favour of the Prayer Book more than a year before, in August 1637, Baillie had thus been at an impasse. He could not argue for its lawfulness on the authority by which it had been introduced, since he was already starting to question the bishops' lawful authority outside the Church's assemblies. Moreover, the extra-legal authority by which the Prayer Book had been introduced ultimately rendered moot the fact that Bishops William Forbes of Edinburgh and John Maxwell of Ross and Archbishop John Spottiswood of St Andrews had tried to ensure that particularly sensitive passages were amended to render them more consonant with existing Scottish practice.[67] As Baillie later asked in his 'Quaeries or doubts about the Scottish service booke', how could Scots accept 'a hudge number of novelties without the pretence of a law'?[68] Moreover, having not yet read the Prayer Book and having been only exposed to negative reactions, he could not construct an argument in favour of conformity based on its contents.

Ultimately, Baillie decided that he could only meditate on ministers' duties in times of disruption and took as his text 2 Timothy 4:1, 'I charge thee therefore before God'. In doing so, Baillie avoided directly engaging with vexed questions of conformity, whilst composing a sermon that may be read as subtle criticism of the Prayer Book. Baillie acknowledged to Spang that, in preaching this sermon, he would have 'spoken no syllable of any conformity, bot pressed these pastorall duties, which would not have pleased all'.[69] Indeed, the content of his sermon might have been displeasing to members of the Scottish episcopate – one of whom had asked Baillie to prepare this sermon – as well as to more vocal critics of the Prayer Book, already convinced that this innovation was ungodly and idolatrous. In the draft sermon, he also explicitly confessed that 'my weikness and Infermities ... will force me to pass sundry [points of doctrine from this verse] ontuchit'.[70] Baillie's insistence on obedience to God's laws led him to tentatively advocate a position of passive obedience. In difficult times, such as those through which Scots were then passing, cases of 'persecutions without' and 'schismes and heresies within', it was a minister's duty to preach and 'be constant, to drau soules from sin both in season and out of season'. In the Scriptural text, when Paul was 'taken ... by the tirannie of the cruell nero' and Timothy 'was to be in the laik danger of marterdome', God would send the 'faithfull pastour directions and comforts'. Accordingly, it was imperative that ministers set their eyes 'towards the lord, its good then to drau neer to God, he will mak a

---

[67] See Donaldson, *Scottish Prayer Book*, pp. 41–59.

[68] NCL, Baill MS 4/2, Robert Baillie, 'Some few Quaeries or doubts about the Scottish service booke', fo. 45r.

[69] Robert Baillie to William Spang, 4 October 1637, *LJB*, vol. I, p. 20.

[70] NLS, Adv.MS.20.6.4, Baillie, Sermons, fo. 46r.

voic come out of heaveen for our comfort and direction'. A minister's duties comprised 'reiding praying Governing, all [are] the actions of our calling at positions to this maintence of exponing and applying the word of God to illuminat the mind'. Preaching was the 'suord of the spirit wherby we arm hearers to chase away the divell', where the 'divell' could, ambiguously, be interpreted as referring either to seditious rebellion in response to the Prayer Book or, equally, to conformity to the Prayer Book. Such equivocations were, however, interspersed with clear, if somewhat lukewarm, reminders that one should 'judg nothing befor the tyme untill the lord come who will bring to light the hidden things and will mak man sort the concell of the hert'.[71] Accordingly, just as Baillie appeared to be moving away from axiomatic conformity in his letters from 1637, this draft sermon confirmed his apprehensions regarding the extent of liturgical changes that bishops might lawfully introduce in Scotland.

After careful consideration of the Prayer Book's content and its significance with regards to established patterns of worship in the Church of Scotland, Baillie explained to Spang that he felt moved 'to disapprove the Book, both for matter and manner'.[72] He had arrived at this decision late in 1637, during conversations with leading opponents of the Prayer Book in Edinburgh. Through his correspondence, we see Baillie as a shrewd scholar, carefully biding his time and keeping lines of communication open with all parties. He did not commit himself to either party too early as the conflicts were still on rocky foundations and, throughout 1637, it was unclear what exactly would come of rioting and sporadic petitioning campaigns. To substantiate his disapproval, he decided to draft a treatise, which had not hitherto been done by colleagues in Scotland, to 'prove the errors that were apparent, or might be deduced by consequence from the Book, to be the minde and avowed doctrine of the booke-makers, by testimonies of these books which Canterburie of late had printed'.[73] Baillie's treatises included lengthy discussions of material written by those responsible for the Prayer Book (but not actually in the Prayer Book itself) because he determined that this was the best way to ascertain the beliefs and motivations of its creators. For models, Baillie looked to Continental accounts of Arminian and Socinian controversies, such as Nicolaus Vedel's *Arcanorum Arminianismi* (1633 and 1634), Festus Hommius's *Specimen controversiarum Belgicarum* (1618) and Nicolaus Bodecherus's *Sociniano Remonstrantismvs* (1624).[74] All these texts laid out statements of doctrinal orthodoxy alongside quotations from authors deemed to have subverted such positions. In his *Specimen*, for example, Hommius

---

71 Ibid., fos 45r, 45v, 49v, 48r.
72 Robert Baillie to William Spang, 27 February [1638], *LJB*, vol. I, p. 34.
73 Ibid. Baillie's claim of novelty may be found at the same point: 'I had thought on a way of opposeing the Book, by God's providence, which had come in the minde of none of that company.' There is no reason to believe that this statement was inaccurate.
74 Ibid., p. 35.

divided the text by each article of the *Confessio Belgica* (1566), by show-ing the 'orthodox' position before contrasting the extent to which claims of divines such as Vorstius, Arminius and Simon Episcopius deviated from these doctrinal standards. In Baillie's case, to furnish his comparative study of the Scottish Prayer Book, he required evidence not only from 'Laudian' divines, but also from Roman Catholic practice. In April 1638, therefore, Baillie wrote again to Spang, requesting 'a Rituale Romanum, Missale, Breviarium, and Pontificale' and also 'Josephus Vicecomes de Ritibus Baptismi', thereby formulating the very best learned polemic.[75]

Reading Catholic tracts alongside treatises written by English and Scottish bishops, such as Laud, William Forbes and James Wedderburn, Baillie became convinced that the new Prayer Book was intended to introduce popish idol-atrous practices. Whether or not his critique is accurate, it is important here to examine the evidence that he mustered to support this conclusion and the methods by which he analysed his findings. Baillie's opposition to the Prayer Book's introduction underpinned his changed position on the law-fulness of defensive arms, as examined in a previous chapter. The worrying shifts in liturgical theology detected by Baillie have since been acknowl-edged as innovative by modern historians. Bryan Spinks, for example, has argued that in the 1630s, theologians such as Samuel Ward and John Forbes of Corse started to discuss the sacraments 'as instruments which actually convey grace' as opposed to seals merely confirming grace.[76] In similar vein, Anthony Milton has claimed that, during the 1630s, English ministers began to emphasize 'that justification was incomplete without the sacramental life of the church'.[77] These changes in discussions of the sacraments were closely linked to the greater authority that clerics accorded to Patristic sources over arguments from Scripture alone.[78] Whilst this shift in sacramental thought may be seen within pre-existing scholarly traditions, Baillie found it almost incomprehensible that Reformed theologians could diverge so widely.

In this context, Baillie criticized the professed 'decencie and uniformitie' that Laud and Charles I had sought to introduce into Scottish worship with the Prayer Book.[79] Individual reforms might have been objectionable for this or that reason, but taken all together this set of comprehensive reforms became dangerously inimical to established practices in the Church of Scotland. The new formalism was unwelcome in itself, but its imposition had

---

[75] Robert Baillie to William Spang, 5 April [1638], *LJB*, vol. I, p. 66.
[76] Bryan D. Spinks, *Sacraments, Ceremonies and the Stuart Divines: Sacramental Theology and Liturgy in England and Scotland, 1603–1662* (Aldershot, 2002), p. 69, and also ch. 2.
[77] Anthony Milton, *Catholic and Reformed: Roman and Protestant Churches in English Protestant Thought, 1600–1640* (Cambridge, 1995), p. 470.
[78] On the Laudians' use of Patristic sources, see Jean-Louis Quantin, *The Church of England and Christian Antiquity: The onstruction of a Confessional Identity in the 17th Century* (Oxford, 2009), pp. 155–70.
[79] [Walter Balcanquhal], *A large declaration concerning the late tumults in Scotland* (London, 1639), pp. 15–16.

been exacerbated because Scots were obliged to 'practice everie one of them [i.e. the Prayer Book's patterns of worship] under the danger to be counted Donatists and Schismaticks if we refused any of them'.[80] Comparing the Prayer Book to Roman Catholic patterns of worship thus alerted Scots to the fact that many of the new aesthetic reforms seemed very close to Catholicism. For instance, Baillie contended that passages in the Prayer Book implied that parishioners should worship the altar itself, by ordering its removal from the congregation to be placed at a church's eastern end. Baillie observed that Laud had printed 'with approbation and applause as much worshipping and adoration even of the altar, as any Papists this day living will require'.[81] The 'Canterburians', just like Roman Catholics, 'do most idolize … our blessed Virgine to whom it is well knowne they give much false worship, then true to the whole Trinity'.[82] Elsewhere, passages in the new Prayer Book also maintained the necessity of offering prayers for the dead, the *limbus patrum*, the doctrine of purgatory and the story of Christ's descent into Hell to deliver 'thence a number of Pagans such as Aristotle, Plato, Socrates'.[83]

To Baillie, evidence of crypto-popery seemed to be rife through the Prayer Book, but in order to substantiate allegations concerning its authors' intentions, he relied heavily on their other writings, setting a methodological precedent for subsequent Scottish and English proceedings against those bishops responsible for Caroline religious policy. Baillie's approach was also conducive to events at the Glasgow Assembly, where those ministers assembled sought to try the 'personall faults' and 'ministeriall errours' of the Scottish bishops.[84] Focusing on English divines, Baillie censured, for example, Anthony Stafford's *The femall glory: or, The life and death of our Blessed Lady, the holy Virgin Mary* (1635) for influencing the Prayer Book's apparent support for the doctrine of the 'invocation of Saints'.[85] Whilst Baillie highlighted passages in which Stafford had attacked puritans for refusing to offer prayers to the Virgin Mary, the fact that Stafford's meditative account of Mary's life used language that left him open to criticism certainly did not necessarily mean that Stafford himself was a Roman Catholic. Baillie also took reintroduction of the sign of the cross at baptism as potentially implying more than the Prayer Book's authors had intended. '[D]oes not this use of the crosse open a doore to all the old ceremonies in baptisme,' namely those implying an infant's regeneration.[86] In the baptismal rubric, before the catechism, Baillie detected an implication that baptized children had all things necessary for salvation, citing Montague's claim that 'children duly baptized

[80] NCL, Baill MS 4/2, Baillie, 'Quaeries', fo. 49r.
[81] Baillie, *Ladensium*, p. 52.
[82] Ibid., p. 60.
[83] Ibid., p. 81. On the controversy over Christ's local descent into Hell, see Quantin, *Church of England and Christian Antiquity*, pp. 114–30.
[84] Peterkin (ed.), *Records*, p. 164.
[85] NCL, Baill MS 4/2, Baillie, 'Quaeries', fos 45v–46v.
[86] NCL, Baill MS 4/2, Baillie, 'Quaeries', fo. 47r.

are put into the state of grace and salvation'. This was effective, yet selective, citation. Montague followed this statement by claiming that regenerated infants may later fall away totally and finally.[87]

Of all aspects of divine worship, however, it was the Canon of the Mass 'whereupon the Papist fo[u]nd love, and the Protestants just hatred is chiefly spent', which Baillie described as 'a meere logomachie of the time'.[88] Yet this war of words had been a point of long-standing and intense debate and the cause of violent conflicts throughout Western Christendom.[89] Amongst all remnants of Roman Catholicism, 'there is none so much beloved by papists, nor so much hated by Protestants, as the Masse, since the reformation of Religion, the Masse hath ever beene counted the great wall of division'. If Baillie was able to prove the Canterburians' affection for the Mass, he hoped he might thereby 'end [his] taske, having set upon the head therof this cape- stone'.[90] According to Baillie, the offertory and the prayer of consecration in the Prayer Book taught that the Mass was a propitiatory sacrifice – a sacrifice of Christ's body and blood that placated God's will – and that the prayer of consecration implied transubstantiation. Whereas the English Book of Common Prayer had changed the arrangement of the prayer of consecration, in the Scottish version, 'our men are so bold as to transplant it from this good ground to the old wicked soyle at the back of the consecration'. Thereafter, the Prayer Book included 'the words of the Masse, whereby God is besought by his omnipotent spirit so to sanctifie the oblations of bread and wine, that they may become to us Christs body and bloud' from whence 'all papists use to draw the truth of their transubstantiation'.[91]

In the Scottish Prayer Book, the explicit passages against transubstantiation found in the English version had been excised with no suggestion that Laud had opposed this decision, nor that he had ever claimed that Rome was guilty of idolatry or heresy. By contrast, Baillie had asserted that throughout all his studies he actually saw that Laud's 'favourites in their writtes' have actually 'absolved [the Roman Church] clearly in formall terms'.[92] Baillie repeated this charge throughout his *Parallel* and *Ladensium*, in which he frequently claimed that the Scottish Prayer Book more closely approximated the Roman liturgy than the English Book of Common Prayer: the Scottish Book 'doth

---

[87] Richard Montague, *Appello Caesarem A just appeale from two vnjust informers* (London, 1625), p. 36.
[88] Baillie, *Parallel*, [p. 23]. NB Numbering in the 1661 edition is inconsistent after p. 30 and resets to [p. 23] until returning to the correct numbering at p. 41. The incorrect pagi- nation, as printed, is given here in square brackets; NCL, Baill MS 4/2, Baillie, 'Quaeries', fo. 48v.
[89] For a history of post-Reformation disputes over the Eucharist see Lee Palmer Wandel, *The Eucharist in the Reformation: Incarnation and Liturgy* (Cambridge, 2006).
[90] Baillie, *Ladensium*, pp. 90, 91.
[91] Ibid., p. 107.
[92] Baillie, *Parallel*, p. 43; Baillie, *Ladensium*, pp. 44–5.

much reform the English'.[93] In his response to Baillie's *Parallel*, the Anglican religious controversialist Laurence Womock seized on this claim about the English book and thanked Baillie for showing how 'cleane the face of our Liturgie is washed from all Popish superstitions'.[94] To Baillie, however, the removal of these passages suggested that Laud, Montagu, John Pocklington and Robert Shelford all agreed with Lutherans and Roman Catholics on the subject of the 'real presence' and the only controversy remained 'the manner of the presence'.[95] These words in the *Parallel* were taken almost verbatim from Baillie's earlier manuscript 'Quaeries' in which he had asked whether it gave cause for concern that 'the divines which now caryes all in England' were prepared to grant the real presence, putting it 'out of all controversies' with Rome, whilst making this the only point 'worthie to be stood on'.[96]

Since Baillie's ideas were almost always presented in the form of critiques of Laudian writers, it is difficult to ascertain his own views on communion. His intense denial of any form of real presence – whether 'spiritual' or 'corporeal' – suggests, however, that he may have ascribed to a form of 'symbolic memorialism' or 'symbolic parallelism'.[97] This latter sacramental theology was closely linked to the Heidelberg Catechism (1563) and subsequent commentary by Zacharias Ursinus on which Baillie had taken notes during his undergraduate studies at Glasgow.[98] For Ursinus, the sacraments were 'holy visible signs and seals' and there was no transubstantiation of the elements, nor conjunction of Christ's body with the elements. Mass was a commemoration and celebration of Christ's propitiatory sacrifice on the Cross. For Baillie, this position was confirmed by surviving communion sermons, wherein he described that Christ, 'immideatly befor his suffering ordainit the holy communion [as] a perpetuall memoriall of his suffering'. Elsewhere, he explicitly meditated on 'that perfect and spotles sacrifice which Christ on the crosse offerit to God and which we in the holy sacrament ordanit to be remberit'.[99]

The growing concord that Baillie detected between Laudian and Roman Catholic authors was exemplified by their disputing the *type* of real presence, whether spiritual or corporal. He substantiated these concerns through an extensive knowledge of medieval liturgical commentaries, liturgies –

---

[93] Baillie, *Parallel*, p. 53. For other examples in the *Parallel*, see pp. 53 (for the inclusion of an extra oblation), 54–5 (implying that the Mass was a propitiatory sacrifice), 66 (alteration in the order of prayers) and 70 (removal of the 'golden sentence' that negated belief in corporal presence).
[94] Laurence Womock, *Beaten oyle for the lamps of the sanctuarie* (London, 1641), [p. 59].
[95] Baillie, *Parallel*, p. 44.
[96] NCL, Baill MS 4/2, Baillie, 'Quaeries', fo. 53r.
[97] Spinks, *Sacraments, Ceremonies and the Stuart Divines*, pp. 100–6. Baillie's sacramental views may have been very similar to those of Spinks's 'Confessional Presbyterian Divines' (roughly a cognate for Stevenson's 'Radical Party'), including Zachary Boyd and George Gillespie.
[98] See EUL, La.III.109, Robert Baillie, Student notebook, [c. 1620], pp. 248–90: 'Ex Catecheticarum explicationum Zachariae Vrsini Prolegomenis'.
[99] NLS, Adv.MS.20.6.4, Baillie, Sermons, fos 60v, 88v.

especially the eleventh-century *Sarum Rite* – and citation of Church Fathers. In debates over the real presence, Montague's writings became a frequent stalking-horse and Baillie even cited Montague's 'written recusancie', which was a manuscript tract probably received from Alexander Cunningham, wherein Montague had expressly defended the 'real and true presence of the verie bodie and blood of our savior'.[100] As indicated elsewhere in Baillie's *Parallel*, the concord that Montague sought between Roman Catholic and Protestant doctrine probably derived from Guillaume Durand's *Rationale divinorum officiorum* (c. 1286) which had denied that prayer at Mass implied consecration of the elements, but rather represented sanctification. Baillie remained unconvinced by this claim, arguing that this change in wording did not negate the implied doctrine of transubstantiation.[101] Debate over the form of Christ's presence in the elements was, as Baillie acknowledged, taken from Montague's reliance on Patristic authorities that described the Eucharist as a sacrifice. 'I hope more will be bold as our censurists to teach the fathers to speake', Baillie wrote, 'that they speake not according to the custome of the scripture.'[102] Patristic writers were valid witnesses of practices of Christian antiquity but, for Baillie, remained authoritative only insofar as their claims conformed to Scripture.

Baillie also denounced the perceived antipathy of Laud and framers of the Prayer Book towards the preached word through citation of Patristic authorities. Whilst post-Reformation worship relied on an interplay of word and sacrament, when challenged, Baillie – like many Scots – leapt to defend sermons as the central element of Protestant worship. Baillie thus recoiled at arguments of English divines, such as Robert Shelford, rector of Ringsfield in Suffolk, who had argued that the 'beauty of preaching (which is a beauty too) hath preacht away the beauty of holinesse'.[103] Drawing on the ordinals of Justin Martyr and Dionysius the Areopagite, the sermons of Cyprian, Basil, Ambrose and Augustine, and canons from the First Lateran Council (1123) and the Second Council of Toledo (527), Baillie found ample evidence 'that in all antiquity, to the very latest and most corrupt times, the care not of reading only, but preaching was seriously recommended to all Bishops and presbyters'.[104] Accordingly, Baillie alleged that Laud was even more hostile to preaching on the Sabbath than Roman Catholics who had sat at the Council of Trent and made 'it needfull to preach every Sabbath'.

---

[100] NCL, Baill MS 4/2, Baillie, 'Quaeries', fo. 53r–v. For Baillie's instructions to Cunningham, see 'My instructions to Mr. Alexander Cunighame [sic]', n.d. *LJB*, vol. I, pp. 225–8. For a modern edition of this tract, see Alexandra Walsham and Anthony Milton, 'Richard Montagu: "Concerning Recusancie of Communion with the Church of England"', in Stephen Taylor (ed.), *From Cranmer to Davidson: A Church of England Miscellany* (Woodbridge, 1999), pp. 69–101.
[101] Baillie, *Parallel*, [pp. 27–8].
[102] NCL, Baill MS 4/2, Baillie, 'Quaeries', fo. 49v.
[103] Robert Shelford, *Five pious and learned discourses* (London, 1635), p. 12
[104] Ibid., p. 24.

Taking this as evidence of a greater Romanizing threat, Baillie argued that the Canterburians avowed 'the great expediency to put down preaching' because of a desire 'to keepe the people in their ancient simplicitie, and so in that old laudable integritie and devotion'.[105] In similar vein, Gillespie had denounced the introduction of set forms of worship in the Church as 'high soaring fancies and presumptuous conceits' that distracted Christians from 'the Word of righteousnesse'.[106] Considering that Scottish worship typically comprised two long sermons every Sunday – much more than was typical of English practice – it is unsurprising that Laud regarded Scottish sermonizing to be excessive. In Baillie's mind, however, any reduction of sermon frequency presaged elimination. This nervousness or alarmism is evident throughout Baillie's polemical writings and is indicative of a broader character of similar works of his day. Much like political pundits today, Baillie would seize on any subtle indication of a nefarious trend and claim that the worst possible outcome was imminent. The Laudians, he wrote, wanted to limit preaching to 'some few of singular learning and eloquence ... only at rare and extraordinary times' and only undertaken in the 'greatest Townes in the most solemne times but once a day'.[107] Adherence to the new Prayer Book thus threatened to turn ministers into readers, parroting an unbiblical script to lead divine worship. For Baillie, Shelford and the Laudians were perverting divine worship by claiming that 'the pithe of godliness, the heart of religion' was the Prayer Book.[108]

III

Although Baillie was certainly concerned with the means by which the Perth Articles and the Prayer Book had been introduced, these anxieties proved, ultimately, secondary to his crucial views regarding the liturgical alterations. More broadly, historians should be cautious when analysing reactions to liturgical change, despite a pronounced willingness to disregard such nuanced views about worship in the Church of Scotland after 1638. As one prominent commentator observed, 'those who would soon be in the van of the covenanting movement had little room for nuanced views' on kneeling, such as those promulgated by Baillie, and all Scottish presbyterians were prepared to label the Prayer Book 'Popish'.[109] By conflating opposition to the Prayer Book

---

[105] Baillie, *Parallel*, p. 25. Cf. NCL, Baill MS 4/2, Baillie, 'Quaeries', fo. 52r. Here, Baillie cites Shelford's *Five pious and learned discourses* (1635) saying that preaching should be kept down so that 'people may be reduced to that old ignorance and simplicity which was in our forefathers'.

[106] [Gillespie], *A dispvte against the English-popish Ceremonies*, sig. A4r.

[107] Baillie, *Ladensium*, pp. 92, 93. On sermons in the post-Reformation Kirk, see Todd, *The Culture of Protestantism*, pp. 24–5.

[108] NCL, Baill MS 4/2, Baillie, 'Quaeries', fo. 52r.

[109] Mullan, *Scottish Puritanism*, p. 233.

and opposition to kneeling under the broad category of 'anti-Catholicism', historiographical orthodoxy has failed to appreciate the variety of opinions that existed on kneeling, or many other facets of worship, in an attempt to emphasize the rhetorical schism opening up between the Scottish episcopate and presbyterian ministers.

A facade of presbyterian unity merely cloaked the diversity of beliefs that characterized worship in the Church of Scotland. Subscribers of the National Covenant continued to hold distinctive views about how worship in the Church of Scotland should be structured. The Covenanters' legislative victory at the Glasgow Assembly in 1638 did not introduce uniform liturgical practice in the Kirk.[110] Reception of the Glasgow Assembly's reforms and the National Covenant itself continued to be coloured by a range of complex perceptions and entrenched behaviours that had gradually shaped worship in the Church since the Reformation.[111] After Baillie joined the Covenanting movement and began writing pieces to justify its actions, the tone of his writings may have changed – not least, because he changed medium from manuscript to print – but he still retained his carefully formulated beliefs on worship. Throughout both his *Ladensium* and *Parallel*, Baillie never denounced kneeling as idolatrous in itself and nor did he ever claim that a particular posture to receive communion was Scripturally warranted. He came closest to doing so in his *Ladensium*, when discussing a manuscript that he had discovered, written by the former bishop of Edinburgh William Forbes. Recounting Forbes's views, Baillie claimed that Forbes had taught that it was proper to 'give outward adoration in the Sacrament ... to adore with our body the blessed Body of Christ, which we with our very body doe receive'.[112] The relationship of kneeling to these acts was, however, only conjectural. As Baillie concluded, 'this was the man who penned our Perth Article concerning geniculation, what hee intended to bring into our Kirke by this ceremony, it is apparent by these Doctrines'.[113] Fragments of later evidence likewise suggest that Baillie had not changed his mind about the theological significance of kneeling. In March 1643, he corresponded with a former minister of Kilpatrick who had been deposed by the Glasgow General Assembly, James Forsyth; attempting to assuage Forsyth's doubts about the National Covenant, Baillie emphasized that 'I remember not that our Covenant tyes yow to call the articles of Perth either Popish or superstitious or idolatrous.'[114]

Baillie and other ministerial colleagues continued to correspond with ministers like Forsyth, who were trying to negotiate their allegiance with the

---

[110] Stevenson, 'Conventicles in the Kirk', p. 112.
[111] Laura A.M. Stewart, 'Authority, Agency and the Reception of the Scottish National Covenant of 1638', in Robert Armstrong and Tadhg Ó hAnnracháin (eds), *Insular Christianity: Alternative Models of the Church in Britain and Ireland, c. 1570–c. 1700* (Manchester, 2013), pp. 88–106.
[112] Baillie, 'Large Supplement', in *Ladensium*, pp. 42, 43.
[113] Ibid., p. 44.
[114] NCL, Baill MS 1, Robert Baillie to James Forsyth, 8 March 1643, p. 381.

Covenants. After subscription of the National Covenant, divisions also persisted over how the godly should react to changes in worship as well as over the potential removal of other established elements of worship considered by some radicals to have been 'superstitious', such as reading the creed, set prayers, bowing in the pulpit and singing doxologies. Whilst few traces of these conflicts are detectable in Baillie's published works, one manuscript account details a 'conference' Baillie had with a few unnamed 'yeomen' from his congregation at the Tron Kirk, Glasgow, a post Baillie held in conjunction with his divinity professorship.[115] It is unclear to whom Baillie exactly referred as 'yeomen', but considering that the Tron Kirk was in the mercantile district of Glasgow, it is likely that these men were minor landowners whose wealth primarily derived from trade. As will emerge, these men were sufficiently alert to the particular implications of elements of divine worship to voice conscientious objections. Discussion of this dispute also sheds light on how Baillie consulted with his congregation and illustrates the extent to which his ministerial duties influenced his writings on worship. This 'conference' occurred a month after Glasgow presbytery had remonstrated with the Town Council to fill vacant ministerial charges to defray the burden shouldered by the current ministers and to combat moral laxity that had arisen in the town. Robert Ramsay enumerated the extensive duties that ministers were expected to fulfil: 'weeklie catechizing', 'erecting of familie worship and instruction of children and servants', the 'visitation of families by the pastors and elders', the 'visitation of ye sick', the 'visitation of schooles speciallie qr onelie english is taucht', the 'pastorall care of some hundreth … disollut young … vaging without dayelie in the streits'. Edward Wright's petition explained that, in Glasgow, 'more vices and great discord both in young ones and in old ones are not taken notice of'.[116] This episode may be read alongside evidence gleaned from the Glasgow Presbytery Records, illustrative of Baillie's practice as a minister. Bridging the divide between learned conferences and popular worship, this discussion also serves as an appropriate way to conclude this chapter.

In April 1643, Baillie held a meeting with a few members of his congregation in Glasgow because they had previously refused to sing a 'conclusion' to prayers: 'Glorie be to God for ever'. No other records of this dispute are extant, but from Baillie's account the aggrieved parishioners had evidently argued that a sung conclusion was 'Popish' and 'Superstitious'.[117] In May

---

115 The copy that will be quoted may be found in NCL, Baill MS 1, Robert Baillie, 'The summe of my conference yesterday with three or four yeomen of my flock who refused to sing the Conclusion', pp. 385–7. For the date, 12 April 1643, see the copy of this manuscript in Baill MS 4/2, fos 129r–130r. For Baillie's appointment at the Tron Kirk, see FES, vol. III, p. 474.

116 Mitchell Library, Glasgow, CH2/171/3/2, Glasgow Presbytery Records, 1641–46, fos 143v, 144r.

117 NCL, Baill MS 1, Robert Baillie, 'The summe of my conference yesterday with three or four yeomen', p. 385.

1645, the Glasgow Presbytery likewise heard the petition of the minister, Robert Tron, who complained that his parishioners disrespected the sung conclusion to the Psalms by refusing to remove their 'bonnets'.[118] At the outset of the conference, Baillie reminded his parishioners not to 'neglect … that duetie whilk yow ought in conscience towards my ministrie, which yow say, and I beleeve yow, is verie dear to yow'. Neglect of one minor aspect of divine worship, Baillie feared, was 'one of the first links of the whole chaine of Brunisme [i.e. Brownism]'. Before long, disgruntled parishioners might seek to discard the Psalms, set prayers, the sacraments and, ultimately, the whole established church.[119] Baillie also denied their claim that a sung conclusion was 'an humane Popish invention', observing that although 'it is a part of the Liturgie and Masse Booke too … this proves it not to be anie worse then the Lords prayer … in these evill books'. Whilst the Prayer Book might be abhorrent as a whole, 'manie things' contained therein are 'no more the worse for the standing in these evil places, than the sunbeams for shining on a dunghill'.[120]

Whilst none denounced the Church of Scotland as a false Church, vituperative characterization of certain aspects of its worship – as either inexpedient or idolatrous – largely determined whether a minister or lay-person would persevere in communion with the national church or retreat to a 'purer' form of worship conducted in a conventicle.[121] Throughout his career as a minister and member of the Glasgow presbytery, Baillie emerged as a strong proponent of reconciliation. When, for instance, he was called away to attend negotiations in Breda with Charles II in 1649, his absence as moderator of Glasgow presbytery was immediately felt. Patrick Gillespie took charge, and ongoing negotiations to readmit supporters of Hamilton's defeated royalist engagement took on a very different tone. Proceedings against David Spense, clerk of Rutherglen session, and the Glaswegian regent, William Willkie, were briskly concluded with decisions against them. Whereas Gillespie heeded calls for a 'chirugion [in Rutherglen] for cutting off ane hudge Lumpe and swelling in thir Kirk', Wilkie remarked in shock at 'a sudden [when] the sentence was pronounced whereas the process shew the contrary'.[122] Given how this chapter has portrayed Baillie as a calculating and open-minded respondent to divergent opinions, it is hardly likely that such decisions would have been made had he remained in charge of the Glasgow presbytery early in 1649. Baillie's approach to the controversial act of kneeling and his careful appraisal of the Prayer Book continued to shape,

---

[118] Mitchell Library, Glasgow, CH2/171/3/2, Glasgow Presbytery Records, 1641–46, fo. 170r.

[119] NCL, Baill MS 1, Robert Baillie, 'The summe of my conference yesterday with three or four yeomen', p. 385.

[120] Ibid., p. 386.

[121] Stevenson, 'Conventicles in the Kirk'.

[122] Mitchell Library, Glasgow, CH2/171/4, Glasgow Presbytery Records, 1647–51, fos 85v, 91r.

and be shaped by, interactions with his parishioners, as well as ministerial colleagues such as Rutherford, Gillespie or Dickson, who agitated for further liturgical reforms after the Covenanters gained political power. The ascendancy of more radical ministers in 1638 was, however, perhaps aided as much by an injection of noble support as by widespread resentment of the Prayer Book. Indeed, noble perceptions of the Prayer Book should not be discounted without further research as a potentially crucial factor influencing their allegiance in the wake of the National Covenant's subscription. Events in 1638 did not mark a triumph of radical opinion over more reluctant voices, such as that of Baillie. Instead, the Covenanting leadership, led by moderates like Baillie, made concerted attempts to accommodate vastly divergent opinions on divine worship within an uncompromising, but subtle, anti-Laudian rhetoric in the years before civil war broke out in England.

6

Biblical Scholarship and the Sermon

The central pillar of intellectual life in seventeenth-century Scotland, the Bible, also lay at the heart of Robert Baillie's writings.[1] Study of early modern Scottish thinkers has, however, often risked historiographical neglect precisely because of a perceived myopic fascination with the Bible. The Victorian scholar Henry Buckle thus dismissed seventeenth-century Scotland as dominated by a 'monkish rabble' – 'the Baillies, the Binnings, the Dicksons ... the Hendersons, [and] the Rutherfords' – who blindly defended Scripture's authority.[2] For Hugh Trevor-Roper, Scotland's four universities were 'the unreformed seminaries of a fanatical clergy', whilst for T.C. Smout, any innovation at Glasgow University was suppressed by 'the most crushingly Calvinist ecclesiastics, such as Robert Baillie'.[3] Even the presbyterian minister and erstwhile Historiographer Royal George Henderson felt obliged to apologize for the fact that 'Scottish culture in the seventeenth century was not very impressive'.[4] More recently, Alasdair Raffe has argued that, in 1660, Scotland 'possessed a common religious culture, the legacy of two decades of presbyterian dominance'.[5] Such assumptions have, in turn, perpetuated a tendency to cast 'Calvinist' or 'Presbyterian' writers as invariably inimical to intellectual diversity whereas 'heterodox' thinkers are portrayed

---

[1] For overviews of the centrality of the Bible in Protestant Scotland, see David George Mullan, *Scottish Puritanism, 1590–1638* (Oxford, 2000), ch. 2; Margo Todd, *The Culture of Protestantism in Early Modern Scotland* (London, 2002), pp. 24–83; G.D. Henderson, 'The Bible in Seventeenth-Century Scotland', in *Religious Life in Seventeenth-Century Scotland* (Cambridge, 1937, reprinted 2011), ch. 1.
[2] H.T. Buckle, *History of Civilization in England* (2 vols, London, 1857–61), vol. II, p. 579. For more recent accounts of Buckle's negative influence over Scottish historiography, see David Allan, *Virtue, Learning and the Scottish Enlightenment* (Edinburgh, 1993), pp. 1–9; Clare Jackson, *Restoration Scotland, 1660–1690: Royalist Politics, Religion and Ideas* (Woodbridge, 2003), pp. 1–6.
[3] Hugh Trevor-Roper, 'The Scottish Enlightenment', in *Studies on Voltaire and the Eighteenth Century*, lviii (Oxford, 1967), pp. 1635–58, at p. 1636; T.C. Smout, *A History of the Scottish People, 1560–1830* (London, 1969), p. 187.
[4] Henderson, *Religious Life*, p. 117.
[5] Alasdair Raffe, 'Presbyterians and Episcopalians: The Formation of Confessional Cultures in Scotland, 1660–1715', *English Historical Review*, 125 (2010), pp. 570–98, at p. 570.

as driving intellectual change.[6] Consequently, our understanding of how Scottish theologians such as Baillie interpreted the Biblical text remains limited to polemical caricature. How did Baillie interpret the Biblical text and from what intellectual traditions did he derive his exegetical approach? Why was teaching and scholarship at the Scottish university so focused on critical and practical analysis of the Bible? And how did a minister's understanding of the doctrinal concept of Scriptural self-sufficiency inform their preaching?

To answer these questions, this chapter illuminates the place of the Bible in Scottish intellectual and religious culture through a study of Baillie's writings. In particular, it addresses Baillie's analysis of the Bible in his Biblical chronology and in his sermons. It is primarily concerned with understanding how Baillie interpreted and communicated Scripture's diverse meanings as well as how he accounted for the numerous textual inconsistencies he encountered. Like many contemporaries, Baillie approached the Bible with preconceptions about its origins and authenticity; in other words, he held a particular set of convictions that may be referred to as a 'doctrine of Scripture'. Baillie's approach was guided by the belief that God had revealed the Biblical text directly to the Prophets and the Apostles and that its message was self-sufficient. Drawing on the Protestant doctrine *sola scriptura*, Baillie was confident that Scripture alone contained all that was necessary to salvation. Such a belief was, for example, enshrined in the Westminster Confession of Faith – adopted by the Church of Scotland in August 1647 – which confirmed that God had declared his 'Will unto his Church', committing it 'wholly unto writing; which maketh the holy Scripture to bee most necessary'.[7] Baillie likewise claimed that Scriptural truths were clear (*perspicuam*) to all Christians 'in whom the Spirit of God [had] roused the ordinary talents of reading, praying and other means of diligent study' so that they could perceive 'all that is necessary for salvation'.[8]

During Baillie's lifetime, however, both Roman Catholic and Protestant scholars alike began to present arguments that threatened to cast doubt on claims that the Bible provided Christians with an uncorrupted record of God's Word.[9] To Reformed Protestants, such scholarship simultaneously threatened the sermon's authority in divine worship. For Roman Catholics, such as the reformer Robert Bellarmine and the ecclesiastical historian Caesar Baronius, Scripture alone was held to be insufficient, meaning that the Roman Church's traditions were also necessary to guide Christians to

---

[6] For a recent manifestation of this trend, see John Robertson and Sarah Mortimer (eds), *The Intellectual Consequences of Religious Heterodoxy, 1600–1750* (Leiden, 2012).

[7] *The confession of faith, and the larger and shorter catechisme* (Edinburgh, 1649), pp. 1–2.

[8] NCL, Baill MS 1, Robert Baillie, 'Commentariolus de praecipuis Pontificiorum erroribus', [n.d], p. 427.

[9] The following paragraph largely follows an outline of this intellectual found in works such as Anthony Grafton, *Defenders of the Text: The Traditions of Scholarship in an Age of Science, 1450–1800* (Cambridge, Mass., 1991); Noel Malcolm, 'Hobbes, Ezra and the Bible: The History of a Subversive Idea', in *Aspects of Hobbes* (Oxford, 2002), pp. 383–431.

salvation. More broadly, Protestant and Roman Catholic theologians also began to apply humanist methods of textual criticism to their study of the Bible's ancient codices. By treating the Hebrew and Greek texts of the Old and New Testament in the same way as other ancient texts, orthodox theologians, such as André Rivet and Louis Cappel sought to uphold Scripture's divine authority by uncovering the divinely inspired original (or ur-text) from which subsequent editions and translations had been derived. Introduction of methods of textual criticism and the concomitant historicization of the Bible had, however, an unintended consequence of highlighting its undeniably human origins. By the middle of the seventeenth century, Isaac La Peyrère, Thomas Hobbes and Baruch Spinoza had all argued that textual inconsistencies in the first five books of the Hebrew Old Testament (the Pentateuch) indicated that they could not have been written by Moses, thus severing the link between God's divine intellect and the Bible.[10] Whilst few seventeenth-century scholars questioned Scripture's divine origins outright, resolute defenders of Scriptural self-sufficiency such as Baillie viewed developments in the textual-critical analysis of Scripture with suspicion. To question the authority of the Hebrew Old Testament, for Baillie, was 'Pyronnian skepticism and true atheism'.[11] 'Against this new religion,' wrote Baillie, 'I wish that our mindes may be well establyshed by the scriptures.'[12]

The means by which Baillie sought to enlighten Christian minds by Scripture were shaped through the interaction of his confessional commitments and his scholarly erudition. Much like early modern scholars who simultaneously deployed scholastic and humanist methods of textual criticism; or, like those early scientific thinkers who seized on the Bible as a starting point from which to understand the natural world; or, like those great works of English Patristic scholarship that contributed to the formation of a distinctive 'Anglican' confessional identity, Baillie's belief in Scriptural self-sufficiency underlay his critical engagement with the Bible in his scholarly work and in his surviving sermons.[13] Baillie's engagement with scholarly debates concerning Old Testament chronology – in his published work and in the lecture theatre – was initiated by the Covenanting regime's official drive to make worship increasingly centred on the word preached.[14]

---

[10]   Malcolm, 'Hobbes, Ezra and the Bible', p. 398.
[11]   Baillie, *Operis Historici et Chronologici*, lib. I, p. 12.
[12]   NCL, Baill MS 1, Robert Baillie 'A Conference by letters with a Canterburian minister anent the Arminian tenet of the Saints apostasie', [1634–36], p. 1.
[13]   Grafton, *Defenders of the Text*, pp. 4–5; Richard A. Muller, 'Calvin and the "Calvinists": Assessing Continuities and Discontinuities between the Reformation and Orthodoxy', *Calvin Theological Journal*, 30 (1995), pp. 345–75, and 31 (1996), pp. 125–60; Jitse M. van der Meer and Scott Mandelbrote, 'Introduction', in Meer and Mandelbrote (eds), *Nature and Scripture in the Abrahamic Religions: Up to 1700* (2 vols, Leiden, 2008), vol. I, pp. 3–34, at p. 6; Jean-Louis Quantin, *The Church of England and Christian Antiquity: The Construction of a Confessional Identity in the 17th Century* (Oxford, 2009).
[14]   Crawford Gribben, 'Introduction', in Gribben and David George Mullan (eds), *Literature and the Scottish Reformation* (Aldershot, 2009), pp. 1–20, at p. 14.

In particular, this legislative programme attempted to improve the quality of ministers entering the profession by standardizing the range of subjects on which candidates were examined. Baillie, therefore, wrote the *Operis Historici*, and taught Biblical chronology to students at Glasgow expressly for the purpose of preparing them to undergo their trials and examination to join the ministry. It is little wonder, then, that we find Baillie implementing in practice, in the pulpit, a method of preaching that adhered to, and even reinforced, his scholarly understanding of the authority of the Biblical text. Biblical studies may have grown rapidly in Glasgow as a result of the pronounced Biblicism of Scottish worship at this juncture, but the two trends were linked together in a far more symbiotic relationship than has hitherto been acknowledged.

Baillie's exegetical method in both his scholarly and homiletic writings demonstrated a careful awareness to present the Bible in light of its self-sufficient authority. Baillie rallied his own erudite knowledge of the Greek, Hebrew and Latin codices of the Bible and meticulous philological scholarship to defend a particularly rigid, even obstinate, conception of Scripture's self-sufficiency. This detailed knowledge of the Biblical text informed the style and content of Baillie's sermons, albeit he rarely addressed Scripture's textual complexities in the pulpit. In practical terms, Baillie taught chronology at Glasgow University and he wrote lectures on the subject, in the first place because ministerial candidates were expected to demonstrate their knowledge of the subject during trials before their admission to a vacant parish charge. The first section of this chapter considers the extent to which Baillie's confessional commitments influenced his scholarly investigation of Biblical chronology in his posthumous *Operis Historici et Chronologici* (1663) by discussing the context of his chronology's composition and the precepts governing its formal organization. The second section explores how Baillie's preaching method was informed by his belief in a Reformed doctrine of Scripture. Although recent accounts of early modern sermon literature have emphasized the emotive elements of a sermon's oral performance, downplaying the dry intellectual rigour that had previously been considered characteristic of early modern preaching, it is still crucial to account for the close relationship between a minister's ideas about Scriptural authority and the style of their sermons.[15] Whereas intellectual innovation has traditionally been ascribed to particular 'heterodox' thinkers, reading of Baillie's works on Biblical authority shows that, in his mind, some of the most worrying challenges to Scriptural self-sufficiency arose from the pulpits of other ministers.

---

[15]   For an overview of this debate in a recent work that emphasizes the affective elements of preaching, see Arnold Hunt, *The Art of Hearing: English Preachers and Their Audiences, 1590–1640* (Cambridge, 2010), pp. 81–3.

I

Baillie's *Operis Historici et Chronologici* presented a sustained defence of Scripture's self-sufficiency based on the belief that the Hebrew Old Testament was the inspired and infallible Word of God.[16] Moreover, it evinces a tension between the pursuit of scholarly inquiry and Baillie's desire to defend the belief that 'the Hebrew and Greek fonts of Scripture are immediately from God'.[17] In this vein, Baillie grappled with problems that stemmed from the introduction of humanist methods of textual criticism into the practice of Biblical exegesis, which were increasingly drawing attention to the fact that the Biblical text had an undeniably human history.[18] Through passages dealing with philological controversies over the relative authority of the Greek and Hebrew Biblical texts, Baillie drew clear lines between 'orthodoxy' and 'heterodoxy'. On points of technical chronology, however, such lines became more blurred as Baillie often disagreed with authors with whom he had elsewhere expressed approval, or vice versa.

Baillie's *Operis Historici et Chronologici* addressed a contemporary philological controversy regarding the origins of Hebrew vowel points as well as the authority of the Hebrew Old Testament in relation to the Greek Septuagint and the Latin Vulgate. Debates over Hebrew vowel points illustrated how developments in scholarly method were starting to challenge Christian conceptions of the Bible's authority, marking a broader transition from Biblical exegesis according to principles of faith, towards a more rigorous, textual exegesis, characteristic of modern Biblical scholarship.[19] In today's accounts, the earliest texts of the Hebrew Old Testament were only consonantal and were consequently rife with ambiguities, variant readings and obscure meanings. Vowel points were only added in the first millennium after Christ's death as a pronunciation aid. This vowel-pointed text, known as the 'Masorah', became standardized around the tenth century and included commentaries and, crucially, variant readings of passages. Thereafter, scholars started claiming either that the Biblical scribe Ezra had composed the pointed text or that the pointed text was that which God had revealed to Moses on Mount Sinai. By the sixteenth century, Protestant discussions of Scriptural self-sufficiency were thus informed by the relatively uncontested belief that the Masoretic text was God's inspired and infallible Word.

Whilst confidence attached to this belief well into the seventeenth and eighteenth centuries – and it may be detected in Baillie's formulation of Scriptural authority – other scholars were increasingly questioning the

---

[16] Baillie defended the Hebrew text of the Old Testament which was reproduced in the so-called 'Second Rabbinic Bible', first printed by Daniel Bomberg in Venice in 1525.

[17] NCL, Baill MS 1, 'Commentariolus', p. 423.

[18] Grafton, *Defenders of the Text*; Malcolm, 'Hobbes, Ezra and the Bible'.

[19] Richard A. Muller, 'The Debate over the Vowel Points and the Crisis in Orthodox Hermeneutics', in *After Calvin: Studies in the Development of a Theological Tradition* (Oxford, 2000), pp. 146–55, at p. 146.

antiquity and divinity of the Hebrew vowel points from the early sixteenth century onwards.[20] By comparing the Masoretic vowel-pointing with the Talmud and Midrash, the Hebrew grammarian Elias Levita concluded in 1538 that the vowel points probably represented a human addition to the text, on account of the Masorah's inclusion of variant readings. If the vowel points were revealed by God, there would have been no textual variations.[21] It was not until the seventeenth century, however, that this controversy entered a new phase amongst Protestant scholars that affected how theologians conceived of Scriptural authority. To explain the existence of textual variants, the Hebraist Johannes Buxtorf I argued that Ezra and the members of the Great Synagogue had fixed the vowel points in the text.[22] Centuries later, when the Massoretes set about compiling an authoritative text, they had evidently acted as editors compiling variant readings accrued through centuries of textual transmission. Regarding the implications that this research had on Protestant doctrine, Buxtorf argued that it was not only the consonants but also the vowel points of the Hebrew text that needed to be immutable, since the latter 'are the soul of the words, the vivifying spirit'. Whereas the Hebrew text needed to be stable and immutable for Buxtorf's doctrinal affirmations, for the French Huguenot scholar Louis Cappel the Masoretic text was fundamentally unstable and susceptible to human corruptions.[23] Cappel's *Arcanum punctuationis revelatum* (1624) and his *Critica Sacra* (1650) presented a devastating series of arguments that undermined the divine origins of the vowel points. Although Cappel thus deemed the text unstable, he nevertheless claimed that a reliable meaning could be extracted from the consonantal text through a rigorous textual-critical method which compared the Hebrew with other ancient translations such as the Chaldean and Samaritan. Shortly afterwards in his prolegomena for the London Polyglot Bible (1657), Brian Walton affirmed Cappel's arguments concerning the relative authority of the Masorah, but stopped short of Cappel's more destabilizing claim regarding the uncertainty of the received Hebrew text. Whereas Cappel had argued that the Masoretic text was fundamentally corrupted, Walton argued that the Hebrew text could be used as the basis to reconstruct the divine original.

It was in this lively intellectual context that Baillie began studying and teaching Biblical chronology. He first composed his Biblical chronology as a series of lectures dictated to his students as divinity professor at Glasgow University. Although the pedagogical context of its initial composition is not evident in the published version, an earlier manuscript contains an extended title, written in Baillie's hand, which describes the work as a 'com-

---

[20] For an overview of this debate, see ibid., pp. 146–55.

[21] Elias Levita, *Massoreth Hamasoreth* (1538).

[22] Johannes Buxtorf, *Tiberias sive commentarius Masorethicus triplex: historicus, didacticus, criticus* (Basel, 1620).

[23] François Laplanche, *L'Écriture, le sacré et l'histoire: Érudits et politiques protestants devant la Bible en France au XVIIe siècle* (Amsterdam, 1986), pp. 229–43.

pendious account' wherein 'common questions and dubious places of chronology from both Testaments are explained briefly and clearly' to students studying theology at Glasgow from 1650 onwards.[24] Instruction in Biblical chronology, controversies and Hebrew was undertaken with practical ends in mind. According to an act of the 1638 Glasgow Assembly, expectant ministers were required to undergo a thorough trial and demonstration of their knowledge, including being 'questioned by the Presbyterie upon questions of controversie, and chronologie [and] anent particular texts of Scripture how they may be interpreted according to the analogie of Faith'. Alongside this foundational act, other official statements were issued in August 1639 and August 1641, reaffirming the Church's commitment to examining prospective ministers thoroughly.[25] In line with these prescriptions, we find Glasgow presbytery, Baillie's local authority, demanding that expectants be examined on these subjects, including chronology.[26] Given the subject's complexities, Baillie's succinct and lucid account of Biblical chronology from the Creation to the reign of Constantine represents an impressive feat – and, certainly, an invaluable resource for young trainees interested in a career in the ministry. By contrast, a pre-eminent humanist scholar such as Joseph Scaliger spent his entire life carefully studying an enormous array of Biblical and pagan sources and accruing technical expertise in subjects such as ancient astronomy and numismatics. Structurally, Baillie's format of brief expositions of controversies over particular elements of Old Testament chronology was probably informed by his study of post-Ramist compendia during his undergraduate arts degree. Post-Ramist pedagogical tracts, such as Bartholomäus Keckermann's posthumous *Systema physicum* (1610), provided lecturers with succinct summaries of subjects suitable for dictation to students. As divinity professor, Baillie was evidently moved to publish similarly structured compendia on Hebrew grammar and religious controversies in 1653 and 1654, as part of a broader movement to produce standard Reformed 'textbooks' for use in Scotland's universities and no doubt intended also to aid expectants as they prepared for their trials before joining the ministry.[27]

Accordingly, Baillie's chapters in *Operis Historici et Chronologici* alternated between two forms. One provided a narrative of events during a particular era, paying special attention to the total length of that period and the time that elapsed between epochal dates. These chapters were mainly based on the Biblical text, albeit at certain points – for instance, when discussing the era from the destruction of the first Temple to the death of Alexander the Great – he admitted that Scripture did not provide sufficient detail and needed

[24]   GUL, MS Gen 375, Robert Baillie, 'Opusculi historici et Chronologici', p. 23.
[25]   Peterkin (ed.), *Records*, p. 37. Also, see acts of the General Assembly dated 29 August 1639 and 7 August 1641.
[26]   For example, see Mitchell Library, CH2/171/3/2, Glasgow Presbytery Records, 1641–46, fo. 108r.
[27]   Baillie, *Appendix Practica*; Baillie, *Catechesis Elenctica Errorum*.

to be supplemented by other ancient authorities.[28] Following each narrative chapter, Baillie addressed controversial points in the preceding chronology, setting out arguments of past scholarship before sometimes – though not always – supplying his own opinion. Between the earlier manuscript of the *Operis Historici* and the published edition, the sections recounting disputed points of chronology underwent substantial revision, indicating Baillie's concern regularly to update his lectures to incorporate the most recent scholarship from the British Isles and abroad. It was in these supplementary sections that Baillie refined the polemical edge of his treatise and particularly engaged with the arguments of Walton, the editor of the London Polyglot Bible (1657), and the Dutch Sinologist Isaac Vossius. In the *addendum* to question IV of the second chapter, for instance, Baillie presented an extended vindication of the chronology found in the Hebrew Masorah as superior to that of the Greek Septuagint.[29] By contrast, Walton's prolegomena for the London Polyglot Bible and Vossius's *Dissertatio de vera aetate mundi* (1659) both challenged Baillie's belief that the Hebrew Old Testament contained a self-sufficient and authoritative account of chronology from Creation to Christ's birth and beyond.

One of Baillie's main challenges in defending the divine authority of the Hebrew text, therefore, was to explain the irrelevance of contradictory readings derived from other ancient translations of Scripture and extra-Biblical sources. In his title, Baillie described his chronology as being an account of 'sacred and profane history' but, in practice, Baillie only selectively cited other ancient sources to verify the authority of the Masoretic text. More broadly, in seeking to prove that 'sacred history was historical', early modern philologists regularly encountered inconsistencies in evidence derived from analysis of ancient coinage, ruins and chronology.[30] Baillie engaged at length with Vossius's *Dissertatio de vera aetate mundi*, for instance, because the Dutch scholar had sought to reconcile chronologies found in pagan sources with those supplied in the Old Testament. Manetho's *Aegyptiaca*, a list of ancient Egyptian pharaohs composed sometime in the first half of the third century BCE, placed the origins of the First Dynasty well before the Biblical date of the Flood, whilst a text written by the Chaldean High Priest Berosus claimed that Chaldean astronomers had traditions of observations stretching back nearly 470,000 years. Such chronologies presented serious challenges to the authority of the Masorah which dated the Earth as only 6,000 years old. Baillie, however, dismissed such claims, referring to Manetho's chronology as a 'fantastic' story. Whilst pagan sources implied that the Old Testament was only an account of the particular history of the Jewish people,

---

[28] Baillie, *Operis Historici et Chronologici*, lib. I, p. 143.
[29] Ibid., lib. I, pp. 7–13; cf. GUL, MS Gen 375, 'Opusculi historici et Chronologia', p. 40.
[30] Peter N. Miller, 'The "Antiquarianization" of Biblical Scholarship and the London Polyglott Bible (1653–57)', *Journal of the History of Ideas*, 62 (2001), pp. 462–82, at p. 464.

Baillie remained adamant that all people of Egypt, Europe, Asia and Africa descended from 'one Moses'.[31]

Whilst Baillie derisively dismissed pagan sources, Vossius aimed to reconcile their chronologies with the Biblical account of sacred history, which alarmed Baillie since it appeared that Vossius was thereby challenging the Bible's pre-eminent status as divine revelation. Seeking to reconcile Christian and pagan chronologies, Vossius argued that the Greek Septuagint was a more authoritative recension of the divine original than the Masorah and, moreover, went so far as to 'ridicule' those Christians and Jews who continued to insist that the Hebrew Old Testament 'comes straight from heaven'.[32] According to Vossius, Moses's original text had been destroyed, along with the Temple that had been destroyed by the Roman emperor Titus's army in 70 CE, obliging scholars to reconstruct its content from the closest related texts which Vossius insisted was the Septuagint rather than the Masorah.[33] In reconciling pagan and Old Testament chronologies, therefore, Vossius drew on the significantly longer chronology found in the Septuagint. In similar vein, Walton had argued in his prolegomena to the London Polyglot Bible that the Hebrew text should be revised through comparison with the newly rediscovered *Codex Alexandrinus* – a fifth-century manuscript of the Greek Bible. Accordingly, Baillie argued that Walton had questioned the integrity of the *Hebraicam veritatem* 'more modestly' than Vossius, 'but bitterly enough'. Indeed, the works of Cappel, Jean Morin, Vossius and Walton denoted an alarmingly emergent 'potent faction of most learned men that contend, along with all their other errors, that the purity of the Hebrew Bibles that now survive, is going to be overthrown by thrusting on it a thousand other errors'.[34] In Biblical chronology, Baillie estimated this account to exceed one thousand errors, as the Greek Septuagint's chronology problematically added over 1,200 years to that of the Hebrew Old Testament.

Biblical scholars such as Vossius and Walton did not directly challenge Scripture's divine authority, but their research clearly demonstrated weaknesses in previous formulations of Scriptural self-sufficiency. Reformed Protestants, in particular, would need to develop a more detailed doctrine of Scripture if no longer able simply to claim that the Masorah was God's revealed Word. Yet such doctrinal alterations were not immediately forthcoming and, in the mid-seventeenth century, beliefs in Scriptural authority were becoming 'increasingly dislocated from the practice of its textual study and interpretation'.[35] In a Scottish context, it appears that these developments were driven by the fact that works of Biblical scholarship like Baillie's

---

[31] Baillie, *Operis Historici et Chronologici*, lib. I, pp. 4–5.
[32] Isaac Vossius, *Dissertatio de vera aetate mundi* (1660), p. 22.
[33] Jorink, "'Horrible and Blasphemous'", pp. 446–50.
[34] Baillie, *Operis Historici et Chronologici*, lib. I, p. 7. This opens an *addenda* to Question IV, entitled 'Vindicatur Chronologia textus Hebraici contra Graeci Interpretis errores in annis Patriarcharum ante fluvium'.
[35] Malcolm, 'Hobbes, Ezra and the Bible', p. 420.

were written for practical ends – namely, to provide preachers with an accessible overview of scholarly debates. Along similar lines, English-language Biblical commentaries were written by Scots in the 1650s, including David Dickson, James Durham and George Hutcheson, ostensibly in an attempt to make the latest formulations of Scripture's self-sufficiency accessible to a wider readership. For Baillie, the Hebrew text was pristine and unambiguous. Sources of ambiguity and confusion in the interpretation of certain passages stemmed from subsequent translation and transmission of the text. The colophon of Baillie's Hebrew grammar underscored this point: 'when interpreters greatly differ from one another, little or no discrepancies often appear to descend from the Hebrew'.[36] Discussing Adam's descendants in his Biblical chronology, Baillie examined readings of Genesis 10:21 which variously interpreted Japhet or Schem as the elder brother. 'By way of this example,' wrote Baillie, 'I wanted to demonstrate the necessity of the Hebrew language and Chronology, to the study of Theology and all the Sacred Scriptures.'[37] Jerome read the passage as *Schemum fratrem Iapheti majorem*, making Schem the elder, whereas the Chaldea paraphrase was translated as *frater Japheti majoris*, making Japhet the elder. English, Dutch and Italian translations did not reach consensus, but merely reproduced ambiguities. The confusion stemmed from unfamiliarity (*imperitus*) with the Hebrew text, which unambiguously read *Achitephet haggadol* – Schem brother of Japhet the Elder. Trusting the presupposition of Scriptural self-sufficiency, namely that God's Word was *clearly* revealed in the Bible, Baillie took such evidence of linguistic clarity to indicate that the modern Hebrew text must be more closely related to the original Hebrew text. If study of the Hebrew text had not clarified this passage, then Baillie maintained that 'this study of Chronology would easily and certainly distinguish and demonstrate this same conclusion'.[38]

Chronology and knowledge of Biblical languages were essential tools in Baillie's effort to uncover Scripture's true meaning and verify its authority. The antiquity of the Hebrew language in the extant Old Testament was inextricably linked to its authority as opposed to that of the Greek Septuagint. Following Cappel, Walton had argued that the Masorah provided an accurate representation of the oral tradition of vocalization and, therefore, was a valuable guide to the divine original.[39] Walton, however, advocated what has been characterized as a 'conservative use' of other ancient versions in order to correct errors in the Hebrew text.[40] For Baillie, such an approach was not conservative, but destructive, of the Hebrew text's meaning. Baillie's emphasis on the internal coherence of the Hebrew text as a means to uncovering

[36] Baillie, *Appendix Practica*, colophon.
[37] Baillie, *Operis Historici et Chronologici*, lib. I, p. 4.
[38] Ibid.
[39] Brian Walton, 'Prolegomena' in *Biblia Sacra Polyglotta* (6 vols, London, 1653–57), vol. I, iii. 8 and iii. 42.
[40] Muller, 'Vowel Points', p. 153.

the correct reading – as exemplified above – prefigured, by at least two decades, the opinions of Francis Turretin and Johann Heidegger who co-wrote the *Formula Consensus Helvetica* (1675).[41] Baillie defended the coherence, clarity and perspicuity of the Hebrew text in his *Operis* by engaging with two central questions: firstly, whether the 'Jews from the days of Ezra adopted the characters of their letters from the Chaldea [script]' and discarded the characters 'in which God wrote the Decalogue on Mount Sinai, and the Script in which Moses and all of the Prophets had written their books'. Secondly, whether the 'accents and vocalization points' were first added to Scripture during Ezra's lifetime 'or whether these were invented in the days of the Masoretes, five hundred years after the birth of Christ'.[42]

Responding to both questions, Baillie defended the conclusions of the Hebraists Johannes Buxtorf I and II, particularly the former's *Tiberias sive commentarius Masorethicus* (1620).[43] Following the Buxtorfs, Baillie argued that Ezra had made the divinely revealed Hebrew text more accessible, having refrained from introducing new Chaldean or Assyrian characters to replace the Samaritan alphabet which – according to Walton and Cappel – had been originally used in sacred texts.[44] There were two scripts of the ancient Jews, one used for common or daily purposes (*Scriptura vulgari*) and the other for more solemn and sacred writings.[45] Samaritan characters were used in the former instance, whilst Hebrew characters as extant in the Masorah were the preserve of rabbis before Ezra. By invoking this distinction between common and sacred scripts, Baillie provided philological refutation of the archaeological evidence that Walton and Cappel had drawn from ancient coins, plates and inscriptions on the Patriarchs' tombs.[46] Baillie argued that such a division of scripts was common in other ancient languages, citing the variety of Egyptian and Greek characters. This argument was reinforced by comparison of Samaritan and Hebrew characters in order to claim that the Babylonian Talmudist Chisda had taught that God had written the letters *Mem* and *Samekh* as closed characters (ie. ם and ס) in the Mosaic Law. As the Samaritan forms of these letters both comprised an open figure, Baillie inferred that the Mosaic Law could not have been written in Samaritan.[47]

Although Baillie claimed that God had revealed his law using the consonantal letters of the Hebrew language, he avoided making the claim that the vowel points were also of divine origin. This tactical silence was not unprecedented amongst Reformed theologians defending the authority of the Hebrew text. The French Protestant theologian Rivet, for instance,

---

[41] Ibid. Turretin and Heidegger's position was also enshrined in the *Formula Consensus Helvetica* (1675).
[42] Baillie, *Operis Historici et Chronologici*, lib. I, p. 196.
[43] Cf. Buxtorf, *Tiberias sive commentarius Masorethicus*, caps iii, xi.
[44] Baillie, *Operis Historici et Chronologici*, lib. I, pp. 196–7.
[45] Ibid., lib. I, p. 197.
[46] Ibid., lib. I, pp. 197–203.
[47] Ibid., lib. I, p. 198.

maintained that Scripture's meaning was clear with or without proof of the Mosaic origins of the vowel points.[48] Baillie implicitly conceded that vowel points were *not* used in the original text of the Decalogue when he concluded that Elias Levita had incorrectly argued that vowel points were the invention of the Masoretes of Tiberius in the fifth century CE.[49] Ezra the Scribe and the Great Synagogue had thus made the Rabbinic Hebrew used in Scripture more accessible to unlearned Jews by introducing the vocalization points, which preserved the Hebrew script's divine origins and disseminated clear and accurate knowledge of the Sacred texts to the whole Jewish population. After Ezra emerged from Assyria, the whole population had accepted the Biblical Hebrew alphabet for common usage, laying aside the vulgar form of Hebrew previously used.[50] It was unproblematic, moreover, that ancient Rabbinic sources referred to the letters that the Decalogue 'was first written in by God [as] Assyrian, because Ezra, coming out of Assyria and Babylon, was the first to make common usage of them'.[51] Moreover, Baillie argued that Cappel and Walton suggested that 'nothing is to be sanctified, glorified and no honour was to be given to the language or to the letters in which God, Moses and the Prophets wrote the Sacred Scripture' by their suggestion that Ezra had introduced scribal errors into the Hebrew text. Baillie was shocked that Cappel might be admired for denying 'all sanctity of the letters of the Hebrew language'; the status of the vowel points was moot.[52]

Disputes over the authority of the Hebrew Old Testament placed Baillie and a well-defined set of opponents in distinct camps. Baillie did not accord much latitude to his opponents – particularly Walton and Cappel – since they fundamentally challenged Scripture's doctrinal status. To Baillie, Walton's arguments implied that Scripture was an insufficient witness to define all points of faith. On questions of technical chronology, however, Baillie's opponents constantly shifted, and his enemies in one instance might well provide his strongest support in others. In this way, Baillie's theological beliefs did not hinder his ability to appraise scholarship more objectively. In the manuscript preface of his *Operis*, Baillie had indicated that sections describing disputed points of chronology were intended to examine questions raised by Scaliger's groundbreaking works of chronology – *De Emendatione Temporum* (1583) and *Thesaurus Temporum* (1606) – and alleviate (*leniens*) the 'Jesuitical difficulties' introduced by Dionysius Petavius in his *Opus de Doctrina Temporum* (1627–29).[53] After composing and further revising his text, however, Baillie came to realize that he was not simply defending a Protestant version of chronology from Jesuitical corruptions and he omitted this preface from the published version.

---

[48] André Rivet, *Isagoge, seu introductio generalis ad Scriptura Sacram Veteris et Novi Testamenti*, in *Operam Theologicorum* (3 vols, Rotterdam, 1651–60), vol. 2, p. 891.
[49] Baillie, *Operis Historici et Chronologici*, lib. I, p. 203.
[50] Ibid., lib. I, p. 202.
[51] Ibid.
[52] Ibid., lib. I, p. 203.
[53] GUL, MS Gen 375, Baillie, 'Opusculi historici et Chronologici', p. 25.

In fact, Baillie often criticized Scaliger's chronological calculations as was evident when he discussed the start of the Babylonian captivity.[54] Baillie insisted that there was 'a great discrepancy' between chronologers and Scriptural interpreters (*Scripturae Interpretes*), 'both old and new, Protestant and Roman Catholic', as to when the Babylonian captivity ended, which in turn determined when it might have begun, given consensus that it lasted for seventy years.[55] Modern scholars remain unclear about precise dating of the 'Exilic period', since terminal dates entirely depend on whether or not one considers the payment of tribute to Nebuchadnezzar in 605 BCE or the later forced deportation of Judeans in 598 BCE to have marked the beginning of a period of 'captivity'. Nevertheless, it is generally accepted that the captivity began with the destruction of Jerusalem in 587/586 BCE.[56] To return to Baillie's reckoning, he summarized the three current opinions on the start date. 'Many grave' authors established the captivity's start from the destruction of Jerusalem in the eleventh year of Zedekiah's reign and the nineteenth of Nebuchadnezzar's reign (587/586 BCE). Others, 'no less grave', placed the epochal date eleven years earlier, in the eighth year of Nebuchadnezzar's reign, or the first year of Jeconiah's reign, which was the eleventh year of Joakim's reign (598 BCE). Finally, another group, 'to which we [i.e. Baillie] add our calculation', preferred the first year of Nebuchadnezzar's reign, which fell partly in Joakim's third and fourth year (605 BCE); thus claiming that Judeans were captive nearly twenty years before the sack of Jerusalem. Baillie had argued that Scaliger, in his *De Emendatione Temporum*, had revealed inconsistencies overlooked by Petavius. In Scaliger's sixth book, for example, it had been argued that the seventy-year captivity had begun in the first year of Jeconiah's reign, when Ezekiel was carried into Babylon, rather than the fourth year of Joakim's reign, when Daniel and others had been deported to Babylon. In his fifth book, however, Scaliger had argued that Daniel and Ezekiel went into exile in Babylon at the same time, 'as if the captivity of Joakim and Jeconiah were one and the same'.[57] Scaliger had confused his calculations because he had misinterpreted the Biblical text and, 'ignoring all Rabbinic commentaries, he contradicted express Scripture' by suggesting that the captivity was dated from the third year that Joakim had paid tribute to Chaldea, in the eleventh and last year of his reign. Rather, according to Baillie, the express words of Scripture indicated that Joakim and Jeconiah were both taken captive in the third year of Joakim's reign and that Daniel and Ezekiel were not taken captive at the same time.[58]

Elsewhere, Baillie criticized *Dictatoria Scaliger nationi toti Chronologorum*,

[54]   Baillie, *Operis Historici et Chronologici*, lib. I, pp. 144–7.
[55]   Ibid., lib. I, p. 144. In fact, Baillie had previously discussed these points in the thirty-first and thirty-fourth chapters of the previous Epoch.
[56]   Rainer Albertz, *Israel in Exile: The History and Literature of the Sixth Century B.C.E.* (Atlanta, Ga., 2003), pp. 1–2.
[57]   Baillie, *Operis Historici et Chronologici*, lib. I, p. 144.
[58]   Ibid., lib. I, pp. 144–5.

as 'no less irritably indignant [than Petavius] of men who did not conform to his interpretation of Chronology and Scripture'.[59] Whilst the foregoing example illustrated how Baillie critically appraised Scaliger's technical chronology on account of inconsistencies with what he took to be Scripture's 'true' reading, in other cases Baillie preferred to cite the consensus of ancient and modern commentators – including Catholics – against Scaliger's sole reliance on one contradictory piece of evidence. To determine the date of the Second Temple's completion, for example, Baillie claimed that Scaliger had followed Sulpicius Severus's *Historia sacra* (c. 403) contrary to the opinion of 'all ancient Hebrews, Latins and Greeks' who had placed it in Darius Hystapsis's reign. Moreover, Baillie denied that Scaliger and followers, including Franciscus Junius, John Reynolds and Ubbo Emmius, had offered any substantial justification for placing 'completion' of the Second Temple in the sixth year of the reign of Darius Nothus (the Persian king who reigned approximately 115 years after Darius Hystaspis).[60] Given his instinctive criticism of Roman Catholics and Jesuits, Baillie's insistence that 'our ancient and communal opinion is embraced by Cappel, Ussher, Petavius, and Henricus Philippi' (the Jesuit author of *Introdvctio Chronologica* (1621)) was remarkable.[61]

II

Baillie's Scriptural erudition and his belief in its self-sufficiency also decisively shaped his preaching style, although this influence was not always evident since Baillie, like many contemporaries, primarily aimed to make his sermons clear, succinct and engaging. In July 1645, however, the close relationship between Baillie's homiletic and scholarly exegesis was revealed in an uncharacteristic digression – probably added in for the published version of the text – in the midst of a sermon preached to the English House of Lords. Amidst a rousing exhortation to beware the deleterious effects of theological error, Baillie started discussing a philological aspect of his chosen text, Isaiah 63:17.[62] According to the King James Bible, the first part of this passage read 'why hast thou made us to erre', implying that God was the author of sin. As Baillie explained, numerous 'famous interpreters' including the Reformed translators of the Old Testament, Franciscus Junius and Immanuel Tremellius, had circumvented this theological problem by translating the

---

[59]   Ibid., lib. I, p. 149.
[60]   Ibid.; Anthony Grafton, *Joseph Scaliger: A Study in the History of Classical Scholarship* (2 vols, Oxford, 1983–93), vol. II, pp. 284–6.
[61]   Baillie, *Operis Historici et Chronologici*, lib. I, p. 149.
[62]   Baillie's text was taken from the King James Bible: 'Lord, why hast thou made us to erre from thy ways, and hardened our hearts from thy fear? Return for thy servants sake, the Tribes of thine Inheritance.'

passage to read that God had 'permitted' Christians to sin.[63] This revised translation had been supported by the Chaldea Paraphrase and approved 'by very Learned and Orthodox Divines', who argued that the Hebrew verb was 'not simply in the active form, not in *Kal*, as they speak, [but] in *Hiphil*, whose signification' often means 'to permit'.[64] While acknowledging this philological solution to an apparent theological inconsistency, Baillie pointed out that the form of the Hebrew verb in this passage (וַנַּעֲתֵנוּ or ṯaṯ·'ê·nū), was never 'exponed of a meer permission'.[65] Consequently, Baillie refused to revise the meaning of the Hebrew text and base his exposition of the doctrine of sin on 'a meer Grammatication' and instead introduced a series of scholastic distinctions concerning the nature of sin to explain the Hebrew text's apparent inconsistency.[66]

It is, nevertheless, likely that Baillie would have refrained from offering such detail to his parishioners in Glasgow or Kilwinning. The sacred texts of the Bible provided a range of examples of how God punished and rewarded humanity that, Baillie believed, might instruct parishioners as to how God's active providence shaped their world. More broadly, early modern preachers actively engaged with numerous Biblical instances to address contemporary political and ecclesiastical concerns, with typological themes from Scripture invoked to edify listeners in various religious, moral, political and social duties.[67] Until recently, scholars working on sermons adopted a defensive tone considering that their subject matter had hitherto been deemed 'one of the most lifeless ancillary aspects of Renaissance literary culture'.[68] In recent years, however, scholarship on the early modern sermon has flowered, with studies proliferating on major figures such as John Donne, the sermon's role in the 'public sphere' and Arnold Hunt's remarkable study on sermon reception.[69] In an English context, it has been claimed that ministers' homiletic style derived from their convictions about Scriptural authority and that this literary genre was actually a dynamic exercise in religious controversy and

---

[63] See Fransciscus Junius, Theodore Beza and Immanuel Tremellius, *Biblia Sacra, sive TestamentvGraftonm Vetvs ab Im. Tremellio et Fr. Ivnio ex Hebraeo Latine redditum, et Testamentvm Novvum, a Theod. Beza e Graeco in Latinum versum* (Amsterdam, 1633), p. 468: 'Quare *sineres* aberrare nos, Iehova, a viis tuis?' (emphasis added).

[64] Baillie, *Errours and Induration*, p. 6.

[65] Ibid., p. 7.

[66] Ibid.

[67] Kevin Killeen, 'Veiled Speech: Preaching, Politics, and Scriptural Typology', in Peter McCullough, Hugh Adlington and Emma Rhatigan (eds), *The Oxford Handbook of the Early Modern Sermon* (Oxford, 2011), pp. 387–403.

[68] Lori Anne Ferrell and Peter McCullough (eds), *The English Sermon Revised: Religion, Literature and History 1600–1750* (Manchester, 2000), p. 3.

[69] See, for example, Jeanne Shami, *John Donne and Conformity in Crisis in the Late Jacobean Pulpit* (Cambridge, 2003); Peter Lake and Michael Questier, *The Antichrist's Lewd Hat: Protestants, Papists and Players in Post-Reformation England* (London, 2002), pp. 335–76; Hunt, *The Art of Hearing*.

rhetorical persuasion.[70] Elsewhere, it has been argued that 'polemical and pedagogical' contexts of early modern Protestantism 'undoubtedly shaped the minds of the preachers as they variously approached' Scripture from the pulpit.[71] In the New Testament, particularly the Pauline epistles, God had appointed preaching and the sacraments as the primary means whereby grace was conveyed to Christians. Accordingly, the Bible was understood to be much more than simply an historical record of Christ's teachings: it was divine revelation, and sermons were therefore intended to make God's grace 'operative' through a particular text, although this operative force derived from the Holy Spirit. Scripture was considered divine, self-sufficient and internally coherent, and difficult passages were to be interpreted primarily by reference to other, clearer, passages. In a Scottish context, sermons helped to make the Bible's diverse meanings accessible to a population in which rural illiteracy rates remained at about 80 per cent and urban illiteracy rates were at 50 per cent.[72]

It remains to be explored how a minister's learned beliefs about Scriptural authority influenced his preaching style, and this section explores this relationship through discussion of Baillie's extant sermons. Baillie's reaction to the new Prayer Book of 1637 and aversion to particular set forms of worship, discussed in the previous chapter, demonstrated that he privileged the sermon as the central component of divine worship in Scotland. This is confirmed by the survival of two enormous manuscripts of sermons, comprising over one million words, written entirely in Baillie's hand. These volumes, however, have remained unstudied. They cover the period of Baillie's ministries in Kilwinning and Glasgow, dating from 1637 to 1639, and 1648 to 1651 respectively, and complement two printed sermons which Baillie preached in London in 1644 and 1645.[73] Drawing together discussion from the previous section, then, this section focuses on analysis of Baillie's preaching style: his training in preaching, the structure of his sermons and their general content. The surviving manuscript material is simply too extensive to allow sufficient space for a more comprehensive account.

The centrality of sermons to Scottish worship notwithstanding, Crawford Gribben has recently observed that scholarly study of preaching in early modern Scotland remains a 'surprising lacunae'.[74] From a seventeenth-century perspective, Calderwood aptly summed up a pastor's duties, declaring

---

[70] Mary Morrissey, 'Scripture, Style and Persuasion in Seventeenth-Century English Theories of Preaching', *The Journal of Ecclesiastical History*, 53 (2002), pp. 686–706.
[71] Carl Trueman, 'Preachers and Medieval and Renaissance Commentary', in McCullough, Adlington and Rhatigan (eds), *Oxford Handbook*, pp. 54–71, at p. 55.
[72] R.A. Houston, 'The Literacy Myth?: Illiteracy in Scotland 1630–1760', *Past and Present*, 96 (1982), pp. 81–102, at p. 87.
[73] See NLS, Adv.MS.20.6.4, Robert Baillie, Sermons, August 1637 to June 1639; NCL, Baill MS 5, Robert Baillie, Sermons from Jan. 1648 to Jun. 1652.
[74] Crawford Gribben, 'Preaching the Scottish Reformation, 1560–1707', in McCullough, Adlington and Rhatigan (eds), *Oxford Handbook*, pp. 271–86, at p. 275.

the 'principall part' being 'to labour in the word & doctrine … And when he preacheth he will haue Gods Word onely to sounde in his owne house, reading nothing but the Canonicall text, & comparing Scripture with Scripture for edification.'[75] Calderwood emphasized the ministerial duty to teach the 'word of God, in season and out of season' (paraphrased from 2 Timothy 4:2) found in *The Second Book of Discipline* (1578), echoing *The First Book of Discipline* (1560) which had stipulated regular sermons – or, at least, reading of Scripture – every Sunday and one other day each week.[76]

Before moving to analyse Baillie's sermons, preliminary remarks are required regarding their composition and the relationship between the words that Baillie may actually have spoken in the pulpit, extant manuscripts and printed versions, since the written or printed texts certainly do not represent verbatim transcriptions. Before the 1620s, many English ministers drew a sharp distinction between reading the printed text of a sermon and listening to a sermon *in situ*. Whereas the former was sufficient for doctrinal instruction, it was only through attendance at sermons that the 'latent force' of the written word could be activated and applied to the parishioner's particular spiritual needs. Yet with the Laudian attack on weekly sermons, discussed in the previous chapter, ministerial attitudes to printed sermons improved and they began to acknowledge the evangelizing potential of print eroding this 'reading/listening' distinction.[77] By the mid-1640s, therefore, Baillie expressed few anxieties that the printed versions of his sermons, respectively published in 1644 and 1645 and respectively preached before the English Houses of Commons and Lords, would be considered an imperfect representation of his live performance.[78] In the dedicatory epistles to his printed sermons, Baillie described the text as comprising the 'Notes of that which to their Honours was preached, without any variation' or 'the Notes of that poor Sermon, without any addition at all, and without any change considerable'.[79] By the 1640s, most preachers did not necessarily prepare a full text of a sermon even when they knew it was likely to be published.[80] This is especially notable in the case of parliamentary fast sermons of which most, but not all, were ordered to be printed by parliamentary ordinance immediately

---

[75] [David Calderwood], *The pastor and the prelate, or reformation and conformity shortly compared* (1628), p. 15.
[76] See *The Second Book of Discipline*, ch. 4; *The First Book of Discipline*, 'The ninth head: Concerning the policy of the church'.
[77] Hunt, *The Art of Hearing*, pp. 27, 21.
[78] On the relationship between print, manuscript and oral media, see D.F. McKenzie, 'Speech-Manuscript-Print', in Peter D. McDonald and Michael F. Suarez (eds), *Making Meaning: 'Printers of the Mind' and Other Essays* (Amherst, 2002), pp. 237–58. In one sense, this agrees with Morrissey's claim that contemporaries regarded oral and printed editions of a sermon as 'different versions of the same oration'. See Mary Morrissey, *Politics and the Paul's Cross Sermons, 1558–1642* (Oxford, 2011), p. 35.
[79] Baillie, *Errours and Induration*, sig. Ar; Baillie, *Satan the Leader in Chief*, sig. Av.
[80] Morrissey, *Paul's Cross Sermons*, p. 38.

following their delivery.[81] The process of expanding and editing a script for publication notwithstanding, Baillie still maintained that the printed text retained characteristics of the oral performance.[82] Indeed, Baillie elided the distinction between oral and print media, confirming in a dedicatory epistle that the text would 'finde in the eyes of others when read, that patience and respect which it had in your ears at the first hearing'.[83]

Baillie's manuscript volumes also contain 'notes' for sermons, many of which are extremely detailed, albeit their prose is significantly less polished than that of Baillie's two printed sermons. Marginal annotations indicate Baillie's confirmation that he had 'notit on' a particular verse, presumably meaning that he had taken notes on a passage in preparation for a future sermon, but that he had not yet preached on the text.[84] In this form, the sermon's preamble discussing the Biblical context of a passage and its division resembles polished prose that may have been recited verbatim. Although most early modern ministers preached from brief notes some, such as Robert Sanderson, prepared a full text.[85] Towards the later sections of sermons, Baillie's notes became more abbreviated, perhaps reflecting greater confidence in extemporizing on a text's applications after initial remarks. A lack of detailed notes regarding the application of doctrine to particular contexts also suggests that Baillie had composed these notes so that they could easily be reused on various occasions. This is further confirmed by a few instances where Baillie indicated in a marginal note that he had 'repetit' a sermon at a later date.[86] The application of doctrinal lessons to particular contexts was meant to affect deep emotive responses in listeners and, therefore, was the part of the sermon that was most carefully tailored. Although general division of the text may have been repeated, Baillie almost certainly adapted a text's applications or 'uses' – those parts only briefly described in some notes – to particular contexts.

Although he was exposed to regular preaching from an early age, Baillie's formal training began during his undergraduate arts degree at Glasgow University. The university's theology curriculum survives only in a late seventeenth-century version, although an early version apparently was

[81] On parliamentary fast sermons, see Hugh Trevor-Roper, 'The Fast Sermons of the Long Parliament', in *Religion, the Reformation and Social Change and Other Essays* (London, 1967), pp. 294–344; John Frederick Wilson, *Pulpit in Parliament: Puritanism during the English Civil Wars, 1640–8* (Princeton, 1969), pp. 3–21.

[82] This qualifies Hunt's claim that, by 1640, printed sermons had lost 'their distinctively oral character and became indistinguishable from other forms of religious literature' (Hunt, *The Art of Hearing*, p. 119).

[83] Baillie, *Satan the Leader in Chief*, sig. Av.

[84] See, for just a selection of examples, NCL, Baill MS 5, Baillie, Sermons, fo. 294v. (Psalm 102:12), 295r (Psalm 102), 358v (Ephesians 1).

[85] Morrissey, *Paul's Cross Sermons*, p. 37.

[86] See, for example, NLS, Adv.MS.20.6.4, Robert Baillie, Sermons, fo. 54v (repeetit Glasgou toun 1 Jun 4 [sic] 1643), 57r ('repeetit in Glasgou and for Mr Ash'), 119v ('repetit in glasgou' [n.d.]).

extant when the nineteenth-century editors of Glasgow University's *munimenta* prepared a published edition. In fact, since the Reformation, young Scots who had entered university had undergone rigorous homiletic training as part of their arts degree curriculum, with all students expected to attend sermons and make notes, which were then reviewed and discussed with tutors.[87] Towards the end of their degree, and certainly during postgraduate theological studies, students also prepared short sermons for presentation and critique by the divinity professor. As the Professor of Divinity at Glasgow during the Restoration, Gilbert Burnet, later explained his method of teaching young ministers: 'On Friday I made the students in course preach a short sermon upon a text that I gave them and ... shewed them what was defective or amiss in the sermon, and how the text ought to have been opened and applied.'[88] Ample evidence is provided in Baillie's student notebook, written around 1620 – forty years before Burnet's tenure – that he had undertaken similar training.[89]

Baillie, in fact, introduced a formal instruction manual into Glasgow's curriculum during his tenure as Professor of Divinity. The student notebook of one of his pupils, James Wodrow – father of the ecclesiastical historian, Robert – contains a copy of a manuscript treatise by James Mitchell of Dykes, entitled 'The severall wayes of preaching', that was presumably dictated to Wodrow by Baillie.[90] Elsewhere a spiritual autobiography written by Mitchell's father also describes Baillie's tutelage of his son that emphasized Mitchell's homiletic talents – his 'three special gifts dispensed to him by the Lord, a notable and tight invention, a great memory, with a nimble and ready expression' – that, in due course, led to Mitchell's recommendation as Baillie's successor at Kilwinning.[91] Before this treatise, there was evidently no set text from which preaching was taught at Glasgow. Accordingly, Mitchell's father recorded that his son was devoted to 'fasting and prayer, and the study of the word of God, and reading thereof ... and among other

---

[87] *Contra* Gribben, 'Preaching the Scottish Reformation', in McCullough, Adlington and Rhatigan (eds), *Oxford Handbook*, p. 281; Cosmo Innes (ed.), *Munimenta alme Universitatis glasguensis: Records of the University of Glasgow from its Foundation till 1727* (4 vols, Glasgow, 1854), vol. II, pp. xviii, 239–41. It does not appear that this earlier curriculum is still extant in the university archives. One of the best descriptions of this theological training is still Henderson's 'Scottish Theological Learning in the Seventeenth Century', in *Religious Life*, pp. 117–39; Innes (ed.), *Munimenta glasguensis*, vol. II, p. 316.
[88] T.E.S. Clarke and H.C. Foxcroft, *A Life of Gilbert Burnet, Bishop of Salisbury* (Cambridge, 1907), p. 82.
[89] EUL, La.III.109, Robert Baillie, Student notebook, pp. 16–110, 126–36.
[90] NLS, Wod.MSS.4, James Wodrow, Student notebook, [c. 1660]. On Baillie's practice of dictating treatises that were copied verbatim by his students and for which he was criticized by the regent, James Veitch, see Robert Baillie to John Young, [1654], *LJB*, vol. III, p. 260.
[91] James Mitchell of Dykes, *Memoirs of the Life of James Mitchell of Dykes ... Containing, His Own Spiritual Exercises, and Some of the Spiritual Exercises of His Two Sons, that Died Before Him* (Glasgow, 1759), p. 89.

fruits of his meditation, invention and pains, he drew up a model and frame of preaching, which he intitled the method of preaching'.[92]

Other pertinent methodological sources for Baillie's preaching are discussed later, but his most important resource remained the Bible. Whilst some efforts have previously been made to argue that a preacher's political commitments might be indicated by the English-language translation they chose to use, Baillie's apparently interchangeable use of both the King James Version and the Geneva Bible undermines such a claim.[93] It is difficult to determine exactly which version Baillie used when preparing sermons, especially since he may have noted quotations from memory. Furthermore, Baillie may also have quoted passages memorized in Latin, Greek or Hebrew and translated *ad hoc* into English. Nevertheless, in cases where a source can be determined with some accuracy, it appears that he used both the King James Version and the Geneva Bible. One example for each case highlights the degree of similarity between Baillie's manuscript and the text of either version. For example, Baillie's text for a sermon on Lamentations 2:17, probably preached in late 1637, was transcribed as 'The lord hes done what he hes devisit,' suggesting that this came from the King James Bible.[94] In another instance, though, there is clear evidence that Baillie used the Geneva Bible when transcribing Luke 22:31 for a fast sermon on 29 August 1649: 'And the lord said Simon Satan hes desirit to *winnou* you'.[95] Since the King James Version reads as 'Satan hath desired to have you, that he may *sift* you as wheat', the Genevan translation of *cribraret* as to 'winnow' was clearly distinct from the more literal translation provided by the King James Version.

Stylistically, Baillie's sermons conformed to the 'doctrine-use' format drawn from several of Philip Melanchthon's works, including his *Dispositio orationis in Epistola Pauli ad Romanos* (1529), and William Perkins's *The Arte of Prophecying* (1592).[96] This style of preaching is evident in all of Baillie's extant sermons and can be illustrated by a fast sermon preached on Psalm 143 on 7 July 1650, which was the Sunday before the General Assembly met to ratify the Treaty of Breda with Charles II.[97] In this psalm, David prays to God for protection in times of persecution. David hopes that he will be able to recognize God's love and kindness and lead his life righteously. After providing a division of the chapter into the distinct petitions that David made, Baillie systematically discussed each of four 'heads' of doctrine found in the text. For example, on the ninth verse – 'Deliver me, O Lord, from mine enemies: I flee unto thee to hide me' – Baillie showed that this contained 'the petition and

[92] Ibid., p. 90.
[93] For example, see Christopher Hill, *Society and Puritanism in Pre-Revolutionary England* (London, 1964), pp. 33, 49, 55, 136.
[94] NLS, Adv.MS.20.6.4, Robert Baillie, Sermons, fo. 50v.
[95] NCL, Baill MS 5, Baillie, Sermons, fo. 190r. Emphasis added.
[96] Greg Kneidel, 'Ars Praedicandi: Theories and Practice', in McCullough, Adlington and Rhatigan (eds), *Oxford Handbook*, pp. 13–15.
[97] For the text of the sermon, see NCL, Baill MS 5, Baillie, Sermons, fos 207r–209r.

its reason'. On this verse, he continued, 'obs[erve] this doctrine': when the godly are threatened by enemies from both within and without, they 'seek deliverance from god. David a verie valiant and wyse warriour yit When he first [saw his] enemies with his eyes ... his hands wer lift up to the lord for help.'[98] Doctrine was thus thoroughly supported through citations from other Scriptural passages before Baillie proceeded to discuss its 'trie fold' uses. As Baillie showed, this passage detailed 'our practic at thes tymes to be praying to be leid for a deliverance', that parishioners must 'hold up holy hands' and pray in a great repentant voice, and, finally, that those who pray must themselves be unblemished in God's eyes.[99]

Along with this practice of dividing texts, Baillie relied heavily on typological exegesis to derive contemporary relevance from Scriptural passages. Typologies did not simply highlight uses to which doctrine could be put, and nor were they a form of Scriptural exemplarity. Rather, a type was a physical mark which early modern Christians perceived as closely connecting two historically separate events.[100] Given parishioners' familiarity with the Bible's extensive repository of tales and tropes, their recitation in the pulpit enabled preachers to draw contemporary parallels through the Biblical idiom, and effectively to communicate political and religious opinions to parishioners. The ease with which Baillie cross-referenced other Scriptural texts suggests that simply alluding to a Biblical figure or event immediately evoked specific connotations amongst his listeners. In a forthcoming article, I discuss how one learned parishioner received and manipulated Baillie's political messages in notes made whilst listening to the sermon. Evidence from this remarkable collection of listener's notes suggests that at least some of Baillie's parishioners were able to understand his meaning clearly and translate implicit contextual remarks into explicit notes about Baillie's political commitments.

Typologies were frequently used to draw implicit messages from Scripture since, like most contemporaries, Baillie usually refrained from identifying the contemporary relevance of a sermon explicitly, despite its clear message. In this way, Baillie critically engaged with Caroline religious policies of the 1630s. As Baillie warned, God would never sleep and let 'his people whos watchman he is be oppresit by ther enemies' which, for his parishioners, should be 'som confort for the praisent in all the praisent confusion of our church'.[101] In the early phase of Covenanting resistance, Baillie preached on the so-called 'Psalms of Degrees', or Psalms 120 to 134, probably during 1638.[102] As summarized in the preface to an earlier sermon on Psalm 121:1,

---

[98] Ibid., fo. 207r.

[99] Ibid., fo. 207v.

[100] Killeen, 'Veiled Speech', in McCullough, Adlington and Rhatigan (eds), *Oxford Handbook*, pp. 389–90. Also, see Charles Kannengiesser, *Handbook of Patristic Exegesis: The Bible in Ancient Christianity* (Leiden, 2006), pp. 228–9.

[101] NLS, Adv.MS.20.6.4, Robert Baillie, Sermons, fo. 11r (second pagination).

[102] This series begins towards the end of the earlier volume when the pagination resets. This later pagination will be indicated with the note '(second pagination)'. See NLS,

this series of Psalms was probably sung by the Israelites during the course of a physical journey – either from Babylon to Jerusalem, or ascending the stairs of the Temple on the way to prayer – which also represented a transition from idolatry to righteousness. As Baillie showed, the Israelites sang these psalms 'to confort a soul lying in the greatest danger, to give grounds of hope to a church most desolat' and when originally sung 'the temple was burnt and distroy, no altar no sacrifice, no ark, no publict meeting for the servic of God', the only thing that remained was 'the promises of a gratious God'.[103] Implicitly applied to the dangers facing the Church of Scotland, the contemporary relevance of Baillie's sermon was unmistakable.

In the pulpit, Baillie fashioned himself as a well-informed guide, leading his listeners through Scripture's manifold meanings. In one vein, this may be cast as a 'quasi-prophetic' identity to endow his interpretations with increased authority. The common adoption of this practice by Reformed preachers was paradoxical given that Reformed theologians acknowledged that the age of Prophets had long ended.[104] Nevertheless, a pastor's command of the Bible – institutionally insured after 1638 by a series of official acts – gave parishioners a sense that their minister had privileged access to knowledge about God's divine will. To maintain this image in society at large, ministers had to appear morally unimpeachable and, therefore, they were often subject to careful oversight by laity and others gathered in the kirk session or the presbytery. Whereas John Milton had chided presbyterians as 'old priest writ large', it might have been more appropriate for him to caricature presbyterian ministers as new saints.[105]

In his sermons, Baillie did not claim privileged access to divine knowledge, but carefully led his listeners through the divisions and uses of his chosen passage. The Holy Spirit worked through the chosen text and, through the preacher's sermon, it was believed to convey grace to the congregation. In his fast-day sermon to the English House of Commons on 28 February 1644 on Zachariah 3:1–2, for example, Baillie explained in more detail this role. All the ills that had recently befallen the godly in Britain had also occurred formerly, yet 'there is no remembrance' of them; 'our ignorance and inconsideration makes all these accidents, and Gods providence about them to be in vain and fruitlesse unto us'. To remedy this situation, 'our mercifull Father' had provided humankind with a record of such passages in Scripture, 'wherein as in a glasse we may behold the cleare Image of our days'. Through a 'judicious comparing of what we read, with what we feele' and by a 'wise

---

Adv.MS.20.6.4, Robert Baillie, Sermons, fo. 2r (second pagination). The dating of these sermons may be established because of the overt statements against defensive arms that Baillie made (fo. 20r (second pagination)).
[103] Ibid., fo. 6v (second pagination).
[104] Mullan, *Scottish Puritanism*, p. 74; Todd, *The Culture of Protestantism*, p. 362.
[105] For the quote from Milton, see 'On the New Forcers of Conscience under the Long Parliament', in F.A. Patterson (ed.), *The Works of John Milton* (New York, 1931), vol. I, p. 71.

paralleling of times with times', Baillie hoped that the MPs would remain patient and feel comforted even 'in our worst dayes'.[106] Baillie stressed that the comfort derived from this typological reading of Scripture was mainly based on God's cyclical providence. In his exposition, Baillie did not act as a prophet *per se*, but rather as a learned interpreter uncovering the mysterious meaning of God's providence. His use of the first-person-plural pronoun in describing his practice emphasized both his elevated stance as interpreter and the need for listeners to participate in the process of Biblical exegesis.

Finally, to set the Scripturalism of Baillie's typological exegesis in perspective, it is useful to contrast his style with that of some contemporaries. The form of his sermons was premised on a strict adherence to the text at hand and its attendant meanings. Yet popular stylistic developments in mid-seventeenth-century Scottish homiletics risked diverting attention away from the self-sufficient Scriptural message by promoting a tendency to discourse on artificially imposed themes or 'heads'. Whilst historians had previously claimed that differences of preaching style rested on the rhetorical theories employed, stylistic differences may have derived from divergent ministerial beliefs about the function of preaching in a local society – though more research about the social context of Scottish preaching is needed in this regard. In the late 1640s, Scottish ministers such as Hugh Binning, Robert Leighton and Andrew Gray had started to preach without explicitly stating the 'heads of doctrine' derived from their text. Baillie denounced these individuals for their apparent failure to foreground the traditional structures of a doctrine-use sermon, comprised of exegetical, doctrinal and applicatory material. In a letter to Spang, Baillie complained about this 'new guyse of preaching' practised by Binning, Leighton and Gray. Baillie denounced their style for deviating from 'the ordinarie way of exponing and dividing a text, of raising doctrines and uses'. Rather, a sermon in this new style 'runs out in a discourse on some common head, in a high, romancing, *unscripturall style*, tickling the ear for the present, and moving the affections in some, bot leaving, as he confesses, little or nought to the memorie and understanding'.[107]

For Baillie, such a style seemed to rely too heavily on human learning and distracted from the clear, simple message of Scripture that ministers were meant to explicate for their parishioners' edification. Whereas Baillie's sermons adhered closely to a text, drawing points of doctrine and usage from individual words as he divided them, Gray and Leighton, for example, began their sermons by discussing the doctrine they wished to address before selectively drawing on a text to show how it illustrated their overarching theme. In 1654, Gray was appointed minister of the Outer High Kirk in Glasgow by Patrick Gillespie on behalf of the dominant 'Protestor' faction,

---

[106] Baillie, *Satan the Leader in Chief*, p. 4.
[107] Robert Baillie to William Spang, Glasgow, 21 July 1654, *LJB*, vol. III, pp. 258–9. Emphasis added.

an appointment opposed by Baillie.[108] More widely, Gilbert Burnet, a dev-
otee of Leighton, claimed that Leighton's weekly sermons as Principal of
Edinburgh University were known throughout Scotland in the 1650s.[109] In
a sermon preached on Romans 7:24 – 'Oh wretched man that I am, who
shall deliver me from my body of this death?' – for example, Gray developed an extended answer to Paul's rhetorical question, supplying a range of
reflections on the different ways in which the godly must 'be helped by the
candle of the Lord' to free themselves from temptation and 'to know these
mysterious subtilities of him whose name is *a deceiver*'.[110] In his discussion,
Gray emphasized how specific words and phrases illustrated his common
theme and tended to infer far more implied meaning than Baillie would
have done. In his first division, for instance, Gray detected a 'sweet and
pleasant emphasis in that word *me*', indicating Paul's belief that, if there
could be any limits to God's grace, 'he was the bounds and limits of infinite
power and grace'. Likewise, in his second division, Gray directed listeners
to perceive that 'a Christian's happiness doth consist in a sweet exchange of
dominion and governments'.[111]

Likewise, Leighton tended to focus on a common doctrinal theme, rather
than the Biblical context of a text. If one compares sermons by both Leighton
and Baillie on Psalm 42, for example, whereas Baillie introduced his text as
'mad[e] by the profit in the tyme of hevie trouble both within and without',
Leighton broadened his focus, beginning with a quote from Job verse 7 ('Man
is born to trouble, as the sparks fly upwards') before suggesting that 'as it is
the corruption and sinfulness of his birth and nature that has exposed him
to trouble, so nature usually sets him at work, to look out for such things as
may preserve and deliver him'.[112] Rather than focusing more closely on his
text, Leighton continued to expand on the implied message – a discourse on
'some common head' – namely, that the Prophet, after suffering affliction,
recognized that 'the light of God's countenance' was a source of assurance.[113]
Whilst Gray's and Leighton's sermon texts – nineteenth-century editions of
manuscript notes similar to Baillie's – appear to be more complete scripts than
Baillie's detailed sermon 'notes', it remains notable that Gray and Leighton
did not divide the words of a text before discussing the doctrine to be derived

[108] On Baillie's opposition to Gray's appointment, see Robert Baillie to William Spang,
Glasgow, 21 July 1654, *LJB*, vol. III, p. 258.
[109] On Leighton's renown see, for example, Gilbert Burnet, *History of His Own Time:
From the Restoration of Charles II to the Treaty of Peace at Utrecht, in the Reign of Queen Anne*
(London, 1838), pp. 89–90.
[110] Andrew Gray, 'The Spiritual Warfare: Sermon 1', in *The Works of the Reverend and
Pious Andrew Gray, Formerly Minister of the Gospel in Glasgow* (Aberdeen, 1839 [reprinted,
1992]), p. 310.
[111] Ibid., pp. 310, 311.
[112] NLS, Adv.MS.20.6.4, Robert Baillie, Sermons, fo. 136v; Robert Leighton, 'Psalm
xlii. 8', in *The Whole Works of Robert Leighton, D.D. Archbishop of Glasgow* (Edinburgh,
1832), p. 376.
[113] Leighton, 'Psalm xlii. 8', p. 376.

from particular words. By contrast, Baillie's primary homiletic focus was to instruct parishioners in the meanings and uses of a particular text.

III

Considering that Baillie's preaching style was derived from his belief in Scripture's self-sufficient authority, it is little wonder that he viewed the apparent innovations in preaching style made by Gray, Binning and Leighton with alarm. To Baillie, these rhetorical changes suggested that attempts were being made to introduce to parishioners a new understanding of Scripture's authority and to disseminate this view through a particularly popular form of sermonizing. Moreover, these stylistic changes might have appeared to Baillie to have simultaneously challenged the criteria by which new ministers were examined and granted a ministerial charge. Whilst it is commonly assumed that popular assumptions about the Bible and its authority derived from scholarly debates that had gradually permeated religious culture, this scenario appears to show the reverse. Three preachers were introducing novel ideas about the Bible's authority through their sermons composed and performed for their local congregations. In reaction, Baillie continued to develop his lectures on Biblical chronology and he even went so far as to publish his *Operis Historici et Chronologici* in order to provide ministers with the scholarly framework in which to combat such affronts to the lodestone of Protestant belief, the principle *sola scriptura*.

Baillie's conviction in Scripture's divine origins and its self-sufficient authority held a dynamic influence over his scholarly and homiletic exegesis but, in turn, the demands of a religion focused on the preached word fundamentally shaped his foray into Biblical scholarship. Baillie constantly refined his understanding of Scriptural authority through reading and engagement with the latest works of Biblical scholarship from Britain and Europe. Whilst the arguments of his *Operis Historici et Chronologici* divided existing scholarship along stark, confessional lines, in discussions regarding issues of technical chronology Baillie demonstrated that he could overlook confessional commitments to praise scholarly acumen. His erudite understanding of the origins and transmission of the Bible's various codices, moreover, provided a subtle framework in which Baillie's talents as a preacher were developed. Despite the noticeable absence of scholarly discussions of doctrinal or philological issues in his extant printed and manuscript sermons, it is nonetheless crucial to appreciate the academic context in which Baillie's preaching style developed so as to situate properly his criticism of preachers, like Gray and Leighton. This chapter has thus drawn together two strands of Biblical exegesis that have hitherto been treated separately. Whereas Max Weber's *Protestant Ethic and the Spirit of Capitalism* (1905) and Perry Miller's *The New England Mind* (1939) treated Protestant preaching as a highly intellectual tradition, devoid of any emotional content, more recently, scholars such as

Hunt and Debora Shuger have emphasized the rhetorical complexities of early modern preaching.[114] This revisionism, however, inadvertently downplayed the relationship between Biblical scholarship and homiletics. Further research is required to explore the relationship between these two enormous fields of study, but considering that a large proportion of Scottish ministers were university educated it is likely that their preaching style derived from their experiences therein. Yet, after their departure from university, practical demands of the profession required that much Biblical scholarship in Scotland remained attuned to issues addressed from the pulpit. In particular, analysis of Baillie's Biblical exegesis suggests that he reacted to challenges to Scriptural authority in unique and creative ways both in his Biblical chronology and in his sermons. With findings in Biblical scholarship exposing inconsistencies in Baillie's conception of Scriptural authority, he shored up his ideas by adamantly defending the belief that the Hebrew and Greek texts accurately preserved God's Word. Far from inhibiting intellectual inquiry, Baillie's confessional beliefs drove him to probe and criticize the latest findings of Biblical scholars from Britain and Europe.

---

[114] Hunt, *The Art of Hearing*, esp. pp. 81–3; Debora K. Shuger, *Sacred Rhetoric: The Christian Grand Style in the English Renaissance* (Princeton, 1988).

7

Record-Keeping and Life-Writing:
The Creation of Robert Baillie's Legacy

In one of his final letters, written in 1661, Baillie exhorted William Cunningham, eighth earl of Glencairn, to obey 'Prince, Countrey, and Mother-Church' after God, so that in the 'true account I may readilie give to the world and posteritie of what is past among us these thirty-six years, your Lordship's just character may be with the fairest of all'.[1] Baillie never began writing the history of the British Civil Wars promised in this letter, but he did bequeath to posterity a detailed account of contemporary events via transcribed copies of his outgoing letters. His decision to transcribe painstakingly a selection of outgoing letters and accompanying documents was motivated by his desire to compile a body of evidence that could be used to prepare an historical account of the Covenanters. In this vein, Baillie showed remarkable historical awareness that has benefitted generations of historians from the 1640s to the present day. He recognized the importance of the conflicts which he witnessed and he decided, quite early on, that he was well placed to document and narrate current events. In his own lifetime, his cousin and a small circle of historians based in northern Europe exploited his letters to these ends. But Baillie's efforts as manuscript collector were also a means by which he unintentionally fashioned his own legacy as detached chronicler, rather than concerned participant.

David Laing's edition of Baillie's *Letters and Journals* is still a valuable resource for scholars of mid-seventeenth-century Britain. Nevertheless, Baillie's practice as contemporary historian, life-writer and manuscript collector remains unstudied. Often, citation of a letter written by Baillie carries with it the tacit assumption that the text survives simply to provide historians with details about an event that fell between 1637 and 1662. Baillie has been variously taken as representative of a 'Scottish' or a 'Covenanting' opinion on a debate in the Westminster Assembly; he has been cited as an 'eyewitness' to treaty negotiations in 1640, 1646 or 1649; and he has been quoted for representative flavour of 'popular' reaction to Laudian liturgical reforms. However heavy-handed such uses of Baillie's letters may be, in one sense they actually perpetuate Baillie's own vision for his collection of documents. In his own day, Baillie had carefully selected and preserved documents that supported a partisan version of events during the British Civil

---

[1]   Robert Baillie to William Cunningham, earl of Glencairn, n.d., *LJB*, vol. III, p. 476.

Wars and Interregnum. What survives, however, constituted little more than a rough narrative outline alongside the documents themselves. The surviving collection, therefore, still includes a wealth of unguarded remarks and other hints about their use and readership that would not have been evident had they been revised for publication. From careful analysis of Baillie's surviving manuscript collections, we may discern his idea of events as he conceived of them and as he hoped others would remember them.

What follows draws on recent work in reader reception, book history and archival studies, and memory studies to inform discussion of the creation and transmission of Baillie's manuscript letters, as well as the origins and manipulation of Baillie's historiographical legacy. Throughout this monograph, Baillie's manuscript letters have loomed large as one of the key sources for establishing the contours of his life. This chapter discusses the material characteristics and formal organization of these manuscripts, highlighting myriad ways in which they have been read and edited by others across the centuries. A collection of documents may tell a story about historical events, but so too do the criteria of selection and editing that informed compilation of the collection in the first place. Looking past their current, modern bindings, and delving past centuries of readership, the physical artefact of Baillie's manuscript letters tells a story about the ways in which Baillie wanted events to be remembered.[2] A collector like Baillie 'actively processed, shaped, and imposed meaning on the very materials [their collections] contained'. These collections, however, were not static repositories of evidence; they were conceived by contemporaries as 'dynamic and creative spaces dedicated to the production of knowledge'.[3] Baillie's manuscripts, moreover, were not created in a vacuum. They were the product and expression of social connections maintained by Baillie during his lifetime. Baillie, like John Aubrey after him, created a manuscript account of his own times through collaboration.[4]

Through Baillie's historical correspondence and his voluminous manuscript collections, he amassed – much like the diarist John Evelyn in his library – a 'more comprehensive representation of his times' than he could have accomplished in a single narrative work.[5] In the process, Baillie was creating a complex and unique record of his life. Centuries of manuscript and print transmission and reception have obscured this characteristic and, indeed, the collection's convoluted textual history has gone some way to muzzling Baillie's distinctive voice. Like Baillie, the Cologne burgher

[2] On the obfuscation of modern archival practices, see Jeffrey Todd Knight, *Bound to Read: Compilations, Collections, and the Making of Renaissance Literature* (Philadelphia, 2013).

[3] Jennifer Summit, *Memory's Library: Medieval Books in Early Modern England* (Chicago, 2008), pp. 15, 238.

[4] Kate Bennett (ed.), *John Aubrey: Brief Lives with An Apparatus for the Lives of our English Mathematical Writers* (2 vols, Oxford, 2015), vol. I, lv.

[5] Kate Loveman, *Samuel Pepys and His Books: Reading, Newsgathering and Sociability, 1660–1703* (Oxford, 2015), p. 280.

Hermann Weinsberg or the Catalan tanner Miquel Parets also created collections of eyewitness testimony illustrative of their own times and their lives, retaining peculiarities or idiosyncrasies of their own lived experience.[6] There was what one commentator has described as a 'sprawling culture' of life-writing in early modern England, found in records as diverse as almanacs and family Bibles. Much like these forms of life-writing, Baillie's manuscript letters were characterized by ongoing, retrospective and accumulative processes of creation and revision.[7] Record-keeping, along the lines practised by Baillie, was itself a form of life-writing that shuns modern expectations of a structured narrative arc and retains the strange grammar of the early modern archive. History-writing and biography were considered inseparable: two sides of the same coin.[8] Consider, for instance, Gilbert Burnet's *History of His Own Times* or Evelyn's *Diary*. Both texts are considered early examples of life-writing, yet they are also important eyewitness records of Restoration Britain. In similar vein, Baillie was writing his own life through the concurrent processes of collection, transcription and narration.

Biography, or an account of his own life, for Baillie, was history. Interpretative problems arose because subsequent generations of readers approached his manuscript letters as history-writing, ignoring the extent to which these letters were also a vital record of Baillie's life. This chapter, therefore, shows how these motivations to document his times and his life could simultaneously inform Baillie's decision to create an archive of letters and other documents. It reconstructs the dynamic textual history of Baillie's manuscript collections, drawing together thematic analysis from preceding chapters and suggesting how re-evaluation of Baillie's life and writings may inform future historiographical use of his correspondence. Libraries and archives alike are central to who we are, because historically they have been central to who we were, 'organizing the individual and collective memories that make up the stories of our lives as individuals, peoples, and nations'.[9] In similar vein, Baillie set out to organize personal and collective memories of the conflicts that erupted in Scotland and soon spread throughout Britain and Ireland. The first two sections explore the origins and compilation of Baillie's manuscript letters, highlighting the rationale that informed Baillie's decision to write to correspondents in the first place, principles of selection that guided creation of the manuscript collections and some comments regarding Baillie's intended aims for the collections. The third section moves from discussion of Baillie's creative efforts to address the reception of his

---

[6] See discussions of these sources in Matthew Lundin, *Paper Memory: A Sixteenth-Century Townsman Writes His World* (Cambridge, 2012) and James Amelang, *The Flight of Icarus: Artisan Autobiography in Early Modern Europe* (Stanford, 1998).

[7] Adam Smyth, *Autobiography in Early Modern England* (Cambridge, 2010), pp. 209, 210.

[8] According to the *OED*, early usage of the term 'biography' referred to a particular form of history-writing.

[9] Summit, *Memory's Library*, p. 239.

letters and manuscript collections during his own lifetime and after his death. Readers mined Baillie's letters for illustrative details and eyewitness narrative whilst avoiding mention of Baillie himself. Following his death in 1662, readers made subtle editorial decisions that further disassociated Baillie's life and creative energies from the manuscripts that he had compiled. The penultimate section explores how editorial decisions further altered the character and meaning of Baillie's manuscript letters in two published editions. Baillie's 'life' was physically separated from the main body of his letters, and the letters were transformed by his nineteenth-century editor, David Laing, into an archive of Covenanting rule in Scotland. Such editorial decisions fundamentally impacted Baillie's legacy. The chapter concludes by arguing that Baillie's paper legacy has shrouded his significant contributions to intellectual culture in the mid-seventeenth century. Whilst not privileging one reading of Baillie over another – indeed he was simultaneously a contemporary chronicler and an engaged participant – future use of Baillie's letters and documents must acknowledge the deeply ambiguous and fretful views of their original compiler.

I

Baillie's manuscript 'letters and journals' mainly comprise a thoughtful and deliberate selection of outgoing correspondence. To better understand the reasons why he selected correspondence for inclusion, we must begin by discussing the reasons lying behind the correspondence itself. When Baillie wrote to his correspondents, he was not just saying things, he was doing something.[10] The majority of Baillie's surviving letters were written to transmit a narrative of the Civil Wars in Britain to his main correspondent, William Spang, based in the Netherlands. This was part of a broader aim to document and preserve a sympathetic account of the Covenanters for posterity. In some cases, Baillie promoted his own version of events, or personal hopes for civil or religious reform. Elsewhere, Baillie acted as advocate for Scottish representatives at the Westminster Assembly trying (in vain) to get foreign divines to write favourable position papers that could be used to influence debate in London. In this regard, many of the letters and documents that survive were selected by Baillie for historical or propagandistic purposes. Such letters made their way into Baillie's manuscript collections because, from an early stage, he decided to create an archive illustrative of Covenanting involvement in – not to mention his own contributions to – the conflicts that tore apart Britain and the religious debates that erupted as a result.

Spang was largely dependent on Baillie for news of the progress of con-

---

[10] William Merrill Decker, *Epistolary Practices: Letter Writing in America before Telecommunications* (Chapel Hill, 1998).

flicts over liturgical reforms and royal power that ignited in Scotland and soon spread throughout the Atlantic archipelago. Baillie, on the other hand, wrote detailed narratives to Spang so that Spang could provide Reformed Christendom with an account that demonstrated the righteousness of the Covenanters' cause. Soon after the Prayer Book Riots, for instance, Baillie explained: 'I shall shew yow the estate of our affaires as they are, at least as I am informed of them; though as yet, they are hinging without any certaintie, so much as propension to settle in any posture, which is knowen to us, or well imaginable to any man.'[11] Early hesitation yielded to a sense of prophetic certainty, when Baillie later wrote that the Glasgow Assembly's reforms 'fitted excellentlie with gifts correspondent to the extraordinarie exigents of the tymes, I wish ye had them well descryved: they could serve our friend [i.e. Spang] for verie good purpose, to be materialls for his Latine storie'.[12] As will be discussed further below, Spang continued to expand his 'Latin storie' to two volumes – *Brevis Narratio Rerum in Regno Scotiae gestarum* (1640) and *Motuum Britannicorum Verax Cushi ex ipsis Joabi et oculati testis prototypis totus translatus* (1647) – as well as forwarding Baillie's correspondence and documents to the German historian Georgius Hornius, which subsequently comprised the evidence for his *Commentarius de Statu Ecclesiae Britannicae hodierno* (1647).

Baillie's historical narrative, to which we will return throughout this chapter, was only one of a range of strategies that he employed in his correspondence with Spang and other foreign intermediaries to promote the Covenanting cause and seek support from abroad. Alongside his historical correspondence, Baillie wrote to Spang to seek assistance in disseminating and popularizing published and manuscript treatises on religious controversies. Baillie was writing largely of his own accord, in no way should his letters be confused with official interests of the Covenanting regime. His letters may, however, be considered 'public' insofar as he intended (or expected) a particular item to be read by multiple recipients. Although English-language works were relatively rare in Continental Europe, since few Europeans could read English, Baillie's record of distributing his own works abroad suggests a fluidity in language barriers that subsisted amongst members of his extended correspondence network.[13] Notably, Baillie never remarked on the potential linguistic restrictions of circulating tracts in English. For instance, in 1640 he wrote to Spang with instructions to distribute his *Ladensium* 'to Rivett, to Tisius [Antoine Thysius], to Voetius, to Paris, to Geneva, to Somer [Saumur], to Tigur'.[14] Five years later, Baillie likewise

---

[11] Robert Baillie to William Spang, 4 October 1637, *LJB*, vol. I, p. 15.
[12] Robert Baillie to William Spang, 12 October 1639, *LJB*, vol. I, p. 187.
[13] Paul Hoftijzer, 'British Books Abroad: The Continent', in John Barnard and D.F. McKenzie (eds), *Cambridge History of the Book in Britain* (6 vols, Cambridge, 1999–2012), vol. IV, pp. 735–43.
[14] Robert Baillie to William Spang, [September 1640], *LJB*, vol. I, p. 247.

sent Spang seven copies of his *Dissuasive from the Errors of the Time* (1645) with directions to forward them to 'Thomas Cunninghame, Mr. Strickland, Apollonius, Spanheim, Dr. Stewart, and Voetius'.[15] Whilst Cunnningham, Strickland and Stewart were Scots, there is no suggestion in this, or other letters, that Apollonius, Spanheim and Voetius might be unable to read his work.[16] Indeed, Voetius and his scholarly circle had often been criticized as Anglophiles for reading English works of practical divinity and even conversing in English.[17] As Baillie himself was connected to Scots and Dutch individuals who were conversant in both vernaculars, it is unsurprising to find a Dutch translation of one of Baillie's pamphlets. It was not uncommon to find Dutch translations of Covenanting tracts in circulation, such as the 1639 translation of *An information to all good Christians*. In similar vein, Baillie's *Review of Bramhall* (1649) was translated into Dutch and reprinted in 1661 as *Ondersoeck van Doctor Brambels waerchouwinge tegens de Kerckenregeringe der Schotten* (Utrecht).[18]

Baillie also used his correspondence network to seek support proactively from divines in the Low Countries and further afield for ecclesiastical reforms. Insofar as Baillie was attached to an international 'Republic of Letters', he largely exploited these links for practical ends. He was less concerned with exchanging learned correspondence, than he was with the pressing religious and political issues over which Britain had descended into civil war. Baillie established correspondence with foreign divines, in similar fashion to correspondence carried out by the New England ministers John Eliot and John Woodbridge, because of a shared sense of godly fellowship that transcended confessional or geographic boundaries.[19] Baillie conceived of the English and Scottish churches as part of a broader community of Reformed Christians that could, if asked, offer advice as to how the structures and doctrine of the British churches might be reformed. The appearance of support from Reformed divines within an international Republic of Letters comforted Baillie when the 'mad' Sectaries threatened to 'subdue our Kingdome' in 1646, because he believed that the godly were 'united, and assisted by all

---

[15] Robert Baillie to William Spang, 29 November 1645, *LJB*, vol. II, p. 327.
[16] Given the close relationships between Baillie, Spang and these divines, it is highly unlikely that these divines did not understand these documents – whether through a translator, or by reading – and did not say anything about these difficulties.
[17] I am grateful for discussions with Anthony Milton on this point. Also, see Keith L. Sprunger, *Dutch Puritanism: A History of English and Scottish Churches of the Netherlands* (Leiden, 1982), pp. 361–2.
[18] The former work was translated and published in the same year as *Informatie aen alle goede Christenen in het coninckrijck van Enghelant*. See the copy in NLS, APS.3.90.8. For a bibliography of English puritan works translated into Dutch, see Jan van der Haar, *From Abbadie to Young: A Bibliography of English, Most [sic] Puritan Works, Translated into the Dutch Language* (2 vols, Veenendaal, 1980).
[19] Alison Searle, '"Though I am a Stranger to You by Face, Yet in Neere Bonds by Faith": A Transatlantic Puritan Republic of Letters', *Early American Literature*, 43 (2008), pp. 277–308.

the power which Ireland, France, Holland, Denmark, and all our friends in England, could make us'.[20]

Idealistic aspirations, however, were thwarted as a result of incessant and subtle theological differences that persisted amongst Reformed divines. Venting his frustration, for instance, over the effect of a letter solicited from the Dutch ecclesiastical assembly (or Classis) at Walcheren, Baillie feared that other assemblies 'shall either not write, or delay too long, or write obscurely; for, as I conceave, they are not at a point, in their own mind, as yett, what to stand at'.[21] Baillie's list of foreign correspondents is admittedly short and his network of Continental divines may appear relatively minor: only three extant letters addressed to Baillie by Continental divines (Voetius and Rivet) and three letters by Baillie to Voetius survive. Yet, through face-to-face contact – in 1641 in London with Rivet and, in 1645 and in 1649, in the Netherlands – and through his extensive exchanges with Spang and other Scots agents abroad, such as David Buchanan in France, Baillie maintained effective links with the wider Reformed community. This is not to mention hints of other letters that were not selected for inclusion in his manuscript collections, including, in 1644, 'Apollonius's letter and questions I had gotten before by another secret means', and, in 1661, a letter that Baillie had received from Voetius in which the Dutch theologian had posed several questions on church government and 'wrote to me concerning Mr W[alter] Bowie's widow'.[22] Evidently, Baillie carried on with Apollonius – minister of the church at Middleburg neighbouring Spang's congregation at Veere – and Voetius in a manner more commonly associated with *epistulae ad familiares*, further suggesting the strength and intimacy of connections that he maintained.

Through Baillie's contact with David Buchanan, for instance, he attempted with varied success to establish links with Huguenot and Swiss Reformed churches. Buchanan's life is difficult to reconstruct though it appears that he had spent a lengthy period of time abroad from his apparent knowledge of French and from Baillie's perception that he was well connected to these communities. For instance, in a letter addressed generically '[f]or Scotland' – indicating a letter that was probably circulated among ministers in Glasgow – Baillie lauded Buchanan as 'a most sincere and zealous gentleman, who hes done, both in write and print, here and over-sea, many singular services to ... the whole cause'.[23] In the first extant letter to Buchanan, Baillie had deemed it 'very expedient' that Buchanan write to 'some of the ministers of Paris,

---

20 Robert Baillie to William Spang, 26 June 1646, *LJB*, vol. II, pp. 376–7.
21 Robert Baillie to William Spang, 17 May [1644], *LJB*, vol. II, p. 183.
22 Ibid.; Robert Baillie to William Spang, 31 January 1661, *LJB*, vol. III, p. 449. Baillie's response to these queries is extant in his manuscripts, see NCL, Baill MS 4/3, 'Reverendissimis doctissimis, ac plurimum dilectis in Christo fratribus S. Theologiae Praefessoribus in Academia Ultrajectina'. For other indications of such correspondence, see *LJB*, vol. II, pp. 197, 313.
23 'For Scotland', 24 April 1646, *LJB*, vol. II, p. 367.

Geneva, and Berne' about the 'true estate of our affairs', and how 'a mighty faction is arisen, to press liberty of conscience for all sects'. Baillie asked that churches in Geneva and Berne might exhort the Westminster Assembly to 'beware of that pernicious liberty', albeit acknowledging the dangers inherent in French Huguenots writing publicly. When Spang's intervention had failed to elicit a response from Frédéric Spanheim, Professor of Theology at Leiden, Baillie asked Buchanan to write to Spanheim and the renowned Huguenot critic of Roman Catholicism Pierre du Moulin, asking them to supply letters 'conceived in the greatest names they could procure [i.e. a national assembly or university]'.[24] Writing to Spang, Baillie reported that Buchanan's requests evidently 'produced a letter from Mr. Drillingcourt [i.e. Charles Drelincourt]' at Paris, a letter from du Moulin 'more to the purpose, and our mind' and, from Spanheim, an explanation that he was 'not disposed to write at this time, except the Universitie [of Leiden] would lay it upon him'.[25]

Typically, Baillie solicited the opinions of foreign divines on theological controversies as they arose in debates at the Westminster Assembly. During the Interregnum, Baillie continued this habit as he wrote to London ministers, such as Edmund Calamy, Jeremiah Whitaker, Simeon Ashe, James Cranford, Samuel Clarke, Lazarus Seaman, William Taylor and Francis Rous MP, asking for support in the Protestor–Resolutioner Controversy and attempting to revive a British network of presbyterian divines.[26] Baillie evidently continued to solicit support throughout his career despite countless failures. His resolve in these matters shows his aspirations for reforms as well as his detached and often quixotic outlook. Instinctively preferring to rest his arguments on external authorities, before Baillie decided to support the Covenanters' armed resistance of Charles I, for example, he wrote to Spang, asking that he 'try the minde of Rivett and Voetius'; as Baillie later wrote, 'we would be refreshed by their incouragement'. Events in Scotland in 1638 should ostensibly have been viewed with universal trepidation, so Baillie wondered why '[a]ll forraigne divines hitherto hes been silent … though popery should swell on Brittaine'.[27]

In a more public context, Baillie asked divines to write letters supporting reforms being debated at the Westminster Assembly. Although such letters sometimes returned forms of support not entirely to Baillie's liking, it has been convincingly argued that Baillie's persistent efforts to isolate congregationalists from the international Reformed community provoked ministers

---

[24] 'Memorandum to David Buchanan', *LJB*, vol. II, pp. 179–80.
[25] Robert Baillie to William Spang, 28 June [1644], *LJB*, vol. II, p. 197. In fact, the university did charge Spanheim with this duty, and he wrote a detailed response to Buchanan's letters, published in London as *Friderici Spanhemii Epistola ad Nobilissimum Virum Davidem Buchananum* (London, 1645). The letter in the published tract is dated February 1645, after Baillie's letter here cited.
[26] For example, *LJB*, vol. III, pp. 204–5, 224–8, 231–2, 235–6, 302–7, 309–10.
[27] Robert Baillie to William Spang, 22 July [1638], *LJB*, vol. I, pp. 92–3, 112.

on both sides of the Atlantic to look to each other for support.[28] Expressing frustration, Baillie bluntly wrote to Buchanan asking that he would 'gett your friends so informed, that they ... would write according to the mind of our Church'. If they could not do so, Buchanan should ensure that 'they may be silent till they see what it may be the will of God to doe with these poor distressed Churches'.[29] It was more difficult than he had believed to get foreign divines from different confessional contexts to write according to the minds of the Scottish commissioners at Westminster. Baillie sought to overcome these challenges by directing attention away from debates over church government and towards issues of theological error that, he believed, might enjoy broader support. Whereas early in his correspondence Baillie had tended to make sweeping requests that divines such as John Ponet, Johannes Cloppenburg, Rivet and Voetius should write works 'which are most profitable for the Reformed Churches', over the course of the 1640s Baillie became increasingly specific amidst the frustrating fortunes of his desired reforms.[30] He even revealed that he was trying to muster support from Gerardus Vossius, a theologian whom Baillie had elsewhere attacked as heterodox.[31] To this end, Baillie requested that Spang ask John Forbes of Corse for assistance in convincing 'his friend Vossius to print that [which] he told me he had readie against the Anabaptists'. Continuing, Baillie offered further praise of Forbes's *Instructiones* – discussed in a previous chapter – and asked Spang whether he could persuade Forbes to write a 'Supplement, wherein he may handle Anabaptisme, Antinomianisme, the Erastian, and the rest of the modern sects'.[32] Indeed, Baillie's request to Vossius suggests that Baillie may have had previous correspondence with him, and perhaps even met him in person since this request came after Baillie's brief journey to the Netherlands earlier in 1645. It also shows that Baillie was clearly tailoring specific requests for works to those best suited to undertake the task.[33] In letters from early 1646, Baillie repeated earlier demands for an anti-anabaptist work from Vossius – 'press Vossius to print what he told me he had beside him against the Anabaptists' – and Forbes, but also added a plea that once Spanheim had finished refuting Amyraut's soteriology, he would go 'on with his *Collegium Anabaptisticum*'.[34] Whatever Baillie's role in providing the requisite impetus, exhortations of Vossius and Spanheim appear to have borne fruit. Vossius published his *De Baptismo disputationes XX* (Amsterdam, 1648)

---

[28] Francis J. Bremer, *Congregational Communion: Clerical Friendship in the Anglo-American Puritan Community, 1610–1692* (Boston, 1994), pp. 164–5.
[29] Robert Baillie to David Buchanan, n.d. [late 1644], *LJB*, vol. II, p. 253.
[30] Robert Baillie to William Spang, 15 July [1641], *LJB*, vol. I, pp. 357–8.
[31] I discuss Baillie's critiques of Vossius in Chapter 6.
[32] Robert Baillie to William Spang, 29 November 1645, *LJB*, vol. II, p. 327.
[33] Along with the evidence that Baillie knew that Vossius had written a tract against anabaptists, Spanheim had previously published *Variae disputationes anti-Anabaptisticae* (Leiden, 1643).
[34] Robert Baillie to William Spang, [January 1646], *LJB*, vol. II, p. 342.

and Spanheim's *Diatribe historica de origine, progressu, sectis et nominibus ana-baptistarum* (Franeker, 1645) was translated into English as *Englands Warning by Germanies Woe* (London, 1646). Spanheim's work also received a critical response from the target of Baillie's anti-anabaptist writings, John Tombes, in his *Refutatio positionis ejusque confirmationis paedo-baptismum esse licitum affirmantis ab Henrico Savage* (London, 1653).

II

The manuscript of Baillie's letters began as a hodgepodge collection of outgoing correspondence before his aims clarified and Baillie began in earnest a life-long practice of historical record-keeping. According to a contemporary index, now-lost correspondence comprised the first seven leaves of Baillie's manuscript letters and included seven items dating from 1636 addressed to local ministers (John Bell and Robert Livingston), his patron (Alexander Cunningham), his daughter (Elizabeth), his cousin (Spang) and an unidentified gentleman, 'Sr. Ja.', probably based in Dublin.[35] Most likely, these earliest entries comprised copies of correspondence that Baillie deemed sufficiently important to save, perhaps for use later in life. Yet with the increased tensions in January 1637 over the looming introduction of a new Prayer Book, Baillie recognized that his correspondence also constituted a valuable source for a history of his own times. He was well placed to comment on affairs as they progressed and he used his pre-existing epistolary link with Spang to share his thoughts and circulate supporting documentation. With little apparent forethought, though great awareness of the importance of documentary preservation, Baillie began to compile an invaluable historical record of Scotland under the Covenanters. I shall now discuss Baillie's practice as archivist of his personal papers, looking at how he began to preserve a selection of correspondence, and indicating likely precedents for his practice, before addressing readership and editorial marks that further help to illuminate Baillie's record-keeping practices.

The practice of transcribing correspondence alongside official documents is not without precedent. Baillie would have been accustomed to such documents from his experiences attending kirk session and presbytery meetings, at which a clerk compiled a register in similar fashion to Baillie's manuscript collections. Alongside an attendance list and committee decisions, a 'session book' also included transcriptions of incoming and outgoing correspondence and other documents illustrative of official proceedings. Baillie's practice as collector and editor also reflected a shift in early modern historiography towards extensive documentation and the production of first-hand accounts or eyewitness testimony alongside a historical narrative.[36]

---

[35] NCL, Baill MS 4/1, [fo. 382r].
[36] Daniel Woolf, *The Idea of History in Early Stuart England: Erudition, Ideology, and 'The Light of Truth' from the Accession of James I to the Civil War* (Toronto, 1990), p. 256.

In a Scottish context, these practices were embraced notably by David Calderwood and John Spottiswood, and, towards the end of the century, by the Scot Robert Wodrow. In an English context, these works and Baillie's manuscript collections may be compared with John Rushworth's *Historical Collections* (1659–1701) and Bulstrode Whitelocke's *Memorials of the English Affairs* (1682). Like Baillie, Whitelocke and Rushworth were able to produce detailed historical narratives furnished by rich documentary evidence, on account of their involvement at the highest governmental levels during the Civil Wars. Unsurprisingly, the ideological animus behind Baillie's letters and the historical collections of Rushworth and Whitelocke are much less pronounced than that found in, for example, Baillie's *Historicall Vindication of the Government of the Church of Scotland* (1646) or Peter Heylyn's critical history of presbyterianism, *Aerius Redivivus* (1670).

Despite striking similarities in method, it must be emphasized that Baillie created this bound archive as a working copy, a dynamic repository of source evidence to be used and with which he (and others, too) could actively engage. It is therefore misleading to refer to Baillie's practice as a collector as one of 'documentary preservation'.[37] Such a label fails to do justice to the creative practices at work in the formation of Baillie's historical collections, instead, conjuring up an image of a static, immutable record. David Laing's edition of Baillie's *Letters and Journals* furthered this misleading perception of the manuscripts themselves, beginning with dramatic flare: 'the Proclamation of our Liturgie is the matter of my greatest affliction … I am greatly affrayit that this aple of contention have banishit peic[e] from our poor Church heireftir for ever'.[38] From this edition, Baillie emerged as a prescient, historically minded contemporary, perfectly placed to bear witness for all of posterity to events that would soon deteriorate into rioting and civil war. By contrast, the manuscript letters begin mid-sentence on a leaf foliated '7', in a heavily edited passage: 'he speks so much to ~~the~~ his honoure ~~of Vossius~~ & comendation of his ~~book~~ story as does greatlie further ~~that~~ sort of ~~natural~~ insinuation which that book hes without so great a testimonie from so divin a mouth'.[39] With no benefit of the hindsight Laing injected into his edition, Baillie's manuscript letters begin with an illuminating passage detailing his engagement in contemporary theological controversies. The first surviving sentences include an obtuse reference to a work by Archbishop James Ussher of Armagh on the little-known medieval saint Gottschalk of Orbais, and Baillie's criticism of Ussher for not speaking out against the Dutch theologian Gerardus Vossius.

As we move through the quarto leaves of the manuscript letters, their *ad hoc* arrangement is inescapable. Baillie's manuscripts portrayed the Prayer

---

[37] As per Lundin's discussion of Hermann Weinsberg's *Gedenkbuch*. See Lundin, *Paper Memory*.

[38] Robert Baillie to William Wilkie, Kilwinning, 2 January 1637, *LJB*, vol. I, p. 1.

[39] NCL, Bail MS 4/1, 'Letters and Journals', fo. 7.

Book Riots and the subsequent conflicts in Scotland as reluctant acts of defiance, the result of exhaustive deliberation, which was painstakingly documented. As Baillie clarified his purpose in gathering together outgoing correspondence and documents, subtle changes may be detected in the physical characteristics of the manuscripts themselves. Items in the manuscript became more frequent and the means of their transcription gradually changed. Between the fragment of Baillie's letter to 'Sr. Ja.' and the next transcribed item there is a gap of four months – from 29 August 1636 to 2 January 1637 – after which items survive on a much more regular basis. Whilst the note to William Wilkie – the first letter in Laing's edition – is in Baillie's hand, the following item, the first lengthy historical letter to his cousin Spang, and most of the subsequent items in these three manuscript volumes are in the hand of an amanuensis. At the outset, Baillie only once varied the practice of using a copyist – unidentified, though perhaps a young and diligent parishioner in Kilwinning at this juncture – and the only other full item in Baillie's hand is his letter of 1637 to the archbishop of Glasgow.[40] Arguably, this item and the letter to Wilkie – in which Baillie infamously wrote 'Bishopes I love' – survive in his difficult hand because Baillie had reproduced them for different reasons. A copyist was probably used to help save time and to make the manuscripts legible for other readers. By contrast, correspondence in his own hand included evidence of Baillie's faithfulness to the Scottish episcopate that would have been exculpatory should early calls for reform have failed and should Baillie have found himself needing to justify his allegiance to the episcopate. Whilst unsure about how his views on episcopacy might sit with other prominent ministers agitating for reform, in 1637 and 1638 Baillie hedged his bets and his manuscript collections became a repository for pieces of paper insurance.

Besides fleeting considerations of self-preservation, Baillie largely selected items for inclusion in his manuscript collections because he perceived them as being valuable to an historical account of the Covenanters. Transcribed letters typically have a distinctive narrative thread running through them, and the tedium of daily life is often, regrettably, absent. Baillie's criteria for selection of correspondence for inclusion are further highlighted through discussion of a Baillie holograph letter, excluded from his collections. There is only one such example that I have been able to locate: a brief note to an unidentified recipient settling his personal debts in case he was killed early in the 1640s.[41] There is an additional sheet appended on which Baillie outlined his outstanding credits and debts. As Baillie wrote to the unnamed recipient, 'the danger of thes onhappy tymes hes mad me by the advys of friends

---

[40] See NCL, Baill MS 4/1, fo. 11r [to the Archbishop of Glasgow].
[41] These two holograph items are in the Macphail Collection in the National Library of Scotland. They were acquired in the early twentieth century. Laing had probably failed in locating this item since they were previously in a private collection.

to assigne to my children the litle thing I have'.[42] The style and content of this letter stands in stark contrast to the lengthy narratives that typify correspondence Baillie selected for transcription. Read alongside Baillie's other surviving testaments from the early 1640s – both included in his manuscript collections – this letter appears as an insignificant addendum: evidence of the practicalities which attended the arrangement of his estate rather than evidence of the extent and disbursement of the estate.

Despite evidence of early indecision and a rush to gather records, Baillie's manuscripts largely show evidence that they were thoughtfully curated. The contents of Baillie MS 4/1, 4/2 and 4/3 were deliberately gathered from disparate sources, bound together and, subsequently, read and edited by Baillie himself. Although the current bindings date from the 1920s, it appears that most of the material was organized in the form in which they currently survive. Nevertheless, there are a few sections that may have been gathered together at a later date or that were appended or prefixed to Baillie's historical collections (by either Baillie or a later editor). The physical make-up and characteristics of all three quarto volumes shed light on the reasons why Baillie had created them and the uses to which these collections may have been put during his lifetime. Baillie MS 4/1 was created on an *ad hoc* basis, with the amount of documentation and its scope rapidly increasing as the crisis in Scotland deepened. This volume has the least consistent chronological order. Documents from the period 1637 to 1643 appear sporadically throughout, suggesting that Baillie's amanuensis transcribed documents when he got access to them. With the greatest number of documents appearing in this volume, it is also notable that Baillie transcribed documents illustrative of both 'Covenanter' and 'Royalist' positions.[43] Predating his promotion to Divinity Professor at Glasgow, during creation of this volume Baillie was able to devote more time towards documenting the ongoing conflicts.

With his translation to Glasgow University and, then, his appointment as one of the Scottish commissioners to the Westminster Assembly, Baillie's personal circumstances changed dramatically. These changes were reflected in his collecting habits and they are evident in the make-up of Baillie MS 4/2. Proportionally, this volume contains the least outgoing correspondence, but it also includes the first clear evidence that Baillie had conceived of these collections as a coherent whole. The first fifty leaves consist of transcriptions of various papers that Baillie had written on theological controversies in Scotland up until he departed for London. These papers originally may have been bound separately before Baillie gathered them together with other relevant material. Baillie had gathered together copies of these personal papers because he thought they might be valuable during debates at the Westminster Assembly. These might even be the same sheets that he had

---

[42]   NLS, MS 1036, Robert Baillie to [?], 21 March [?1642], fos 131r, 132r.
[43]   Although 'Royalist' documents usually appeared well after other documentation of the event described. For instance, see NCL, Baill MS, 1 fos 230v, 231r.

been asked to gather together in 1640 'for the convinceing of that praevalent faction [i.e. of Canterburian bishops]' during negotiations that resulted in the Treaty of London (1641).[44] Baillie probably feared (with good reason) carrying too many of his personal papers during the treacherous journey south and, therefore, thought it shrewd to make copies. This also helps to explain why some of the tracts, like Baillie's 'Meditation on the Canterburian faction' and his speech against Arminianism delivered at the Glasgow Assembly, survive elsewhere in his collections.[45]

Baillie's concern not only to collect but to preserve letters and documents reflected a discernible shift in his conception of the manuscript letters. The creation of these collections became an end in itself, not simply some haphazard exercise in record-keeping. Indeed, in Baillie MS 4/2 we find, for the first time, that Baillie gave a title and overarching description to the collection in his own hand: 'Letters and Papers from Nov. 1643 to Jun 1647'.[46] Despite his residence in a relatively unknown and enormous capital like London, Baillie made every effort to find a suitable copyist to assist as he carried on gathering what few meagre pieces of official material he could access. The sections of his London correspondence – transcribed in a neat, italic hand – include very little supplementary material. On his return to Edinburgh in April 1645, the hand of the copyist changed, and the number of supplementary documents balloons.[47] Changes in hand that reflected his movements suggest that Baillie had transcribed these documents and letters soon after their dated composition, if not before the letters were sent. Throughout his travels, Baillie prioritized transcribing outgoing correspondence and whatever documents he could find. Letters were sometimes transcribed around other documents or additional space was left in the manuscript indicating that Baillie made every effort to transcribe documents when he had access to them.[48] It is little wonder, then, that in the midst of controversies surrounding the Westminster Assembly it was Baillie – not Calderwood or Rutherford or Gillespie – who was asked to write a historical defence of the Church of Scotland.[49]

As the conflicts progressed, the propagandistic value of Baillie's historical collections – his manuscript letters – gradually aligned in more meaningful ways with his collecting and transcription habits. Baillie MS 4/3, therefore,

---

[44] Robert Baillie to Lillias Baillie, 5 November 1640, *LJB*, vol. I, p. 269.
[45] See, for example, Baill MS 4/2, fos 116r, 102v.
[46] Baill MS 4/2, fo. 43r.
[47] NCL, Baill MS 4/2, fo. 148r.
[48] For instance, a rather long letter to Spang is split and includes cross-references in the text: 'vide p. 113, the rest of Spangs lettre'. See, NCL, Baill MS 4/1, fos 113v, 119r (for the cross-reference). Also, see NCL, Baill MS 4/1, fo. 255r. Also see, Baill MS 4/3, fo. 76r for a blank left after some 'Animadversions' on the Western Remonstrance of 1650 before the start of a transcribed letter to Spang.
[49] See Baillie's exchanges with Alexander Henderson and David Calderwood in 1646 in *LJB*, vol. II, pp. 371–3.

is the first and only volume to begin with a title in Baillie's hand: 'Letters & Papers from March 1648 to 1660'.[50] By this juncture, it appears that Baillie had a much clearer purpose in mind: he was gathering this material together to write a history of the Covenanting movement. Whether or not this idea had originated with Baillie, in 1648 initial efforts were made to gather together material for an official 'History of the late troubles' and, in 1649, Baillie claimed that his name was put forward to write 'the Storie of the tymes'.[51] In Baillie MS 4/3, the organization and presentation of documents became clearer. Baillie made fewer interventions to correct spelling or other typographical errors – suggesting that he was consistently employing the same copyists who had become accustomed to his handwriting. And, notably, this final volume included the greatest number of marginal annotations in Baillie's hand that are best described as commentary.

Baillie, evidently, re-read his collections and made comments on the documents themselves in an attempt to organize his thoughts for a historical treatise that he never began to write. This section, therefore, concludes with a few remarks on the ways in which the first reader of these collections – Baillie himself – engaged with the text. Unlike modern archival practice that is focused on documentary preservation, an early modern collector like Baillie conceived of his manuscript collections in fluid terms: as a group of rough notebooks to be edited, amended and altered in line with his own thoughts on the transcribed documents.[52] These collections were created to be read, annotated and used – in ways reminiscent of Renaissance humanist reading habits and the sociable note-taking habits of later seventeenth-century scientific thinkers.[53]

Baillie's historical collections were gathered together in a rough, heavily edited format intended to serve as a resource for himself. Typically, his editorial interventions consisted in the correction of typographical errors or the addition of missing words which the copyist could not decipher.[54] He also added dates, titles or the names of recipients alongside longer descriptions of items. In some cases, these headings are neatly framed in the text, suggesting that space might have been left or that Baillie had included the title *before* the copyist had reproduced the document.[55] Elsewhere, cramped and sloppy addition of titles appear redolent of Baillie's hopes that these documents

---

[50] NCL, Baill MS 4/3, [n.p.].
[51] Robert Baillie to William Spang, 27 March 1648, *LJB*, vol. III, p. 60; Robert Baillie to William Spang, 14 September 1649, *LJB*, vol. III, p. 96.
[52] Bibliographic methods are typically conceived in similar terms, prioritizing 'collated' and 'perfect' volumes over those wanting pages. See Knight, *Bound to Read*, pp. 4–7.
[53] Elizabeth Yale, *Sociable Knowledge: Natural History and the Nation in Early Modern Britain* (New Haven, 2016).
[54] For example, Baillie's letter to Spang dated 27 February 1638, the day before the first subscriptions of the National Covenant, includes many blank spaces left by the copyist in which Baillie has supplied the missing word(s). See NCL, Baill MS 4/1, fos 44r–46r.
[55] For example, NCL, Baill MS 4/1, fos 105v–106r, 114r, 116r.

might enjoy wider readership as a sort of historical library of the Covenanters. For instance, Baillie added in the title 'Hemmersons Instructions for defensive armes' alongside the rather verbose heading for Alexander Henderson's important intervention in debates over armed resistance in 1639.[56] Elsewhere, Baillie squeezed in headings for a series of letters and documents related to debates he had held with parishioners over liturgical changes early in 1643.[57]

Archival signposting also took the form of critical commentary. Baillie commonly added contextual information to manuscripts in order to clarify content in the document itself; such a practice was common in the volume of his surviving manuscript sermons dating from 1648. This practice suggests another way in which manuscript production and collection were sociable acts: handwritten documents were immediately related to current events and developing social relations.[58] Laing's edition of the *Letters and Journals* does not adequately represent the extent to which the manuscripts were a work-in-progress. Two early notes suggest that Baillie viewed the documents as separate from his own thoughts. His immediate opinions could be added in in his own hand, such as on 4 October 1637 when he described 'my feirs ... [of] ane ecclesiastik separation but nou I am mor affrayit for a bloudie civill warr', or, at the end of a letter dated 22 July 1638 to Spang, when he added the remark, 'this day ... the serving maids in Edinburge began to drau doun the bishops prid when it was at the most'.[59] Before the transcription of a royal proclamation circulated in England, describing the 'seditious practises' of some in Scotland, Baillie included the sardonic annotation, 'strang[e] proclamation in all the parish churches of Ingland'.[60] These marginalia indicate that Baillie was increasingly aware that other writers might benefit from reading his historical collections. In another context, he might have been considering his documents for wider readership when he edited his conference on Arminian theology with John Creighton to remove evidence of Creighton's identity. Deletions included the original title Baillie had given to this collection of letters – 'To his reverend and loving cousinge Mr Jhon Chreighton preacher Att Pasiley' – renamed in Baillie's hand with the generic title, 'A conferenc by letters with a canterburian minister ~~for~~ anent the Arminian tenet of the Saintes apostasie'.[61] Throughout, Baillie replaced the friendly address 'Cousin' with the formal 'Sir', and he altered his valediction from 'your cousin' to 'loving friend'. More substantial deletions indicate that Baillie's letters were written in the midst of another controversy with 'yor schoolemaster ... Mr Jhone Hay' who was also convinced of the

---

[56] The title, in its entirety, reads 'The tymes requyre that the poynts following be pressed upon the people both by the preachers in publick and by vnderstanding and well affected professors in privat conference 1639'. See NCL, Baill MS 4/1, fo. 131r.
[57] NCL, Baill MS 4/2, fos 124r, 126r, 127r, 129r.
[58] Cf. Bennett, 'Introduction', in *Aubrey Brief Lives*, vol. I, lv, lxxxvi.
[59] NCL, Baill MS 4/1, fos 15v, 96v.
[60] NCL, Baill MS 4/1, fo. 137v.
[61] NCL, Baill MS 4/2, fo. 2r.

dubious tenet of the Saints' apostasy.[62] Elsewhere, Baillie expressed reluctance to answer Creighton, perhaps since Baillie was unconvinced of the value of these protracted disputes over an insignificant theological point. As Baillie wrote, '[t]he reasone why I delay it so long this my thrid lybell wes my doubt [that] long I had whither to make any aunswer at all and now when it comes it will be so evill written That it cannot I feir be gotten weill redd for I had so litle pleasur in this task'.[63]

III

It is, therefore, unfounded to suggest that Baillie would have been 'abhorred' to learn of the wide readership that his letters have enjoyed since his death.[64] Baillie wrote to Spang (not to mention others) so that his letters could be circulated, read widely and discussed. Spang read and, conceivably, may have translated Baillie's letters into Latin or Dutch to augment readership even further. Baillie's letters formed the basis of three historical accounts of the British conflicts published in his lifetime. After his death, historians interested in the Church of Scotland continued to read and mine Baillie's manuscripts for illustrative quotations and more. In the process, Baillie's biography became disassociated from the content of the valuable historical sources that he had preserved. Readers and editors subtly altered aspects of Baillie's life substantiated in his letters – such as his professed affinity for episcopacy – affirming the orthodox credentials of the historical collections as a whole. Through these changes, Baillie's manuscript collections became a site for contests over the evolving identity of the Church of Scotland whilst his contributions to such debates in his own lifetime were forgotten.

In fact, it was the ambiguity of Baillie's personal ideological commitments, and the resulting appropriations of Baillie's historical collections in the decades following his death, that led the historian Andrew Stevenson to baulk at the task of producing an edition in the eighteenth century. Writing in 1753, Stevenson admitted that Baillie's manuscript collections had enjoyed widespread readership amongst specialists, but he decided against publication because 'those collections were not prepared for publick view; they contain only a heap of unconnected letters and papers, which the principal thought proper to preserve ... they are so interspersed as quite to marr the thread of the history'.[65] Baillie evidently set out to gather together these paper artefacts to further a particular ideological cause. As he explained in the preface to

---

[62] NCL, Baill MS 4/2, fo. 11v. For the edited letter, see Baill MS 1, p. 15.
[63] NCL, Baill MS 4/2, fo. 38v. For the edited letter, see Baill MS 1, p. 53.
[64] David Stevenson, 'Mere Hasty Babblements? Mr Robert Baillie', in *King or Covenant? Voices from Civil War* (East Linton, 1996), pp. 17–39.
[65] Andrew Stevenson, *The History of the Church and State of Scotland* (2 vols, Edinburgh, 1753–57), vol. I, 'Preface'.

his *Historical Vindication*, the manuscript collections he gathered would 'let the world know the plaine truth' about significant events, such as the Prayer Book Riots of 1637, that had hitherto been recounted 'in no other habit then of monstrous tragedies'.[66] Despite such prophetic certainty in print, a problem remained: Baillie's manuscript letters comprised the building blocks for a history, not the finished edifice. He had gathered evidence with the tacit purpose of defending his own actions and those of his compatriots throughout the tumultuous decades of the 1640s and 1650s. Yet, in their surviving form, there is no narrative path guiding readers through the gnarled undergrowth of documents that he had collected.

As a result, early readers used his manuscript letters to forward specific and, sometimes, divergent, ideological programmes. In the first place, Baillie's letters furnished his cousin Spang and Spang's correspondent Hornius with source material for three Latin histories of the Civil Wars. Spang's and Hornius's uses of Baillie's letters in published Latin histories of the British conflicts unearthed a latently partisan tone, blurring the boundaries between epistolary correspondence and polemical tracts. Spang, for instance, had claimed that his first historical work on the Covenanters had been 'ploughed up from Scottish writings' that had not been previously translated into Latin. When studying the 'greatest authors in their pure and simple verity', Spang continued, one may better know the 'elegant colour' of their writings as well as the precise language used to 'graphically depict' their conflict.[67] Likewise, Hornius set out to satisfy a 'yearning desire' amongst his readers to know the true character of the state of churches in Britain through discussion of 'all types of writings' that had sprung forth from the conflicts.[68] Unlike Spang, who was less forthcoming in identifying Baillie as his primary source, Hornius singled out 'the writings of Robert Baillie, pastor of Kilwinning, delegate to the Westminster Assembly, and author of the compendium, *Ladensium Autokatakrisis*' as his source for an account of the foundations and progress of bishops in Scotland and 'The Synod of Glasgow's acts and decrees against them'.[69] Despite Spang and Baillie's close friendship, Spang's use of Baillie's letters did not amount to slavish transcription. Spang took Baillie's accounts and fashioned a swift narrative that glossed over any hints of early indecision (often stirred up by Baillie personally) amongst Covenanting elite, so evident in Baillie's letters. Spang ignored Baillie's dissent to the vote *abjuring* episcopacy in Scotland – as well as ignoring Baillie's description of the support aired for his dissent. By contrast, Spang merely recounted that 'Prelacy was judged to be abjured by a unanimous vote.' Spang, then, moved swiftly from the conclusions of the Glasgow Assembly to recount the proceedings of the

---

66 Baillie, *Historicall Vindication*, sig. B2r.
67 [William Spang], *Brevis et fidelis narratio*, sig. A2r.
68 Georgius Hornius, *De Statu Ecclesiae Britannicae hodierno, liber commentarius* (Danzig, 1647), 'Praefatio ad Lectorem'.
69 Ibid.

Scottish Parliament of 1641, when Charles I 'personally enacted ... to abjure prelacy and all acts passed in the time of episcopacy'.[70]

Spang's decision to downplay Baillie as his primary source – describing his account instead as written 'from eyewitness testimony' – presaged the ways in which later generations separated Baillie's historical collections from the life of their collector. Later commentators realized that his sources were problematic because they could be cited effectively by both presbyterian and episcopalian authors. Cross-confessional citation of Baillie's letters after 1662 indicated at least one common intellectual foundation for these apparently irreconcilable identities.[71] On the one hand, the apologist for presbyterian nonconformity John Brown of Wamphray drew on Baillie's historical collections, especially through citation of Spang's *Historia Motuum*. Whilst Brown explicitly cited Spang's treatise, it is possible that Brown might have accessed Baillie's original letters if he and Spang had crossed paths during Brown's exile in the Low Countries in 1663. Perhaps it was through readings of Baillie's letters, preserved by Spang, that Brown had gleaned evidence for his account, detailing 'all the discipline which was tyranny over consciences, and over men's persons and estates'. As Brown recounted, with the subscription of the National Covenant, 'the Lord awaketh, as one after wine, and looketh through the cloud with compassion on a long tossed and sorely afflicted church'.[72]

On the other hand, the future bishop of Salisbury, Gilbert Burnet, appears to have relied on Baillie's manuscript letters for passages in his *History of His Own Time*. Burnet probably saw Baillie's manuscript collections during his time as Divinity Professor at Glasgow University from 1669 to 1674. At this juncture, Burnet was writing his historical works on the Reformation and his biographical accounts of the first two dukes of Hamilton. With Baillie, like the first duke of Hamilton, Burnet would have found a man who had striven to maintain a *via media* throughout the conflicts.[73] Baillie's historical collections would have provided Burnet with documentary evidence to support his objective 'to lay open the good and bad of all sides and parties'.[74] With these balanced intentions in mind, Burnet's brisk account of the period of Covenanting rule described the ways in which the 'war corrupted both sides': a lament discernible throughout Baillie's historical correspondence. In a passage reminiscent of a Baillie letter, Burnet recounted how, during the Interregnum, members of the dominant Protestor faction 'preached often,

---

[70] *Motuum*, sig. *6r.

[71] This should be read alongside the arguments for divergent confessional cultures emerging after 1662. See Alasdair Raffe, *The Culture of Controversy: Religious Arguments in Scotland, 1660–1714* (Woodbridge, 2012).

[72] John Brown of Wamphray, *Apologetical Reltion* (1845), p. 35.

[73] Gilbert Burnet, 'Autobiography', in *A Supplement to Burnet's History of my own time*, p. 479.

[74] Gilbert Burnet, *History of His Own Time: From the Restoration of Charles II to the Treaty of Peace at Utrecht, in the Reign of Queen Anne* (London, 1838), vol. I, p. 4.

and very long and seemed to carry their devotions to a greater sublimity than others did … and they often proposed several expedients for purging [the church]'.[75] In similar language, Baillie had described the same scene in which Protestors were 'bent as ever to purge the Church … the Moderator's sermon ran on the necessitie of taking up the too-long neglected work of purging'.[76]

Brown and Burnet appear to have taken inspiration from Baillie's descriptions, perhaps at second hand, but in Matthew Craufurd's enormous manuscript 'History of the Church of Scotland', begun in 1677, we find evidence of unabashed plagiarism. Craufurd was a nonconforming presbyterian minister of Eastwood and subsequently Professor of Ecclesiastical History at Edinburgh University.[77] Craufurd's 'History' owes a staggering debt to Baillie's manuscript letters. Although he set out to cover the years 1560 to 1688 in his 'History', the vast majority of the two folio volumes comprise material on the years covered by Baillie's manuscripts. Sections covering 1637 to 1662 comprise over 75 per cent of the manuscript's total length, despite covering only about 20 per cent of the total chronological scope. Craufurd made little effort to disguise his borrowings from Baillie. Compare, for instance, Craufurd's and Baillie's descriptions of the proclamation introducing the Scottish Prayer Book in 1637:

> In february 1637 there was a proclamation by sound of Trumpet commanding all subjects Ecclesiastick and civill to conforme to the Liturgie against Easter.[78]

> [I]n the breaking up of the Winter Session, there was a Proclamation, by sound of trumpet, commanding all subjects, ecclesiastick and civil, to conform themselves to the Liturgie against the nixt Pasch.[79]

Yet the opinions, the hesitations and the critiques of the Covenanting government that Craufurd found in Baillie's letters would have been disconcerting for a minister of Craufurd's stalwart, nonconformist principles.[80] Craufurd probably acquired Baillie's manuscripts through his association with nonconformists in Ayrshire.[81] After a period of exile, Craufurd began preaching under the protection of John Maxwell of Pollock. He also came into contact with Baillie's surviving relatives: James Walkinshaw, husband

---

[75] Ibid., vol. I, pp. 69, 63, 116–17.

[76] Robert Baillie to William Spang, 19 July 1654, *LJB*, vol. III, pp. 244–5.

[77] For the manuscript, see NCL, Cra MS 1, Matthew Craufurd, 'History of the Church of Scotland from the earliest dawning of the light of the Gospell after the Apostles time to the year 1688' [dated 17 September 1726].

[78] NCL, Cra MS 1, Matthew Craufurd, 'History', pp. 50–1.

[79] *LJB*, vol. I, pp. 15–16.

[80] The following may all be found in the unpaginated 'Vita Authoris' prefixed to the 'History', see NCL, Cra MS 1, Craufurd, 'History', 'Vita Authoris'.

[81] Laing, 'Preface', in *LJB*, vol. I, viii–ix. Further discussion of the provenance of Baillie's letters may be found in Thomas Carlyle, 'Baillie the Covenanter', in Henry Duff Traill (ed.), *The Works of Thomas Carlyle: Critical and Miscellaneous Essays IV* (reprinted Cambridge, 2010), vol. XXIX, pp. 226–60, at pp. 229–30.

of Baillie's youngest daughter, Margaret; and William Eccles, husband of Baillie's daughter Lilias. As I have argued throughout this biography, Baillie's opinions about church government, liturgical reform, monarchical power and Reformed theology often led him to disagree with contemporaries. His letters highlighted deep-seated ideological fissures within the Covenanting movement – fissures that this biography has only begun to probe in any depth. Drawing on Baillie's manuscripts, therefore, Craufurd took liberties with biographical details concerning the deceased Principal and silently excised (or simply disregarded) passages in his letters that did not conform to his opinions.

Considering that Craufurd relied so heavily on Baillie's letters elsewhere, it is striking that he chose to use a different source for his account of the Glasgow General Assembly. By doing so, Craufurd portrayed the Assembly as a clear triumph for presbyterianism. By contrast, Baillie's meandering account of the Assembly included much commentary about his personal misgivings about the reforms that were implemented alongside notes about the heavy-handed tactics that were deployed to insure that these reforms passed. For instance, Craufurd briskly recounted the opening of the Assembly with Hamilton's arrival on 16 November 1638 (Baillie placed his arrival on 17 November) and the days following during which there were 'severall conferences betuixt him [i.e. Hamilton] and the said Noblemen and Gentlmen about the maner and way of holding the said assembly'.[82] Baillie's account began with a lengthy introductory preface, written with benefit of hindsight and containing personal reflections on the disappointments that he had faced during the Assembly. Baillie's account, moreover, did not brush over these 'severall conferences', explaining that 'the wysest of the ministrie consulted upon the ordering of affairs'. This included discussion about procedures for convening a general assembly and the nomination of a moderator.[83] Likewise, Craufurd's account of the vote to abjure and remove episcopacy presented the act as a *fait accompli*. Rather than recounting the debates, his section on the session of 8 December 1638 largely consists of a transcription of the act of the Assembly itself. This act, Craufurd wrote, was made 'after much debateing to and fro' – none of which was detailed.[84] By contrast, Baillie's account presented this act as the Assembly's fatal misstep: a moment when caution was thrown to the wind and a radical group of Covenanters managed to hijack anti-Laudian sentiment to overturn the Scriptural institution of episcopacy.[85] Although relying on another source, Craufurd appears unsure whether to ignore Baillie altogether and instead included a lengthy and awkwardly worded passage describing the vote as one in which 'the wholl Assembly most unanimously, without contradiction of any one (*and with the*

---

82 NCL, Cra MS 1, vol. I, p. 175.
83 'History of the Glasgow Assembly', *LJB*, vol. I, p. 121.
84 NCL, Cra MS 1, vol. I, p. 246.
85 'History of the Glasgow Assembly', *LJB*, vol. I, pp. 156–8.

hesitation of one allenarly) professing full perswasing of minde did voices, That all Episcopacy different from that of a pastour over a particular flock was abjured in this Kirk and to be removed out of it'.[86]

Elsewhere, Craufurd betrayed his desire that his critical source – Baillie – would have identified with his own nonconformist principles. Problematically, Baillie's letters end with Baillie conforming to the restored episcopate. Notwithstanding this evidence, Craufurd included 'R. Baillie' in his list of Glaswegian ministers ejected from their livings in 1662. This is the only reference to Baillie's ejection that I have been able to locate and, on balance, it looks to be a mistake, if not a deliberate fabrication. In earlier chapters, I have argued that it was highly likely that Baillie would have continued in his role as Principal of Glasgow University had he survived any longer into the Restoration. Given Baillie's experiences of the Interregnum, moreover, it appears unlikely that he would have countenanced nonconformity. Throughout the last years of his life he had come to be at odds with ministers such as John Carstairs, Patrick Gillespie, James Guthrie and James Fergusson, who would go on to play significant roles in Restoration nonconformist circles. By contrast, it was amongst such nonconformist ministers that Craufurd flourished and, indeed, through whom he had gained access to Baillie's manuscripts. Considering the dissonance between Craufurd's own political views and those of Baillie, it is unsurprising to see Craufurd amending or overlooking certain aspects of Baillie's career. This decision was doubtless made to affirm Baillie's credentials as the historical voice of nonconformist presbyterians after the Restoration.

IV

Over one hundred years after Baillie's death, the selection of correspondence that he had carefully preserved was first published in an imperfect edition. From this first edition to David Laing's 1840s edition, still widely in use today, the 'letters and journals' emerged as a historical source in their own right, figuratively and literally separated from the life and writings of the man who had assembled them in the first place. In the first edition, through deletion and addition of documents, the orthodox presbyterian character of the collections was ensured. In Laing's edition, through the naming of the documents as the *Letters and Journals* and the addition of numerous documents from other sources, Baillie's manuscript collections were transformed into an archive for the Covenanting movement as a whole. Rushing to press, Laing was only able to publish an accompanying 'memoir' of Baillie's life in a supplementary volume. Despite many illuminating details, this supplement was often discarded or bound separately since it is common to find it missing from surviving editions of Laing's *Letters and Journals*. If Baillie's voice survived

---

[86] NCL, Cra MS 1, vol. I, p. 253. My emphasis.

these editorial interventions, he now survived as the mouthpiece of a move-ment with which he had maintained a tumultuous relationship.

Before Aiken's and Laing's editions, Baillie's manuscript letters had enjoyed reasonably broad manuscript circulation. Numerous manuscript copies were created in the eighteenth century that are still extant.[87] Transmission of Baillie's manuscript letters through scribal publication created, and was indicative of, widespread interest within academic circles.[88] Robert Wodrow, James Fall (Principal of Glasgow University) and Baillie's descendants can be identified as creators of copies made after 1700. Historians and others, however, appear to have been content to read a copy rather than the origi-nals, preserved in the Church of Scotland's archives after 1737. This trend suggests an ambivalent attitude towards manuscript sources: historians of this earlier generation were content to use a copy so long as the source of the copy was known (or thought) to be authentic. It also suggests that more value was placed on the information contained in Baillie's manuscript letters, rather than the circumstances of the manuscripts' creation. At the back of Baillie MS 4/3, for instance, there are reader's notes in the hand of Baillie's grandson and namesake – the 'R.B.' who had compiled a library list at Carnbrae dated 22 July 1708.[89] Although written on blank leaves bound together with one of the original volume, these notes include page numbers that correspond to the copy now preserved under the shelfmark Baillie MS 2 at New College Library – a copy made around 1701. Elsewhere, Wodrow considered it sufficient to list 'Baileys Letters' as a source for the period 1637 to 1662, rather than listing individual items under headings for the corresponding year as he had done for other source material.[90] None of these transcriptions included copies of the missing correspondence from Baillie MS 4/1, suggesting that these letters had been removed before the originals were copied in an effort to emphasize their credentials as a source on the Covenanting period alone. To these and other readers, it appears that Baillie's manuscript letters were just a source – albeit, a valuable one – containing illustrative details about the high-political and ecclesiastical conflicts of the mid-seventeenth century.

The first edition of Baillie's letters appeared in 1775, edited by an oth-erwise unknown schoolmaster from Anderston in Glasgow named Robert Aiken. In addition to omitting the interspersed documents from his edition, Aiken also excluded over two hundred letters that might have detracted from Baillie's impeccably 'presbyterian' credentials, not to mention countless other

---

[87]   Laing, 'Preface', in *LJB*, vol. I, ix. Copies may be found in the following locations: British Library, London [BL] MS Harl. 6004; NCL, Baill MS 2 [1701 transcription]; NCL, Baill MS 3 [1728 Robert Wodrow transcription]; NLS, MS.1908, Robert Baillie, Letters to William Spang, 1637–43 [Society of Antiquaries volume]; Glasgow University Special Collections, MS Gen 1239–41 [transcribed between 1768 and 1770, from 1701 transcription].

[88]   For instance, see Stevenson, *History of the Church and State of Scotland*, vol. I, 'Preface'.

[89]   See the list from the back of NCL, Baill MS 1, [n.p.]

[90]   See, NLS, Wod.Qu.CVIII, Robert Wodrow, 'Library List', fo. 199r.

sections deleted from individual items.[91] Such editorial decisions, in part, subsequently led Thomas Carlyle and Laing to dismiss as absurd speculation that Aiken's edition of Baillie's letters had been 'undertaken on the counsel of [William] Robertson and [David] Hume'.[92] Whereas Robertson's *History of Scotland* (1759) had defended the Act of Settlement (1690) as establishing a Presbyterian Church integral to Scottish liberty, he had portrayed the pre-1690 Church as structured according to a series of 'makeshifts', blurring the line between episcopacy and presbytery.[93] By contrast, Aiken's editorial decisions brought this confessional divide into focus. These decisions marked the early signs of a revival of a vigorously triumphalist presbyterian historiography spearheaded by evangelical ministers such as Thomas M'Crie who cast the Covenanters as proponents of civil liberty.[94] For his part, Aiken reassured readers that 'nothing has been left out that throws the smallest light upon the history of those times'.[95] In practice, Aiken excluded any letters suggesting that Baillie was ever sympathetic to episcopacy or that the Church's ministry had been seriously divided under the Covenanting regime. For instance, Aiken left out Baillie's letter to William Wilkie in which he had famously confessed 'Bishopes I love', and had instead started his edition with the earliest extant letter to Spang from January 1637.[96] Most letters relating to the Protestor–Resolutioner controversy were likewise excluded, probably to avoid potential impressions of the Church of Scotland as rife with internal divisions during the 1650s. Letters in which Baillie had asked James Wood to circulate his correspondence to the future Restoration bishop Andrew Honyman were similarly left out.[97] Most notably, Aiken also excluded correspondence between Baillie and James Sharp – subsequently archbishop of St Andrews from 1661 – in which Baillie had urged Sharp to supplicate Charles II for a presbyterian settlement.

Aiken's exclusions provided Laing with grounds to produce a new edition of Baillie's correspondence, noting in the preface to the first volume of his edition that Aiken's edition 'has no claim to be regarded otherwise than as a Selection from Baillie's Letters'.[98] Laing was a celebrated antiquarian

---

[91] In his preface to the edition, Aiken claimed explicitly that he had only printed a selection of extant letters. Aiken's edition contained 201 letters whilst Laing's edition contained 443. See, Robert Aiken (ed.), *Letters and Journals written by the deceased Mr. Robert Baillie, Principal of the University of Glasgow* (2 vols, Edinburgh, 1775), vol. I, sig. a2r.

[92] Carlyle, 'Baillie', p. 230. This unfounded folk-attribution was repeated, for example, in William Orme, *Bibliotheca Biblica: A Select List of Books on Sacred Literature; with Notices, Biographical, Critical, and Bibliographical* (Edinburgh, 1824), pp. 16–17.

[93] Colin Kidd, *Subverting Scotland's Past: Scottish Whig Historians and the Creation of an Anglo-British Identity, 1689–c. 1830* (Cambridge, 1993), pp. 185, 196, 198.

[94] Ibid., pp. 201–3.

[95] Aiken (ed.), *Letters*, vol. I, sig. a2r.

[96] Robert Baillie to William Wilkie, 2 January 1637, *LJB*, vol. I, p. 2.

[97] For example, Robert Baillie to James Wood, 1 April 1652, *LJB*, vol. III, p. 176.

[98] Laing, 'Preface', in *LJB*, vol. I, x.

and bibliophile, best known as the editor of John Knox's *Works* (1846–64) and closely associated with leading Edinburgh literati such as Sir Walter Scott. Laing's edition of Baillie's letters should, however, be discussed in the context of the historicist turn that attended the growth of Romanticism in Scotland and the attendant rise in popularity of antiquarian publications. Laing's intellectual preoccupations reflected a positivist turn in historiography, exemplified by the work of Leopold von Ranke, which claimed to reconstruct past societies 'as they actually were'.[99] In similar vein, Scott's *Waverley Novels* (1814–31) helped to engrain a demythologized version of Scotland's national past in popular culture. Like Robertson – who had been Principal of Edinburgh University whilst Scott had studied as an undergraduate – Scott's fictional accounts of Scottish history were presented in a critical light, as illuminating an earlier stage in the development of civilization. Otherwise, Scott, Laing and Thomas Thomson were responsible for the consolidation of Scotland's national records office and initiating the serial publication of historical documents through the Bannatyne Club (est. 1823), which were sold by subscription to members. In this series, Scott, Laing and other antiquaries sought to disseminate otherwise rare documents illustrative of Scotland's past. Their aim was to continue to deconstruct triumphalist presbyterian historiographies of Scotland's history or the Ossianic forgeries that had alleged discovery of an ancient 'Scottish' civilization. By editing and publishing numerous volumes of historical source material, antiquaries like Laing provided ample evidence that the Scottish past did not easily fit into one simple narrative.

Dismantling myths about Scotland's past, Laing established a new framework in which to understand the Covenanters at the heart of which lay his edition of Baillie's *Letters and Journals*. A deconstructive intent is evident in Laing's remarks concerning editorial method. According to Laing, his edition was undertaken with the purpose of 'preserving, in an accessible form, the more valuable remains of our National History and Literature', an objective that was consonant with the aims of the Bannatyne Club which had financed transcription of Baillie's letters.[100] In contrast to Aiken, who had appeared to judge the 'truth' or authenticity of his edition insofar as Baillie adhered to a presbyterian ideal type, Laing believed that the 'genuine character, of such documents' was established through inclusion of 'those local and personal details ... however unimportant in themselves'.[101] Laing, like many of his antiquarian colleagues, sought to present readers with historical sources unmediated by editorial interventions. The historical value and authenticity of documents derived from presenting information from a seemingly distant and murky past in an accessible, published form. As editor, Laing's task was

---

[99]   Stephen Bann, *Romanticism and the Rise of History* (Boston, 1995), ch. 2; Marinell Ash, *The Strange Death of Scottish History* (Edinburgh, 1980), p. 41.
[100]   Laing, 'Preface', in *LJB*, vol. I, x.
[101]   Ibid.

thus to make Baillie's antiquated orthography and his illegible, handwritten letters accessible to a wider public. In the event, demand for the proposed edition of Baillie's letters was so great that the Bannatyne Club offered an extra print-run for sale to non-members.[102] Laing also decided to use the modernized spelling of the 1701 transcription extant in Baillie's papers in the Church of Scotland archives as his working text to avoid reproducing Baillie's 'wretched' Scots orthography.[103] Laing included descriptive footnotes identifying individuals, acts, events, publications and geographic locations. Thomas Carlyle remarked with esteem the speed with which Laing had completed his edition, though Laing was forced to enlist David Meek – editor of George Gillespie's journal of the Westminster Assembly – to assist with specialist knowledge of the period.[104] Producing his edition within three years, Laing's inclusion of notes – however sparse – remains admirable and would have assisted readers in explicating more obscure references.

Laing's editorial influence is most evident in the documents included and excluded in the appendices of each volume. Laing went to considerable lengths to locate extant manuscripts produced by Baillie; my own research has not been able to add any items of significance to this list. Nevertheless, the documents that Laing appended to Baillie's *Letters and Journals* suggest that his intention was to publish an edition that would provide a comprehensive source for a general history of the Scottish Covenanters.[105] As Laing explained in the preface to his edition, constraints of space precluded publication of all material contained in the three manuscript volumes of Baillie's letters. In lieu of publishing all available documentation, Laing included a hand-list of the papers which Baillie had transcribed at the beginning of each appendix, followed by 'a Selection of such contemporary Papers *as seemed most worthy of notice*'.[106] Laing's appendices largely comprised correspondence, official papers and memoranda found in manuscript collections unrelated to Baillie, such as the Wodrow Papers now preserved in the National Library of Scotland. Laing's appendices for Baillie's *Letters and Journals* thus reproduced a selection of manuscripts that 'chiefly refer to the state of Ecclesiastical Affairs in Scotland' between 1637 and 1662, as opposed to including documents simply because they had 'been collected by Baillie'.[107] Laing used the publication of Baillie's letters as an occasion to transcribe and publish a selection of previously unpublished documents related to the Covenanting regime.

Laing's editorial achievement was commendable and produced one of the

---

[102]   Ibid., vol. I, xi. Carlyle also remarked on the speed with which Laing's edition was produced, see Carlyle, 'Baillie'.
[103]   Laing, 'Preface', in *LJB*, vol. I, vii.
[104]   Ibid., vol. I, xi.
[105]   For another account of Laing's practice as an editor, see Jane Dawson and Lionel K.J. Glassey, 'Some Unpublished Letters from John Knox to Christopher Goodman', *Scottish Historical Review*, 84 (2005), pp. 166–201.
[106]   Laing, 'Preface', in *LJB*, vol. I, xi–xii. My italics.
[107]   Ibid., vol. I, xii.

first, and easily the most extensive, printed edition of documents pertaining to the Covenanters. Despite compiling his edition in only three years, Laing's transcription remains reliable and, having compared it to the manuscript original, his choosing to base his edition on the 1701 transcription did not corrupt his text significantly. Praising his edition of Baillie's letters, M'Crie commented to Laing that 'I feel satisfied that on nothing you have ever written will you reflect with greater pleasure, at any period of life, than in this well timed, judicious, candid, and excellent humour.'[108] To modern historians, however, Laing's decision to exclude certain documents as extraneous may appear puzzling. In some respects, Baillie's record of his own involvement in political and religious affairs became transformed, in Laing's edition, into the voice of a narrator, with his letters providing a framework to contextualize the documents appended to each volume. Baillie's role as commentator, as opposed to historical actor, was also emphasized through Laing's exclusion of documents that reflected his direct involvement. For example, Laing excluded a brief treatise of Latin maxims on the rights of civil magistrates that Baillie had composed whilst agonizing over his decision to support the Covenanters' war effort in 1639, and also left out a treatise on the lawfulness of episcopacy that Baillie had prepared shortly after the Glasgow General Assembly of 1638, at which most Covenanters had denounced the institution as unlawful.[109]

Whilst exclusions stand out, Laing's decisions on which items to include in the *Letters and Journals* also significantly altered the make-up of the manuscript letters, overriding Baillie's original decisions regarding documentary inclusion and exclusion. Laing decided to include *all surviving correspondence* either to or from Baillie in his edition. Whilst this decision may be justified, Laing's choice to rearrange all letters in strict chronological order, interpolating additional correspondence surviving outside the original manuscript letters amongst those items, and to place a selection of documents in appendices, completely undermined any effort to preserve the organization of the original manuscripts. Three examples of this editorial practice stand out. In all cases, Baillie probably excluded this correspondence because it illustrated embarrassing disputes and private workings of the highest echelons of Covenanting government that he preferred to be forgotten. First, Laing included letters exchanged between Baillie and Wariston on the vexed issue of church patronage. Whilst illuminating in itself of the ways in which Baillie and Wariston disputed and justified their divergent positions on this thorny issue, the letters show a messy, overly intellectual exchange on a delicate matter. This subject matter stands in stark contrast to Baillie's typical epistolary narrative which included no more than brisk summaries of debates. Second, Laing helpfully included three surviving responses from Spang to

[108] EUL, La.IV.17, Thomas M'Crie to David Laing, 6 December 1842, fo. 5678v.
[109] See, NCL, Baill MS 4/1, 'Theses de Majestatis jure', fos 62v–64r; NCL, Baill MS 4/2, 'A Discourse anent Episcopacy', fos 103r–116r.

Baillie dating from 1649. Yet the inclusion of these three items in Laing's edition may lead a reader to believe that Baillie had made this decision. In reality, it appears that Baillie exhibited a certain decorum and carefully protected his correspondents' letters from preservation. Finally, and in similar vein, Baillie did not include a letter dated 17 December 1653 from Lauderdale, written while the statesman was imprisoned in the Tower of London. Lauderdale explicitly claimed to avoid discussion of 'publick concerns' and, instead, simply recollected Baillie's kindness and friendship during his imprisonment. Considering that Baillie was gathering his manuscript letters together for the express purpose of sharing the material contained therein, it is unsurprising that Baillie would have chosen to exclude such a personal letter.

V

Baillie's correspondence still leaves an indelible mark on the historiography of mid-seventeenth-century Britain. Yet it is only through careful reconstruction of the contexts of their creation, transmission and reception that the full significance of these documents may be appreciated. Drawing together thematic analysis from preceding chapters, this chapter has offered a revised analysis of the documents that comprise Baillie's oft-cited *Letters and Journals*. Analysis has shown how the act of life-writing in the mid-seventeenth century was inextricably linked with the practice of history-writing. Baillie's decision to create an archive of his *times* simultaneously created an archive of his *life*. Hitherto, consideration of archival practices has not played a significant role in accounts of the origins of the genre of biography.[110] More often, such narratives look at intellectual trends that led writers to think of an individual life as a discrete and coherent unit. This esoteric, rise-of-the-individual thesis certainly has merit, but it neglects the constituent parts that comprise a life recounted. Indeed, the fundamental materials for such accounts are the physical archive itself – the repositories of papers and other ephemera that provide the empirical data from which a biography is born. However, the archive itself is not a source of unmediated information and it is crucial that historians attend to the circumstances that shaped the archive itself. This chapter drew into focus moments when Baillie's paper legacy became a site of contention, being used to forward opposed ideological platforms. These contested interpretations of Baillie's historical collections were stabilized, in effect, by removing Baillie's life from the collections he had amassed. Garnering accolades from men of such divergent ecclesiastical positions, Baillie's life and writings eschewed entrenched historiographical tendencies to compartmentalize post-Reformation Scottish thinkers as either presbyterian or episcopalian. This chapter has provided essential background that will hopefully inform future citation of the *Letters and Journals*.

[110] With the notable exception of Adam Smyth's *Autobiography in Early Modern England*.

Centuries of readership, revision and editing have shaped the Baillie that has been transmitted to us in the form of Laing's *Letters and Journals*. Neither a hero nor a villain, then, Robert Baillie quietly vanished from the records he had painstakingly gathered, only to be replaced by caricature – the dutiful letter-writer, the virulent critic, the unashamed time-server and the embarrassing vacillator. The myths that emerged to explain this period in Scottish history of regrettable violent extremism and intemperate religious belief had no place for a character like Baillie. As interest in the Covenanters declined early in the twentieth century, Baillie likewise was consigned to a place of relative neglect and those few commentators relied on recycled facts and hagiographic narratives to fill out his biography. We read, then, of Principal Baillie's comments on a riot in Edinburgh or Baillie's description of the Solemn League and Covenant without any acknowledgement of the role that he took in the very events that he had described. Through contingencies related to textual transmission and shifting historiographical trends, Baillie's *life*, his biography, that he so clearly and vividly detailed, has largely been forgotten. In its place, we have become accustomed to reading about the period in which Baillie lived, described by a man consigned to a footnote.

Conclusion

After 'presbyterian' and 'episcopalian' confessional identities became entrenched by the Act of Settlement (1690) which established presbyterianism as the state religion, Scots on both sides of the divide sought to claim Robert Baillie as their own. In 1747, for example, the staunch episcopalian and Jacobite Thomas Ruddiman offered Baillie unexpected praise as the 'only [Covenanter], who had the Courage and Conscience to deny, that the first Subscribers to that [Negative] Confession did abjure Episcopacy'. For Ruddiman, Baillie was 'one of the most learned, and I say too little, when I add, the most honest in that famous Convention [i.e. the 1638 Glasgow Assembly]'.[1] In this light, Baillie could be refashioned as a brave critic of Covenanting Scotland's dangerous radicalism: a minister with principled beliefs who had refused to succumb to the prevalent anti-episcopal hysteria of 1638. By contrast, nearly a century later, in December 1842, the secessionist minister Thomas M'Crie wrote to David Laing thanking him for publishing his new edition of Baillie's *Letters and Journals*. As M'Crie wrote, 'I have perused with the highest anticipation and delight your masterly and elaborate Memoir of Baillie ... I rejoice to think that we have been furnished with such an Antidote to the numerous misrepresentations which have issued from Jacobite and deeply prejudiced pens.'[2]

M'Crie expressed hope for an 'antidote' to misrepresentations of Baillie, but in the end, Laing's edition achieved this by silencing Baillie's distinctive voice. This biography has sought to recover Baillie's voice by situating his vast and understudied corpus of writings in context. Baillie was a characteristically nuanced and dynamic thinker, steeped in the broader intellectual traditions of Reformed Europe. Far from exemplifying a 'typical' Covenanter, analysis of Baillie's ideas has revealed the superficiality that attaches to most claims regarding the unity of the Covenanting movement. There was no uniform 'Covenanting ideology' that integrated swathes of Scottish presbyterians, much less their English and Irish sympathizers. Whilst a majority of

---

[1] Thomas Ruddiman, *An answer to the Reverend Mr. George Logan's late treatise on government: in which (contrary to the manifold errors and misrepresentations of that author) the ancient constitution of the Crown and Kingdom of Scotland, and the hereditary Succession of its Monarchs are asserted and vindicated* (Edinburgh, 1747), p. 115.

[2] EUL, La.IV.17, Thomas M'Crie to David Laing, 6 December 1842, fo. 5678r–v.

the Church of Scotland's ministers agreed in 1638 to subscribe the National Covenant, seeking to preserve the Church's liberties from Laud's perceived 'innovations', subscribers such as Baillie remained deeply divided over the extent of reform. Beyond Baillie's conviction that Laud and his associates were intent on returning Scotland, and then England, to the Roman Catholic fold, Baillie and many Covenanting compatriots could not agree on their reforming objectives. Disagreements over the precise definition of, *inter alia*, membership in the visible church, the *locus primus* of ecclesiastical power or the rigidity with which doctrinal orthodoxy ought to be enforced, persisted throughout the 1640s and eventually erupted in the Protestor–Resolutioner schism of 1651.

Through the pages of this biography, I have sought to restore Baillie to centre stage. He was a calculating thinker, who was guided by principle and fervent belief rather than obeisance to the wishes of those in positions of political power. Baillie was cautious and non-committal, sometimes to a fault, as in 1643, when he tried to convince his parishioner, James Forsyth, to subscribe the National Covenant. Explaining that subscription did not entail denunciation of the Perth Articles as 'idolatrous', nor did it entail an 'absolute' denunciation of episcopacy, Baillie acknowledged that his dissent over the abjuration of episcopacy at the Glasgow Assembly 'is miscalled my haesitation'.[3] Evidently, Baillie had developed a reputation for indecision, leading to one parishioner questioning why he preferred to study, read and reflect on pressing political or religious matters before he made up his mind. Baillie did not have recourse to a detailed confessional document that outlined what he ought to think about monarchical power, church government, Reformed theology, liturgical forms and the Bible. Without uniform definition of these beliefs, it is to be expected that diversity flourished behind a facade of unity, yet tendencies to assign Scottish ministers into one of two neatly organized parties has contributed to the neglect of subtle dissonances.

Taking Baillie's writings as a point of departure, we have uncovered further evidence of intra-Covenanting divisions and suggested points at which Baillie's views influenced the course of events in the British Civil Wars. Whilst Samuel Rutherford's *Lex Rex* subjected monarchy to the collective will of the people, Baillie bolstered claims that Charles I and II ruled by divine right and claimed the Scottish throne through an inalienable hereditary right. George Gillespie, likewise, vested the Church's powers of censure and ordination in the people of a particular congregation, whereas Baillie refused to devolve these powers from preaching presbyters. In fact, at particularly fraught junctures, Baillie even retained the belief that a temporary episcopate provided the best recourse for the preservation of ecclesiastical unity. The rigid appearance of Baillie's delineation between 'orthodoxy' and 'heterodoxy' in his works on controversial theology also evaporates when probing particular contexts in which he formulated his biting polemic.

---

[3]   NCL, Baill MS 1, Robert Baillie to James Forsyth, 11 April 1643, p. 382.

Indeed, Baillie's plea that Scripture provided a self-sufficient witness for all matters of Christian doctrine was little more than a plea to cite proof-texts selectively to support his own doctrinal aims. This was most evident in Baillie's defence of kneeling at communion, an important instance when Baillie admitted that the Biblical text remained unclear on the particulars of worship. Although Baillie showed a relentless obsession with uncovering the 'true' meaning of the Biblical text, in both his academic and homiletic exegesis, this did not lead to intellectual stagnation. In fact, Baillie's deeply engrained beliefs about Scriptural authority provided a dynamic framework in which his scholarly and homiletic exegesis was formulated. More widely, his engagement with the latest works of Biblical scholarship situated Baillie as an active, but peripheral, participant in an erudite international Republic of Letters. Moreover, despite the noticeable absence of discussions of phil-ological complexities in his extant sermons, Baillie's refined understanding of the origins and transmission of the Biblical text provided a basis for his preaching style.

Moving beyond the fact that Baillie's tracts provoked extreme responses of adulation and denunciation, it is crucial to ask what Baillie was *doing* in publishing his works in his chosen format. Biography allows the historian to approach a subject with care and sympathy, appreciating the practical, pro-fessional and personal motivations underlying extant works – alongside, of course, their discursive context. The task of the historian is to take the 'life residue', the extant words on paper, and reconstruct a convincing portrait of the individual who gave expression to these words. Biography presents the opportunity to interrogate the nature of the sources themselves in a unique context. As the prominent scholar of biography Leon Edel wrote, 'biography has been wedded always … to the document, to the fact and anecdote'.[4] The task of the historian is to read against the grain of these documents in order to understand better the circumstances and reasons why these sources survive, the form in which they survive, and how such considerations might add fur-ther depth and breadth to our understanding of the *meaning* of these sources. Just as biography is the organization of human memory, historical biography reorganizes surviving relics of human memory into a convincing and rounded narrative of lived experience. Insofar as I have reconstructed Baillie's life in the preceding pages, I have attempted to reflect the surviving characteristics of source material. For this reason, this biography did not proceed chrono-logically, but instead grew organically around thematic discussions that tran-scended Baillie's career.

To come to terms with the raw material that remains evincing Baillie's life, we need to begin by acknowledging the various roles and duties that Baillie took on himself during his vibrant career. Baillie wrote tracts such as *Ladensium Autokatakrisis* and *A Dissuasive from the Errours of the Times* with two audiences in mind. On the one hand, these treatises were catered to a

---

[4]   Leon Edel, *Writing Lives* (1959), p. 23.

non-specialist audience proficient in reading English; perhaps Baillie even hoped that his tracts would be read aloud to others. The text of these treatises contained little more than a succinct summary of Baillie's case against particular theological errors. On the other hand, Baillie accepted that learned ministers and laity would require further proof of his claims. Accordingly, Baillie complemented an austere text with extensive marginal citations of verbatim and paraphrased evidence, often with further narrative linking individual pieces of evidence. Baillie's decisions regarding the format were influenced by his career as a lecturer at Glasgow University. Lecturers such as Baillie would have prized brief summaries of complex subjects because they taught students by dictating a text verbatim while students took notes. In the lecture theatre, there was little room for more than perspicuous summaries of controversies and Baillie's published tracts prepared explicitly for teaching undergraduates suggests that this pervaded his writing style.

Alongside this pedagogical context, in analysing his engagement with religious controversies it is crucial to account for Baillie's practice as a minister, preaching God's Word and exercising discipline over his flock. In the post-Reformation Church of Scotland, the minister and parish church session investigated, examined and censured members of the parish church for moral transgressions. Although the vast majority of cases addressed by sessions would have dealt with adultery, drunkenness and profanity, it was not uncommon for ministers to ensure that their flock remained orthodox in their doctrinal beliefs and their practice of piety. In such cases, the ultimate objective was rehabilitation and reintegration of transgressors back into a congregation, as opposed to banishment and excommunication. We may detect the same impetus for rehabilitation throughout many of Baillie's most acerbic treatises. He demonstrated a conviction in his role as informed guide to divine knowledge and, much like contemporary polemicists in 1640s London, Baillie was merely trying to convince wayward Christians to repent and return to their flock. Variously, Baillie's tracts were aimed at 'convincing' the Laudians of the errors of their ways; they were intended to 'dissuade' suggestible Londoners from accepting the errors of congregational ministers such as John Cotton; they were cast as an 'antidote' to the deceptive rhetoric of Arminian theologians such as John Goodwin. Setting out to denounce as 'heterodox' or 'erroneous' the writings of prominent figures such as Cotton, Bramhall or Goodwin, Baillie kept his ministerial duties at the front of his mind. Indeed, his most detailed and, by far, his lengthiest engagements with controversial topics such as kneeling and Arminian theology were undertaken in manuscript 'conferences' by letters with David Dickson and John Crichton, both of whom had begun to mislead their respective flocks and threaten the Church of Scotland's standing as a unified, national church.

Drawing together Baillie's writings on myriad themes was his pervasive desire to maintain or, after 1638, to re-establish peace and unity in the Church of Scotland. Undergirding his controversial works was a peculiarly irenic vision, rigidly doctrinaire but subtly inclusive. For Baillie, accommodation of theological diversity needed to occur within a clearly defined 'orthodox' framework. This apparent contradiction, however, should not be taken to discount Baillie's pleas as disingenuous. Whilst historiographical attention continues to be diverted towards the writings of decidedly 'heterodox' individuals such as Thomas Hobbes and Baruch Spinoza to uncover the driving forces of intellectual change, the writings of the 'orthodox' multitude has tended to be neglected and denigrated as unoriginal and stagnant.[5] Thinkers such as Baillie are dismissed because their ideas about religious uniformity and their willingness to pry into the private lives of individual parishioners appear at first glance as offensive to our own political and religious sensibilities. Indeed, this historiographical tendency has perpetuated entrenched views of pre-Enlightenment Scotland as hopelessly divided, intolerant and parochial. But reorienting ourselves to Baillie's prevalent concerns as a minister and lecturer, it becomes apparent that foremost in his mind was his desire to preside over a flock who worshipped devoutly and who maintained a highly disciplined, austere lifestyle. Baillie was a renowned religious controversialist, but he did not set out to add fuel to the fires of religious schism; rather, he chose to douse those flames. If Reformed Christians throughout Britain and Europe approached their faith with 'a simplicitie and meeknesse of spirit' then divisive issues could be set aside, and Protestant reunion secured to counter the looming threat of the Roman Antichrist and its Habsburg crusaders.[6] Although such an approach to doctrinal pluralism may appear alien to modern ideals that celebrate religious diversity, in post-Reformation Europe, at a time when schism and warfare were rampant, Baillie gave voice to an aspiration for peace that resonated with some, but that most of his contemporaries were not prepared to heed.

[5] See, for example, Sarah Mortimer and John Robertson (eds), *The Intellectual Consequences of Religious Heterodoxy, c. 1600–1750* (Leiden, 2012).
[6] NCL, Baill MS 1, Robert Baillie to John Rae, 14 June 1643, p. 379.

Bibliography

Manuscripts

British Library, London, United Kingdom
MS Harl 6004, Robert Baillie, Letters and Journals [Transcripts].

Edinburgh University Library, Edinburgh, United Kingdom
Dc.5.67 Robert Baillie, Treatises (1643).

David Laing Papers
La.I.298, Letters between Robert Baillie and Archibald Johnston of Wariston
    [1638–39].
La.III.109, Robert Baillie, Student notebook, [c. 1620].
La.III.543, Robert Baillie, Sermon notes, [c. 1650–51].
La.IV.17, Thomas M'Crie to David Laing, 6 December 1842, fo. 5678v.

Glasgow University Library Special Collections, Glasgow, United Kingdom
MS Gen 1239–41, Robert Baillie, Letters and Journals [Transcriptions].
MS Gen 375, Robert Baillie, Treatises [c. 1650s]:
—'Oratio In academia Glasguensis comitiis habita a R.B. anno. 1627 cum In
    regentium numuerum solemiter cooptaretur De mente agente' [1627].
—'Opusculi historici et Chronologia Libri Duo in quibs historia sacra et
    profana compendiose deducitur ex ipsis fontibus a creatione ad mortem
    Joannis Evangelistae et et quaestiones ac dubia chronologica quae ex utro-
    que testamento moveri solent breviter et perspicue explicantur sacrae theo-
    logia studiosis in academia Glasguensi anno 1650 et aliquot sequentibus' [*c.*
    1650].
—'Theses a sacrae theologiae studiosis diebus lunae hora locoque solitis discu-
    tiendae.' [n.d.].
—'Ex primariis philosophiae partibus Thesum sylloge de quibus cum bono Deo
    respondere conabimur Dignissimis viris Dominis academiae moderatoribus
    quando et vbi dignitatibus convenire videbitur', [n.d.].
—'Parergeticorvm diatriba tertia. Contra Vorstium et Socinianos, dei simplici-
    tatem, divinorum attributorum primum, ebertentes' [n.d.].
—'Parergeticorvm Diatriba quarta De Episcopatu' [*ante* 1643].

National Library of Scotland, Edinburgh, United Kingdom
MS.1036, Letters from Robert Baillie concerning debts.
MS.1908, Robert Baillie, Letters to William Spang, 1637–43.

231

MS 15948, Samuel Rutherford and Thomas Sydserff, 'Ane discussing of some arguments against cannons and ceremonies in God's worshipe'.

Advocates' Manuscripts
Adv.MS.20.6.4, Robert Baillie, Sermons August 1637 to June 1639.

New College Library, Edinburgh, United Kingdom
Robert Baillie Papers
Baill MS 1 Treatises [c. 1634–58]:
—'A Conference by letters with a Canterburian minister anent the Arminian tenet of the Saints apostasie' [1634–36].
—'Duorum studiosorum de geniculatione; quam vocant, per literas Collatio' [n.d.]
—'A peacable [sic] consideration of a paper against Kneeling' [n.d.]
—'A freindlie Conference betuixt tuo Ministers D and B anent the gesture of Communicants in the act of receiving the holie elements of the Lords supper' [c. 1634–36].
—Robert Baillie to John Rae, 14 June 1643.
—Robert Baillie to John Rae, [n.d.].
—Robert Baillie to James Forsyth, 8 March 1643.
—Robert Baillie to James Forsyth, 11 April [1643].
—'The summe of my conference yesterday with three or four yeomen of my flock who refused to sing the Conclusion' [1643].
—'Commentariolus de praecipuis Pontificiorum erroribus' [n.d.].
—'Parergeticorum Diatriba secunda de Congregationum independentia seu de Presbyteriorum et Synodorum auctoritate' [n.d.].
—'Theses a sacrae Theologiae studiosis debus lunae hora locoque fontis discutiendae' [n.d.].
—'Tractatus de formali caussa justificationis seu potius de justitia Christi imputata et hominis inhaerente' [c. 1658].
—'Oratio in Academiae Glasguensis comitiis habita a R.B. anno 1627 cum in Regentium numerum soelmniter cooptaretur De mente agente' [1627].
—'Ex primariis Philosophiae partibus Thesium Sylloge, de quibus cum bono Deo respondere conabimur dignisimis viris Dominis Academiae moderatoribus quando, et ubi ipsorum dignitatibus convenire videbitur' [n.d.].
—Oratio in Laudem linguae Hebraeae in Academiae Comitiis dum promoverentur ordines annon CIC ICC XXIX recitata' [1629].
Baill MS 2 Robert Baillie's Letters and Journals Transcripts [3 vols in 4 parts, 1701].
Baill MS 3 Robert Baillie's Letters and Journals Transcripts [3 vols in 4 parts, 1728].
Baill MS 4 Robert Baillie's Letters and Journals, Contemporary transcript [3 vols].
Baill MS 5 Robert Baillie, Sermons from Jan. 1648 to Jun. 1652 [1 vol.].

Printed primary sources

Abbott, W. and Crane, C.D. (eds), *The Writings and Speeches of Oliver Cromwell* (4 vols, Cambridge, Mass., 1937–47).

Aiken, Robert (ed.), *Letters and Journals written by the deceased Mr. Robert Baillie, Principal of the University of Glasgow* (2 vols, Edinburgh, 1775).

Anderson, James R. (ed.), *The Burgesses and Guild Brethren of Glasgow, 1573–1750* (Edinburgh, 1925).

Baillie, Robert, *Ladensium autokatakrisis, the Canterburians self-conviction: or, An evident demonstration of the avowed Arminianisme, poperie, and tyrannie of that faction, by their owne confessions; With a postscript to the personat Jesuite Lysimachus Nicanor, a prime Canterburian* ([Glasgow], April 1640). Also printed Amsterdam, April 1640.

——*Prelacie is miserie: or, The suppressing of prelaticall government and establishing of provintiall, and nationall sinods, is a hopefull meanes to make a flourishing Church, and happie kingdome* ([London], 1641).

——*A parallel or briefe comparison of the liturgie with the masse-book, the breviarie, the ceremoniall, and other romish ritualls. VVherein is clearly and shortly demonstrated, not onely that the liturgie is taken for the most part word by word out of these antichristian writts; but also that not one of the most abominable passages of the masse can in reason be refused by any who cordially imbrace the liturgie as now it stands, and is commented by the prime of our clergie. All made good from the testimonies of the most famous and learned liturgick writers both romish and English. By R.B.K. Seene and allowed* (London, 1641).

——*The unlawfulnesse and danger of limited episcopacie· VVhereunto is subioyned a short reply to the modest advertiser and calme examinator of that treatise. As also the question of episcopacie discussed from Scripture and fathers* (London, 1641).

——*Ladensium autokatakrisis, the Canterburians self-conviction: or, an evident demonstration of the avowed Arminianisme, poperie, and tyrannie of that faction, by their owne confessions; with a postscript for the personat Jesuite Lysimachus Nicanor, a prime Canterburian. The third edition augmented by the author, with a large supplement. And corrected in typographicke faults, not these onely which in a huge number did escape through negligence and ignorance that printer at Amsterdam, but these also, which in the very first edition were but too many. Helped also in sundry materiall passages, wherein the author hath received better information* ([London], 1641).

——*The life of William now Lord Arch-Bishop of Canterbury, examined. Wherein his principall actions, or deviations in matters of doctrine and discipline (since he came to that sea of Canturbury) are traced, and set downe, as they were taken from good hands, by Mr. Robert Bayley, a learned pastor of the Kirk of Scotland, and one of the late commissioners sent from that Nation. Very fitting for all judicious men to reade, and examine, that they may be the better able to censure him for those thing [sic] wherein he hath done amisse. Reade and judge* (London, 1643). This is a reissue of the expanded 1641 edition of *Ladensium Autokatakrisis* under a different title.

——*Satan the leader in chief to all who resist the reparation of Sion. As it was cleared in a sermon to the Honourable House of Commons at their late solemn fast, Febr. 28. 1643. By Robert Baylie, minister at Glasgow. Published by order of the House of Commons* (London, [1644]).

——*Errours and induration, are the great sins and the great judgements of the time. Preached in a sermon before the Right Honourable House of Peers, in the Abbey-Church at Westminster, July 30. 1645. the day of the monethly fast: by Robert Baylie, minister at Glasgow* (London, 1645).

——*A dissvasive from the errours of the time: vvherein the tenets of the principall sects, especially of the Independents, are drawn together in one map, for the most part, in the words of their own authours, and their maine principles are examined by the touch-stone of the Holy Scriptures* (London, 1645). This went through a second impression in London, 1645 and two further impressions in London, 1646.

——*An historicall vindication of the government of the Church of Scotland, from the manifold base calumnies which the most malignant of the prelats did invent of old, and now lately have been published with great industry in two pamphlets at London. The one intituled Issachars burden, &c. written and published at Oxford by John Maxwell, a Scottish prelate, excommunicate by the Church of Scotland, and declared an unpardonable incendiary by the parliaments of both kingdoms. The other falsly intituled A declaration made by King James in Scotland, concerning church-government and presbyteries; but indeed written by Patrick Adamson, pretended Archbishop of St. Andrews, contrary to his own conscience, as himselfe on his death-bed did confesse and subscribe before many witnesses in a write hereunto annexed* (London, 1646).

——*Anabaptism, the true fountaine of Independency, Brownisme, Antinomy, Familisme, and the most of the other errours, which for the time doe trouble the Church of England, unsealed. Also the questions of pædobaptisme and dipping handled from Scripture. In a second part of the Disswasive from the errors of the time* (London, 1647).

——*A revievv of the seditious pamphlet lately pnblished [sic] in Holland by Dr. Bramhell, pretended Bishop of London-Derry; entitled, His faire warning against the Scots discipline· In which, his malicious and most lying reports, to the great scandall of that government, ar fully and clearly refuted. As also, the Solemne League and Covenant of the three nations justified and maintained. By Robert Baylie, minister at Glasgow, and one of the commissioners from the Church of Scotland, attending the King at the Hague* (Delft, 1649).

——*A review of Doctor Bramble, late Bishop of Londenderry, his Faire warning against the Scotes disciplin. By R.B. G.* (Delft, 1649). This tract is also reprinted in *Three treatises concerning the Scotish discipline* (The Hague, 1661; London, 1662).

——*A Scotch antidote against the English infection of Arminianism. Which little book may be (through Gods blessing) very useful to preserve those that are yet found in the faith, from the infection of Mr John Goodwin's great book* (London, 1652).

——*Appendix practica, ad Ioannis Buxtorsii epitomen grammaticæ hebrææ. In gratiam tyronum qui in sacri textus penetralia, absque longis ambagibus, & prosundiori scrutinio manduci desiderant. Una cum quæstionibus aliquot Hebraicis grammaticæ usum demonstrantibus,in collatione cum originali versionum chaldaicæ, Græcæ, Latinæ, cum vulgatæ tum Tremellii ac interlinearis Montani: etiam Gallicæ Bezæ, Italicæ 'Deodati, Belgicæ Dordracenorum, & Anglicanæ tam veteris quam novæ, in textibus aliquot illustribus; ubi interpretes cum longissime a seinvicem, sæpe tamen parum aut nihil ab Hebræo descedere videntur* (Edinburgh, 1653). Second impression published Edinburgh, 1654.

——*Catechesis elenctica errorum qui hodie vexant Ecclesiam, ex nudis sacræ Scripturæ testimoniis, in brevibus ac claris quæstionibus ac responsionibus proposita. In gratiam studiosæ juventutis academiæ Glasguensis. Imprimatur, Edm. Calamy. Imprimatur, Edm. Calamy* (London, 1654).

——*The Dissvvasive from the errors of the time, vindicated from the exceptions of Mr. Cotton and Mr. Tombes* (London, 1655).

——A parallel of the liturgy, with the Mass-book, the breviary, the ceremonial, and other Romish rituals. Wherein is clearly and shortly demonstrated, not onely that the liturgy is taken for the most part word for word out of these Antichristian writs; but also that not one of the most abominable passages of the Mass can in reason bee refused by any who cordially imbrace the liturgy as now it stands, and is commented by the prime of our clergy. All made good from the testimonies of the most famous and learned liturgick writers both Romish and English (London, 1661).

——Ondersoeck van Doctor Brambels, Gewesen Bisschop van Londenderry in Irelant, waerschouwinge tegens de Kercken-regeringe der Schotten. Door Robert Bailie, Professor der Theologie inde Universiteyt tot Glasgou in Schotlandt Overgeset uyt het Engelsch. Gedruckt tot Delft by Michiel Stael, vvonende aen de Turf-merckt (Utrecht, 1661). NLS APS.3.90.8.

——Operis Historici et Chronologici Libri Duo; In quibus Historia Sacra et Profana compendiose deducitur ex ipsis fontibus, a creatione Mundi ad Constantinum Magnum, et quaestiones ac dubia Chronologica, quae ex utroque Testamento moveri solent, breviter et perspicue explicantur et vindicantur (Amsterdam, 1663). Reprinted in Amsterdam, 1668 and Basel, 1669.

——The Letters and Journals of Robert Baillie, A. M. Principal of the University of Glasgow. M.DC.XXXVII. – M.DC.LXII, ed. David Laing (3 vols, Edinburgh, 1841–42).

[Balcanquhal, Walter], A large declaration concerning the late tumults in Scotland (London, 1639).

Baxter, Richard, Aphorismes of Justification (London, 1649).

Bertius, Petrus, Hymenaeus desertor. Siue de sanctorum apostasia problemata duo (Frankfurt, 1612).

Bilson, Thomas, The Trve difference between Christian Svbiection and Vnchristian Rebellion (London, 1585).

Binning, Hugh, The Works of the Rev Hugh Binning, ed. M. Leishman (Edinburgh, 1851).

Boyd, Robert, Epistolam Pauli Apostoli ad Ephesios Praelectiones supra CC. Lectione varia, multifaria Eruditione, et Pietate singulare refertae (London, 1652).

Bramhall, John, A fair warning to take heed of the Scottish discipline ([Delft], 1649).

[Brutus, Stephanus Junius], Vindiciae contra Tyrannos: sive, De principis in populum, populique in principem, legitima potestate (Basel, 1579).

Buchanan, George, De jure regni apud Scotos dialogus (Edinburgh, 1579).

Burnet, Gilbert, History of His Own Time: From the Restoration of Charles II to the Treaty of Peace at Utrecht, in the Reign of Queen Anne (London, 1838).

Buxtorf, Johannes, Tiberias sive commentarius Masorethicus triplex: historicus, didacticus, criticus (Basel, 1620).

Cabeljavius, Petrus, Apologetica rescriptio pro libertate ecclesiae in exercenda disciplina spirituali (Amsterdam, 1642).

Calderwood, David, Perth assembly. Containing 1. The proceedings thereof. 2 The proofe of the nullitie thereof. 3 Reasons presented thereto against the receiving the fiue new articles imposed. 4 The oppositenesse of it to the proceedings and oath of the whole state of the land. An. 1581 5 Proofes of the unlawfulnesse of the said fiue articles, viz. 1. Kneeling in the act of receiving the Lords Supper. 2. Holy daies. 3. Bishopping. 4. Private baptisme. 5. Private communion. ([Leiden], 1619).

——The pastor and the prelate, or reformation and conformity shortly compared (1628).

——*The History of the Kirk of Scotland*, ed. T. Thomson and D. Laing (8 vols, Edinburgh, 1842–49).

Cameron, John, *ΤΑ ΣΩΖΟΜΕΝΑ sive opera partim ab auctore ipso edita, partim post ejus obitum vulgata* (Geneva, 1642).

The confession of faith, and the larger and shorter catechisme (Edinburgh, 1649).

Cotton, John, *The way of Congregational churches cleared. In the former, from the historical aspersions of Mr. Robert Baylie, in his book, called a disswasive from the errors of the time* (London, 1648).

Cranford, James, *Haereseo-machia: or, The mischiefe which heresies doe, and the means to prevent it* (London, 1646).

Cunningham, Thomas, *The Journal of Thomas Cunningham of Campvere, 1640–1654*, ed. E.J. Courthope (Edinburgh, 1928).

Descartes, René, *Epistola Renati Des-Cartes ad celeberrimum virum D. Gisbertum Voetium* (Amsterdam, 1643).

Edwards, Thomas, *The first and second part of Gangraena, or, A catalogue and discovery of many of the errors, heresies, blasphemies and pernicious practices of the sectaries of this time, vented and acted in England in these four last years* (London, 1646).

The First Book of Discipline (1560).

Franck, Richard, *Northern Memoirs, Calculated for the Meridian of Scotland: To which is added the contemplative and practical angle, writ in the year 1658* (Edinburgh, 1821).

Gardiner, S. R. (ed.), *The Constitutional Documents of the Puritan Revolution, 1625–1660* (Oxford, 1906).

——*Letters and Papers relating to the First Dutch War, 1652–1654* (6 vols, 1899–1930).

Gillespie, George, *A dispute against the English-popish ceremonies, obtruded vpon the Church of Scotland* ([Leiden], 1637).

——*Reasons for Which the Service Booke, Urged upon Scotland Ought to Bee Refused* (Edinburgh, 1638).

——*An assertion of the government of the Church of Scotland* (Edinburgh, 1641).

——*The Presbyterian's Armoury: Works of Mr. George Gillespie*, ed. W.M. Hetherington (2 vols, Edinburgh, 1846).

Grant, Francis J., Herald, Rothesay and Clerk, Lyons (eds), *The Commissariot Record of Glasgow, Register of Testaments, 1547–1800* (Edinburgh, 1901).

Gray, Andrew, *The Works of the Reverend and Pious Andrew Gray, Formerly Minister of the Gospel in Glasgow* (Aberdeen, 1839 [reprinted, 1992]).

Heylyn, Peter, *A Briefe and Moderate Answer*, in Joyce Lee Malcolm (ed.), *The Struggle for Sovereignty: Seventeenth-Century English Political Tracts* (Indianapolis, 1999).

Honyman, Andrew, *Seasonable case of submission to the church-government as now re-established by law* (Edinburgh, 1662).

Hornius, Georgius, *De Statu Ecclesiae Britannicae hodierno, liber commentarius* (Danzig, 1647).

Innes, Cosmo (ed.), *Munimenta alme Universitatis glasguensis: Records of the University of Glasgow from its Foundation till 1727* (4 vols, Glasgow, 1854).

James VI and I, *The vvorkes of the most high and mightie prince, Iames by the grace of God King of Great Britaine, France and Ireland, defender of the faith, &c* (London, 1616).

Johnson, Samuel and Boswell, James, A Journey to the Western Islands of Scotland and the Journal of a Tour to the Hebrides, ed. Peter Levi (London, 1984).

Junius, Fransciscus, Beza, Theodore and Tremellius, Immanuel, Biblia Sacra, sive Testamentvm Vetvs ab Im. Tremellio et Fr. Ivnio ex Hebraeo Latine redditum, et Testamentvm Novvum, a Theod. Beza e Graeco in Latinum versum (Amsterdam, 1633).

Kirkton, James, The Secret and True History of the Church of Scotland, ed. Charles Kirkpatrick Sharpe (Edinburgh, 1817).

Leighton, Robert, The Whole Works of Robert Leighton, D.D. Archbishop of Glasgow (Edinburgh, 1832).

Le Long, Jacques, Bibliotheca Sacra in Binos Syllabos Distincta (Paris, 1723).

The Liturgy of John Knox: Received by the Church of Scotland in 1564 (Glasgow, 1889).

Maccovius, Johannes, Volumen Thesium theologicarum per locos communes disputatarum in academia Franequerana (Franeker, 1639).

Mackenzie, George, Religio Stoici (Edinburgh, 1663).

Maitland, John, The Lauderdale Papers, 1639–1667, ed. Osmund Airy (3 vols, London, 1884–85), vol. I.

Maxwell, John, The burthen of Issachar: or, The tyrannical power and practices of the Presbyteriall-government in Scotland (London, 1646).

M'Crie, Thomas (ed.), The Life of Mr. Robert Blair, Minister of St. Andrews (Edinburgh, 1848).

Middleton, Thomas, An appendix to the history of the Church of Scotland (London, 1677).

Milton, John, Milton's Sonnets with Introduction, Notes, Glossary and Indexes, ed. A.W. Verity (Cambridge, 1916).

Mitchell of Dykes, James, Memoirs of the Life of James Mitchell of Dykes ... Containing, His Own Spiritual Exercises, and Some of the Spiritual Exercises of His Two Sons, that Died Before Him (Glasgow, 1759).

Montague, Richard, Appello Caesarem A just appeale from two vnjust informers (London, 1625).

——'Concerning Recusancie of Communion with the Church of England', ed. Anthony Milton and Alexandra Walsham, in Stephen Taylor (ed.), From Cranmer to Davidson: A Church of England Miscellany (Church of England Record Society, 7) (Woodbridge, 1999), pp. 69–101.

Mullan, David George (ed.), Religious Controversy in Scotland, 1625–1639 (Edinburgh, 1998).

Nicoll, John, A Diary of Public Transactions and Other Occurrences, Chiefly in Scotland, 1650-67, ed. David Laing (Edinburgh, 1836).

Paraeus, David, In divinam Ad Romanos S. Pavli Apostoli Epistolam Commentarivs (Frankfurt, 1613).

Peterkin, Alexander (ed.), Records of the Kirk of Scotland, Containing the Acts and Proceedings of the General Assemblies from the Year 1638 Downwards (Edinburgh, 1843).

Rivet, André, Isagoge, seu introductio generalis ad Scriptura Sacram Veteris et Novi Testamenti, in Operam Theologicorum (3 vols, Rotterdam, 1651–60).

Rivius, Johann, De erroribus pontificiorum seu de abusibus ecclesiasticis (Basel, 1546).

Ruddiman, Thomas, *An answer to the Reverend Mr. George Logan's late treatise on government: in which (contrary to the manifold errors and misrepresentations of that author) the ancient constitution of the Crown and Kingdom of Scotland, and the hereditary Succession of its Monarchs are asserted and vindicated* (Edinburgh, 1747).

Rutherford, Samuel, *Exercitationes apologeticae pro divina gratia* (Amsterdam, 1636).

——*A peaceable and temperate plea for Pauls Presbyterie in Scotland* (London, 1642).

——*Lex, rex The law and the prince: a dispute for the just prerogative of king and people* (London, 1644).

——*A Survey of the Survey of that Summe of Church-Discipline Penned by Mr. Thomas Hooker* (London, 1658).

——*Influences of the Life of Grace* (London, 1659).

——*Letters of Samuel Rutherford*, ed. Andrew Bonar (Edinburgh and London, 1891).

Sagittarius, Caspar, *Introdvctionis in Historia Ecclesiasticam Tomvs II* (Jena, 1720).

Scot, William, *An Apologetical Narration of the State and Government of the Kirk of Scotland since the Reformation*, ed. David Laing (Edinburgh, 1846).

The Second Book of Discipline, ed. James Kirk (Edinburgh, 1980).

Shelford, Robert, *Five pious and learned discourses* (London, 1635).

[Spang, William], *Rerum nuper in Regno Scotiae gestarum historia, seu verius commentarius* (Danzig, 1641).

Spanheim, Frédéric, *Friderici Spanhemii Epistola ad Nobilissimum Virum Davidem Buchananum* (London, 1645).

Strang, John, *De interpretatione et perfectione scripturae* (Rotterdam, 1663).

Three treatises concerning the Scotish discipline (The Hague, 1661).

Tombes, John, *An addition to the Apology for the two treatises concerning infant-baptisme…In which the author is vindicated from 21 unjust criminations in the 92 page of the book of Mr. Robert Baille, minister of Glasgow, intituled Anabaptisme* (London, 1652).

Van Dixhoorn, Chad, *The Minutes and Papers of the Westminster Assembly, 1643–1652* (5 vols, Oxford, 2012).

Vines, Richard, *The Authour, Nature, and Danger of Heresie* (London, 1662).

Vossius, Isaac, *Dissertatio de vera aetate mundi* (1660).

Walch, Johann Georg, *Bibliotheca theologica selecta litterariis adnotationibvs instrvcta, tomvs tertivs* (Jena, 1762).

Walton, Brian, *Biblia Sacra Polyglotta* (6 vols, London, 1653–57).

Watson, Richard, *Akolouthos or A second faire warning to take heed of the Scotish discipline, in vindication of the first* (The Hague, 1651).

White, Francis, *An examination and confutation of a lawlesse pamphlet, intituled, A briefe answer to a late treatise of the Sabbath-day* (London, 1637).

Wodrow, Robert, *The History of the Sufferings of the Church of Scotland from the Restoration to the Revolution*, ed. Robert Burns (4 vols, Glasgow, 1830–35).

——*Collections upon the Lives of the Reformers and Most Eminent Ministers of the Church of Scotland* (2 vols, Glasgow, 1834–45).

Womock, Laurence, *Beaten oyle for the lamps of the sanctuarie; or The great controversie concerning set prayers and our liturgie, examined in an epistle to a private friend: with an appendix that answers the paralell, and the most materiall objections of others against it* (London, 1641).

Secondary sources

Abbott, W.M., 'James Ussher, Ussherian Episcopacy, 1640–1656 – the Primate and his "Reduction" Manuscript', *Albion*, 22 (1990), pp. 237–59.

Adams, Sharon, 'James VI and the Politics of South-West Scotland, 1603–1625', in Julian Goodare and Michael Lynch (eds), *The Reign of James VI* (East Linton, 2000), pp. 228–40.

——'The Making of the Radical South-West: Charles I and his Scottish Kingdom, 1625–1649', in John Young (ed.), *Celtic Dimensions of the British Civil Wars* (Edinburgh, 1997), pp. 53–74.

Albertz, Rainer, *Israel in Exile: The History and Literature of the Sixth Century B.C.E.* (Atlanta, Ga., 2003).

Allan, David, *Virtue, Learning and the Scottish Enlightenment* (Edinburgh, 1993).

Anderson, James R. (ed.), *The Burgesses and Guild Brethren of Glasgow, 1573–1750* (Edinburgh, 1925).

Armstrong, Brian G., *Calvinism and the Amyraut Heresy: Protestant Scholasticism and Humanism in Seventeenth-Century France* (London, 1969).

Armstrong, Robert and Ó hAnnracháin, Tadhg (eds), *Insular Christianity: Alternative Models of the Church in Britain and Ireland, c. 1570–c. 1700* (Manchester, 2013).

Ash, Marinell, *The Strange Death of Scottish History* (Edinburgh, 1980).

Ashton, Robert, *Counter-Revolution: The Second Civil War and its Origins, 1646–8* (London, 1994).

Bangs, Carl, *Arminius: A Study in the Dutch Reformation* (Nashville, 1971).

Bann, Stephen, *Romanticism and the Rise of History* (Boston, 1995).

Barth, Karl, *Church Dogmatics: The Doctrine of God*, trans. G.W. Bromiley (Edinburgh, 1957).

Baskerville, Stephen, *Not Peace but a Sword: The Political Theology of the English Revolution* (London, 1993).

Beeke, Joel R., 'Gisbertus Voetius: Toward a Reformed Marriage of Knowledge and Piety', in Carl Trueman and R. Scott Clark (eds) *Protestant Scholasticism: Essays in Reassessment* (Carlisle, 1999), pp. 227–43.

Bejczy, István, '*Tolerantia*: A Medieval Concept', *Journal of the History of Ideas*, 58 (1997), pp. 365–84.

Bell, M. Charles, *Calvin and Scottish Theology: The Doctrine of Assurance* (Edinburgh, 1985).

Benedict, Philip, *Christ's Churches Purely Reformed: A Social History of Calvinism* (London, 2002).

Bennett, Kate (ed.), *John Aubrey: Brief Lives with An Apparatus for the Lives of our English Mathematical Writers* (2 vols, Oxford, 2015).

Bevan, Jonquil, 'Scotland', in John Barnard and D.F. McKenzie (eds), *Cambridge History of the Book in Britain* (6 vols, Cambridge, 1999–2012), vol. IV, pp. 687–700.

Bonet-Maury, G., 'John Cameron: A Scottish Protestant Theologian in France', *Scottish Historical Review*, 7 (1909–10), pp. 325–45.

Bots, Hans and Waquet, Françoise, *La République des lettres* (Paris, 1997).

Boys, Jayne E.E., *London's News Press and the Thirty Years War* (Woodbridge, 2011).

Brachlow, Stephen, *The Communion of Saints: Radical Puritan and Separatist Ecclesiology, 1570–1625* (Oxford, 1988).

Bremer, Francis J., *Congregational Communion: Clerical Friendship in the Anglo-American Puritan Community, 1610–1692* (Boston, 1994).

Brown, Keith M., *Kingdom or Province? Scotland and the Regal Union, 1603–1715* (London, 1992).

——*Noble Power in Scotland from the Reformation to the Revolution* (Edinburgh, 2011).

Brown, Peter Hume, *History of Scotland* (3 vols, Cambridge, 1905).

Buckle, H.T., *History of Civilization in England* (2 vols, London, 1857–61).

——*On Scotland and the Scotch Intellect*, ed. H.J. Hanham (Chicago, 1970).

Buckroyd, Julia, 'The Resolutioners and the Scottish Nobility in the Early Months of 1660', *Studies in Church History*, 12 (1975), pp. 245–52.

Burgess, Glenn, *Politics of the Ancient Constitution: An Introduction to English Political Thought, 1603–1642* (London, 1992).

——*Absolute Monarchy and the Stuart Constitution* (London, 1996).

——'Religious War and Constitutional Defence: Justifications of Resistance in English Puritan Thought, 1590–1643', in Robert von Friedeburg (ed.), *Widerstandsrecht in der frühen Neuzeit: Eträge und Perspektiven der Forschung im deutsch-britischen Vergleich* (Berlin, 2001), pp. 185–206.

——'England and Scotland', in Burgess, Howell A. Lloyd and Simon Hodson (eds), *European Political Thought 1450–1700: Religion, Law and Philosophy* (London, 2007), pp. 332–75.

——*British Political Thought, 1500–1660: The Politics of the Post-Reformation* (Basingstoke, 2009).

Burns, J.H., *The True Law of Kingship: Concepts of Monarchy in Early-modern Scotland* (Oxford, 1996).

Burrell, S.A., 'The Covenant Idea as a Revolutionary Symbol – Scotland 1596–1637', *Church History*, 27 (1956), pp. 338–50.

——'The Apocalyptic Vision of the Early Covenanters', *Church History*, 43 (1964), pp. 1–24.

Butin, Philip, 'Reformed Ecclesiology: Trinitarian Grace according to Calvin', *Studies in Reformed Theology and History* (Princeton, 1995).

Cairns, John, 'Alexander Cunningham's Proposed Edition of the Digest', *Tijdschrift voor Rechtsgeschiedenis*, 69 (2001), pp. 81–117.

——'Alexander Cunningham, Book Dealer', *Journal of the Edinburgh Bibliographical Society*, 5 (2010), pp. 11–35.

Cameron, James, 'The Piety of Samuel Rutherford (c. 1601–61): A Neglected Feature of Seventeenth-Century Scottish Calvinism', *Nederlands Archief voor Kerkeschiedenis*, 65 (1985), pp. 153–9.

Campbell, Alexander D., 'Episcopacy in the Mind of Robert Baillie, 1637–1662', *Scottish Historical Review*, 93 (2014), pp. 29–55.

Cant, R.G., *The University of St Andrews: A Short History* (Edinburgh, 1970).

Carlyle, Thomas, 'Baillie the Covenanter', in *Critical and Miscellaneous Essays* (7 vols, London, 1839–69), vol. VI, pp. 206–37.

Clark, Stuart, *Thinking with Demons: The Idea of Witchcraft in Early Modern Europe* (Oxford, 1997).

Clarke, T.E.S. and Foxcroft, H.C., *A Life of Gilbert Burnet, Bishop of Salisbury* (Cambridge, 1907).

Coffey, John, *Politics, Religion and the British Revolutions: The Mind of Samuel Rutherford* (Cambridge, 1997).

——'The Problem of "Scottish Puritanism", 1590–1638', in Elizabethanne Boran and Crawford Gribben (eds), *Enforcing Reformation in Ireland and Scotland, 1550–1700* (Aldershot, 2006), pp. 66–90.

——*John Goodwin and the Puritan Revolution: Religion and Intellectual Change in 17th-Century England* (Woodbridge, 2006).

——'George Buchanan and the Scottish Covenanters', in Caroline Erskine and Roger Mason (eds), *George Buchanan: Political Thought in Early Modern Britain and Europe* (Farnham, 2012), pp. 189–203.

Coffey, John, Chapman, Alister and Gregory, Brad S., *Seeing Things their Way: Intellectual History and the Return of Religion* (Notre Dame, 2009).

Collins, Jeffrey R., 'Redeeming the Enlightenment: New Histories of Religious Toleration', *The Journal of Modern History*, 81 (2009), pp. 607–36.

Constable, Giles, 'The Imitation of the Divinity of Christ', in *Three Studies in Medieval Religious and Social Thought* (Cambridge, 1995), pp. 145–68.

Cowan, E.J., 'The Making of the National Covenant', in John Morrill (ed.), *The Scottish National Covenant in its British Context* (Edinburgh, 1990), pp. 68–89.

——'The Covenanting Tradition in Scottish History', in Edward J. Cowan and Richard J. Finlay (eds), *Scottish History: The Power of the Past* (Edinburgh, 2002).

Cowan, I.B., 'The Five Articles of Perth', in Duncan Shaw (ed.), *Reformation and Revolution: Essays Presented to Hugh Watt* (Edinburgh, 1967), pp. 160–75.

——'The Covenanters: A Revision Article', *Scottish Historical Review*, 47 (1968), pp. 35–52.

Craig, W.L., *The Problem of Divine Foreknowledge and Future Contingents from Aristotle to Suarez* (Leiden, 1988).

Davidson, John and Gray, Alexander, *The Scottish Staple at Veere: A Study in the Economic History of Scotland* (London, 1909).

Davies, Godfrey and Hardacre, Paul H., 'The Restoration of the Scottish Episcopacy, 1660–1661', *The Journal of British Studies*, 1 (1962), pp. 32–51.

Davies, Julian, *The Caroline Captivity of the Church* (Oxford, 1992).

Dawson, Jane and Glassey, Lionel K.J., 'Some Unpublished Letters from John Knox to Christopher Goodman', *Scottish Historical Review*, 84 (2005), pp. 166–201.

Daybell, James, 'Recent Studies in Seventeenth-Century Letters', *English Literary Renaissance*, 36 (2006), pp. 135–70.

Decker, William Merrill, *Epistolary Practices: Letter Writing in America before Telecommunications* (Chapel Hill, 1998).

Devine, T.M. and Jackson, Gordon (eds), *Glasgow* (2 vols, Manchester, 1995).

Dibon, Paul, 'Communication in the Respublica Literaria of the 17th Century', *Res Publica Litterarum*, 1 (1978), pp. 42–55.

Donald, Peter, *An Uncounselled King: Charles I and the Scottish Troubles, 1637–1641* (Cambridge, 1990).

Donaldson, Gordon, *The Making of the Scottish Prayer Book of 1637* (Edinburgh, 1954).

——'The Emergence of Schism in Seventeenth-Century Scotland', in Derek Baker (ed.), *Schism, Heresy and Religious Protest* (Cambridge, 1972), pp. 277–94.

Dunthorne, Hugh, 'Resisting Monarchy: The Netherlands as Britain's School of Revolution in the Late Sixteenth and Seventeenth Centuries' in Robert Oresko, G.C. Gibbs and H.M. Scott (eds), *Royal and Republican Sovereignty in Early Modern Europe: Essays in Memory of Ragnhild Hatton* (Cambridge, 1997), pp. 138–42.

Durkan, John, 'The French Connection in the Sixteenth and Early Seventeenth Centuries', in T.C. Smout (ed.), *Scotland and Europe, 1200–1850* (Edinburgh, 1986), pp. 18–44.

Durkan, John and Kirk, James, *University of Glasgow, 1451–1577* (Glasgow, 1977).

Edelstein, Dan, *The Enlightenment: A Genealogy* (Chicago, 2010).

Eglinton, James, 'Scottish–Dutch Reformed Theological Links in the Seventeenth Century', *Dutch Crossing*, 37 (2013), pp. 131–48.

Escott, Harry, *A History of Scottish Congregationalism* (Glasgow, 1960).

Fasti Ecclesiae Scoticanae (7 vols, Edinburgh, 1915–28).

Ferrell, Lori Anne, 'Kneeling and the Body Politic', in Donna B. Hamilton and Richard Strier (eds), *Religion, Literature, and Politics in Post-Reformation England, 1540–1688* (Cambridge, 1996), pp. 70–92.

Ferrell, Lori Anne and McCullough, Peter (eds), *The English Sermon Revised: Religion, Literature and History 1600–1750* (Manchester, 2000).

Ferris, Ina, 'Printing the Past: Walter Scott's Bannatyne Club and the Antiquarian Document', *Romanticism*, 11 (2005), pp. 143–60.

Fincham, Kenneth, *Prelate as Pastor: Ehe Episcopate of James I* (Oxford, 1990).

Fissel, Mark Charles, *The Bishops' Wars: Charles I's Campaigns against Scotland, 1638–1640* (Cambridge, 1994).

Ford, Alan, *James Ussher: Theology, History, and Politics in Early-Modern Ireland and England* (Oxford, 2007).

Ford, John D., '*Lex, rex iusto posita*: Samuel Rutherford on the Origins of Government', in Roger Mason (ed.), *Scots and Britons: Scottish Political Thought and the Union of 1603* (Cambridge, 1994), pp. 262–90.

——'The Lawful Bonds of Scottish Society: The Five Articles of Perth, the Negative Confession and the National Covenant', *Historical Journal*, 37 (1994), pp. 45–64.

——'Conformity in Conscience: The Structure of the Perth Articles Debate in Scotland, 1618–38', *Journal of Ecclesiastical History*, 46 (1995), pp. 256–77.

Ford, M., 'Importation of Printed Books', in L. Hellinga and J.B. Trapp (eds), *A History of the Book in Britain* (6 vols, Cambridge, 1999–2012), vol. III, pp. 179–201.

Foster, W.R., *Bishop and Presbytery: The Church of Scotland, 1661–1688* (London, 1958).

Friedeburg, Robert von, *Self-Defence and Religious Strife in Early Modern Europe: England and Germany, 1530–1680* (Aldershot, 2002).

Furey, Constance, *Erasmus, Contarini, and the Religious Republic of Letters* (Cambridge, 2006).

Furniss, Tom, 'Reading the Geneva Bible: Notes toward an English Revolution?', *Prose Studies: History, Theory, Criticism*, 31 (2009), pp. 1–21.

Gellera, Giovanni, 'The Philosophy of Robert Forbes: A Scottish Scholastic Response to Cartesianism', *Journal of Scottish Philosophy*, 11:2 (2013), pp. 191–211.

Goldgar, Anne, *Impolite Learning: Conduct and Community in the Republic of Letters, 1680–1750* (New Haven, 1995).

Goldie, Mark, 'The Political Thought of the Anglican Revolution', in Robert Beddard (ed.), *The Revolutions of 1688* (Oxford, 1991), pp. 102–36.

Goudriaan, Aza, *Reformed Orthodoxy and Philosophy, 1625–1750: Gisbertus Voetius, Petrus van Mastricht, and Anthonius Driessen* (Leiden, 2006).

Goudriaan, Aza and van Lieburg, Fred (eds), *Revisiting the Synod of Dordt (1618–1619)* (Leiden, 2011).

Grafton, Anthony, *Joseph Scaliger: A Study in the History of Classical Scholarship* (2 vols, Oxford, 1983–93).

——*Defenders of the Text: The Traditions of Scholarship in an Age of Science, 1450–1800* (Cambridge, Mass., 1991).

Grant, James, *History of the Burgh and Parish Schools of Scotland* (2 vols, London and Glasgow, 1876).

Gribben, Crawford and Mullan, David George (eds), *Literature and the Scottish Reformation* (Aldershot, 2009).

Grosjean, Alexia, *An Unofficial Alliance: Scotland and Sweden 1569–1654* (Leiden, 2003).

Grosjean, Alexia and Murdoch, Steve (eds), *Scottish Communities Abroad in the Early Modern Period* (Leiden, 2005).

Ha, Polly, *English Presbyterianism, 1590–1640* (Stanford, 2011).

Haar, Jan van der, *From Abbadie to Young: A Bibliography of English, Most [sic] Puritan Works, Translated into the Dutch Language* (2 vols, Veenendaal, 1980).

Henderson, G.D., *Religious Life in Seventeenth-Century Scotland* (Cambridge, 1937, reprinted 2011).

——'The Idea of the Covenant in Scotland', in *The Burning Bush* (Edinburgh, 1957), pp. 61–74.

Hill, Christopher, *Society and Puritanism in Pre-Revolutionary England* (London, 1964).

Hoftijzer, Paul, 'British Books Abroad: The Continent', in John Barnard and D.F. McKenzie (eds), *Cambridge History of the Book in Britain* (6 vols, Cambridge, 1999–2012), vol. IV, pp. 735–43.

Hotson, Howard, *Commonplace Learning: Ramism and its German Ramifications, 1543–1630* (Oxford, 2007).

Houston, R.A., 'The Literacy Myth?: Illiteracy in Scotland 1630–1760', *Past and Present*, 96 (1982), pp. 81–102.

——*Scottish Literacy and the Scottish Identity: Illiteracy and Society in Scotland and Northern England, 1600–1800* (Cambridge, 1985).

——*The Population History of Britain and Ireland, 1500–1750* (Cambridge, 1995).

Hoy, W.I., 'The Entry of Sects into Scotland', in D. Shaw (ed.), *Reformation and Revolution: Essays Presented to the Very Rev. Hugh Watt* (Edinburgh, 1967), pp. 178–211.

Hughes, Ann, *Gangraena and the Struggle for the English Revolution* (Oxford, 2006).

Hughes, Sean, '"The Problem of Calvinism": English Theologies of Predestination c. 1580–1630', in Susan Wabuda and Caroline Litzenberger (eds), *Belief and Practice in Reformation England: A Tribute to Patrick Collinson from his Students* (Aldershot, 1998), pp. 229–49.

Hunt, Arnold, *The Art of Hearing: English Preachers and Their Audiences, 1590–1640* (Cambridge, 2010).

Israel, Jonathan, *Radical Enlightenment: Philosophy and the Making of Modernity, 1650–1750* (Oxford, 2001).
——*Enlightenment Contested: Philosophy, Modernity, and the Emancipation of Man 1670–1752* (Oxford, 2006).
——*Democratic Enlightenment: Philosophy, Revolution and Human Rights 1760–1790* (Oxford, 2011).
Jackson, Clare, *Restoration Scotland, 1660–1690: Royalist Politics, Religion and Ideas* (Woodbridge, 2003).
——'Buchanan in Hell: Sir James Turner's Civil War Royalism', in Caroline Erskine and Roger Mason (eds), *George Buchanan: Political Thought in Early Modern Britain and Europe* (Farnham, 2012), pp. 205–27.
——'Latitudinarianism, Secular Theology and Sir Thomas Browne's Influence in George Mackenzie's *Religio Stoici* (1663)', *The Seventeenth Century*, 29 (2014), pp. 73–94.
Kannengiesser, Charles, *Handbook of Patristic Exegesis: The Bible in Ancient Christianity* (Leiden, 2006).
Kaplan, Benjamin, *Divided by Faith: Religious Conflict and the Practice of Toleration in Early Modern Europe* (Cambridge, Mass., 2007).
Kaplan, Lawrence, *Politics and Religion during the English Revolution: The Scots and the Long Parliament 1643–1645* (New York, 1976).
Kearney, Hugh, *Scholars and Gentlemen: Universities and Society in Pre-Industrial Britain, 1500–1700* (London, 1970).
Kidd, Colin, *Subverting Scotland's Past: Scottish Whig Historians and the Creation of an Anglo-British Identity, 1689–c. 1830* (Cambridge, 1993).
Killeen, Kevin, 'Hanging up Kings: The Political Bible in Early Modern England', *Journal of the History of Ideas*, 72 (2011), pp. 549–70.
Kim, Joong-Lak, 'Firing in Unison? The Scottish Canons of 1636 and the English Canons of 1640', *Records of the Scottish Church History Society*, 28 (1998), pp. 55–77.
——'The Scottish-English-Romish Book: The Character of the Scottish Prayer Book of 1637', in Michael J. Braddick and David L. Smith (eds), *The Experience of Revolution in Stuart Britain and Ireland: Essays for John Morrill* (Cambridge, 2011), pp. 14–32.
Knight, Jeffrey Todd, *Bound to Read: Compilations, Collections, and the Making of Renaissance Literature* (Philadelphia, 2013).
Lachman, D.C., *The Marrow Controversy, 1718–1723: An Historical and Theological Analysis* (Edinburgh, 1988).
Lake, Peter, *Moderate Puritans and the Elizabethan Church* (paperback edn, Cambridge, 2004).
Lake, Peter and Questier, Michael, *The Antichrist's Lewd Hat: Protestants, Papists and Players in Post-Reformation England* (London, 2002).
Langley, Chris, *Worship, Civil War and Community, 1638–1660* (London, 2015).
Laplanche, François, *L'Écriture, le sacré et l'histoire: Érudits et politiques protestants devant la Bible au XVIIe siècle* (Amsterdam, 1986).
Leeuwen, Th. Marius van and Stanglin, Keith D. (eds), *Arminius, Arminianism, and Europe: Jacobus Arminius (1559/60–1609* (Leiden, 2009).
Lim, Paul Chang-Ha, *In Pursuit of Purity, Unity and Liberty: Richard Baxter's Puritan Ecclesiology in its Seventeenth-Century Context* (Leiden, 2004).

——Mystery Unveiled: The Crisis of the Trinity in Early Modern England (Oxford, 2012).

Lockhart, Brian R.W., The Town School: A History of the High School of Glasgow (Edinburgh, 2010).

Loewenstein, David and Marshall, John (eds), Heresy, Literature and Politics in Early Modern English Culture (Cambridge, 2006).

Lundin, Matthew, Paper Memory: A Sixteenth-Century Townsman Writes His World (Cambridge, 2012).

Lüthy, Christoph, 'David Gorlaeus' Atomism, or: The Marriage of Protestant Metaphysics with Italian Natural Philosophy', in Lüthy, John E. Murdoch and William R. Newman (eds), Late Medieval and Early Modern Corpuscular Matter Theories (Leiden, 2001), pp. 245–90.

McCallum, John, Reforming the Scottish Parish: The Reformation in Fife, 1560–1640 (Farnham, 2010).

McCoy, F.N., Robert Baillie and the Second Scots Reformation (Berkeley, 1974).

McCullough, Peter, Adlington, Hugh and Rhatigan, Emma (eds), The Oxford Handbook of the Early Modern Sermon (Oxford, 2011).

MacDonald, Alan R., The Jacobean Kirk, 1567–1625: Sovereignty, Polity and Liturgy (Aldershot, 1998).

Macinnes, Allan I., Charles I and the Making of the Covenanting Movement, 1625–1641 (Edinburgh, 1991).

——'Covenanting Ideology in Seventeenth-Century Scotland', in Jane Ohlmeyer (ed.), Political Thought in Seventeenth-Century Ireland (Cambridge, 2000), pp. 191–220.

——The British Revolution, 1629–1660 (Basingstoke, 2005).

——'The 'Scottish Moment, 1638–45', in J.S.A. Adamson (ed.), The English Civil War: Conflict and Contexts, 1640–49 (Basingstoke, 2009), pp. 125–52.

——The British Confederate: Archibald Campbell, Marquess of Argyll, c.1607–1661 (Edinburgh, 2011).

McKay, W.D.J., An Ecclesiastical Republic: Church Government in the Writings of George Gillespie (Edinburgh, 1997).

McKenzie, D.F., 'Speech-Manuscript-Print', in Peter D. McDonald and Michael F. Suarez (eds), Making Meaning: 'Printers of the Mind' and Other Essays (Amherst, 2002), pp. 237–58.

Mackenzie, Kirsteen, 'A Glimpse Behind the Censor: Baillie and the Covenanting Printing Press', Notes and Queries, 60 (2013), pp. 42–3.

Maclehose, James, The Glasgow University Press, 1638–1931 (Glasgow, 1931).

Macleod, James, Scottish Theology: In Relation to Church History since the Reformation (Edinburgh, 1974).

McMahon, George I.R., 'The Scottish Courts of High Commission, 1610–1638', Records of the Scottish Church History Society (1965), pp. 193–209.

Makey, Walter, The Church of the Covenant, 1637–1651: Revolution and Social Change in Scotland (Edinburgh, 1979).

Malcolm, Noel, 'Hobbes, Ezra and the Bible: The History of a Subversive Idea', in Aspects of Hobbes (Oxford, 2002), pp. 383–431.

——'The Name and Nature of Leviathan: Political Symbolism and Biblical Exegesis', Intellectual History Review, 17 (2007), pp. 21–39.

Mann, Alastair J., *The Scottish Book Trade, 1500–1720: Print Commerce and Print Control in Early Modern Scotland* (East Linton, 2000).

——'A Spirit of Literature: Melville, Baillie, Wodrow, and a Cast of Thousands: The Clergy in Scotland's long Renaissance', *Renaissance Studies*, 18 (2004), pp. 90–108.

Marshall, John, *John Locke, Toleration and Early Enlightenment Culture* (Cambridge, 2006).

Marwick, James D., *Early Glasgow: A History of the City of Glasgow from the Earliest Times to the Year 1611* (Glasgow, 1911).

Mason, Roger, 'Scotching the Brut: Politics, History and the National Myth of Origin in Sixteenth-Century Britain', in Mason (ed.), *Scotland and England, 1286–1815* (Edinburgh, 1987), pp. 60–84.

Maxwell, William D., *A History of Worship in the Church of Scotland* (Oxford, 1955).

Meer, Jitse M. van der and Mandelbrote, Scott (eds), *Nature and Scripture in the Abrahamic Religions: Up to 1700* (2 vols, Leiden, 2008).

Meier, Hans, 'Love, Law and Lucre: Images in Rutherford's Letters', in M. Arn and H. Wirtjes (eds), *Historical and Editorial Studies in Medieval and Early Modern English for Johan Gerritson* (Groningen, 1985), pp. 77–96.

Mijers, Esther, 'The Scottish–Dutch Context to the Blaeu Atlas: An Overview', *Scottish Geographical Journal*, 121 (2005), pp. 311–20.

Miller, Peter N., 'The "Antiquarianization" of Biblical Scholarship and the London Polyglott Bible (1653–57)', *Journal of the History of Ideas*, 62 (2001), pp. 463–82.

Milton, Anthony, '"The Unchanged Peacemaker"? John Dury and the Politics of Irenicism in England, 1628–1643', in Mark Greengrass, Michael Leslie and Timothy Raylor (eds), *Samuel Hartlib and Universal Reformation: Studies in Intellectual Communication* (Cambridge, 1994), pp. 95–117.

——*Catholic and Reformed: The Roman and Protestant Churches in English Protestant Thought, 1600–1640* (Cambridge, 1995).

——(ed.), *The British Delegation and the Synod of Dort (1618–1619)* (Woodbridge, 2005).

——*Laudian and Royalist Polemic in Seventeenth-Century England: The Career and Writings of Peter Heylyn* (Manchester, 2007).

Moore, Jonathan, *English Hypothetical Universalism: John Preston and the Softening of Reformed Theology* (Grand Rapids, 2007).

Morrill, John, 'The Religious Context of the English Civil War', *Transactions of the Royal Historical Society*, 5th Series, 34 (1984), pp. 155–78.

——'A British Patriarchy? Ecclesiastical Imperialism under the Early Stuarts', in Anthony Fletcher and Peter Roberts (eds), *Religion, Culture and Society in Early Modern Britain: Essays in Honour of Patrick Collinson* (Cambridge, 1994), pp. 209–37.

Morrissey, Mary, 'Scripture, Style and Persuasion in Seventeenth-Century English Theories of Preaching', *The Journal of Ecclesiastical History*, 53 (2002), pp. 686–706.

——*Politics and the Paul's Cross Sermons, 1558–1642* (Oxford, 2011).

Mortimer, Sarah, *Reason and Religion in the English Revolution: The Challenge of Socinianism* (Cambridge, 2010).

Mortimer, Sarah and Robertson, John (eds), *The Intellectual Consequences of Religious Heterodoxy, c. 1600–1750* (Leiden, 2012).

Mulder, M.J., 'The Transmission of the Biblical Text', in M.J. Mulder and H. Sysling (eds), *Mikra: Text, Translation, Reading and Interpretation of the Bible in Ancient Judaism and Early Christianity* (Assen, 1988), pp. 87–135.

Mullan, David George, *Episcopacy in Scotland: The History of an Idea, 1560–1638* (Edinburgh, 1986).

——'"Uniformity in Religion": The Solemn League and Covenant (1643) and the Presbyterian Vision', in W. Graham (ed.), *Later Calvinism: International Perspectives* (Kirksville, 1994), pp. 249–66.

——'Theology in the Church of Scotland, 1618–1640: A Calvinist Consensus?', *Sixteenth Century Journal*, 26 (1995), pp. 595–617.

——'Arminianism in the Lord's Assembly, Glasgow, 1638', *Records of the Scottish Church History Society*, 26 (1996), pp. 1–30.

——'Masked Popery and Pyrrhonian Uncertainty: The Early Scottish Covenanters on Arminianism', *Journal of Religious History*, 21 (1997), pp. 159–77.

——*Scottish Puritanism, 1590–1638* (Oxford, 2000).

Muller, Richard A., *God, Creation, and Providence in the Thought of Jacob Arminius* (Grand Rapids, 1991).

——*Post-Reformation Reformed Dogmatics* (4 vols, Grand Rapids, 1993).

——'Calvin and the "Calvinists": Assessing Continuities and Discontinuities between the Reformation and Orthodoxy', *Calvin Theological Journal*, 30 (1995), pp. 345–75, and 31 (1996), pp. 125–60.

——*The Unaccommodated Calvin: Studies in the Formation of a Theological Tradition* (Oxford, 2000).

——*After Calvin: Studies in the Development of a Theological Tradition* (Oxford, 2003).

Murdoch, Steve, *Network North: Scottish Kin, Commercial and Covert Associations in Northern Europe, 1603–1746* (Leiden, 2006).

Nenner, Howard, 'The Trial of Charles I and the Failed Search for a Bounded Monarchy', in Gordon J. Schochet (ed.), *Restoration, Ideology, and Revolution* (Washington DC, 1990), pp. 1–21.

——'Loyalty and the Law: The Meaning of Trust and the Right of Resistance in Seventeenth-Century England', *Journal of British Studies*, 48 (2009), pp. 859–70.

Niebuhr, H. Richard, *Christ and Culture* (New York, 1951).

Nijenhuis, W., *Adrianus Saravia (c. 1532–1613): Dutch Calvinist, First Reformed Defender of the English Episcopal Church Order on the Basis of the Ius diuinum* (Leiden, 1980).

Orr, D. Alan, *Treason and the State: Law, Politics, and Ideology in the English Civil War* (Cambridge, 2002).

Osborne, Grant, *The Hermeneutical Spiral: A Comprehensive Introduction to Biblical Interpretation* (Downers Grove, Il., 2006).

Patterson, W.B., *King James VI and I and the Reunion of Christendom* (Cambridge, 1997).

Paul, R.S., *The Assembly of the Lord: Politics and Religion in the Westminster Assembly and the 'grand debate'* (Edinburgh, 1985).

Paul, Sir James Balfour (ed.), *The Scots Peerage: founded on Wood's edition of Sir Robert Douglas's peerage of Scotland: containing an historical and genealogical account of the nobility of that kingdom* (9 vols, Edinburgh, 1904–14).

Pearl, Valerie, 'London Puritans and Scotch Fifth Columnists: A Mid-Seventeenth-Century Phenomenon', in A.E.J. Hollaender and W. Kellaway (eds), *Studies in London History Presented to P.E. Jones* (London, 1969), pp. 317–31.

Plomer, Henry R., *A Dictionary of the Booksellers and Printers Who Were at Work in England, Scotland and Ireland from 1641 to 1667* (London, 1907).

Prior, Charles W.A., *A Confusion of Tongues: Britain's Wars of Reformation, 1625–1642* (Oxford, 2012).

Prior, Charles W.A. and Burgess, Glenn (eds), *England's Wars of Religion, Revisited* (Farnham, 2011).

Quantin, Jean-Louis, 'The Fathers in Seventeenth-Century Anglican Theology', in Irena Backus (ed.), *The Reception of the Church Fathers in the West: From the Carolingians to the Maurists* (2 vols, Leiden, 1997), vol. II, pp. 987–1008.

——*The Church of England and Christian Antiquity: The Construction of a Confessional Identity in the 17th Century* (Oxford, 2010).

Rademaker, C.S.M., *Life and Work of Gerardus Joannes Vossius (1577–1649)*, trans. H.P. Doezema (Assen, 1981).

Raffe, Alasdair, 'Presbyterians and Episcopalians: The Formation of Confessional Cultures in Scotland, 1660–1715', *English Historical Review*, 125 (2010), pp. 570–98.

——*The Culture of Controversy: Religious Arguments in Scotland, 1660–1714* (Woodbridge, 2012).

Reid, David, 'Prose after Knox', in R.D.S. Jack (ed.), *The History of Scottish Literature: Origins to 1660 (Medieval and Renaissance)* (Aberdeen, 1988), pp. 183–99.

Reid, H.M.B., *The Divinity Professors in the University of Glasgow* (Glasgow, 1923).

Reid, Steven J., *Humanism and Calvinism: Andrew Melville and the Universities of Scotland, 1560–1625* (Farnham, 2011).

Robertson, Jean, *The Art of Letter Writing: An Essay on the Handbooks Published in England during the Sixteenth and Seventeenth Centuries* (London, 1942).

Rose, Jacqueline, *Godly Kingship in Restoration England: The Politics of the Royal Supremacy, 1660–1688* (Cambridge, 2011).

Ross, I.S., *Lord Kames and the Scotland of his Day* (Oxford, 1972).

Russell, Conrad, 'Arguments for Religious Unity in England, 1530–1650', *Journal of Ecclesiastical History*, 18 (1967), pp. 201–26.

Salmon, J.H.M., *The French Religious Wars in English Political Thought* (Oxford, 1959).

Schneider, Carol G., 'Roots and Branches: From Principled Nonconformity to the Emergence of Religious Parties', in Francis J. Bremer (ed.), *Puritanism: Transatlantic Perspectives on a Seventeenth-Century Anglo-American Faith* (Boston, 1993), pp. 167–200.

Schneider, Gary, 'Politics, Deception and the Workings of the Post: Some Features of Epistolarity in Early Modern England', *Explorations in Renaissance Culture*, 28 (2002), pp. 99–127.

——*The Culture of Epistolarity: Vernacular Letters and Letter Writing in Early Modern England, 1500–1700* (Newark, 2005).

Searle, Alison, "'Though I am a Stranger to You by Face, Yet in Neere Bonds by Faith": A Transatlantic Puritan Republic of Letters', *Early American Literature*, 43 (2008), pp. 277–308.

Shagan, Ethan, 'Beyond Good and Evil: Thinking with Moderates in Early Modern England', *The Journal of British Studies*, 49 (2010), pp. 488–513.

——*The Rule of Moderation: Violence, Religion and the Politics of Restraint in Early Modern England* (Cambridge, 2012).

Shami, Jeanne, *John Donne and Conformity in Crisis in the Late Jacobean Pulpit* (Cambridge, 2003).

Sharpe, Kevin, *The Personal Rule of Charles I* (London, 1992).

Shelford, April, *Transforming the Republic of Letters: Pierre-Daniel Huet and European Intellectual Life, 1650–1720* (Rochester, 2007).

Shriver, F., 'Orthodoxy and Diplomacy: James I and the Vorstius Affair', *English Historical Review*, 85 (1970), pp. 449–74.

Shuger, Debora K., *Sacred Rhetoric: The Christian Grand Style in the English Renaissance* (Princeton, 1988).

Skinner, Quentin, *The Foundations of Modern Political Thought* (2 vols, Cambridge, 1978).

——*Visions of Politics* (3 vols, Cambridge, 2002).

Smart, I.M., 'The Political Ideas of the Scottish Covenanters, 1638–88', *Journal of the History of Political Thought*, 1 (1980), pp. 167–93.

Smith, David, *Constitutional Royalism and the Search for Settlement, c. 1640–1649* (Cambridge, 1994).

Smout, T.C., *A History of the Scottish People, 1560–1830* (London, 1969).

Sommerville, J.P., 'Absolutism and Royalism', in *The Cambridge History of Political Thought, 1450–1700*, ed. J.H. Burns and Mark Goldie (Cambridge, 1991), pp. 347–73.

Spalding, James and Brass, Maynard, 'Reduction of Episcopacy as a Means to Unity in England, 1640–1662', *Church History: Studies in Christianity and Culture* (1961), pp. 414–32.

Spicer, Andrew, '"Laudianism" in Scotland? St. Giles' Cathedral, Edinburgh, 1633–39: A Reappraisal', *Architectural History*, 46 (2003), pp. 95–108.

Spinks, Bryan D., *Sacraments, Ceremonies and the Stuart Divines: Sacramental Theology and Liturgy in England and Scotland, 1603–1662* (Aldershot, 2002).

Sprunger, Keith L., *Dutch Puritanism: A History of English and Scottish Churches of the Netherlands in the Sixteenth and Seventeenth Centuries* (Leiden, 1982).

Spurlock, R. Scott, *Cromwell and Scotland: Conquest and Religion, 1650–1660* (Edinburgh, 2007).

——'The Problems with Religion as Identity: The Case of Mid-Stuart Ireland and Scotland', *Journal of Irish and Scottish Studies*, 6 (2013), pp. 1–30.

Stam, F.P. van, *The Controversy over the Theology of Saumur, 1635–1650* (Amsterdam, 1988).

Stevenson, Andrew, *The History of the Church and State of Scotland* (2 vols, Edinburgh, 1753–57).

Stevenson, David, *The Scottish Revolution, 1637–1644: The Triumph of the Covenanters* (London, 1973, reprinted edn, 2003).

——'Conventicles and the Kirk, 1619–37: The Emergence of a Radical Party', *Records of the Scottish Church History Society*, 18 (1973), pp. 99–114.

——'The Radical Party in the Kirk, 1637–45', *Journal of Ecclesiastical History*, 25 (1974), pp. 135–65.

——*Revolution and Counter-Revolution in Scotland, 1644–1651* (London, 1977, reprinted edn, 2003).

——*Alasdair MacColla and the Highland Problem in the Seventeenth Century* (Edinburgh, 1980).

——*Scottish Covenanters and Irish Confederates: Scottish–Irish Relations in the Mid-Seventeenth Century* (Belfast, 1981).

——'The "Letter on Sovereign Power" and the Influence of Jean Bodin on Political Thought in Scotland', *Scottish Historical Review*, 61 (1982), pp. 25–43.

——'A Revolutionary Regime and the Press: The Scottish Covenanters and their Printers, 1638–51', *The Library*, 7 (1985), pp. 315–37.

——'The National Covenant: A List of Known Copies', *Records of the Scottish Church History Society*, 23 (1988), pp. 255–99.

——*The Covenanters: The National Covenant and Scotland* (Edinburgh, 1988).

——'The Solemn League and Covenant: A List of Signed Copies', *Records of the Scottish Church History Society*, 25 (1995), pp. 154–87.

——'Mere Hasty Babblements? Mr Robert Baillie', in *King or Covenant?: Voices from Civil War* (East Linton, 1996), pp. 17–39.

——'Baillie, Robert (1602–1662)', *Oxford Dictionary of National Biography* (online edn, May 2008) [www.oxforddnb.com/view/article/1067].

Stewart, Laura A.M., *Urban Politics and the British Civil Wars: Edinburgh, 1617–1653* (Leiden, 2006).

——'"Brothers in Treuth": Propaganda, Public Opinion and the Perth Articles Debate in Scotland', in Ralph Houlbrooke (ed.), *James VI and I: Ideas, Authority, and Government* (Aldershot, 2006), pp. 151–68.

——'The Political Repercussions of the Five Articles of Perth: A Reassessment of James VI and I's Religious Policies in Scotland', *The Sixteenth Century Journal*, 38 (2007), pp. 1013–36.

——'Power and Faith in Early Modern Scotland', *Scottish Historical Review* Supplement (2013), pp. 25–37.

——'Authority, Agency and the Reception of the Scottish National Covenant of 1638', in Armstrong and Ó hAnnracháin (eds), *Insular Christianity*, pp. 88–106.

Summit, Jennifer, *Memory's Library: Medieval Books in Early Modern England* (Chicago, 2008).

Todd, Margo, *The Culture of Protestantism in Early Modern Scotland* (London, 2002).

——'The Problem of Scotland's Puritans', in John Coffey and Paul Chang-Ha Lim (eds), *The Cambridge Companion to Puritanism* (Cambridge, 2008), pp. 174–88.

Torrance, J.B., 'Covenant or Contract? A Study of the Theological Background of Worship in 17th-century Scotland', *Scottish Journal of Theology*, 23 (1970), pp. 51–76.

——'The Covenant Concept in Scottish Theology and Politics and its Legacy', *Scottish Journal of Theology*, 34 (1981), pp. 225–43.

——'The Concept of Federal Theology – Was Calvin a Federal Theologian?', in Wilhelm Neuser (ed.), *Calvinus Sacrae Scripturae Professor* (Grand Rapids, 1994), pp. 15–40.

Torrance, Thomas F., *Scottish Theology: From John Knox to John McLeod Campbell* (Edinburgh, 1996).

Trevor-Roper, Hugh, 'Scotland and the Puritan Revolution', in *Religion, the Reformation and Social Change* (London, 1967), pp. 392–444.

——'The Scottish Enlightenment', in *Studies on Voltaire and the Eighteenth Century*, lviii (Oxford, 1967), pp. 1635–58.

——'The Religious Origins of the Enlightenment', in *The Crisis of the Seventeenth Century: Religion, the Reformation and Social Change* (Indianapolis, 1967), pp. 179–218.

——'The Fast Sermons of the Long Parliament', in *Religion, the Reformation and Social Change and Other Essays* (London, 1967), pp. 294–344.

Tyacke, Nicholas, 'Puritanism, Arminianism and Counter-Revolution', in Conrad Russell (ed.), *The Origins of the English Civil War* (London, 1973), pp. 119–43.

——*Anti-Calvinists: The Rise of English Arminianism, 1590–1640* (Oxford, 1987).

——'The Puritan Paradigm of English Politics, 1558–1642', *Historical Journal*, 53 (2010), pp. 527–50.

Usher, R.G., *The Rise and Fall of the High Commission* (rev. edn, Oxford, 1968).

Vallance, Edward, *Revolutionary England and the National Covenant: State Oaths, Protestantism, and the Political Nation, 1553–1682* (Woodbridge, 2005).

Von Rohr, John, *The Covenant of Grace in Puritan Thought* (Atlanta, 1986).

Walsham, Alexandra, 'The Parochial Roots of Laudianism Revisited: Catholics, anti-Calvinists and "Parish Anglicans" in Early Stuart England', *Journal of Ecclesiastical History*, 49 (1998), pp. 620–51.

——*Charitable Hatred: Tolerance and Intolerance in England, 1500–1700* (Manchester, 2006).

Wandel, Lee Palmer, *The Eucharist in the Reformation: Incarnation and Liturgy* (Cambridge, 2006).

Watts, Sylvia, 'The Impact of Laudianism on the Parish: The Evidence of Staffordshire and North Shropshire', *Midland History*, 33 (2008), pp. 21–42.

Webster, Tom, *Godly Clergy in Early Stuart England: The Caroline Puritan Movement, c. 1620–1643* (Cambridge, 1997).

White, Peter, 'The Rise of Arminianism Reconsidered', *Past and Present*, 101 (1983), pp. 34–54.

——*Predestination, Policy and Polemic: Conflict and Consensus in the English Church from the Reformation to the Civil War* (Cambridge, 1992).

Wickenden, Nicholas, *G.J. Vossius and the Humanist Concept of History* (Assen, 1993).

Wilson, John Frederick, *Pulpit in Parliament: Puritanism during the English Civil Wars, 1640–8* (Princeton, 1969).

Winship, Michael P., *Making Heretics: Militant Protestantism and Free Grace in Massachusetts, 1636–1641* (Princeton, 2002).

Witt, J.R. de, *Jus divinum: The Westminster Assembly and the Divine Right of Church Government* (Kampen, 1969).

Woolf, Daniel, *The Idea of History in Early Stuart England: Erudition, Ideology, and 'The Light of Truth' from the Accession of James I to the Civil War* (Toronto, 1990).

Wormald, Jenny, *Lords and Men in Scotland: Bonds of Manrent, 1442–1603* (Edinburgh, 1985).

Young, John R., *The Scottish Parliament, 1639–1661: A Political and Constitutional Analysis* (Edinburgh, 1996).
——'The Scottish Parliament and the War of the Three Kingdoms, 1639–1651', *Parliaments, Estates and Representation*, 21 (2001), pp. 103–23.
——'The Scottish Parliament and the Covenanting Heritage of Constitutional Reform', in Allan I. Macinnes and Jane H. Ohlmeyer (eds), *The Stuart Kingdoms in the Seventeenth Century: Awkward Neighbours* (Dublin, 2002), pp. 226–50.
——'Charles I and the 1633 Parliament', in Keith M. Brown and Alastair J. Mann (eds), *Parliament and Politics in Scotland, 1567–1707* (Edinburgh, 2005), pp. 101–37.

Unpublished dissertations

Holfelder, Kyle David, 'Factionalism in the Kirk during the Cromwellian Invasion and Occupation of Scotland, 1650 to 1660: The Protester-Resolutioner Controversy', Ph.D. thesis, University of Edinburgh (1998).
Langley, Christopher R., 'Times of Trouble and Deliverance: Worship in the Kirk of Scotland, 1645–1658', Ph.D. thesis, University of Aberdeen (2012).
MacKenzie, Kirsteen M., 'Presbyterian Church Government and the "Covenanted Interest" in the Three Kingdoms, 1649–1660', Ph.D. thesis, University of Aberdeen (2008).
McMahon, George I.R., 'The Scottish Episcopate, 1600–1638', Ph.D. Thesis, University of Birmingham (1972).
Powell, Hunter, 'The Dissenting Brethren and the Power of the Keys, 1640–1644', Ph.D. thesis, University of Cambridge (2011).
Shepherd, Christine Mary, 'Philosophy and Science in the Arts Curriculum of the Scottish Universities in the 17th Century', Ph.D. thesis, University of Edinburgh (1974).
Vernon, Elliot, 'The Sion College Conclave and London Presbyterianism during the English Revolution', Ph.D. thesis, University of Cambridge (1999).
Wells, Vaughan T., 'The Origins of Covenanting Thought and Resistance: c. 1580–1638', Ph.D. thesis, University of Stirling (1997).

Index

253

St Andrew Studies in Scottish History

Previously published

I

Elite Women and Polite Society in Eighteenth-Century Scotland
Katharine Glover

II

Regency in Sixteenth-Century Scotland
Amy Blakeway

III

Scotland, England and France after the Loss of Normandy, 1204–1296
'Auld Amitie'
M.A. Pollock

IV

Children and Youth in Premodern Scotland
edited by Janay Nugent and Elizabeth Ewan

V

Medieval St Andrews: Church, Cult, City
Edited by Michael Brown and Katie Stevenson